AUTHENTIC RESTORATION
GUIDE

CHALLENGER & BARRACUDA

RESTORATION GUIDE

1967–1974

Paul Herd

MBI Publishing Company

First published in 1997 by MBI Publishing Company, PO Box 1, 729 Prospect Avenue, Osceola, WI 54020-0001 USA

The information in this book is true and complete to the best of our knowledge. All recommendations are made without any guarantee on the part of the author or Publisher, who also disclaim any liability incurred in connection with the use of this data or specific details.

We recognize that some words, model names and designations, for example, mentioned herein are the property of the trademark holder. We use them for identification purposes only. This is not an official publication.

MBI Publishing Company books are also available at discounts in bulk quantity for industrial or sales-promotional use. For details write to Special Sales Manager at Motorbooks International Wholesalers & Distributors, 729 Prospect Avenue, PO Box 1, Osceola, WI 54020-0001 USA.

Library of Congress Cataloging-in-Publication Data
Challenger & Barracuda restoration guide, 1967-1974/
Paul A. Herd.
p. cm.
Includes index.
ISBN 0-7603-0207-3 (pbk.: alk. paper)
1. Barracuda automobile--Conservation and restoration--Handbooks, manuals, etc. 2. Challenger automobile--Conservation and restoration--Handbooks, manuals, etc. I. Title.
TL215.B22H47 1997
629.222'2--dc21 96-51127

On the front cover: Moulin Rouge was just one color of a mind-blowing palette offered by Plymouth for 1970. Who would have thought a pink AAR 'Cuda could look so right? Paula Smith is the lucky owner. *Dan Lyons*

On the back cover: Top: The tire-shredding 440 Six Pack topped the Challenger displacement heap for 1970. *Chrysler Historical photo*
Lower left: Virtually nothing remained of the 1969 Barracuda for 1970, save some engine options. *Chrysler Historical photo*
Lower right: A 340 under the hood made the 1968 Formula S a spirited performer. *Chrysler Historical photo*

Printed in the United States of America

Contents

Acknowledgments

This book would not have been possible if it were not for the insistence of many individuals. I would like to thank all of those that attended the Street Machine Nationals in Springfield, Missouri, and allowed me to photograph their cars. Thanks to Lisa Finch and the rest at Special Events for so gracefully allowing me to attend the show. A special thanks to John Justice and Kathy Slobe and all the rest at R and R Auto Salvage, for answering my questions and allowing me to do research at the yard. The illustrations used in this book would not have been possible without the assistance of William Coughlin and Marilyn Hobbs and the legal staff at Chrysler Motors. And to Jim Stimac and Brandt Rosenbusch at Chrysler Historical Collection for digging through negatives to find the original factory photos used in this book. Special thanks to Barbara Hillick and all those at Year One for supplying photos of their products.

On a personal note, I would like to thank my friends and family who were there to lean on for support with the loss of my mother during the writing of this book. A special thanks to Randy and Jean, who have been there longer than I can remember. To Kim, whose warm smile and cheerful words brighten even the darkest of my days, she is a true friend. To Stacy, a nurse's aide at the hospital where my mother was, thanks for just taking time to sit and talk—it helped more than you know. And finally, last but not least, thanks to Kathy H. and the rest in my Sunday School class and church family, it is through you that I can see the Lord working every day. It is in memory of my mother Blanche Herd that I dedicate this book.

Year One
P.O. Box 129
Tucker, GA 30085
1-800-950-9503-Phone-USA
1-800-680-6806-FAX-USA
770-493-6568-Atlanta area and over seas
770-496-1949 FAX Atlanta area and over seas FAX

R & R Auto Salvage
Route 2, Box 196G
Verona, MO 65769
417-678-5551

Introduction

By all rights Firebirds and, yes, even the Mustang, should be called "fish cars" instead of pony cars. The Plymouth Barracuda was released to the public on April 2, 1964, a whole 15 days before the release of the famous Ford. While the fastback design of the Barracuda was hailed by magazine reviewers at the time, it was overshadowed by the reports on the Mustang. The Barracuda just got lost in the shuffle.

The 1964-1966 Barracuda offered only one body style—the fastback. In 1967, the Barracuda was completely restyled and was offered in two-door hardtop and convertible form in addition to the fastback. The new design also featured a wider engine bay that allowed the big-block powerplant to be installed. In a decade when visible horsepower was a strong selling point, the addition of a mega-cube big-block helped to strengthen the Barracuda's racy image.

In 1964 Dodge was offered its own version of the Barracuda, but passed and decided instead to rework the Coronet, a model that would later become known as the Charger. In 1970, Dodge did finally offer its own version of the Barracuda. Called the Challenger, it and the all-new Barracuda had strong design ties with the 1969 Camaro. In fact, undetected by most viewers in the original version of the movie *Vanishing Point*, it is not a Challenger that hits the bulldozers at the end of the movie but a white Chevrolet Camaro.

The new body styling of both the Barracuda and Challenger provided for a two-door hardtop or convertible only; there was no fastback. The all-new styling also allowed for the easy installation of the 440-ci engine and the 426 Hemi. However, tight restrictions from safety zealots and environmentalists killed off the big-blocks and the convertible after the 1971 model year. It was shortly after the introduction of the 1972 models that Chrysler made the decision to ax the Barracuda and Challenger lines. This explains the lack of options available and the limited design changes in these two models up through their demise in 1974.

No matter whether it's a 1967 six-cylinder coupe or a 1970 Hemi convertible, the Plymouth Barracuda and the Dodge Challenger were unique models. Built in a time when ETs—not MPGs—were the primary interest of buyers, and the sound of a free-flowing dual exhaust system was better then anything that could be heard on the radio; there will never be anything like them again. If you are one of the proud owners of one of the 250,000 Barracudas or 165,500 Challengers built, consider yourself blessed. Compare that to the millions of Mustangs built and you'll see just how special your car really is.

Chapter 1

Decoding VINs and Fender Tags

Vehicle Identification Number

By federal law, every automobile sold or made in the United States must have a vehicle identification number, or VIN for short. The format for decoding the VIN plate remained constant throughout the eight-year run of the Barracuda and Challenger, but the plate's location did change.

On 1967 Barracudas, the plate is riveted to the left front door hinge pillar. For 1968 through 1974 models, it is attached to the driver's side of the instrument panel and is readable through the windshield.

The first four digits of the VIN are considered the body number. Decoding the body number can tell you whether your 1970 Challenger R/T is in fact an R/T and not a redone plain-Jane Challenger. The VIN plate breaks down like this:

First character: Model line (B for Barracuda, J for Challenger)

Second digit: Price class (H for High, S for Special, P for Premium)

Third and fourth digits: Body style (23 for hardtop, 27 for convertible, 29 for fastback)

A typical 1967-style VIN plate.

INCLUDES SOME SPECIAL AND STANDARD EQUIPMENT TO AGREE WITH CAR ORDERED
1234567890
ABCDEFGHJKLMNPQRSTVWXYZ
SO NUMBER BODY TRM PNT
INCLUDES DATE AND MONTH OF YEAR AND ORDER NUMBER
BODY CODE NUMBER
TRIM CODE NUMBER
PAINT CODE NUMBER

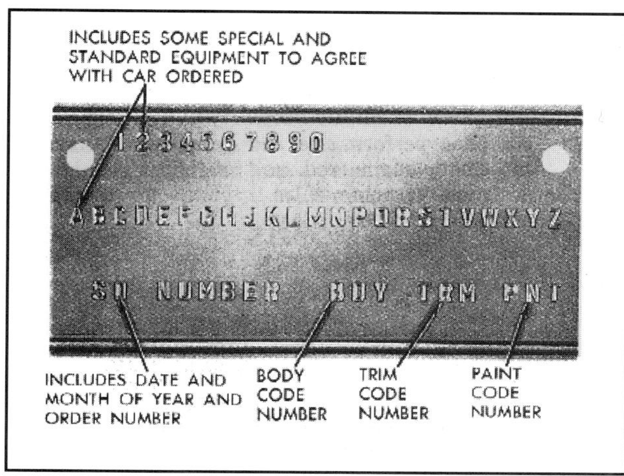

The typical format of the 1967-1968-style fender tag.

CHRYSLER CORPORATION

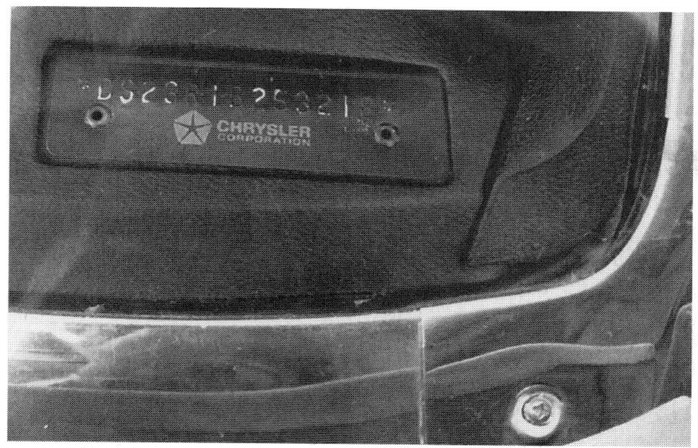

As the fifth digit reveals, this VIN plate belongs to one the few 1971 Hemi Cudas made.

CODE PLATE INTERPRETATION

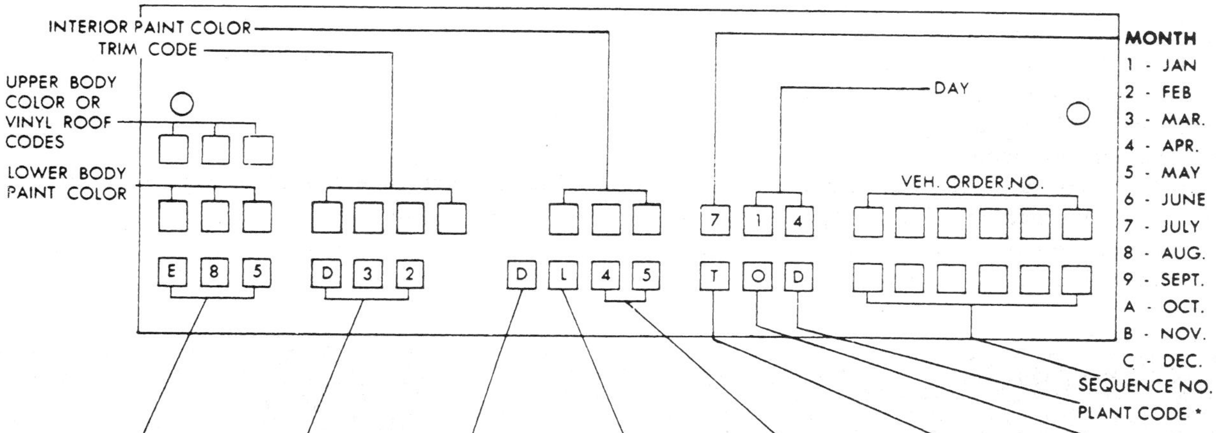

INTERIOR PAINT COLOR
TRIM CODE
UPPER BODY COLOR OR VINYL ROOF CODES
LOWER BODY PAINT COLOR
DAY
VEH. ORDER NO.
7 1 4
E 8 5
D 3 2
D L 4 5
T O D
MONTH
1 - JAN
2 - FEB
3 - MAR.
4 - APR.
5 - MAY
6 - JUNE
7 - JULY
8 - AUG.
9 - SEPT.
A - OCT.
B - NOV.
C - DEC.
SEQUENCE NO.
PLANT CODE *

ENG. CODES	TRANS CODES	CAR LINE	PRICE CLASS	BODY TYPE	ENG. CODE	MODEL YEAR
E-22-198	D13-A230 F/S	V-VALIANT	H-HIGH	21-2 DR. SED.	B-198 CU. IN.	0-1970
E-24-225	D14-A903	L-DART	K-POLICE	23-2 DR. H/TOP	C-225 CU. IN.	1-1971
E-25-225	D15-230 C/S	B-BARRACUDA	L-LOW	29-2 DR. SPORTS H/TOP	E-SPL. 6 CYL.	2-1972
E-44-318	D21-A833	J-CHALLENGER	M-MEDIUM	41-4 DR. SED.	G-318 CU. IN.	
E-55-340	D34-A904	R-SATELLITE	P-PREMIUM	43-4 DR. H/TOP	H-340 CU. IN.	
E-57-360	A998	W-CORONET CHARGER	S-SPORT	45-2 SEAT WGN.	K-360 CU. IN.	
E-63-400	D35-A727	P-PLYMOUTH	T-TAXI	46-3 SEAT WGN.	M-400 - 2 Bbl.Carb.	
E-68-400		D-DODGE			P-400 - 4 Bbl. Carb.	
E-85-440		C-CHRYSLER			T-440 CU. IN.	
E-86-440		Y-IMPERIAL			U-440 HI. PERF.	
E-87-440					V-440 6 BBL.	
					Z-SPL. 8 CYL.	

* ASSEMBLY PLANT, A - LYNCH ROAD, B - HAMTRAMCK, C - JEFFERSON, D - BELVEDERE, F - NEWARK, G - ST. LOUIS, R - WINDSOR

A 1968-1974 fender tag layout.

1967-1974 Engine VIN Code Letters

Code Letter	Engine Displacement	Model Years Used
B	225-ci 1-bbl six-cyl.	1967-1969
C	225-ci six-cyl.	1970-1972
D	273-ci 2-bbl V-8	1967
E	273-ci 4-bbl V-8	1967
F	318-ci 2-bbl V-8	1968-1969
G	318-ci 2-bbl V-8	1970-1974
H	383-ci 4-bbl 330-hp V-8	1967-1970
H	340-ci 4-bbl V-8	1969–1970
J	340-ci 3x2-bbl V-8	1970-1971
J	360-ci 4-bbl V-8	1974
L	383-ci 2-bbl V-8	1970-1971
M	426 Hemi— 440-ci 4-bbl (Special engine)	1968—1969
N	383-ci 4-bbl High Performance	1970-1971
P	340-ci 4-bbl V-8	1968-1969
R	426 Hemi	1970-1971
U	440-ci 4-bbl	1970 only
V	440-ci 3x 2-bbl V-8	1970-1971

Fender tags should be painted the same color as the inner fender, and not be bright, as shown here.

Fifth character: **Engine code** (see chart)
Sixth digit: Model year (7 for 1967, 8 for 1968, 9 for 1969, 0 for 1970, 1 for 1971, 2 for 1972, 3 for 1973, 4 for 1974)
Seventh character: Assembly plant (see chart)
Eighth through thirteenth digits: Serial number (all begin at 100001 each year)

1967-1974 Barracuda/Challenger Body Numbers

Model	Two-Door Hardtop	Convertible	Fastback
1967-1969 Barracuda	BH23	BH27	BH29*
Cuda (1969 only)	BH23	BH27	BH29
1970-1974 Barracuda	BH23#	BH27 (1970-1971)	N/A
1970-1974 Cuda	BS23	BS27 (1970-1971)	N/A
Barracuda Gran Coupe	BP23	N/A	N/A
1970-1974 Challenger	JH23#	JH27 (1970-1971)	N/A
1970-1974 Challenger	JS23		
R/T ('70-'71) Rally ('72-'74)	JS23	JS27 (1970-1971)	JP29
1970 Challenger S.E.	N/A	N/A	JP29

* = 1968 Hemi Barracuda is coded BO29.
\# = 1970-1971 two-door coupes (rear quarter-windows do not roll down) are coded BH21 for Barracuda or JH21 for Challenger.

Fender Tags

All Chrysler products used a fender tag that carries vital information about the car. Two different layouts were used, one for 1967-1968 and the other for 1969 on. Of the two, the latter style carries more information about the options on the car. Both layouts hold information about the original powerplant, transmission, exterior color, and interior trim.

The fender tag was usually attached to the inner left-hand fender. Tags are read from left to right, from the bottom line up. The accompanying illustrations will help with further tag decoding.

1967-1974 Assembly Plant VIN Code

Assembly Plant	1967 VIN	1968-1974 VIN
Lynch Road	1	A
Hamtrack	2	B
Jefferson	3	C
Belvedere	4	D
Los Angeles	5	E
Newark	6	F
St. Louis	7	G
Wyoming	8#	P#
Windsor	9	R

= Some exports.

1967-1968 Barracuda Tire Codes (Fender Tag)

Tire Size	Code
6.95x14 WSW	23
D70x14 BSW	26
D70x14 WSW	27
D70x14 RS	28
E70x14 RS	38
E70x14 WSW	39

Key: WSW, white sidewall; BSW, black sidewall; RS, red stripe

1967-1968 Barracuda Engine Codes (Fender Tag)

Engine Size	Code
225 six-cylinder	21
273 V-8 2-bbl	31
273 V-8 4-bbl	32
318 V-8 2-bbl	41
340 V-8 4-bbl	52
383 V-8 4-bbl	62

Cars with a options like this AAR may use two fender tags.

Chapter 2

Powerplants

Both big-blocks and small-blocks were available in Barracudas and Challengers. Standard in all but Cuda and Challenger R/T or Rally models was a slant-six six-cylinder, so called because the block was tilted over to one side.

A short block is the engine minus the induction system (carburetor and intake) and cylinder heads. The casting number is the best way to identify the bare block. This number is cast into the sides of the block. When used with the casting date, which is located below the casting number, it can tell you if the block is right for the model year of your car. The date is straightforward and easy to read. For example, it might be 11-09-70, which would mean November 9, 1970. However, this block would be for a 1971 model, not a 1970 model. The casting date and model year will not always match.

Usually, if the block is cast after July, it is intended for use in the following model year. If it is cast before July, then the model year and casting year will match. For example, the casting date of 10-14-67 would be September 10, 1967, and would be for the 1968 model. A block cast on April 12, 1969, would have the date of 4-12-69, and would be for a 1969 Barracuda.

Blocks can be quickly identified by their casting number. A 318-ci block is shown. The casting date (arrow) can further pinpoint the model year. This block was cast on October 22, 1968, so it was for use in a 1969 model.

Here is the location of the six-cylinder engine identification numbers.

1967-74 Chrysler Engine Block Casting Numbers

Engine Displacement	Casting Numbers
225-ci	1967: T-22; 1968-1972: 2128418,2202843-6, 2022857, 2205528, 2463430-1
273-ci	2463930
318-ci	2536030
340-ci 4-bbl	2780930-340
340-ci 3x2-bbl	3577130TA
383-ci (all)	2468130,2120429
440-ci (1969-1971)	2536430
426 Hemi	2468330

The engine identification number, or EIN for short, can further identify engines for 1968-and-later model years. The location of the EIN varies with engine family type. On six-cylinder engines, the EIN can be found at the front on the passenger's side, just below the cylinder head. On small-blocks (273-ci, 318-ci, 340-ci, and 360-ci) the EIN is on the driver's side at the front of the block, just below the cylinder head.

For big-blocks and Hemi engines beginning with the 1968 model year, the EIN is at the rear of the block on the passenger's side near the oil pan flange. For the 1967 model year, an identification number on the 383-ci big-block will be at the front of the block on the passenger's side just below the distributor.

The breakdown for the 1968-1974 EIN consists of 13 digits plus character codes and looks like this:

First letter or first two letters: Plant code (PM, Mound Road; PT, Trenton; MV or MN, Maryland; and W, Windsor).

Next three digits: The cubic-inch displacement (225, 318, 340, 383, 426, 440).

Next four digits: This code represents the 10,000-day calendar. See calendar charts for more information.

Last four digits: These are the daily sequential number of engines built.

If the letter "S" or the letters "HP" follow the displacement code, this denotes a high-performance block. The letter "H" shows it is a Hemi block. Note that a few 1973-1974 engines used a slightly different pattern. These exceptions gave the date as the last digit of the year (3 for 1973, 4 for 1974) followed by the month and day code (1109 for November 9). This type of date code followed the plant code and was placed before the displacement.

Here is the location of the 1968-1974 small-block engine identification numbers.

The location of the 1968-1974 big-block engine identification numbers.

In 1967 models, a different system was used to code the block. However, the same basic information was found in the 1967 coding system. It begins with the letter "C" indicating the 1967 model year, followed by the engine displacement. Next is the build date (month and day), followed by the body code. For example, the code C383414A would be for a 1967 383-ci engine built April 14, 1967. Note that some 318-ci small-blocks may have the code CC318. This suggests a Canadian-built engine, which is completely different from the U.S. version. It is the same engine used in 1966 U.S. and Canadian models. The Canadian block is much heavier than its United States cousin.

Beginning with 1968 models, the last eight digits of the VIN are stamped on the engine, on a pad on the passenger's side of the block near the oil pan flange. If the numbers match those on the instrument panel, then you have a "number-matching" block. Note that some 1968 models did use the entire 13-digit VIN on the block instead of just the last eight.

The upper block pad can identify the model year and a high-performance block. Location of this pad varies with the engine family. On the small-block this pad is found on the front of the block under the left-hand cylinder head. On the six-cylinder engines the pad is on the passenger side of the block. On the 383-ci engine it's found at the front of the block just to the right of the distributor. On the 440 and Hemi block, the pad is to the left of the distributor.

A single letter on the pad shows the model year (C=1967, D=1968, E=1969, F=1970, G=1971, H=1972, J=1973, and K=1974). Engine displacement follows, and below this is the upper engine (heads, intake, and such) assembly date, including the day and month. If the block is a high-performance version, then the letters HP will appear. You may also find this pad blank, which in-

The six-cylinder vehicle identification number (VIN) engine pad location.

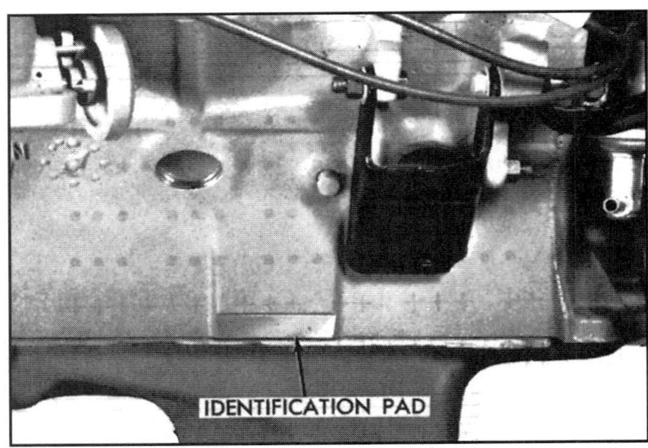

Here is the eight-cylinder VIN engine pad location.

Special symbols on the engine pad indicate undersized bearings or oversized bores.

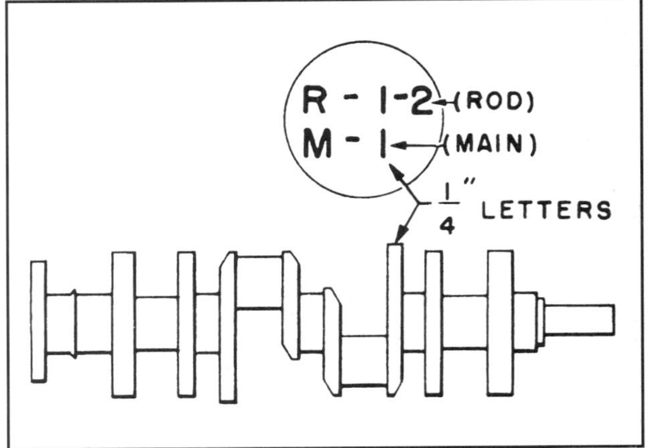

Internal markings on the crankshaft denote undersized bearings; the location for big-block engines is shown in this example. Marks for small-blocks are on counterweight number eight.

dicates that the original engine was replaced under warranty. Warranty engines usually have a tag riveted to the block just above the freeze plug.

Other letters and symbols may appear on the upper engine pad when oversized bores or undersize bearings are used. On six-cylinder engines, big-blocks, and Hemis, a Maltese cross will indicate 0.001-inch undersized main bearings. Any numbers following the cross indicate the specific bearings that were undersized. The cross is not used with small-blocks; instead, the letter "M" shows the undersized main bearings. The letter "X" after the cross or the letter "M" indicates all main bearings are undersized by 0.010 inch.

The letter "R" may appear instead, or with the code for undersized bearings. It suggests 0.001-inch undersized rod bearings. If numbers follow, they indicate which rod bearings are undersized; otherwise, all are undersized by 0.001 inch. "RX" indicates that all rod bearings are undersized by 0.010 inch.

The letter "A" on the block pad suggests an overbore of 0.020 inch. Otherwise, the bore is standard size.

A diamond symbol on the pad shows that all tappets are oversized by 0.008 inch. Warranty engines may have the undersize/oversize symbols but won't have the series code. You also may find the codes for the undersized rod and main bearings on a crankshaft counterweight. If the block has the markings for undersized bearings, then these markings will be found on the crankshaft.

As with blocks and cylinder heads, intake manifolds have a casting number and casting date. Number 2806178 is for a 1969 440-ci big-block. The date translates as March 31,1969.

Cylinder head casting numbers can be found on one of the runners. The one shown here is for a big-block. The casting date can also be found on a runner. This four-digit date, 6169, translates as June 1,1969, so this is for a 1969 model.

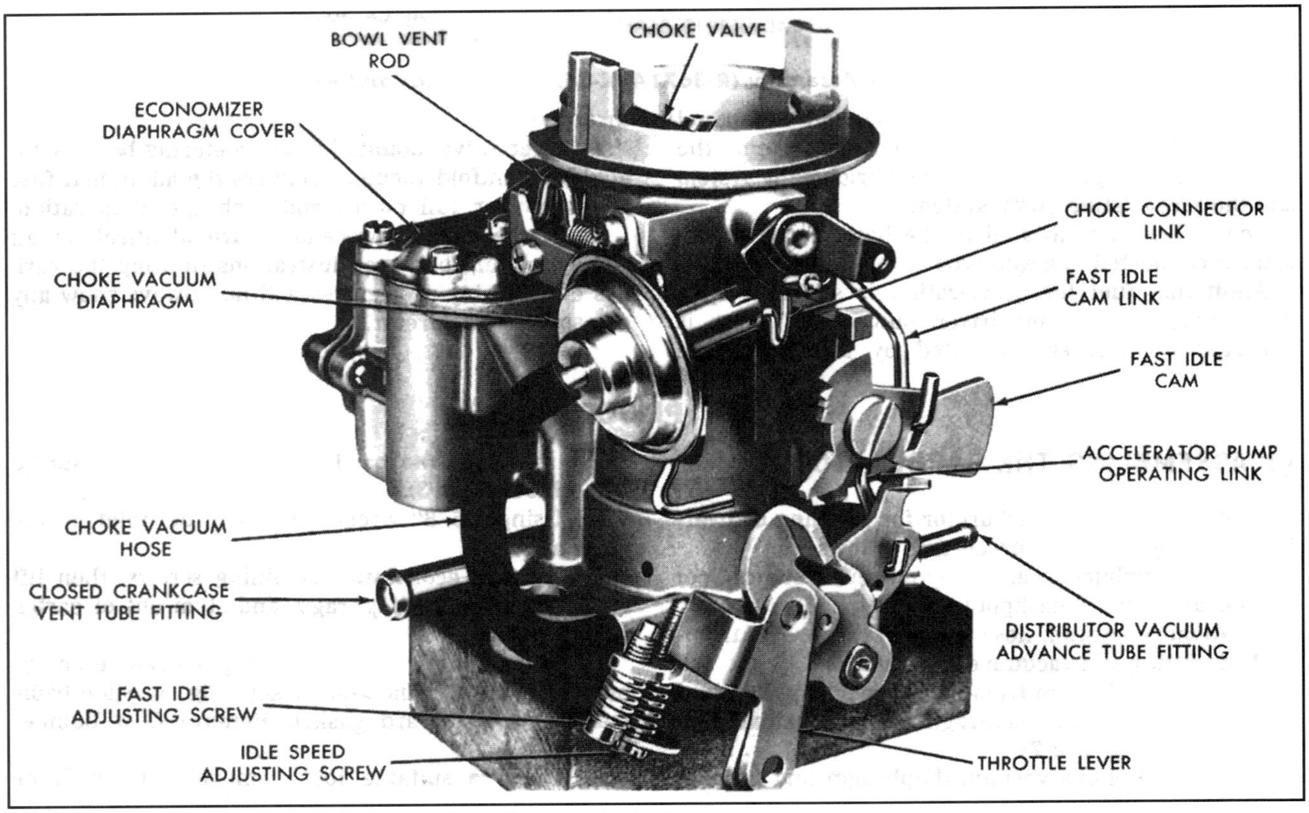

The 1967 Holley 1920 1-barrel carburetor without the Clean Air Package.

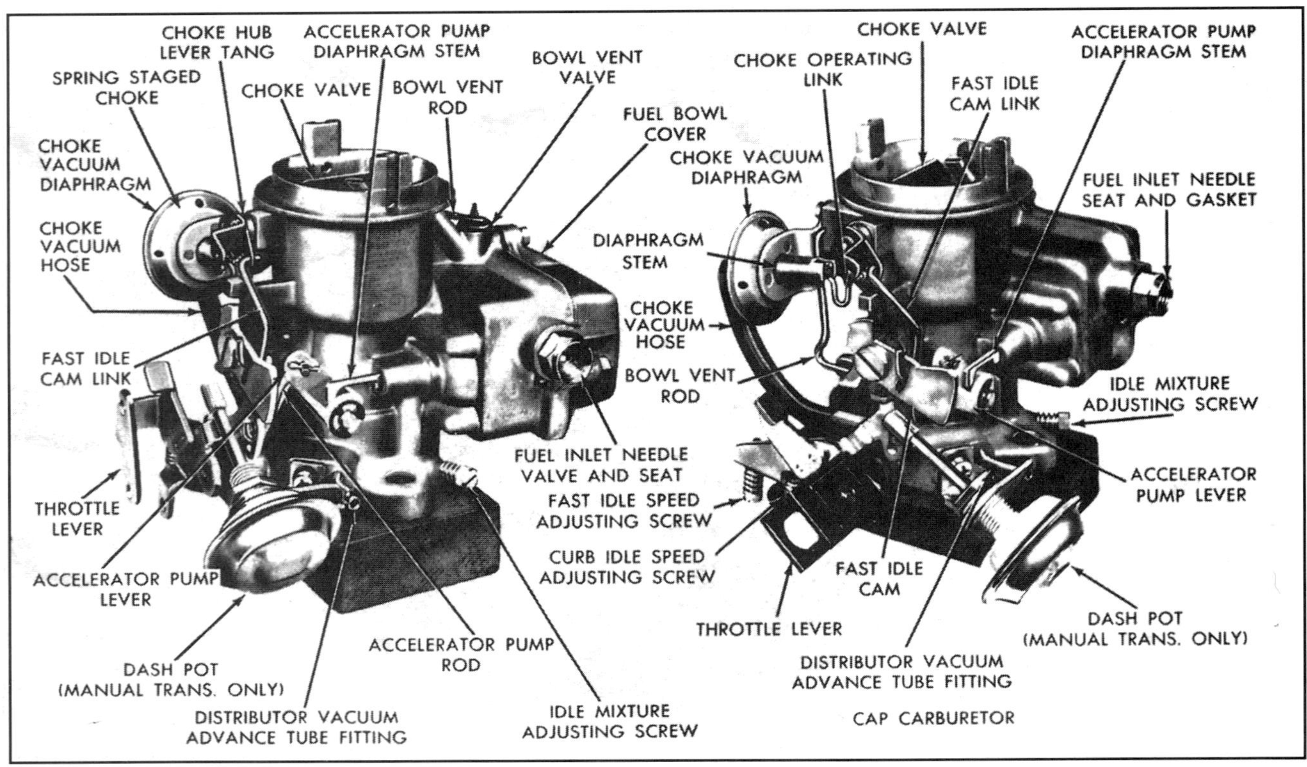

The Holley 1920 1-barrel carburetor with the Clean Air Package.

Painting the Engine

All cylinder blocks should be painted with a high-temperature paint. All 273-ci engines were painted Chrysler Red along with the 1968 318-ci and 340-ci engines. All 1967-1968 383-ci engines were painted a medium blue-green. For 1969 all 383s and the rare 440 were painted Hemi Orange. This color was also used on 1969 to late-built 1971 340s and all 440s installed in Cudas and Challengers. During the two years that the 426 Hemi was available, it was painted Street Hemi Orange. This color is brighter than the Hemi Orange. To duplicate the factory look, paint all Hemi blocks with Ditzler EQE-60626 orange paint. When applied to a four-barrel 383 or 440, then add the DX-265 flatting agent from Ditzler. The formula is one part flatting agent to three parts of paint.

Most 1970-1971 383 four-barrels and 440s were painted Hemi Orange, although some with the Shaker Hood option were painted turquoise. All 383-ci powerplants with a two-barrel carburetor were painted turquoise. Beginning in late 1971, all 318s and 340s were painted Chrysler Blue. This medium-blue color was also used on all 1974 360-ci engines. Although not officially available, one 340-ci 3x2-barrel Trans-Am Challenger was built in 1971. It is uncertain if this block was painted blue like production engines or Hemi Orange. My belief would be that the engine was pulled from the stock pile of 1970 engines and it would be painted Hemi Orange.

Cylinder Heads

All cylinder heads were made from cast-iron and are painted the same color as their matching cylinder block. Cylinder heads can be identified by their casting numbers, which can be found on a runner. High-performance heads like the 340 T/A heads have large valves and ports to allow free breathing and use a special casting, while high-output versions of the 383 and 440 use the same heads as lower-powered production models. Most cylinder heads used stamped steel covers painted the same color as the cylinder head and block, though there were some exceptions that used chrome valve covers.

Chrome-plated valve covers were part of the Formula S package when ordered with a 383-ci engine on 1967 and 1968 models. A chrome-plated oil filler cap and a breather cap completed the look. The 1967 273-ci four-barrel also used special valve covers featuring a black crinkle finish and aluminum cooling fins. All other valve covers, including those on the Trans-Am versions, were painted the same color as the rest of the engine. An exception was the 1970-1971 Hemi, which used special wide valve covers with provisions for the spark plug wires; these valve covers were matte black. It also used an unpainted oil filler cap and a gloss black emissions cap; no chrome valve covers were installed on the street editions of the 426 Hemi.

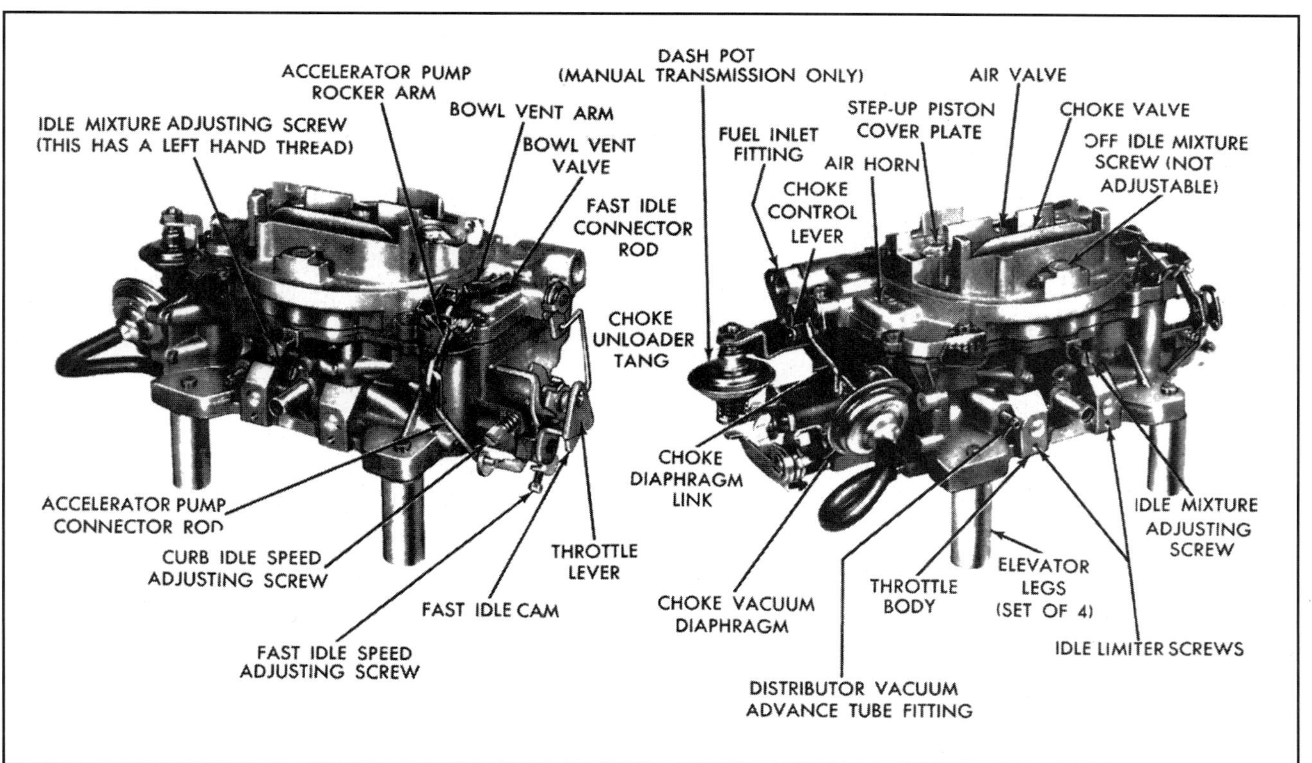

Two views of the Carter AVS 4-barrel carburetor.

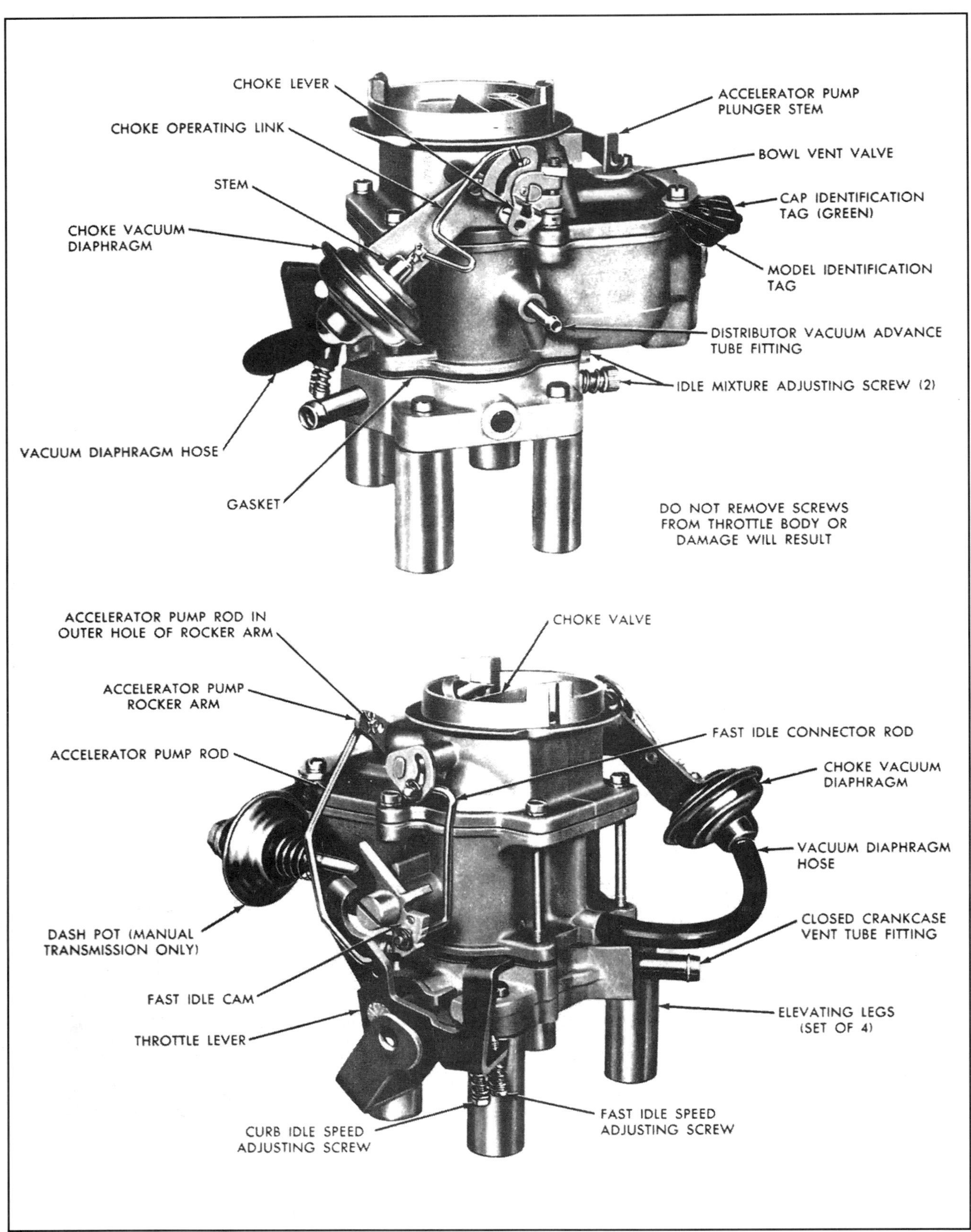

The Carter BBD 2-barrel carburetor with the Clean Air Package.

1967-1974 Chrysler Cylinder Head Casting Numbers

Displacement	Casting Number	Years Used	Intake Valve Diameter	Exhaust Valve Diameter	Notes
225-ci six-cyl.	2121476	1967-1969	1.625	1.365	# = With A.I.R.
	2843169	1970-1971	1.625	1.365	
	3614850 #	1972	1.625	1.365	
	3698995	1972	1.625	1.625	
273-ci V-8	2658920	1967	1.78	1.56	
318-ci V-8	2843675	1968-1974	1.78	1.56	
340-ci 4-bbl	2531894	1968-1971	2.02	1.60	
	3418915	1972	1.88	1.60	
	3671587	1973	1.88	1.60	
340-ci 3x2-bbl	3577053	1970-1971	2.02	1.60	Open chamber
360-ci 4-bbl	3671587	1974	1.88	1.60	
383 or 440-ci 4-bbl or 3x2-bbl	2406516	1967	2.08	1.60	
	2843906	1968-1970	2.08	1.75	
	3462346	1971	2.08	1.75	
426 Hemi	2780559	1968	2.25	1.94	
		1970-1971	2.25	1.94	1968 drag race only

Hemis used twin Carter AFB 4-barrel carburetors.

Induction Systems

The induction systems include the intake manifold, the carburetor or carburetors, and the air cleaner assembly. Intake manifolds are identified by a casting number and casting date, which can be found on an intake runner. The date is usually just below the casting number. All intakes except those used on the Hemi were made of cast-iron. Hemi intakes were made of cast-aluminum. All intakes, including the Hemis, should be painted to match the cylinder block.

Carburetors

Carburetors are identified by the manufacturer model part number. The location of the number varies with the type and brand of the carburetor. Both Carter and Holley carburetors were installed on Barracudas and Challengers. Application will depend on engine size, transmission type, and emission controls; certain options will require a special carburetor.

1967-1974 Intake Manifold Casting Numbers

Engine	Carburetor Type	Casting Number	Model Years
225-ci six-cyl.	1-bbl	2205901	1967-1968
225-ci six-cyl.	1-bbl	2899959	1969-1972
225-ci six-cyl.	2-bbl	2806815	1967-1972*
273-ci V-8	2-bbl	2536559	1967
273-ci V-8	4-bbl	2536563	1967
318-ci V-8	2-bbl	2468960	1968-1969
318-ci V-8	2-bbl	2951185	1970-1971
318-ci V-8	2-bbl	3698431	1972#
318-ci V-8	2-bbl	2951185	1972*
318-ci V-8	2-bbl	3698431	1973-1974
340-ci V-8	4-bbl	2531915	1968-1969
340-ci V-8	4-bbl	3462848	1970
340-ci V-8	3x2-bbl	3418682	1970-1971
340-ci V-8	4-bbl	3512100	1971
340-ci V-8	4-bbl	3671918	1972#
340-ci V-8	4-bbl	3614025	1972
340-ci V-8	4-bbl	3671918	1973
383-ci V-8	4-bbl	2205968	1967
383-ci V-8	4-bbl	2806301	1968-1969
383-ci V-8	2-bbl	2951670	1970-1971
383-ci V-8	4-bbl	2951666	1970-1971
426 Hemi	2x4-bbl	2780543	1970-1971
440-ci V-8	4-bbl	2806178	1969
440-ci V-8	4-bbl	2951736	1970
440-ci V-8	3x2-bbl	2946276	1970-1971

* = Export models only; # = With NOX emissions.

One- and Two-Barrel Carburetors

A Holley model 1920 one-barrel carburetor was standard on all 225-ci engines from 1967 to 1972. The Holley part number is stamped on the top of the bowl or just below the air horn at the front of the carburetor. The 1967 273-ci two-barrel was the standard V-8 and it used a Carter-built Ball and Ball Dual Downdraft (BBD) with a 1 1/4-inch bore. The Carter part number appears on a tag attached to the top of the bowl at the front, just below the air horn.

The 1967 318-ci engine, including Canadian-built cars, also used a two-barrel BBD model carburetor. However, Canadian and United States cars used different part numbers. BBD carburetors continued to be used on 318-ci engines until the end of the 1974 model year. The tag location is the same as with the 1967 carburetor used on the 273-ci two-barrel powerplant.

The 1970 and 1971 models were available with a 383-ci two-barrel powerplant. In 1970, two different carburetors were used. Those models with automatic transmissions and *without* air conditioning and *without* California emissions, use a model 2210 series carburetor made by Holley. This model was listed as number R4371A and it is stamped on the side of the air horn or the side of the bowl. All other 1970 383-ci two-barrels used a Carter BBD with a 1 1/2-inch bore. For 1971 the 383-ci two-barrel was available only with an automatic transmission. The part number will appear on a tag attached to the top of the bowl just below the air horn.

Four-Barrel Carburetors

The 1967 273-ci four-barrel used a Carter AFB model four-barrel carburetor. This model, using a different part number, was also used with the 383-ci engine, and all Hemi engines also used this model. The manufacturer's part number can be found on a tag attached to the side of the bowl or stamped into the base of the carburetor on the foot pad.

For 1968 the 340-ci and the 383-ci used a Carter AVS series four-barrel carburetor, but each engine used a different part number. The AVS continued to be standard equipment into the 1970 model year. However, certain options, such as California emissions and the fresh air package, used a Holley model 4160 four-barrel. The Holley part number is stamped on the air horn. The 1969 and 1970 models with the 440-ci also used both Carter AVS and Holley 4160 models, dependent on options used on the car.

In 1971, all 383-ci engines used the Holley carburetor. All 440-ci powerplants used the Carter AVS series model, and the 340-ci engine used a Carter Thermo-Quad carburetor that continued with the 1972 and 1973 340s and the 360-ci in 1974. The manufacturer's part number for the Thermo-Quad will appear on a

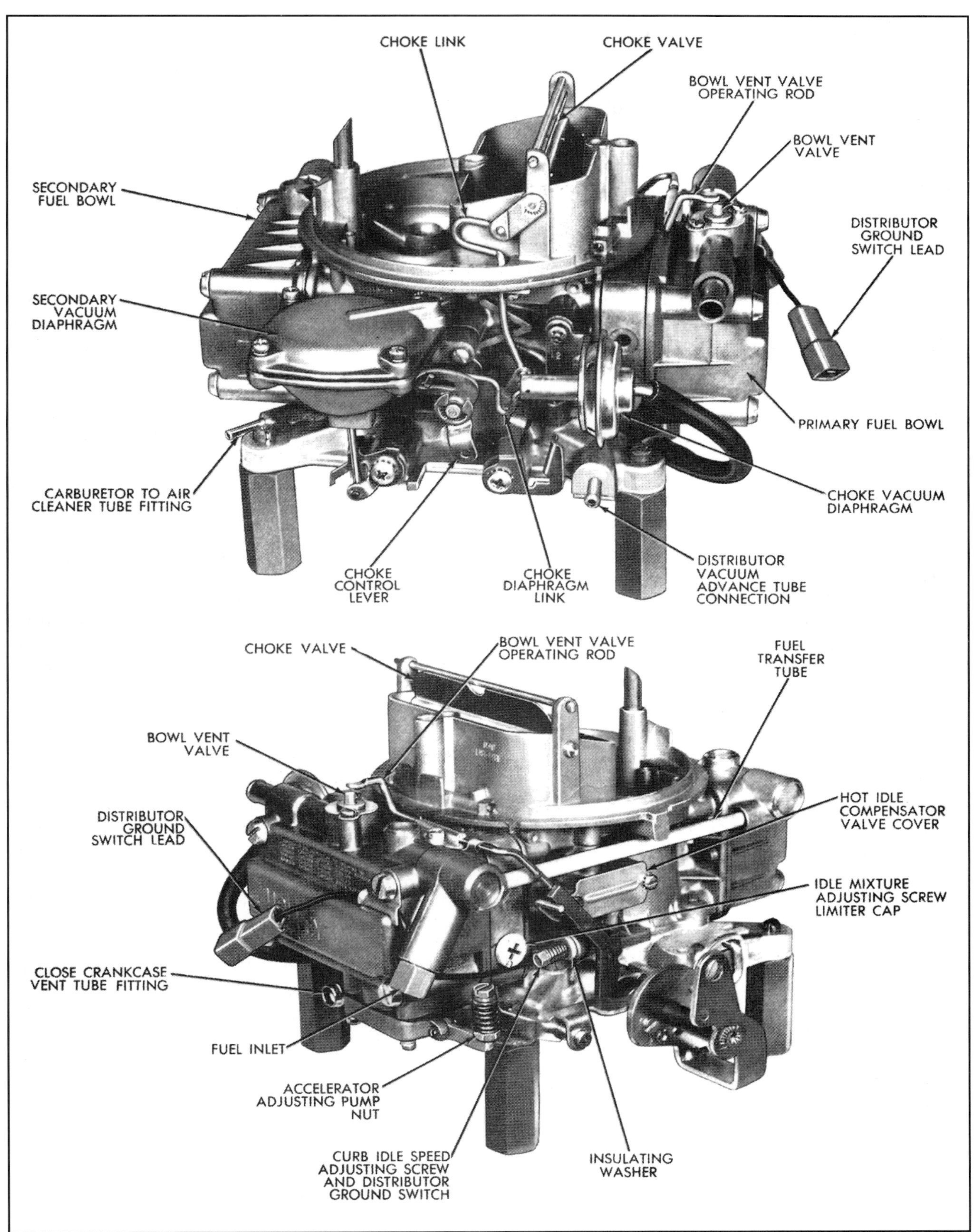

Two views of the Holley 4160 model 4-barrel carburetor.

The 426 Hemi, in all its glory with a Shaker Hood, sitting in a Barracuda. Notice the matte-finished valve covers.

small tag attached to the top of the carburetor just below the air horn.

Multiple Carburetors

All 1970-1971 440 3x2-barrel engines and the 340 3x2-barrel powerplants used Holley 2300 series model carburetors. As with the one-barrel carburetors, transmission type affects their usage, though only the center carburetor is affected. The front and rear carburetors are the same with both transmission types. The model number is stamped on the air horn. Also on the air horn is the code number in black ink. As previously mention, the Hemi engine used two Carter AFB four-barrel carburetors; transmission type affected only the rear carburetor.

Three Holley 2-barrels were used on 440- and 340-ci engines.

1967 Barracuda Carburetor Model Identification Numbers

Displacement	Carburetor Type	Manufacturer and Model No.	Model Number Manual Trans.	Automatic
225-ci six-cyl.	1-bbl	Holley 1920	R3671A#	R3672A#
			R3675A	R3676A
225-ci six-cyl.	2-bbl	Carter BBD	4300S	4301S
Export				
273-ci V-8	2-bbl	Carter BBD	4113SA	4114SA
	4-bbl	Carter AFB	4115SA#	4116SA#
			4294S	4295S
			4304S#	4305S#
383-ci V-8	4-bbl	Carter AFB	4298S	4299S
			4309S#	4310S#

= With Clean Air Package

1968 Barracuda Carburetor Model Identification Numbers

Displacement	Type	Manufacturer and Model No.	Model Number Manual Trans.	Automatic
225-ci six-cyl.	1-bbl	Holley 1920	R3919A	R3920A
225-ci six-cyl.				
Export	2-bbl	Carter BBD	4300S	4301S
318-ci V-8	2-bbl	Carter BBD	4420S	4421S
340-ci V-8	4-bbl	Carter AVS	4424S	4425S
383-ci V-8	4-bbl	Carter AVS	4426S	4401S

1969 Barracuda Carburetor Model Identification Numbers

Displacement	Type	Manufacturer and Model No.	Model Number Manual Trans.	Automatic
225-ci six cyl.	1-bbl	Holley 1920	R4161A	R4162A
225-ci six cyl.				
Export	2-bbl	Carter BBD	4300S	4301S
318-ci V-8	2-bbl	Carter BBD	4607S	4608S
340-ci V-8	4-bbl	Carter AVS	4612S	4639S
383-ci V-8	4-bbl	Carter AVS	4615S	4616S
440-ci V-8	4-bbl	Carter AVS	n/a	4618S or 4640S

1970 Chrysler Single One- and Two-Barrel Carburetor Model Numbers

Displacement	Type	Manufacturer and Model No.	Model Number Manual Trans.	Automatic
225-ci six-cyl.	1-bbl	Holley 1920	R4351A	R4352A
			R4353A#	R4354A#
			R4361A*	R4362A*
225-ci six-cyl.	2-bbl	Carter BBD	4300S*	4301S*
318-ci V-8	2-bbl	Carter BBD	4749S	4750S
			4721S#	4722S#
383-ci V-8	2-bbl	Carter BBD	N/A	4728S+
383-ci V-8	2-bbl	Holley	N/A	2200R

= California cars only ; * = Export cars only; 2-bbl standard in some countries.
+ = Air conditioning, manual transmission not available with 383-ci.

1970 Chrysler Multiple-Carburetor Model Identification Numbers

Engine	Type	Manufacturer and Model No.	Identification Numbers and Position Front	Center	Rear
340-ci V-8	3x2-bbl	Holley 2300	R4789A **84**	R4791A ^ **82**	R4790A **85**
				R4792A* **83**	
426-ci Hemi	2x4-bbl	Carter AFB	4742S	Not used	R4745^
					R4746*
440-ci V-8	3x2-bbl	Holley 2300	R4382A **45**	R4375A^ **47**	R4383A **46**
			R4175A# **44**	R4376A* **48**	R4365A **73**
				4144A^# **50**	
				4145A*# **55**	

^ = Manual transmission; * = Automatic transmission; # = California cars.
Numbers in **bold** are in black on side of air horn.

1970 Chrysler Four-Barrel Carburetor Model Numbers

Displacement	Manufacture	Model	Manufacturer Model Numbers Manual Trans.	Automatic
340-ci	Carter	AVS	4933S	4934S
			4936S#	4937S#
383-ci 335 HP	Holley	4160	R4736A	R4737A
			R4738A+	R4739A+#
			R4367A	R4368A
			R4217A#	R4218A#
383-ci 330 HP	Carter	AVS	n/a	4736S
				4732S**
				4734S#
440-ci	Carter	AVS	4737S	4738S
			4739S#	4741S**
				4740S#

= California cars; + = With Shaker Hood option; ** = With air conditioning

Big-blocks in 1970 and 1971 with a single 4-barrel and without a fresh air hood used a twin-snorkel air cleaner.

1971 Chrysler Single One-and Two-Barrel Carburetor Model Numbers

Displacement	Type	Manufacturer and Model No.	Model Number	
			Manual Trans.	**Automatic**
225-ci six-cyl.	1-bbl	Holley 1920	R4655A	R4656A
318-ci V-8	2-bbl	Carter BBD	4957S	4985S
			4959S*	4950S*
		Rochester 2GV		7041180
383-ci V-8	2-bbl	Carter BBD	4961S	4962S

* = Export cars only

^ = With Air conditioning

1971 Chrysler Four-Barrel Carburetor Model Identification Numbers

Displacement	Manufacturer	Model	Manufacturer Model Number	
			Manual Trans.	**Automatic**
340-ci V-8	Carter	T-quad	TQ4972S	TQ4973S
383-ci V-8	Holley	4160	R6191A	R4668A
			R6193A+	R4739A+

+ = Use with Shaker Hood option.

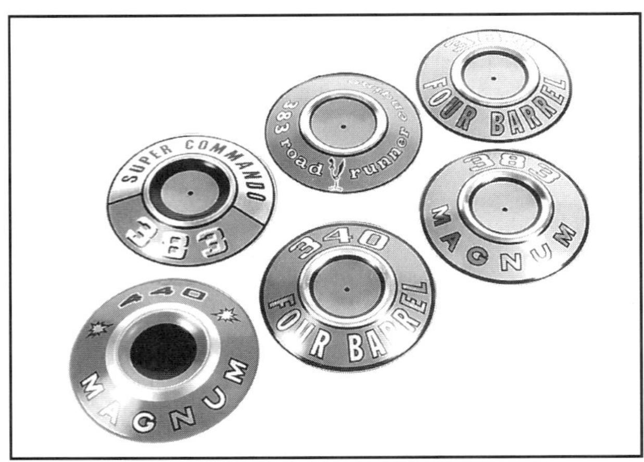

Right
1967-1971 air cleaners used colored pie tins. *Year One*

1971 Chrysler Multiple-Carburetors Model Identification Numbers

Engine and Position		Type and Model	Manufacturer Front	Model Identification Numbers Center	Rear
340-ci V-8	3x2-bbl	Holley 2300	4789A **84**	4791A^ **82** 4792* **83**	4790A **85**
440-ci V-8	3x2-bbl	Holley 2300	4671A **36**	4669A^ **34** 4670A* **35**	4672A **37**
426 Hemi	2x4-bbl	Carter AFB	4771S	n/a	4969S^ 4970S*

^ = Manual transmission; * = Automatic transmission.

Numbers in **bold** are on air horn in black ink

1972 Barracuda and Challenger Carburetor Model Numbers

Displacement	Type	Manufacturer and Model	Manufacturer Model Numbers Manual Trans.	Automatic
225-ci six-cyl.	1-bbl	Holley 1920	R6155A R6153A#	R6156A R6154A#
318-ci V-8	2-bbl	Carter BBD	6150S 6152S#	6149S 6151S#
340-ci V-8	4-bbl	Carter T- Quad	TQ6138S	TQ6139S

= California cars only.

1973 Barracuda and Challenger Carburetor Model Identification Numbers

Displacement	Type	Manufacturer and Model	Manufacturer Model Number Manual Trans.	Automatic
318-ci V-8	2-bbl	Carter BBD	6316SA 6343SA#	6317SA 6344SA#
340-ci V-8	4-bbl	Carter T- Quad	TQ6318S TQ6339S#	TQ6319S TQ6340S#

= California cars only.

Air Cleaner Assembly

All air cleaners used a replaceable heavy-duty micronic dry element. The 1967 273-ci 2-bbl and the 1968-1974 318-ci 2-bbl used a semi-gloss black-painted, silenced air cleaner of single-snorkel design. Six-cylinder engines also used a silenced air cleaner, but it is much taller and narrower than those used on the V-8s. Exports used a special air cleaner assembly that looked like the U.S. unit, but was designed to fit the 2-bbl carburetors and has no provisions for the emission controls.

The 1967 273-ci four-barrel used a chrome-plated unsilenced air cleaner (without a snorkel) with a red appliqué that read "273 Commando." The 1967 383 also used an unsilenced air cleaner. It was larger in diameter than the one used on the 273 but not as tall; it was painted in a black crackle finish and included a red pie tin that read "383 Commando."

1974 Barracuda and Challenger Carburetor Manufacturer Model Numbers

Displacement	Type	Manufacturer and Model	Manufacturer Model Number	
			Manual Trans.	Automatic
318-ci V-8	2-bbl	Carter BBD	6464S	6465S
			6466S#	6467S#
360-ci V-8	4-bbl	Carter T- Quad	TQ6452S	TQ6453S
			TQ6454S#	TQ6455S#

= California cars.

Throttle Return Spring Color Codes
Spring Identification

Model Years	Number of coils	Color Code	Part Number
1967-1968 (six-cyl.)	30	Blue	2843757
1967-1968 (V-8)	39	White with Black stripe	2806462
1967-1968 (V-8)	49	Green with Orange stripe	2899327
1968	38	Red with Blue stripe	2946611
1969 (six-cyl.)	34	Violet	2951448
1969 (340-ci)	33	Black	2946695
1969-1971 (six-cyl. exports)	34	Green	2951471
1969 (318-ci)	45	Gray	2951473
1969	33	See Note 1	See Note 1
1969	38	Yellow	2946694
1970-197 (six-cyl.)	16	Orange	3462704
1970-1971	33	Red	3462753
1970	45	Gray	3462752
1970	38	Yellow	2946694
1970	34	Blue	3418815
1970 (Hemi front carburetor)	22	Green with Blue stripe	2863722
1970 (Hemi rear carburetor)	18	Red with White stripe	2946617
1970-1972 (six-cyl.)	34	Blue	3462754
1971-1972 (318-ci)	33	Red	3462751

Note 1: Four different springs in 1969 had 33 coils: Black = 2946695; Green = 2951472; Red = 2946696; Blue = 2946697.

A Challenger with a Hemi but without a Shaker Hood used this air cleaner.

For 1968 and 1969, both the 340 and the 383 used an unsilenced air cleaner. They were finished in the same manner as the 1967 383, but the pie tins were replaced. They were still red, but those on the 340 read "340 Four Barrel" while the 383 now read "383 Super Commando." California Barracudas were the exception in 1968, where a dual-snorkel air cleaner was used due to noise restrictions, and it could be hard to find today. The 440 used the unsilenced air cleaner with a pie tin that read "440 Super Commando" even in California.

All 1970 engines except those with four-barrel or multiple carburetors used a single-snorkel air cleaner with heated air ducts. Those cars with a 340-ci or 440-ci engine with a single four-barrel used the redesigned unsilenced air cleaner. It is larger in diameter than the one used on earlier models, and the lid is flat; it looks a lot like a silenced air cleaner with the snorkel removed. The 383 used a large, dual-snorkel air cleaner assembly, with a flat lid. Both the unsilenced and the twin-snorkel designs were painted like the unsilenced unit of previous years.

Pie tins were still used in 1970, but now they were orange instead of red. The tin used on the 340 read "340 Four Barrel," and those with the 383-ci 330-hp engine read "383 Four Barrel" in both the Challenger and Barracuda. Cudas used a different pie tin than those in a Challenger R/T when equipped with a 383- or 440-ci engine. Those in the Dodge read "383 Magnum" and "440 Magnum," depending on the engine. Pie tins used with the Plymouth read "383 Super Command" and "440 Super Commando."

The air cleaner applications and pie tins continued unchanged into 1971, except that both 440 pie tins were deleted as this engine was no longer available. Also removed was the 383 four-barrel pie tin; all 383-ci four-barrel V-8s were consider high-output versions in 1971. Two different pie tins were used as identification; Challengers used the 383 Magnum tin and the Barracuda used the 383 Super Commando tin.

For 1972 the 340 air cleaners were restyled to a large, single-snorkel design painted Street Hemi Orange. Pie tins were replaced with decals that read "340 Four-Barrel 340." This design and color continued into 1973. The 1974 360-ci four-barrel also used this style of air cleaner, but the assembly was painted Chrysler Blue to match the cylinder block.

Cars equipped with a 426 Hemi used unique air cleaners. As with the Plymouth B-bodies, Cudas with the 426 Hemi came standard with the fresh air package, which in the E-body line was called the Shaker Hood. The fresh air hood was not standard on Challengers with the 426 Hemi. Hemi Challengers, on the other hand, used a large, oval, open-element design, and the top of the cover was painted Street Hemi Orange to match the block. The bottom portion of the air cleaner

AAR and T/A cars used this air cleaner. An AAR model is shown.

The Shaker Hood option used an air cleaner that doubled as a hood scoop.

assembly was painted flat black and a decal that read "426 HEMI" was used for identification on the cover.

The 440-ci 3x2-barrel and the 340-ci 3x2-barrel powerplants also used a large, oval, open-element air cleaner. The cover was painted Hemi Orange and the bottom pan was flat black. Decals are used as identification on the covers. Those on Plymouths read "340 Six Barrel" or "440 Six Barrel," while on the Dodge, the decal read "340 Six Pack" or "440 Six Pack."

When the Shaker Hood, or the fresh air package as Chrysler called it, was ordered, a special air cleaner was required. This air cleaner supported a divided scoop that stuck up through an opening in a special hood. The air cleaner assembly itself is painted gloss black, but the portion that stuck up out of the hood is painted one of four different colors: flat black, Astrotone Silver (with any exterior color), Blue Fire Metallic (with blue exterior colors), or Rally Red (with red exterior colors). The flat black paint is listed as Ditzler DDL 9355 Organosol Black. Astrotone Silver is listed as Medium Textured Argent Silver DNA-8575. The Shaker Hood option was limited to models with the 426 Hemi when production began. Then it was expanded to include models with the 440 3x2-barrel in late June 1969, and the 340-ci and 440-ci four-barrel powerplants in late July or early August 1969.

The Shaker Hood option was standard in all Cudas with a 426 Hemi, of which a total of 664 were built, and only 14 were convertibles. A total of 1,391 1970 Barracudas (including the Hemis) were built with the Shaker Hood; most were hardtops, and only 22 were convertibles. Only 189 1970 Challengers were built with the Shaker Hood, and this total includes 15 S.E. models and 5 convertibles. This low number is mainly due to a shortage of the Challenger Shaker Hood at the factories, where the Trans Am's fiberglass hood was installed instead.

In its last year of production as an option, a total of 817 Barracudas were built with the Shaker Hood, including 115 with the 426 Hemi. On the Challenger line only 224 cars, including 11 convertibles, were ordered with the Shaker Hood. The hood was still not standard with Hemi models but was available for the base Challenger models with a four-barrel powerplant. The Shaker Hood option was canceled shortly before the end of the 1971 production line, thus no 1972-1974 cars with a Shaker Hood were built.

An air cleaner service decal used on 1968-1971 unsilenced air cleaners and 1970-1971 dual-snorkel air cleaners. It is positioned on the front of the air cleaner on the driver's side.

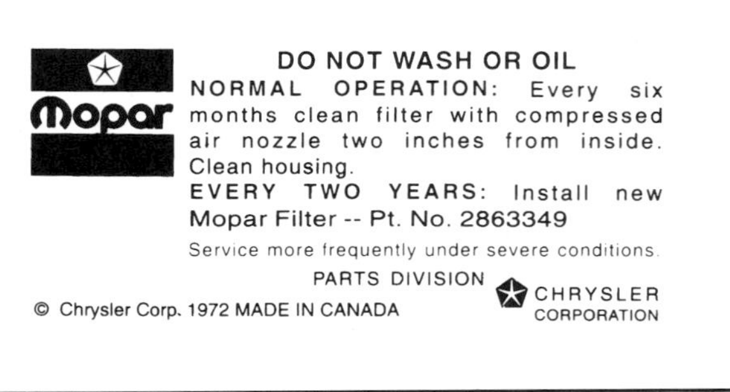

A service decal for the 1972-1973 340-ci, and 1974 360-ci engines. It should be positioned on front of air cleaner facing the driver's side.

This decal was used instead of a pie tin on 1972-1973 models.

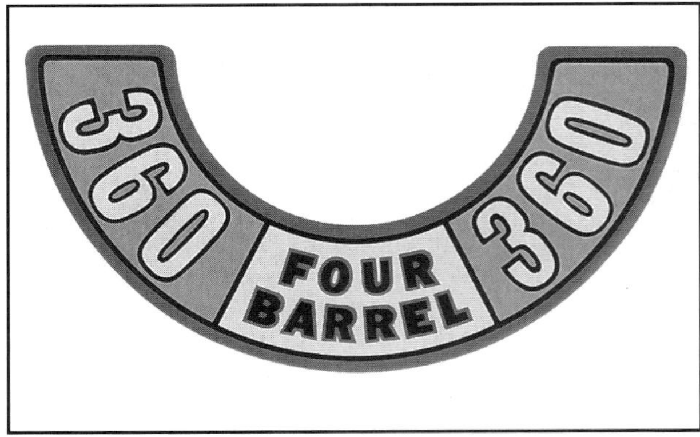

In 1974, the 340-ci engine was replaced with a 360-ci engine, which used this decal.

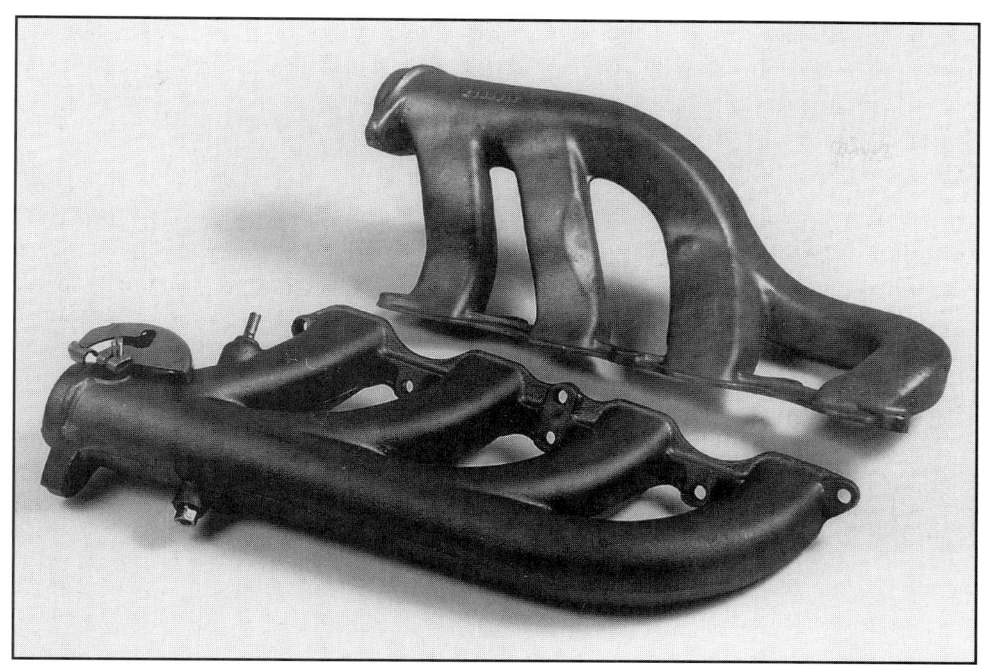

Hemis used header-like exhaust manifolds. *Year One*

Cars with a 340 3x2-barrel used exhaust pipes that exited in front of the rear tires.

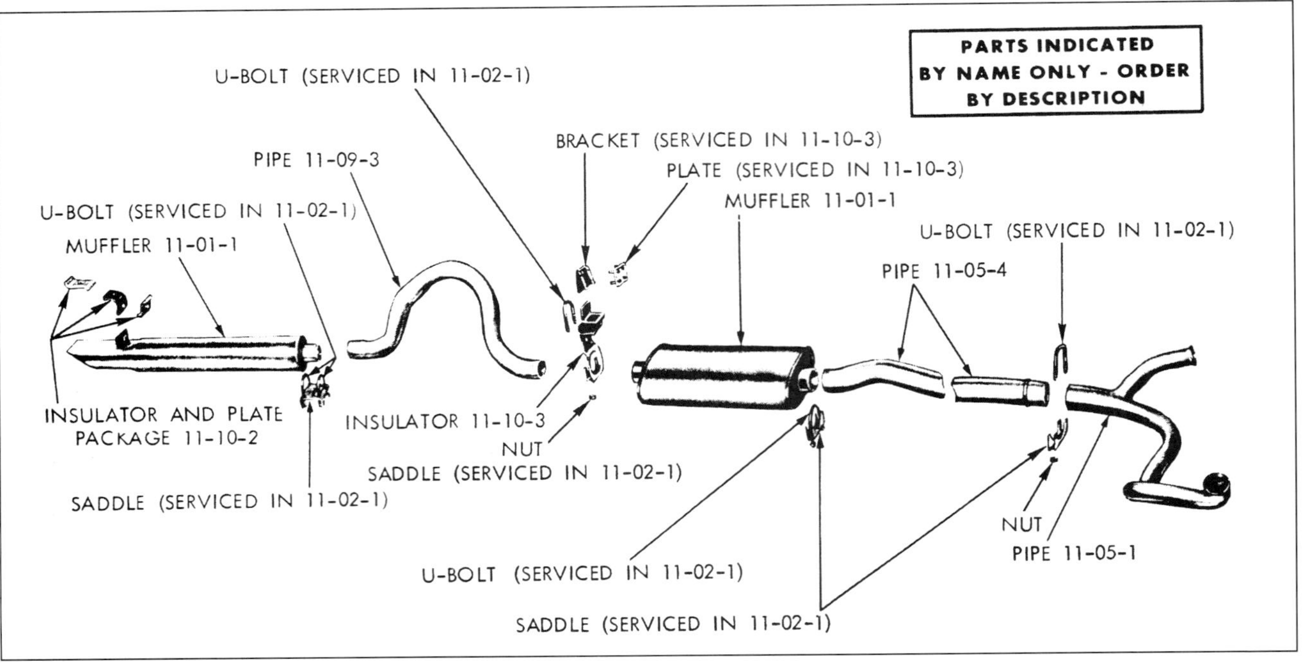

The 1967 273-ci 4-barrel with the Powerpack exhaust system.

1967-1974 Chrysler Exhaust Manifold Casting Numbers

Displacement	**Years Used**	**Casting Numbers**		
			Driver's Side	**Passengers Side**
Notes				
225-ci six-cyl.	1967-1968	2268760	n/a	n/a
225-ci six-cyl.	1969	2658350	n/a	n/a
225-ci six-cyl.	1969-1972	2658350	n/a	Export only
225-ci six-cyl.	1970-1972	2951840	n/a	Not for export
273-ci	1967	2780945	2465769	n/a
318-ci	1968	2780945	2465769	n/a
318-ci	1969	2780945	2843953	n/a
318-ci	1970	2951916	2946085	n/a
318-ci	1971	3512077	2946085	n/a
318-ci	1972-1974	3512077	2843953	n/a
340-ci	1968-1970	2863553	2863549	n/a
340-ci	1971-1972	3418621	3418623	n/a
340-ci	1973	3751084	3418623	n/a
360-ci	1974	3741084	3418623	Except Calif.
360-ci	1974	3671584	3671635	Calif. only
383-ci	1967	2899002	2863900	For Barracuda only
383-ci/440-ci	1968-1969	2946729	2863900	For Barracuda or Dart GT only
383/440-ci	1970-1971	2951865	2899879	N/A
383-ci 2-bbl	1970-1971	2951865	2899970	2-bbl engines
426 Hemi	1970	3418351	2780508	N/A
426 Hemi	1971	3418351	3577281	N/A

Exhaust Systems

Dual exhaust was standard with all models except those with a one- or two-barrel carburetor, where single exhaust is used. However, the 1967 Barracuda with a 273-ci four-barrel did use a single exhaust system with a special free-flowing muffler. The casting number and date is the best way to identify the exhaust manifold. All manifolds should have a fresh-cast appearance. This can be accomplished by finishing with an ultra-high-temperature cast-iron gray paint. Several companies offer this paint, including Eastwood.

At the factory, exhaust manifolds were installed when the engine was painted, thus some overspray found its way onto the manifolds—and it was quickly burned off. This look could be duplicated by using an ultra-high-temperature paint the same color as the block and letting a fine mist of paint fall onto the inner edges of the manifold. Despite being authentic, this can end up looking sloppy on a show car.

Either aluminum-coated or zinc-coated mufflers were installed on the 1967-1969 Barracudas. The aluminum-coated muffler will have a dull aluminum appearance while the zinc-coated muffler will have a dull gold finish. The 1970-1974 models used mufflers mounted at the rear of the car, where resonators would normally be located. This includes both single- and dual-exhaust systems. Chrome extensions were part of the dual-exhaust package all eight years, but they were not used with a single-exhaust system.

The 1970 Trans-Am models used a special setup with two short headpipes that empty into two rectangular, free-flowing mufflers. The large-diameter tailpipes exited at the sides of the car just in front of the rear wheels, giving the car a racy look. Special hangers were used to mount the tailpipes to the underbelly of the car. An orange paint mark was used to identify the driver's-side tailpipe hanger, a detail many restorers leave off.

Emission Controls

Due to federally mandated standards, every Barracuda and every Challenger built came with some type of emission-controls system, although cars for sale in California used extra emission controls. Typically, emission controls used on California cars one year became standard equipment for all states the next year.

Crankcase Ventilation

Two types of ventilation were installed in 1967 models. All states, except California, used the Standard Ventilation System (SVS). This setup consisted of a PCV valve mounted on the passenger-side valve cover and a hose connected from this valve to a provision on the carburetor. With the SVS setup, the oil filler cap doubled as

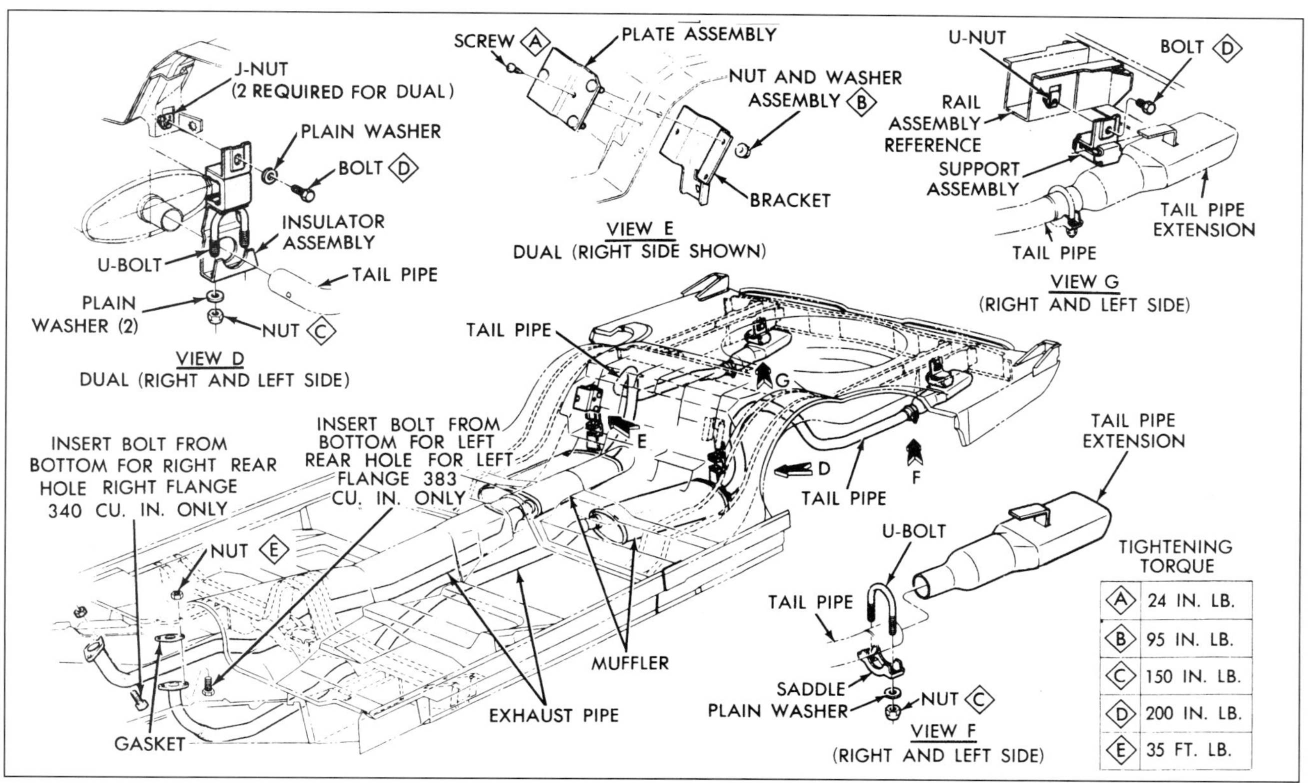

The 1968-1969 Barracuda dual-exhaust system.

a breather cap. The breather cap was painted gloss black on all but the 383, where it was chrome-plated.

Mandatory in 1967 California cars was the Closed Ventilation System (CVS) except those with the 383-ci engines, where only the SVS setup was used. This setup was similar to the SVS but used a closed-type oil breather cap. This cap has a provision for a hose that is routed to a provision on the underside of the air cleaner. The CVS setup was made standard in 1968 models for all 50 states. The cap was painted semi-gloss black, except those with the 383-ci or 440-ci powerplants in 1968 and 1969.

In 1970, cars sold in California used a different oil breather cap than the other 49 states. This is due to the ECS, or Evaporative Control System (see below), that required an extra provision for a hose that was routed to the gas tank. In 1971 this cap was standard in all 50 states. The cap was painted gloss black. Export cars in 1971- 1974 continued to use the older style of breather with only one provision.

Clean Air Package (CAP)

The CAP was mandatory in cars sold in California, in addition to the CVS in 1967. Unlike the CVS, other components of the engine are affected. Hoses were routed from a vacuum control to a modified carburetor and distributor, all of which worked to reduce the emissions in the exhaust. Just as with the CVS, this setup was made standard in 1968 for all states, where it was known as the Cleaner Air System (CAS).

Heated Air System (HAS)

The HAS was part of the CAS package in 1970 for all engines with a silenced air cleaner. Warm air was directed into the engine by duct work routed from the exhaust manifold to a diaphragm on the air cleaner. When underhood temperatures were above 100 deg, the doors would open and cold air would be directed into the carburetor. In 1972, HAS was standard on all engines.

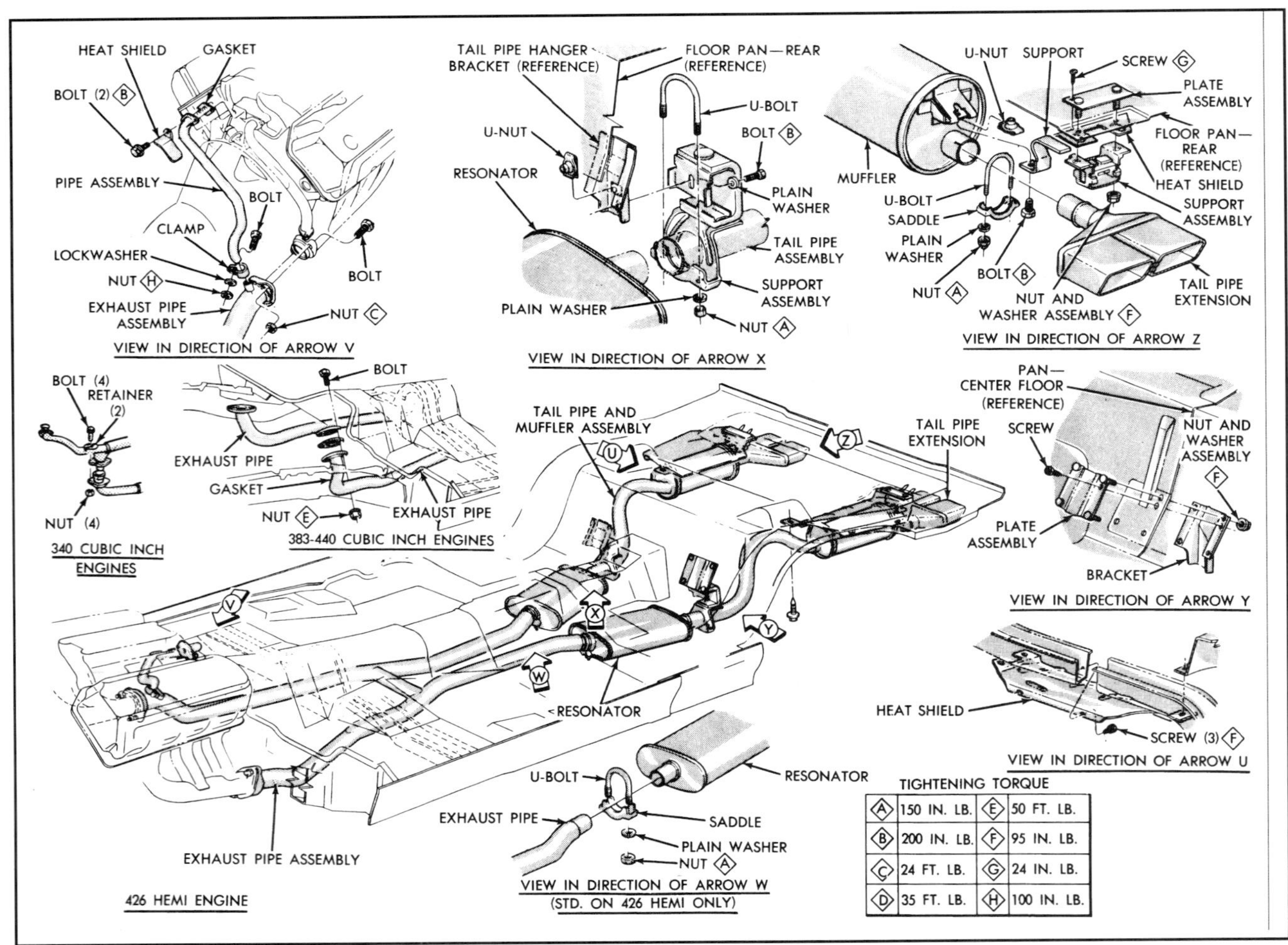

A	150 IN. LB.	E	50 FT. LB.
B	200 IN. LB.	F	95 IN. LB.
C	24 FT. LB.	G	24 IN. LB.
D	35 FT. LB.	H	100 IN. LB.

The 1970-1974 Barracuda or Challenger dual exhaust.

28998 **45**

THIS VEHICLE HAS
CHRYSLER CLEANER AIR SYSTEM
TO REDUCE VEHICLE EMISSIONS
REGULAR SERVICE IS REQUIRED TO
MAINTAIN LOWEST VEHICLE EMISSIONS

IDLE SETTINGS
- **RPM = 700 IN NEUTRAL**
- **TIMING = TDC**
- **MIXTURE = 14.0 TO 14.4 A/F RATIO**

This emission decal was used with: the 1968 340 four-speed; the 1969 383 four-speed; and the 1969 to early 1970 318-ci with an automatic. It was positioned on the left-hand inner fender to the rear of the washer jar, except on 1970 models. On 1970 models, the position is the left-hand inner fender near the hood hinge.

28998 **46**

THIS VEHICLE HAS
CHRYSLER CLEANER AIR SYSTEM
TO REDUCE VEHICLE EMISSIONS
REGULAR SERVICE IS REQUIRED TO
MAINTAIN LOWEST VEHICLE EMISSIONS

IDLE SETTINGS
- **RPM = 750 IN NEUTRAL**
- **TIMING = TDC**
- **MIXTURE = 14.0 A./F. RATIO OR HIGHER**

This decal was used with: the 1969 340-ci with a four-speed; early 1970 318s with manual transmissions; and early 1970 383 four-barrels with manual transmission. The change occurred around March 10, 1970. See the previous decal for placement.

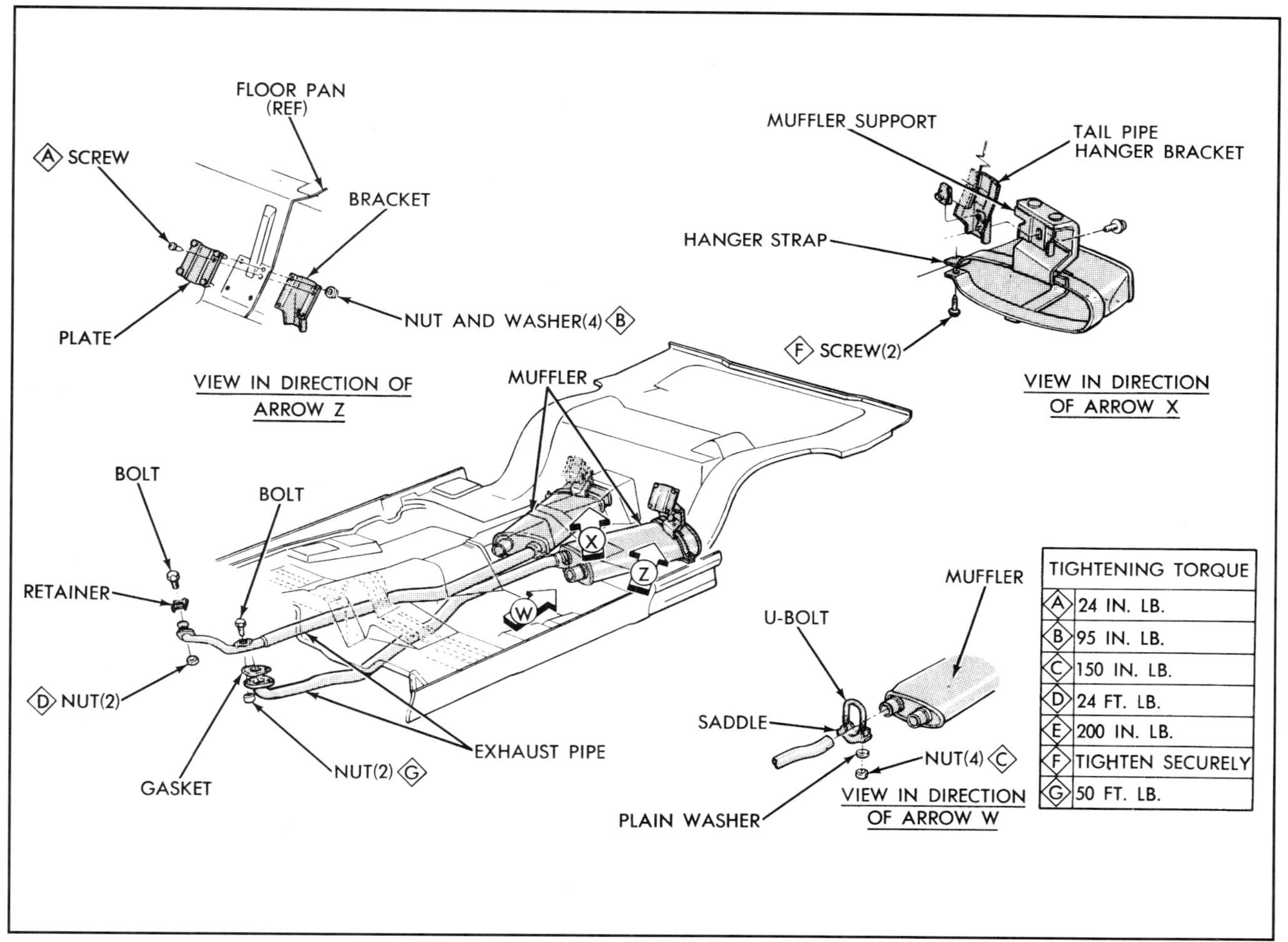

TIGHTENING TORQUE	
A	24 IN. LB.
B	95 IN. LB.
C	150 IN. LB.
D	24 FT. LB.
E	200 IN. LB.
F	TIGHTEN SECURELY
G	50 FT. LB.

The Trans-Am-style exhaust system.

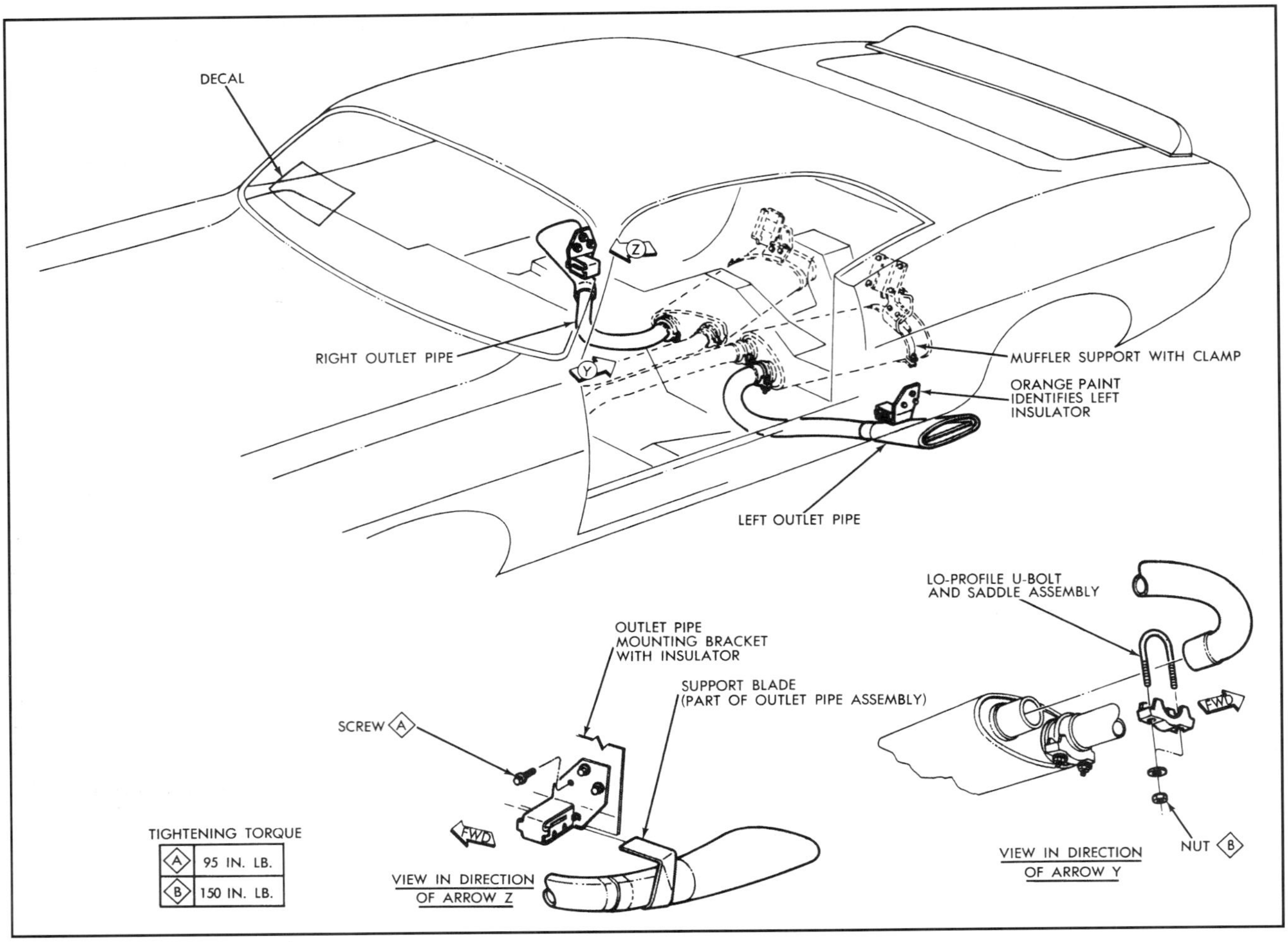

DECAL
RIGHT OUTLET PIPE
MUFFLER SUPPORT WITH CLAMP
ORANGE PAINT IDENTIFIES LEFT INSULATOR
LEFT OUTLET PIPE
LO-PROFILE U-BOLT AND SADDLE ASSEMBLY
OUTLET PIPE MOUNTING BRACKET WITH INSULATOR
SUPPORT BLADE (PART OF OUTLET PIPE ASSEMBLY)
SCREW A
FWD
TIGHTENING TORQUE

A	95 IN. LB.
B	150 IN. LB.

VIEW IN DIRECTION OF ARROW Z
VIEW IN DIRECTION OF ARROW Y
NUT B

The Trans-Am-style exhaust pipes.

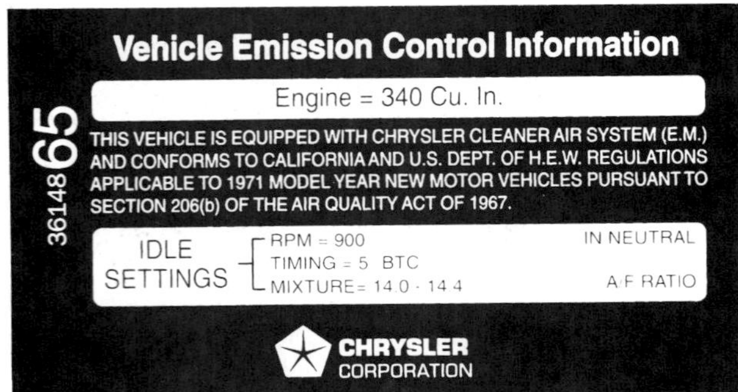

This blue-and-white decal was used on 1970 340-ci four-barrel cars sold in California. It was positioned on the left-hand inner fender near the hood hinge.

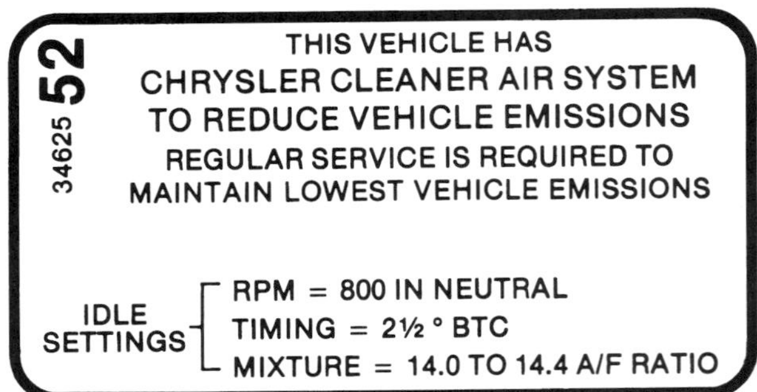

This decal was used on early (until approximately March 10, 1970) 1970 models with the 440 four-barrel with an automatic. It was positioned on the left-hand inner fender near the hood hinge.

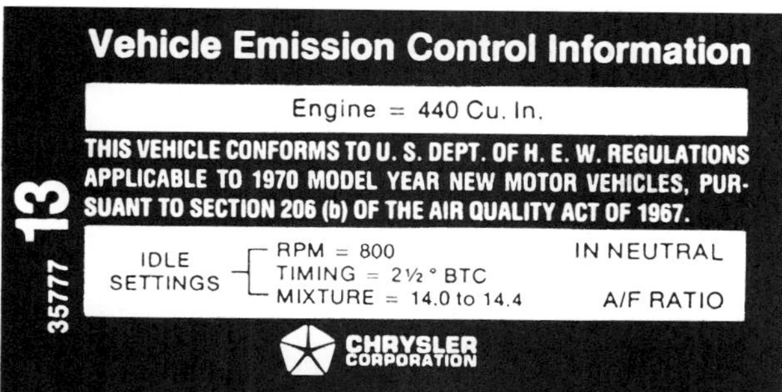

Although timing data and position stayed the same, the decal was changed in March 1970. Shown is that for a 1970 440 four-barrel with an automatic. Compare with the previous decal. This decal is green and white.

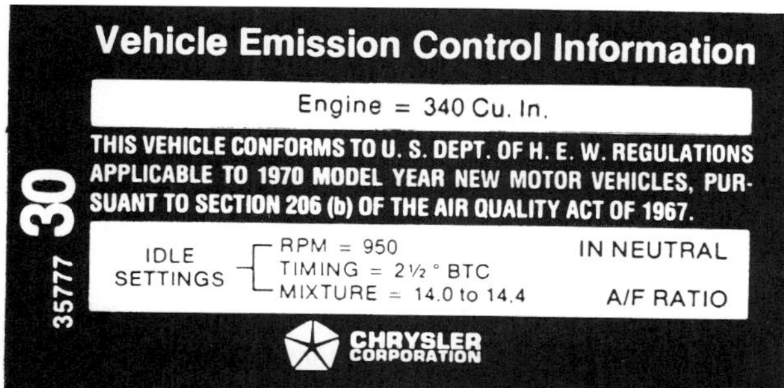

An emission decal for 1970 (all year long) models with the 340 3x2-barrel with an automatic transmission. Its position was the left-hand inner fender near the hood hinge. This decal is green and white.

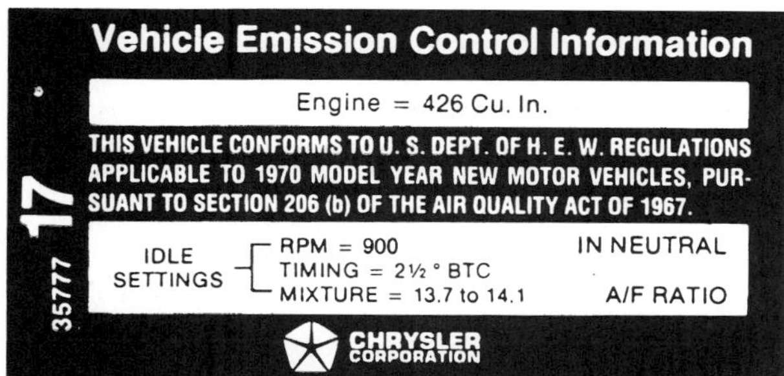

This green and white emission decal was used on late-1970 426 Hemis with automatic transmission. Its position is the same as the early style.

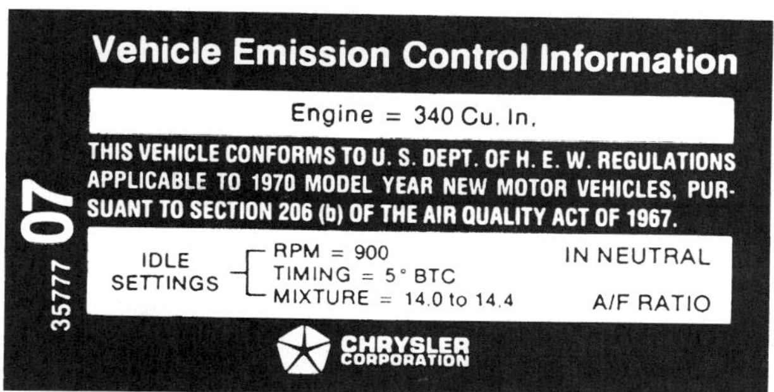

This decal was used on late-1970 (after March 10, 1970) models with a 340 four-barrel with a manual transmission. Its position was the left-hand inner fender near the hood hinge. The decal is green and white.

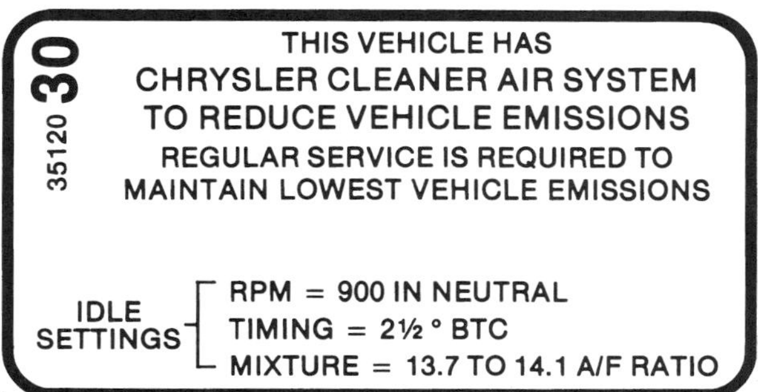

This was used on early 1970 (up to March 10, 1970) models with the 426 Hemi with an automatic transmission. Its position is the left-hand inner fender near the hood hinge. The decal is white with black lettering.

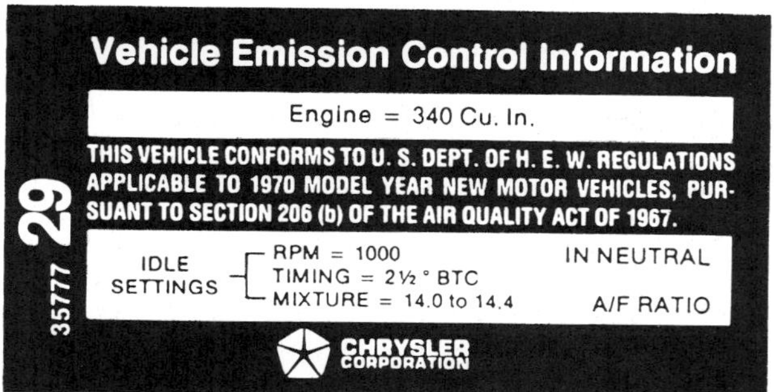

This emission decal was used for 1970 models with a 340 3x2-barrel with a manual transmission. Its position is the left-hand inner fender near the hood hinge. This decal is green and white.

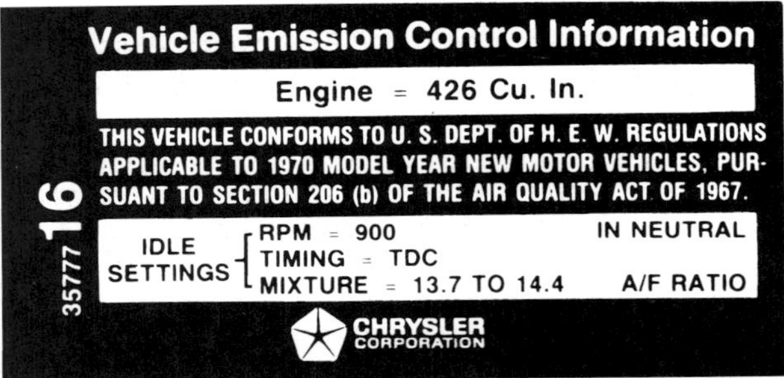

This green-and-white emission decal is for late-1970 (after March 10, 1970) models with the 426 Hemi with a four-speed. Its position is on the left front inner fender near the hood hinge.

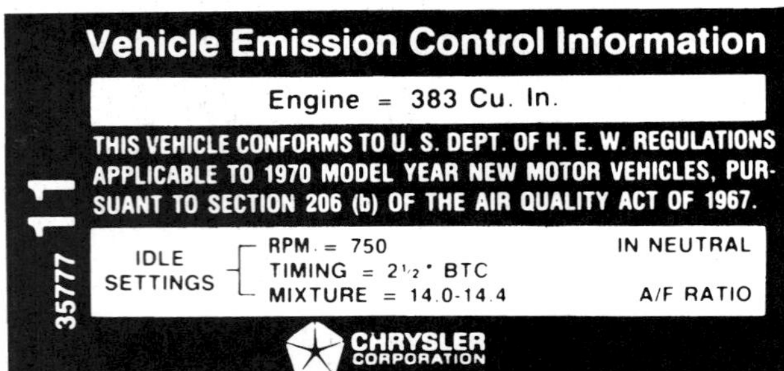

This was used on late-1970 (after March 10, 1970) models with a 383-ci four-barrel with automatic transmission. The decal is green and white.

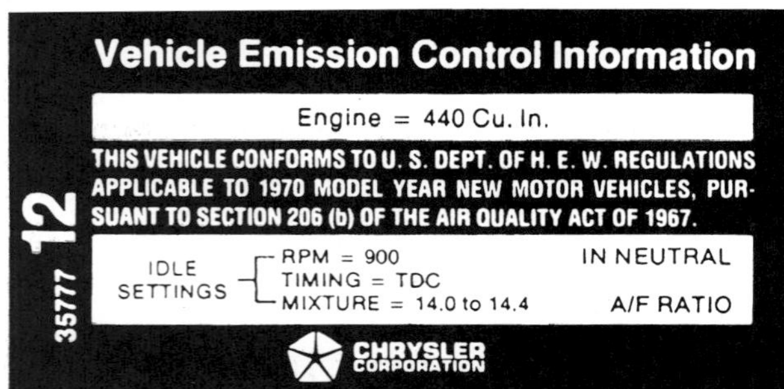

An emission decal for a late-1970 (after March 10, 1970) 440 four-barrel with automatic transmission.

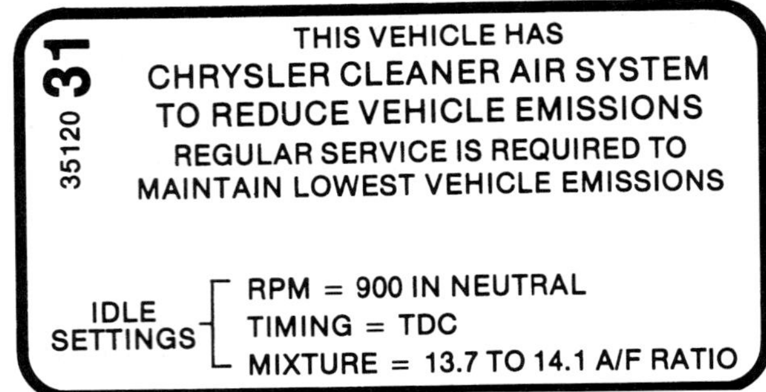

This is an early (before March 10, 1970) 1970 Hemi emission decal.

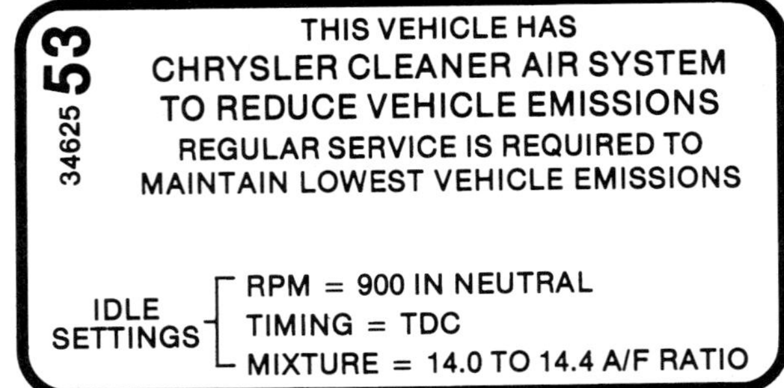

An emission decal for an early 1970 (before March 10, 1970) 440 four-barrel with four-speed.

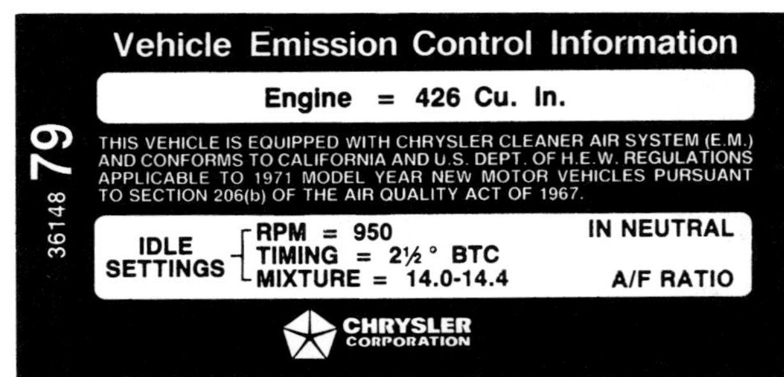

Emission decals for 1971 were blue and white. Shown A decal for a 1971 426 Hemi with automatic transmission, which should be positioned on left front inner fender near the hood hinge.

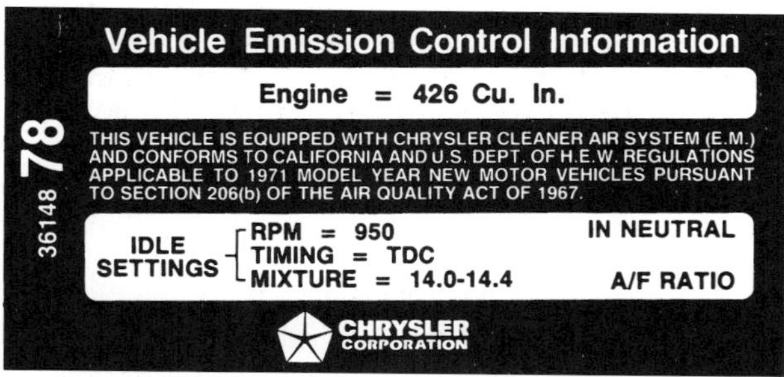

The emission decal for the 1971 Hemi with a four-speed is blue and white.

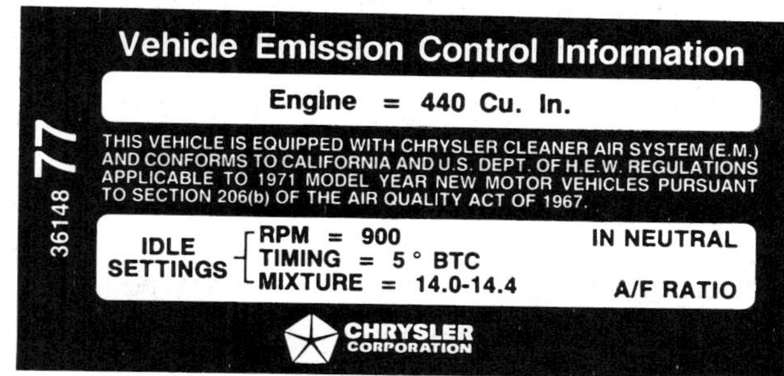

The only 440 emission decal for 1971 models.

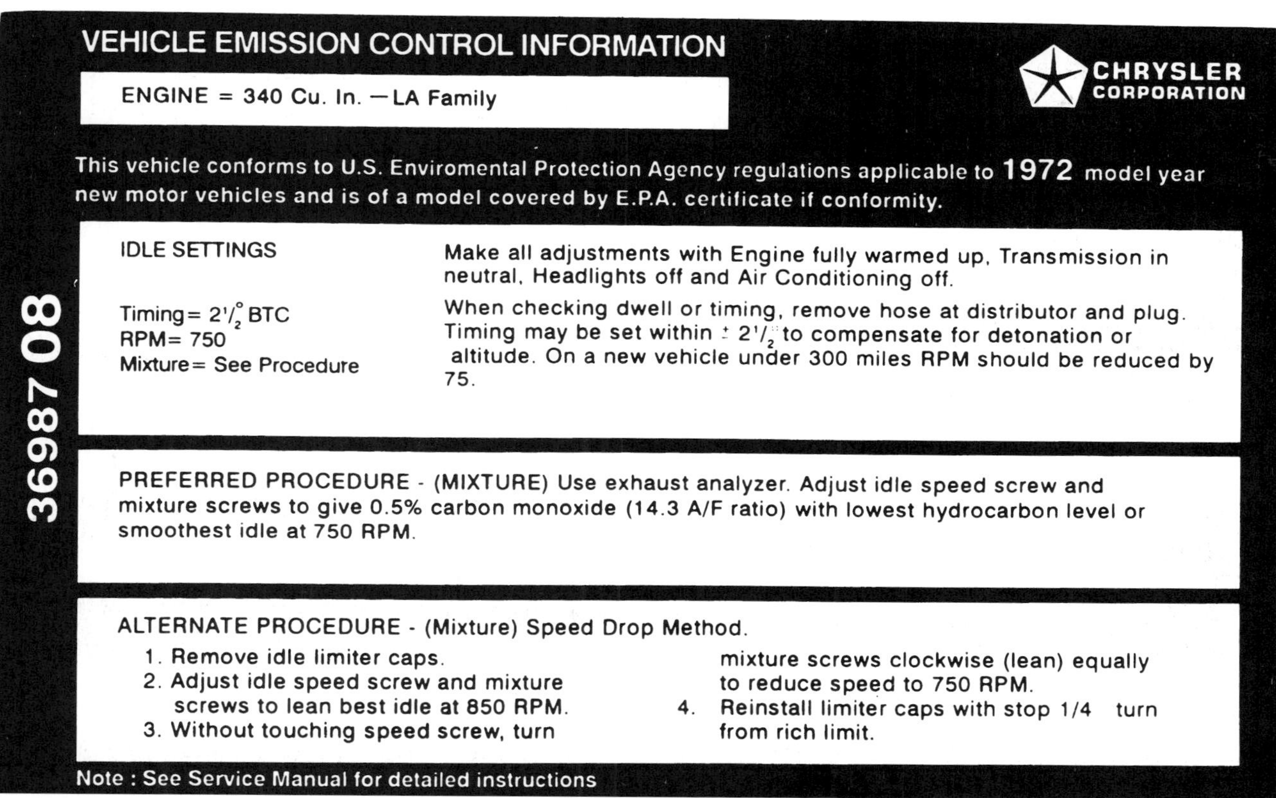

The 1972 emission decal is larger than previous versions.

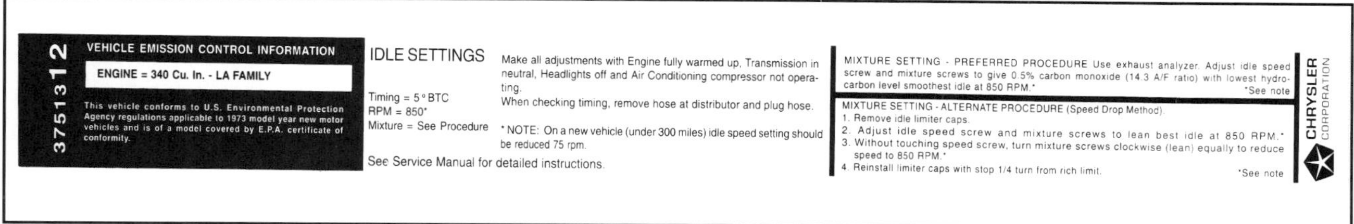

An emission decal for the 1973 340-ci with a four-speed.

Evaporation Control System (ECS)

The ECS was mandatory in 1970 California cars; it was designed to reduce fuel vapors from entering the air. It consisted of a special gas tank with an extra provision for vapor lines. Four lines are routed from the tank to a vapor-liquid separator. A steel line was routed under the car to a vacuum hose connected to a provision on a special breather cap on the valve cover. Another hose was routed from the breather to a provision on the carburetor. Spring ring clamps were used at each end of the hose. A special gas cap was also required with the emission package. Beginning with the 1971 models, the ECS option was made standard for all 50 states.

NOX System

This appeared in 1971 models as mandatory equipment for California-bound cars. It was used in addition to the CAS and the ECS packages. Special components for the transmission, a special camshaft (with more valve overlap), and a 185degree thermostat were required. Two distinct configurations were used, the selection made based on the transmission used.

With manual transmissions, a switch was mounted on the transmission so it sensed which gear,the car was in. In any gear below high gear the switch remained closed and a circuit to ground was completed. This activated a solenoid that cut off the vacuum from the carburetor and the distributor, canceling the normal spark advance. In high gear the switch opened and the vacuum was returned to normal. Because a cold car needs more advance, a temperature sensor was mounted on the firewall. If the underhood temperature was below 70 degree, the control unit opened the switch, creating normal advance in all gears.

In an automatic transmission, a speed switch is mounted in line with the speedometer cable. It worked much the same way the manual transmission did, by cutting off normal advance vacuum during certain driving conditions. When the underhood temperature is above 70 degree and car speed is below 30 miles per hour, or during acceleration, the vacuum to the carburetor and distributor is shut off. Below 70 degree, or over 30 miles per hour under a nonload condition, the vacuum returns to normal.

All of this was done to reduce the nitrous oxide emissions coming out of the exhaust, a condition which is most prevalent during gear changes or acceleration. Of the two, the most noticeable change (lack of performance) was felt in cars with a manual transmission. This package was canceled for 1972 models, and the Exhaust Gas Recirculation (EGR) package took its place.

Exhaust Gas Recirculation

The EGR was standard equipment on all cars in all 50 states in 1973. Two types were used: The 318-ci engine used a ported type, while the 340 used a floor-jetted type.

In the ported type, a port in the carburetor body drew a vacuum from the intake manifold. The port is connected to a tee that connects it to an EGR valve. The valve controlled the mixture of exhaust gases with the fuel-air mixture flowing to the carburetor. A temperature control unit mounted to the firewall recali-

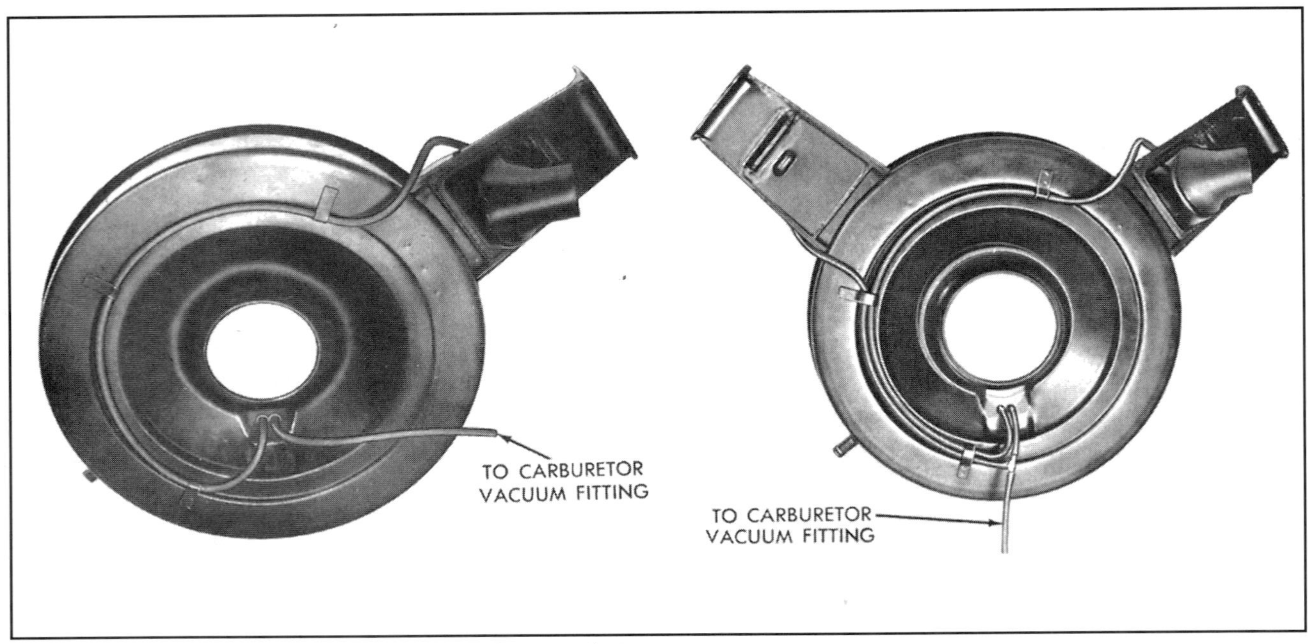

The routing of vacuum hoses on air cleaners with the Heated Air System.

brated the gases for better driveability during cold conditions. Color-coded, striped hoses were used to connect the components.

With the 340-ci engine, exhaust gases were introduced into the intake manifold through jets under the carburetor. An orifice in each jet controlled the fuel-air mixture. For 1974, both the 318- and the 360-ci engines used the ported system—except in California. In California cars, both V-8s used the venturi method (which used a vacuum amplifier) that dumped the gases into the carburetor.

Orifice Spark Advance Control

This system also replaced the NOX system and was used in all 50 states with all engines in 1973 models. This package consisted of a valve mounted on the firewall. Two color-coded hoses ran from this valve: a black hose to the carburetor, and a red-striped hose to the distributor.

Cooling System

The cooling system consisted of a: tube-and-spacer-type radiator core, a 16-psi pressure cap, a water pump, and a fan blade. There were three different systems used:

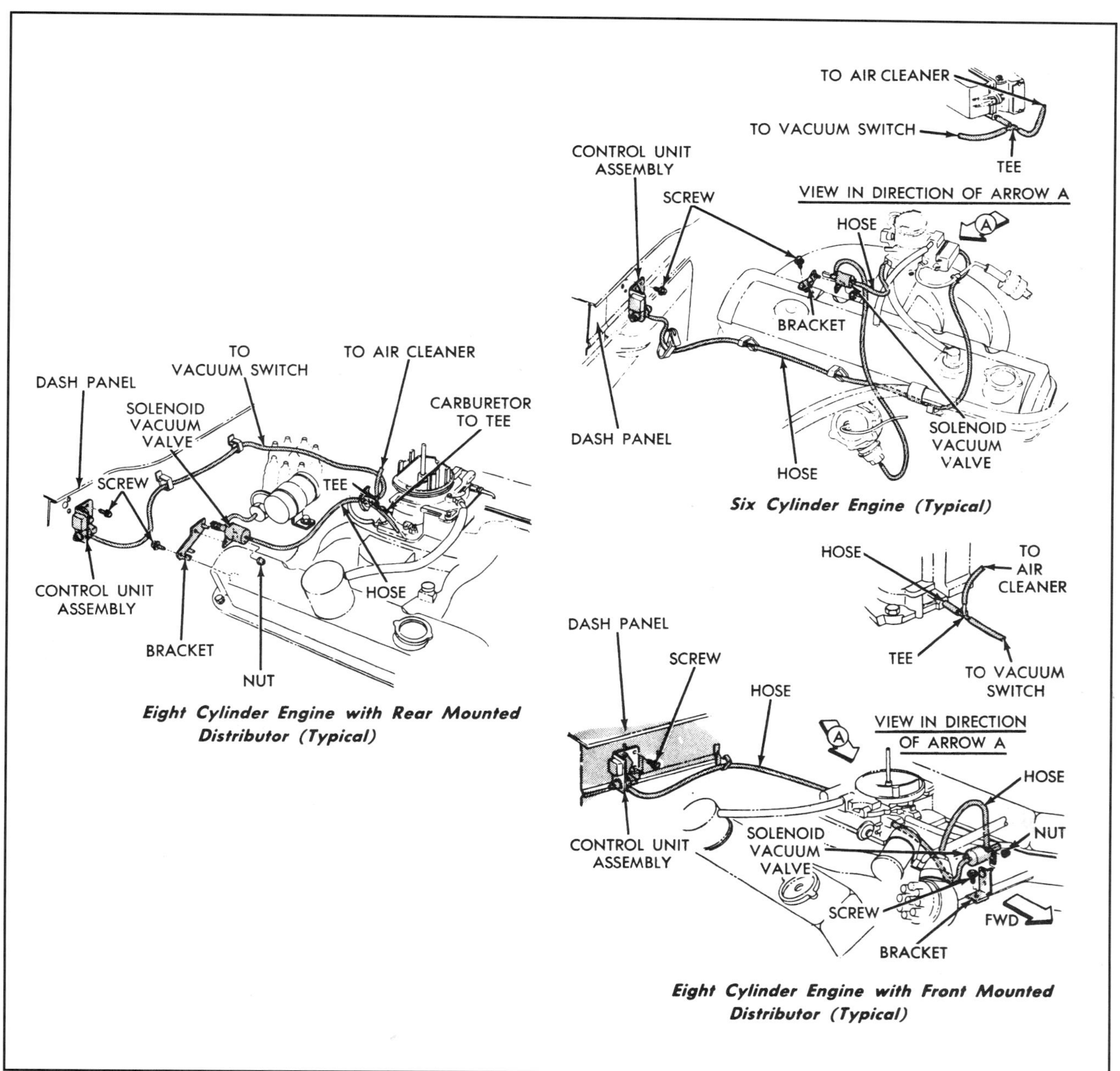

These are the various hose routings with the NOX system and automatic transmissions.

1967 Barracuda Radiator Core Identification Numbers

Displacement	System	Shroud Used	Transmission	Identification Number
225-ci six-cyl.	Std.	No	Manual	2785980
225-ci six-cyl.	Std.	No	Automatic	2785978
273-ci V-8	Std.	No	All	2785973
273-ci V-8	A/C	Yes	All	2785971
273-ci V-8	Calif. cars	Yes	All	2785970
383-ci V-8	Std.	Yes	All	2785929

1968 Barracuda Radiator Core Identification Numbers

Displacement	System	Shroud	Transmission	Identification Number
225-ci six-cyl.	Std.	No	Manual	2898021
225-ci six-cyl.	Std.	No	Auto	2898023
225-ci six-cyl.	A/C or Max Cool	Yes	Auto	2898067
318/340-ci V-8	Std.	No #	Manual	2898026
318/340-ci V-8	Std.	No #	Auto	2898028
318/340-ci V-8	A/C or Max Cool	Yes	All	2898031
383-ci	Std.	Yes	All	2898033

= Yes with 340-ci engine.

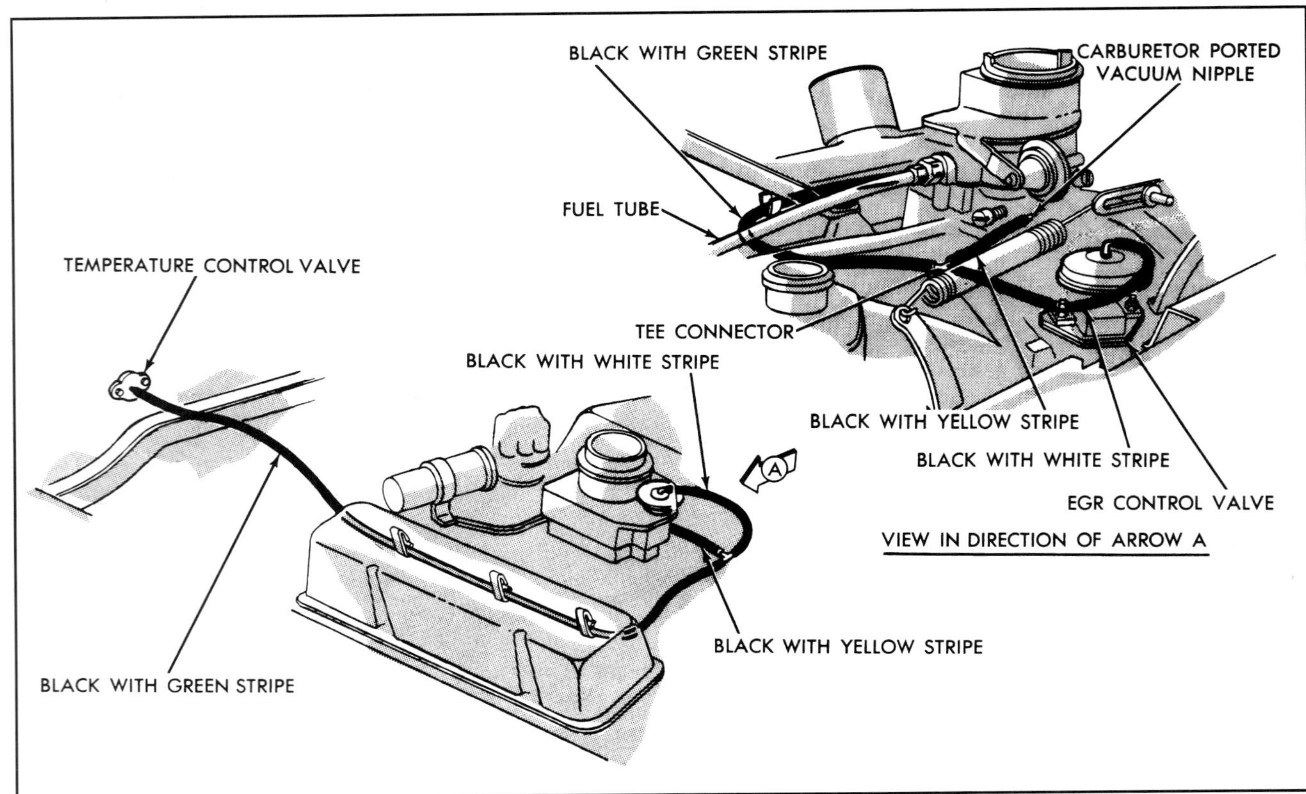

The EGR hose routes with the ported system.

1969 Barracuda Radiator Core Identification Numbers

Displacement	System	Shroud	Transmission	Identification Number
225-ci six-cyl.	Std.	No	Manual	2949074
225-ci six-cyl.	Std.	No	Auto	2949073
225-ci six-cyl.	A/C	Yes	Auto	2949072
225-ci six-cyl.	Max Cool	Yes	All	2949075
318-ci V-8	Std.	No	Manual	2949071
318-ci V-8	Std.	No	Auto	2949031
318-ci V-8	A/C	Yes	Auto	2949067
318-ci V-8	Max Cool	Yes	All	2949068
340-ci V-8	Std.	Yes	All	2949066
340-ci V-8	A/C or Max Cool	Yes	All	2949068
383-ci	Std.	Yes	All	2949065

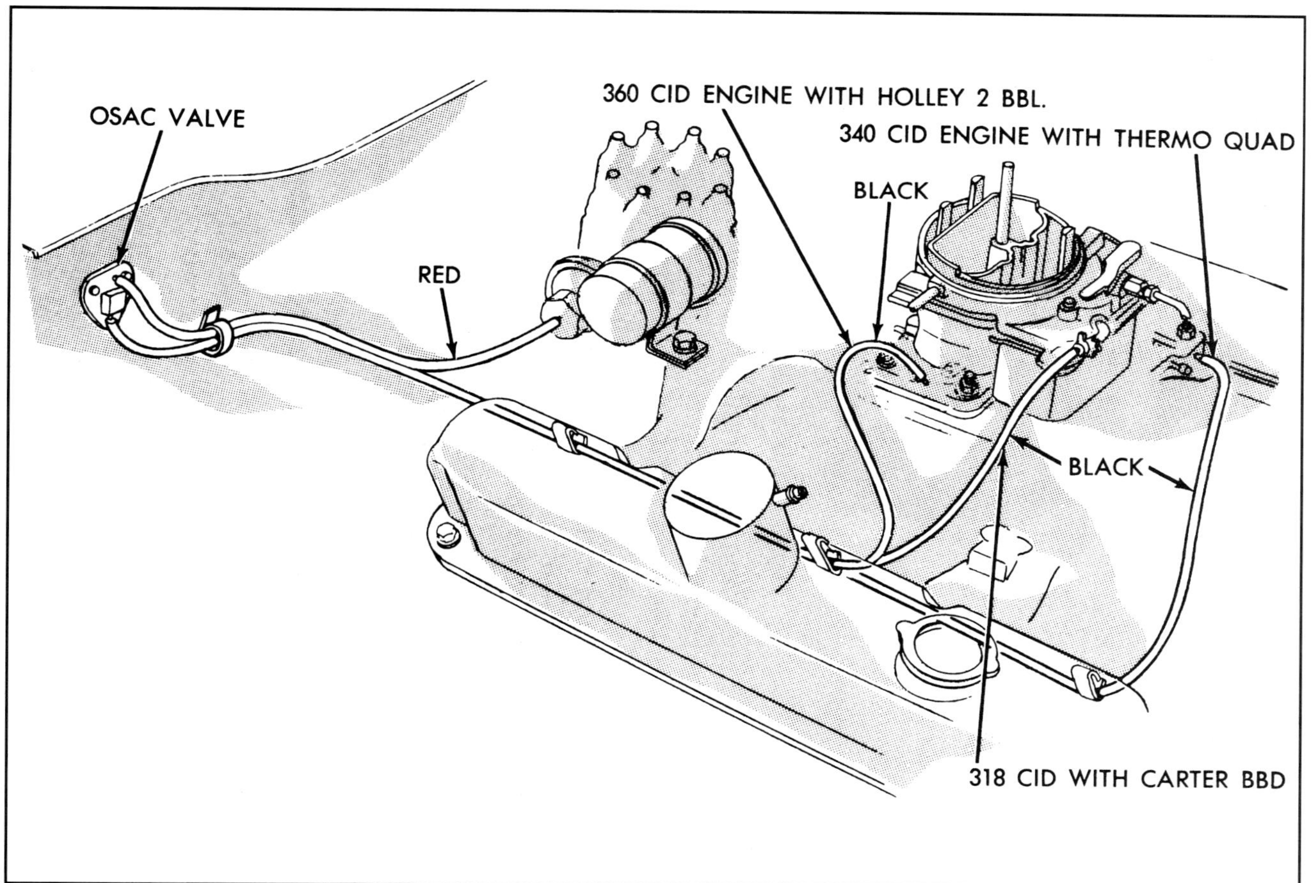

The OSAC valve vacuum hose routing.

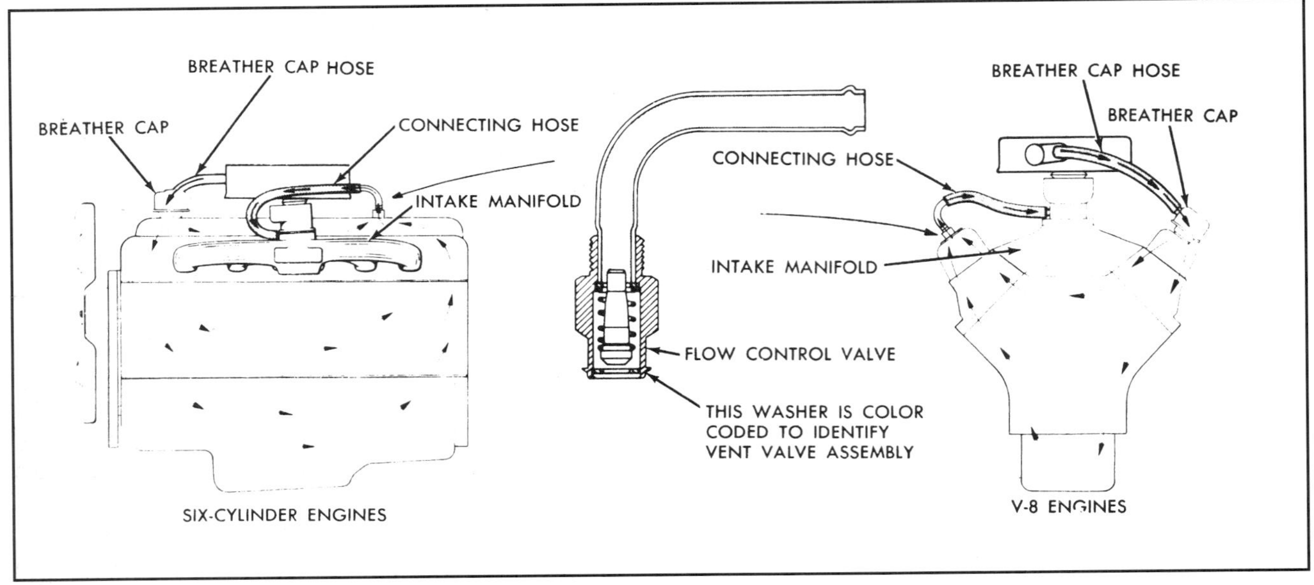

A look at the closed-crankcase ventilation system.

1970 Barracuda/Challenger Radiator Core Identification Numbers

Displacement	System	Shroud	Transmission	ID Number
225-ci six-cyl.	Std.	No	Manual	2998936
225-ci six-cyl.	Std.	No	Auto	2998937
225-ci six-cyl.	A/C	Yes	Auto	2998938
225-ci six-cyl.	Max Cool	Yes	All	2998939
318-ci V-8	Std.	No	Manual	2998946
318-ci V-8	Std.	No	Auto	2998947
318-ci V-8	A/C	Yes	Auto	2998948
318-ci V-8	Max Cool	Yes	All	2998949
340-ci V-8	Std.	Yes	All	2998974
340-ci V-8	A/C	Yes	All	2998974*
340-ci V-8	Max Cool	Yes	All	2998949
383-ci 2-bbl	Std.	No	Auto	2998957
383-ci 2-bbl	A/C	Yes	Auto	2998958
383-ci 2-bbl	Max Cool	Yes	Auto	2998956
383-ci 4-bbl	Std.	Yes#	Manual	2998954
383-ci 4-bbl	Std.	Yes#	Auto	2998960
383-ci 4-bbl	A/C	Yes	All	2998961
383-ci 4-bbl	Max Cool	Yes	All	2998956
426 Hemi	Std.	Yes	All	2998956*
440-ci V-8	Std.	Yes	Manual	2998958
440-ci V-8	Std.	Yes	Auto	2998961
440-ci V-8	A/C	Yes	All	2998961*
440-ci V-8	Max Cool	Yes	All	2998956

* = Air conditioning not available with 3x2-bbl or 2x4-bbl; # = Not with 330-horse-power setup.

The radiator core part number is stamped into the top of the tank.

Right
This yellow-with-black print decal was used on cars sold with a 180-degree thermostat. It was placed on the C-shaped cross-member forward of the radiator top on the passenger's side.

USE ONLY 180° THERMOSTAT
USE MOPAR ANTIFREEZE (PERMANENT TYPE ONLY). PROTECT RADIATOR TO 15° F. FOR SUMMER OPERATION.

IMPORTANT
PROTECTED TO — 20° F WITH MOPAR ANTIFREEZE (ETHYLENE GLYCOL TYPE)
DATE ______________
CHECKED BY DEALER: ______________

WARNING
ALWAYS MAKE SURE COOLANT HAS PROPER AMOUNT OF RUST INHIBITOR. SEE OWNER'S MANUAL FOR COOLING SYSTEMS RECOMMENDATIONS.

The yellow with black and red print anti-freeze warning decal was affixed to the left-hand side of the C-shaped cross-member, forward of the radiator top. It was used in 1967 to mid-1969 models. For correctness, information should be filled in the blanks. Note that anti-freeze was checked by the dealer, not the factory.

1971 Barracuda/Challenger Radiator Core Identification Numbers

Displacement	System	Shroud	Transmission	ID Number
225-ci six-cyl.	Std.	No	Manual	3443984
225-ci six-cyl.	Std.	No	Auto	3443945
225-ci six-cyl.	A/C	Yes	Auto	3443944
225-ci six-cyl.	Max Cool	Yes	All	3443981
318-ci V-8	Std.	No	Manual	3443973
318-ci V-8	Std.	No	Auto	3443972
318-ci V-8	A/C	Yes	Auto	3443971
318-ci V-8	Max Cool	Yes	All	3443970
340-ci V-8	Std.	Yes	All	3443969
340-ci V-8	A/C	Yes	All	3443969*
340-ci V-8	Max Cool	Yes	All	3443970
383-ci 2-bbl	Std.	No	Auto	3443961
383-ci 2-bbl	A/C	Yes	Auto	3443960
383-ci 2-bbl	Max Cool	Yes	Auto	3443959
383-ci 4-bbl	Std.	Yes	Manual	3443962
383-ci 4-bbl	Std.	Yes	Auto	3443961
383-ci 4-bbl	A/C	Yes	All	3443940
383-ci 4-bbl	Max Cool	Yes	All	3442959
426 Hemi	Std.	Yes	All	3443959*
440-ci V-8	Std.	Yes	All	3443959*

*= Air conditioning not available

IMPORTANT
PROTECTED TO —20° F WITH CHRYSLER ANTIFREEZE (ETHYLENE GLYCOL TYPE)
DATE ________________
CHECKED BY DEALER: ________________

WARNING
ALWAYS MAKE SURE COOLANT HAS PROPER AMOUNT OF CHRYSLER ANTI-FREEZE. SEE OWNER'S MANUAL FOR COOLING SYSTEMS RECOMMENDATIONS.

The anti-freeze decal was changed around January 1, 1969. Though subtle, the wording on the right-hand side was changed. Its placement is the same as the previous version.

IMPORTANT :
PROTECTED TO -20° F WITH MOPAR
ANTIFREEZE (ETHYLENE GLYCOL TYPE)
DATE
CHECKED BY DEALER

WARNING:
ALWAYS MAKE SURE COOLANT HAS PROPER AMOUNT OF MOPAR ANTIFREEZE SEE OWNERS MANUAL FOR COOLING SYSTEM RECOMMENDATIONS

The anti-freeze decal was changed again for 1973 models and used again in 1974. It was affixed to passenger's side of C-shaped cross-member forward of the radiator.

1972 Barracuda/Challenger Radiator Core Identification Numbers

Displacement	System	Shroud	Transmission	ID Number
225-ci six-cyl.	Std.	No	Manual	3574645
225-ci six-cyl.	Std.	No	Auto	3574644
225-ci six-cyl.	Max Cool	Yes	All	3574642
318-ci V-8	Std.	No	All	3574631
318-ci V-8	A/C	Yes	Auto	3574627
318-ci V-8	Max Cool	Yes	All	3574624
340-ci V-8	Std.	Yes	All	3574628
340-ci V-8	A/C	Yes	All	3574626
340-ci V-8	Max Cool	Yes	All	3574624

1973 Barracuda/Challenger Radiator Core Identification Numbers

Displacement	System	Shroud	Transmission	ID Number
318-ci V-8	Std.	No	Manual	3673922
318-ci V-8	Std.	No	Auto	3673926
318-ci V-8	A/C	Yes	Auto	3673924
318-ci V-8	Max Cool	Yes	All	3673925
340-ci V-8	Std.	No	Manual	3673931
340-ci V-8	Std.	No	Auto	3673932
340-ci V-8	A/C	Yes	All	3673924
340-ci V-8	Max Cool	Yes	All	3673925

1974 Barracuda/Challenger Radiator Core Identification Numbers

Displacement	System	Shroud	Transmission	ID Number
318-ci V-8	Std.	Yes	All	3692926
318-ci V-8	A/C	Yes	Auto	3692935
318-ci V-8	Max Cool	Yes	All	3692925
360-ci	Std.	Yes	All	3692932
360-ci	A/C	Yes	All	3692935
360-ci	Max Cool	Yes	All	3692925

The fan blade used with thermal drive.

(1) standard, (2) with air conditioning, and (3) maximum cooling. Some engines, like the 1967-1969 383-ci and 1970-1971 multiple-carburetor engines, came standard with maximum cooling and were not available with air conditioning.

Radiator

Several different radiator cores were used, and they sometimes changed with the model years. The core can be identified by an identification number on top of the tank. The transmission, engine size, and options such as air conditioning can determine which core is used. All radiator cores should be finished in semi-gloss black.

Fan Blades

There are three basic designs of fan blades: the standard fan that used a spacer, the Thermal-Drive

1967 Barracuda Fan Usage

Engine	System	Diameter	Number of Blades	Width	Drive Type	Spacer Length	Fan Part Number
225	Std.	16	4	1 1/2	Solid	1.06	2121971
225	Calif.	17	4	1 1/2	Solid	1.06	1947907
225	A/C	17	7	1 1/2	Solid	1.06	2863200
273	Std.	17	4	1 3/4	Solid	2.00	2658984
273	Calif.	17	7	1 3/4	Solid	2.00	2658970
273	A/C in Calif.	17	7	2 1/4	Thermal	n/a	2658973
273	A/C	17	7	1 3/4	Solid	2.00	2658970
383	Std.	18	7				2863203
383	Calif.	18	7				2863202

A/C = Air conditioning; Calif. = California cars [Clean Air Package (CAP) mandatory in California].

1968 Barracuda Fan Usage

Engine	System	Diameter	Number of Blades	Width	Drive Type	Spacer Length	Fan Part Number
225	Std.	17	4	1 1/2	Solid	1.06	1947907
225	A/C	17	7	1 1/2	Solid	1.06	2863200
318	Std.	18	7	2	Solid	1.86	2863227
318	A/C	18	7	2 1/4	Thermal		2863215
318	Max Cool	18	7	2 1/4	Solid	2.00	2863227
340	Std.	18	7	2 1/4	Solid	2.00	2863213
340	A/C	18	7	2 1/4	Thermal		2863215
383	Std. *	18	7	1 1/2	Solid		2863213

A/C = Air conditioning; * = Air conditioning not available with this engine. Max Cool std.

1969 Barracuda Fan Usage

Engine	System	Diameter	Number of Blades	Width	Drive Type	Spacer Length	Fan Part Number
225	Std.	17	4	1 1/2	Solid	1.06	1947907
255	A/C	17	7	1 1/2	Solid	1.06	2863200
318	Std.	18	7	2	Solid	2.38	2863224
318	A/C	18	7	2 1/4	Thermal		2863215
318	Max Cool	18	7	2 1/4	Solid	2.00	2863227
340	Std. or A/C	18	7	2 1/4	Thermal		2863215
383 or 440	Std. *	18	7	1 1/2	Solid	.70	2863224

* = Air conditioning not available with 383-ci or 440-ci.

1970 Barracuda and Challenger Fan Usage

Engine	System	Diameter	Number of Blades	Width	Drive Type	Spacer Length	Fan Part Number
225	Std.	17	4	1 1/2	Solid	1.06	1947907
225	A/C	17	7	1 1/2	Solid	1.06	2863200
318	Std.	18	4	2	Solid	2.20	2265034
318	A/C	18 1/2	7	2 1/4	Thermal		2863216
318	Max Cool	18	7	2 1/4	Torque		2863227
340*	Std. or A/C	18 1/2	7	2 1/4	Torque		2863216
383	Std.	18	7	1 1/2	Solid	.70	2863224
383	A/C	18 1/2	7	2 1/4	Thermal		2863216
426*	Std.	18 1/2	7	2 1/4	Torque		2863216
440*		18 #	7	1 1/2#	Solid	1.60#	(1)
		18 **		2 1/4**	Torque**	**	(2)
		18 +		2 1/4+	Thermal+	+	

* = Air conditioning not available with multiple carburetors; # = With automatic transmission; ** = With manual transmission; + = Air conditioning; (1) With automatic part number 2863224; (2) with manual or with A/C part number 2863216.

1971 Barracuda and Challenger Fan Usage

Engine	System	Diameter	Number of Blades	Width	Drive Type	Spacer Length	Fan Part Number
225	Std.	17	4	1 1/2	Solid	1.06	1947907
225	Max Cool	17	7	1 1/4	Solid	1.06	2863200
225	A/C	17	7	1 1/2	Solid	1.06	2863200
318	Std.	18	4	2	Solid	2.20	2265034
318	A/C	18 1/2~	7#	2 1/4#	Thermal		~
		18 1/4^	5^	2.31^			^
318	Max Cool	18	7	2 1/4	Torque		2863227
340*	Std. or A/C	18 1/2	7	2 1/4	Torque		2863216
383	Std.	18	7	1 1/2	Solid	.70	2863224
383	A/C	18 1/2	7	2 1/4	Thermal		2863216
426*	Std.	18 1/2	7	2 1/4	Torque		2863216
440*	Std.	18 #					
		18 **	7	1 1/2#	Solid	1.60#	(1)
		18 +		2 1/4**	Torque**	**	(2)
				2 1/4+	Thermal+	+	

* = Air conditioning not available with multiple carburetors;
# = With automatic transmission;
** = With manual transmission;
+ = Air conditioning; (1) With automatic part number 2863224; (2) With manual or with A/C part number 2863216;
~ = Except with 2.71 or 2.76 rear axle fan part number 2863216;
^ = With 2.71 or 2.76 rear axle only. Flex blade type fan part number 3462150.

1972 Plymouth Barracuda and Dodge Challenger Fan Usage

Engine	System	Diameter	Number of Blades	Width	Drive Type	Spacer Length	Fan Part Number
225	Std.	17	4	1 1/4	Solid	1.72	1947907
318	Std.	18	4	2	Solid	2.20	2265034
318	Calif.	18 1/2	7	2 1/2	Solid	2.20	2863224
318	A/C#	18	7	2 1/4	Thermal		2863216
318	A/C^	18 1/4	5	2.31	Thermal		3462150
318	Max Cool	18	7	2 1/4	Solid	2.00	2863227
340	Std. or A/C	18 1/2	7	2 1/2	Torque		2863216

= Except with 2.71 or 2.76 rear axle; ^ = With 2.71 or 2.76 rear axle only. Flex blade fan.

1973 Plymouth Barracuda and Dodge Challenger Fan Usage

Engine	System	Diameter	Number of Blades	Width	Drive Type	Spacer Length	Fan Part Number
318	Std.	18 1/2	4	2 1/4	Solid	1.72	2863214
318	A/C#	18	7	2 1/4	Thermal		2863216
318	A/C^	18 1/4	5	2.70	Solid	2.20	3462139
318	Max Cool	18	7	2 1/4	****		2863216
340	Std. or A/C	18 1/2	7	2 1/2	Torque		2863216

= Except with 2.71 or 2.76 rear axle;
^ = With 2.71 or 2.76 rear axle only. Flex blade fan;
**** = Torque Drive without A/C. Thermal drive with A/C.

1974 Plymouth Barracuda and Dodge Challenger Fan Usage

Engine	System	Diameter	Number of Blades	Width	Drive Type	Spacer Length	Fan Part Number
318	Std.	18 1/2	4	2 1/4	Solid	1.72	2863214
318	A/C or	20	5	n/a	Solid	n/a	3462190
318	Max Cool						
360	Std. or A/C	20	7	n/a	Thermal		3462149

Part Number 3462190 is a Flex-blade fan.
Part Number 3462149 is an aluminum-blade fan.

(usually used with air conditioning), and the torque fan (usually used on high-performance engines). No matter what type is used, all fan blades should be painted semi-gloss black to duplicate the fresh factory look.

Fans are identified by their diameter, number of blades, and what type of drive they use. The Thermal-drive can be identified by a thermostatic spring in the center face of the drive. This drive should have a look of unpainted cast-aluminum and the spring should be painted flat black. The torque drive looks similar to the Thermal-drive, but has no center spring. Instead, the drive is sealed and filled with silicone. This drive operated normally at low speeds, but limited fan speed at highway speeds. Note the same fan may be used with all drive types in some applications.

Water Pumps

There are three basic water pumps: those on six-cylinder engines, those on small-blocks (273, 318, 340, and 360-ci), and those that fit the big-blocks (383 and 440-ci) and the Hemi. Before 1969, the small-block water pump housings were made of cast-iron. Beginning in 1970, the housing was made of aluminum and a pentastar (Chrysler logo) was cast into the lower passage tube of big-block water pumps. On those models with factory-installed air conditioning, usually using a different water pump, the housing is the same but the insides are different. All water pumps were painted the same color as the cylinder block. Note that bypass hoses were installed on the engine when it was painted at the factory, thus engine paint is sometimes found on the clamps, especially on the small-blocks.

1967-1974 Water Pump Casting Numbers

Engine	Years Used	System	Casting Number	Impeller Specifications Diameter	Impeller Specifications Number
225-ci	1967-1968	Both	2128284	3.50	Six
225-ci	1969-1972	Both		3.50	Six
273-ci	1967	Std.	2402794	4.20	Ten
273-ci	1967	A/C	2942794	3.50	Six
318-ci	1968-1969	Std.	2942794	4.20	Ten
318-ci	1968-1969	A/C	2942794	3.50	Six
318-ci	1970-1974	Std.	3420038	4.38	Eight
318-ci	1970-1974	A/C	3420038	3.70	Six
340-ci	1968-1969	Std.	2402794	4.20	Ten
340-ci	1968-1969	A/C	2402794	3.50	Six
340-ci	1970-1973	Std.	3420037	4.38	Eight
340-ci	1970-1973	Std.	3420037	3.70	Six
360-ci	1974	Std.	3780109	4.38	Eight
360-ci	1974	A/C	3780109	3.70	Six
383/440-ci or Hemi	1967-1971**	Std.	2780987	4.38	Eight
383/440-ci	1967-1971*	A/C	2780987	3.50	Six

** = 440-ci available only 1969-1971; Hemi available 1970-1971.

* = Air conditioning not available on 1967-1969 or 1970-1971 Hemi, or 1970-1971 440 3x2-bbl, or 1970-1971 340 3x2-bbl.

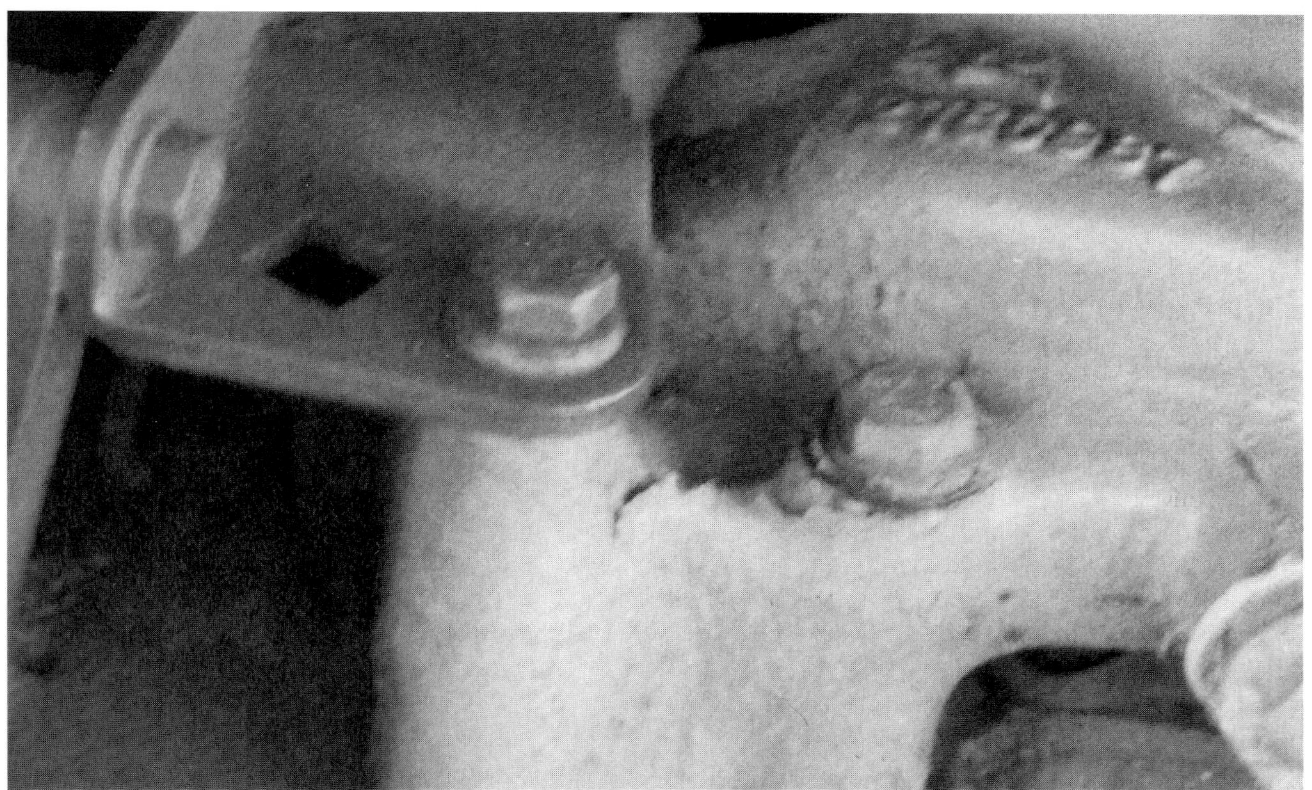

Water pumps can be identified by a casting number.

1967 Barracuda Fan Belts

Engine	Without A/C	Length	With A/C	Length
225-ci	2843277*	57 1/2	2264463	n/a
273-ci 2-bbl	2806216	46 1/2	2658391^	n/a
273-ci 4-bbl	2806217		2658391^	n/a
383-ci	2532648		Option n/a	

Belt runs from engine to alternator to fan.
* = Heavy-duty belt available as option; ^ = With A/C and CAP only—without A/C and CAP Standard belt is used.

1968 Barracuda Fan Belt Usage

Engine	Without A/C	Length	With A/C	Length
225	2843277	57 1/2	2264463	n/a
318	2806216	46 1/2	2863564	n/a
340	2899096	n/a	2863564	n/a
383	2843221	n/a	Option n/a	

Belt runs from engine to alternator to fan.

1969 Barracuda Fan Belt Usage

Engine	Without A/C	Length	With A/C	Length
225-ci	2532659	57	n/a	
318-ci	2806216	46 1/2	2863564	48
340-ci	2806216	46 1/2	2863564	48
383/440	2806216	46 1/2	n/a	

Belt runs from engine to alternator to fan. Some engines don't use a different belt with air conditioning.

1970 Barracuda and Challenger Fan Belts

Engine	Without A/C	Length
225-ci	2843277	57 1/2
318-ci	3418943	47 1/2
340-ci^	3418943	47 1/2
383/440^-ci	2806216	46 1/2
426 Hemi	2658895	43

Some engines don't use a different belt with A/C; ^ = A/C n/a with 3x2-bbl setups.
Part number 2532659 (57 inches long) used with 46- or 60-amp alternators.

1971 Barracuda and Challenger Fan Belt Usage

Engine	Without A/C	Length	With A/C	Length
225-ci	2532659	57 .	n/a	
318-ci	2128751	41 1/2	n/a	
340-ci^	2128751	41 1/2	n/a	
383/440-ci^	2806216	46 1/2	15551006	53 1/2
426 Hemi	2658895	43	Option n/a	

^ = Air conditioning not available with 340 3 x 2-bbl or 440 3x2-bbl.
Some engines don't use a another belt with A/C.

1972 Barracuda and Challenger Fan Belt Usage

Engine	Without A/C	Length	With A/C
225-ci	3671682	56 3/4	n/a
318/340-ci	3418943	47 1/2	n/a

1973-1974 Barracuda and Challenger Fan Belt Usage

Engine	Without A/C	Length	With A/C
318/340-ci	3671524	47 3/4	n/a

1967 Barracuda Radiator Hoses

Engine	Without Air Conditioning		With Air Conditioning	
	Upper Hose	Lower Hose	Upper Hose	Lower Hose
225-ci	1881812	2806196	1881812	2806196
273-ci	2806066	2806067#	2806066	2806067
383-ci	2863209	2863207	Option n/a	

= Used until January 1, 1967, after part number 2863205.

1968 Barracuda Radiator Hoses

Engine	Without Air Conditioning		With Air Conditioning	
	Upper Hose	Lower Hose	Upper Hose	Lower Hose
225-ci	2806195	2806196	2806195	2806196
318-ci	2863211	2863205	2863212	2863205
340-ci	2863211	2863205	2863212	2863205
383-ci	2863209	2863207	Option n/a	

1969 Barracuda Radiator Hoses

Engine	Without Air Conditioning		With Air Conditioning	
	Upper Hose	Lower Hose	Upper Hose	Lower Hose
225-ci	1881805	2863235	1881805	2863235
225-ci #	1719639	2863235	1717639	2863235
318-ci	2863211	2863205	2863212	2863205
340-ci	2863211	2863205	2863212	2863205
383-ci	2863209	2863243	Option n/a	

= Canadian cars only

1970 Plymouth Barracuda and Dodge Challenger Radiator Hoses

Engine	Without Air Conditioning		With Air Conditioning	
	Upper Hose	Lower Hose	Upper Hose	Lower Hose
225-ci	2863241	2863278	2863291	2863278
318-ci	1881806	3462165	3462102	3462165
340-ci *	1881806	3462165	3462102	3462165
340-ci **	3462193	3462165	3462193	3462165
383-ci	1881804	2863256	2863257	2863256
426-ci	3462184	2863256	Option n/a	
440-ci	1881804	2863256	2863257	2863256

* = Without Shaker Hood or AAR T/A models only.
** = With Shaker Hood, AAR Cuda, and Challenger T/A.
Air conditioning not available with 340 3x2-bbl, 440 3x2-bbl, or Hemi powerplants.

1971 Plymouth Barracuda and Dodge Challenger Radiator Hoses

Engine	Without Air Conditioning		With Air Conditioning	
	Upper Hose	Lower Hose	Upper Hose	Lower Hose
225-ci	2863241	2863278	2863291	2863278
318-ci	1881806	3462165	3462102	3462165
340-ci *	1881806	3462165	3462102	3462165
340-ci **	3462118	3462165	3462118	3462165
383-ci	1881804	2863256	2863257	2863256
426-ci	3462184	2863256	option n/a	
440-ci	1881804	2863256	2863257	2863256

* = Without Shaker Hood, or AAR T/A models only.
** = With Shaker Hood, AAR Cuda, or Challenger T/A.
Air conditioning not available with 340 3x2-bbl, 440 3x2-bbl, or Hemi powerplants

1972 Plymouth Barracuda and Dodge Challenger Radiator Hoses

Engine	Without Air Conditioning		With Air Conditioning	
	Upper Hose	Lower Hose	Upper Hose	Lower Hose
225-ci	3462175	2863278	1881812	2863278
318-ci	1881806	1881810	3462102	1881810
340-ci	3462118*	1881810	3462102	1881810
	3462123**	1881810	3462102	1881810

* = Before August 16, 1972; ** = From August 16, 1972-on.

1973-1974 Plymouth Barracuda and Dodge Challenger Radiator Hoses

Engine	Without Air Conditioning		With Air Conditioning	
	Upper Hose	Lower Hose	Upper Hose	Lower Hose
318-ci	3462153	3462137	3462102	3462137
340-ci (1973)	3462200	3462137	3462102	3452200
360-ci (1974)	3462200	3462137	3462102	3452200

Chapter 3

Frames, Suspension, and Steering

Frames

All Barracudas and Challengers used a unibody construction and a front subframe. The front subframe was made up of two side-members and three cross-members that supported the engine, transmission, and front suspension. The front cross-member is an end piece. The second cross-member, commonly called a K-member because of its shape, supported the engine and the front suspension.

Four basic K-members were used, and their usage is dependent on the engine used: one is for the six-cylinder engines, one is for all small-blocks, one is for the big-blocks, and the last one is for the Hemi. However, on the 1970-1974 models, a single K-member fit

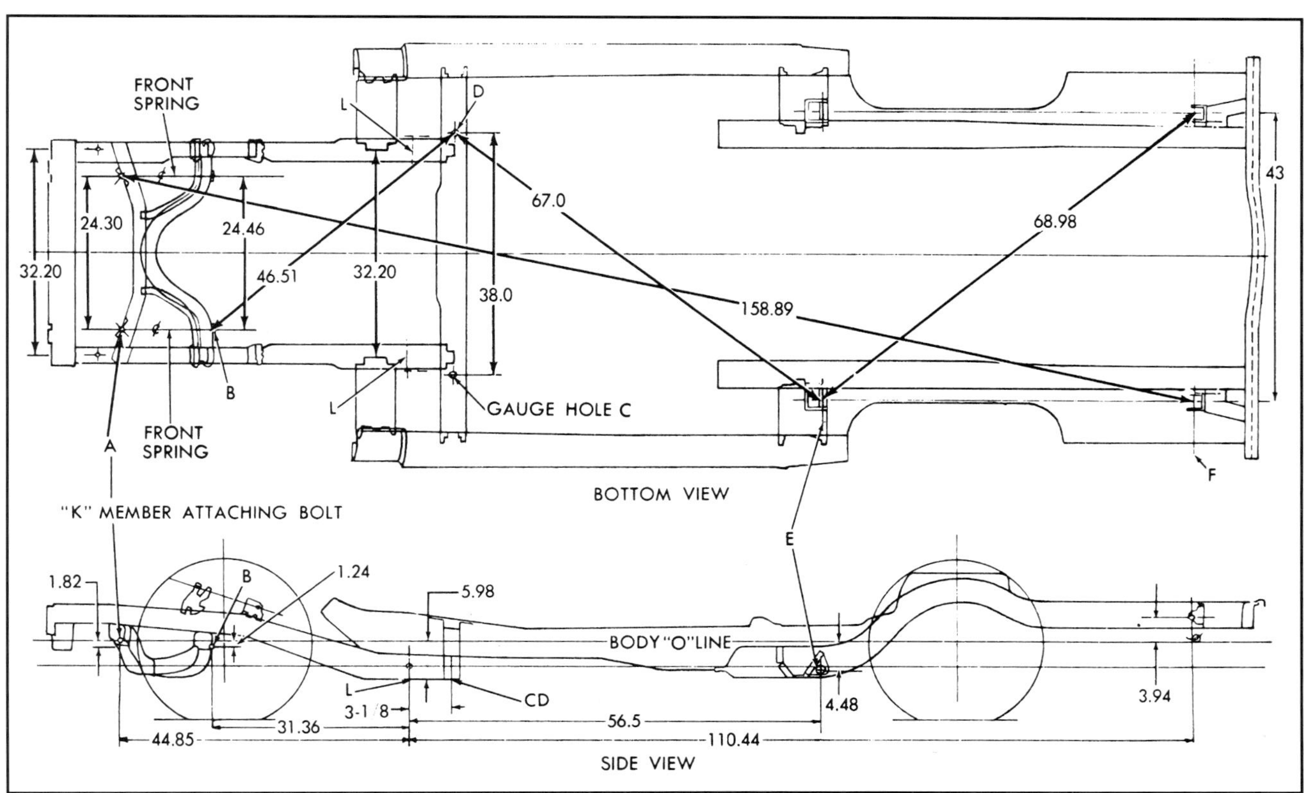

1967-1969 Barracuda body frame dimensions.

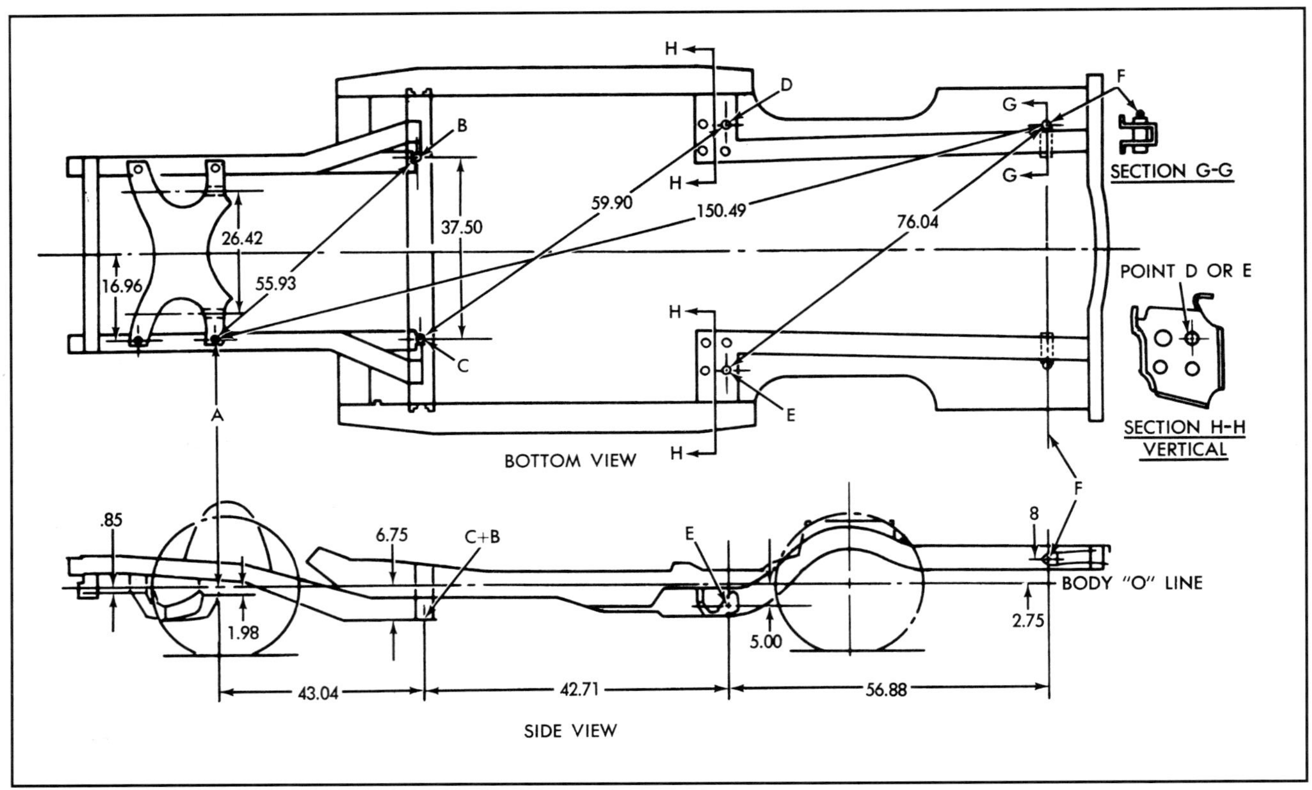

1970-1974 Barracuda and Challenger body frame dimensions.

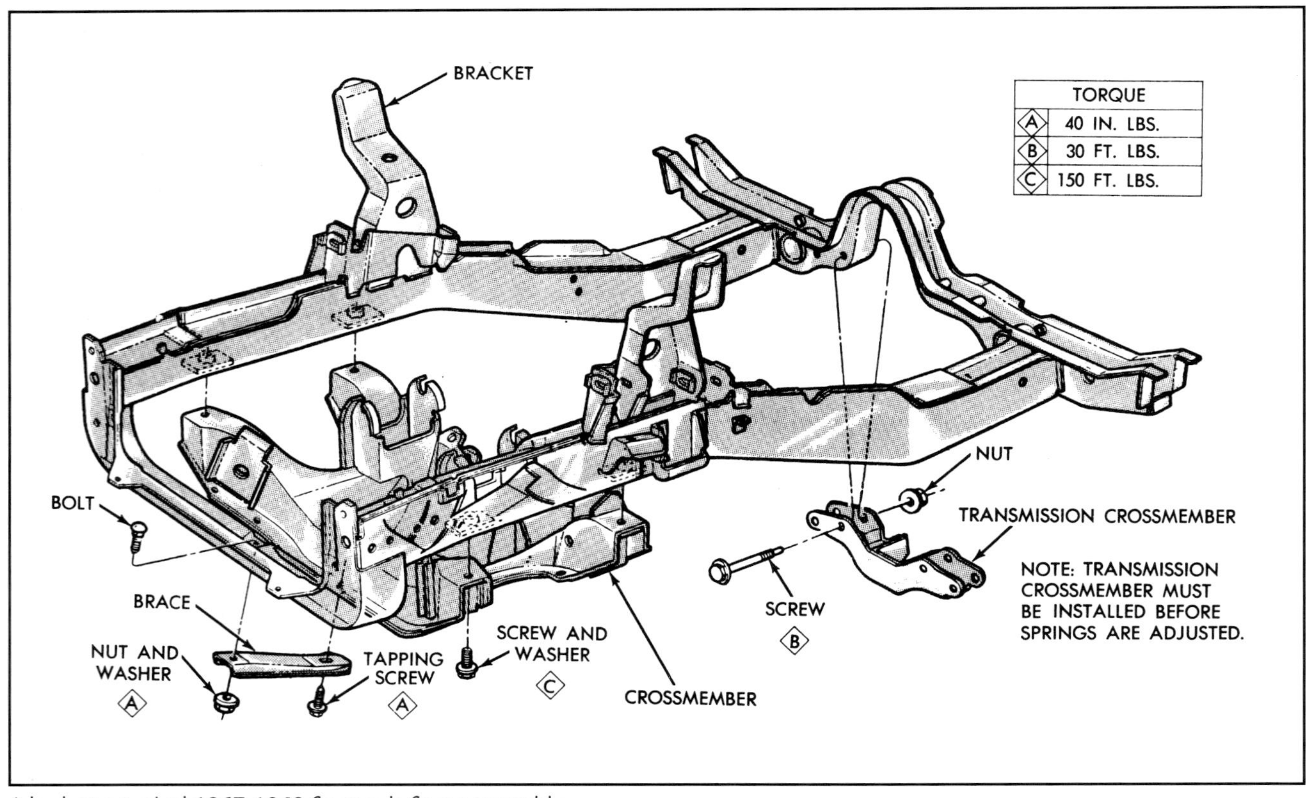

A look at a typical 1967-1969 front sub-frame assembly.

both small-blocks and big-blocks. Trans-Am models with the 340-ci 3x2-bbl powerplants are listed as using a special cross-member, yet there is no apparent physical difference between it and a regular V-8 K-member. A small, round, metal tag is welded to the bottom of the K-member, and the last two digits of the part number are stamped upside-down in the tag's face.

K-members should be painted semi-gloss black; a clear coat can be used for protection of the paint but it may change the gloss incorrectly. A better method is to

1967-1969 A-Body and 1970-1974 E-Body K-Members

Model Year	Six-Cylinders	273, 318, 340, 360-ci	383, 440-ci	426 Hemi
1967	2768375	2768548	2881925	Not produced
1968	2883982	2883980	2883984	2836891
1969	2962082	2925976	2925946	Not produced
1970	2962010	3466477 #	3466477	3583076
		3583052 **		
1971	3583070	3583074	3583074	3583076
		3583052		
1972	3583098	3583078	3583078	Not produced
1973	Not produced	3583074	3583074	Not produced
1974	Not produced	3526799	3526799	Not produced

= Except AAR or T/A models; ** = AAR or T/A models only.

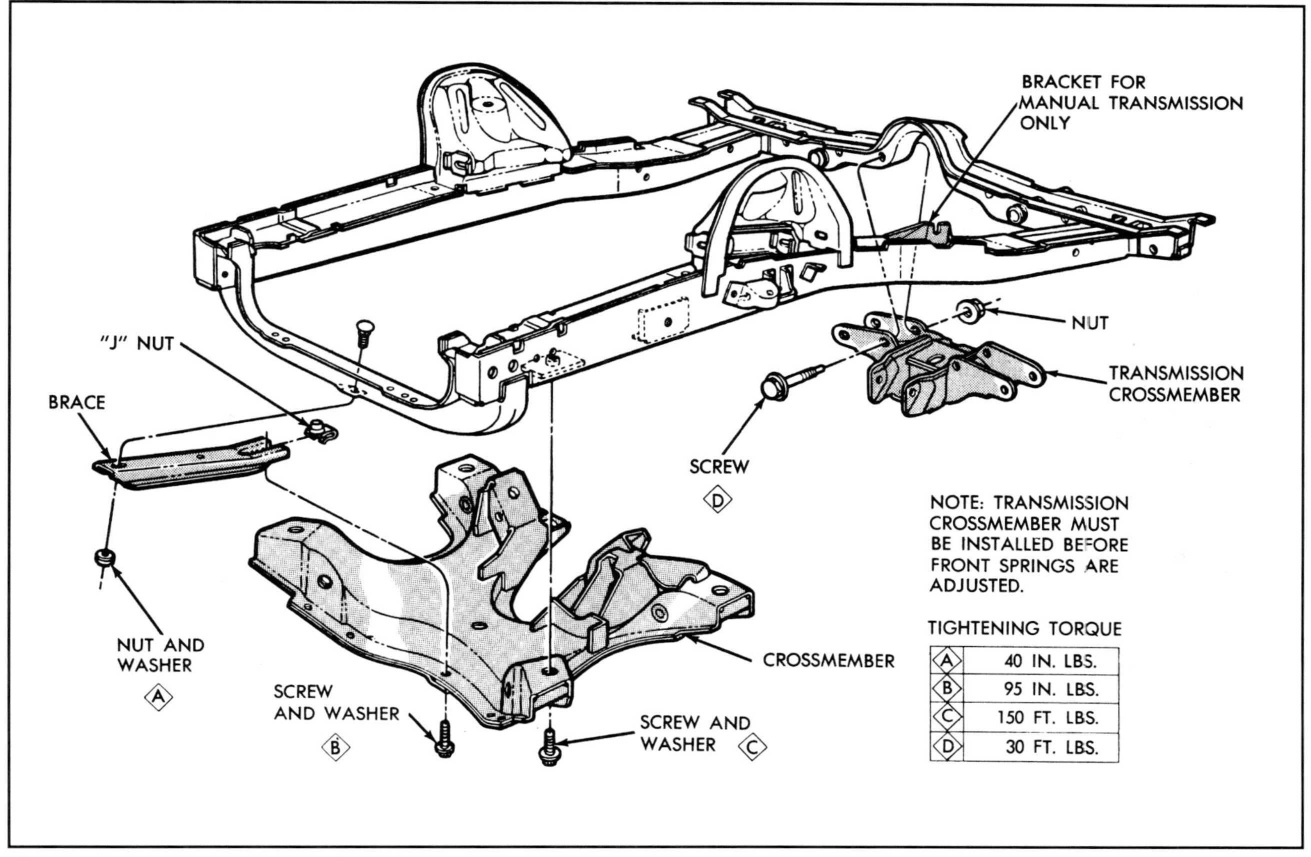

The late-1970 to 1974 front sub-frame.

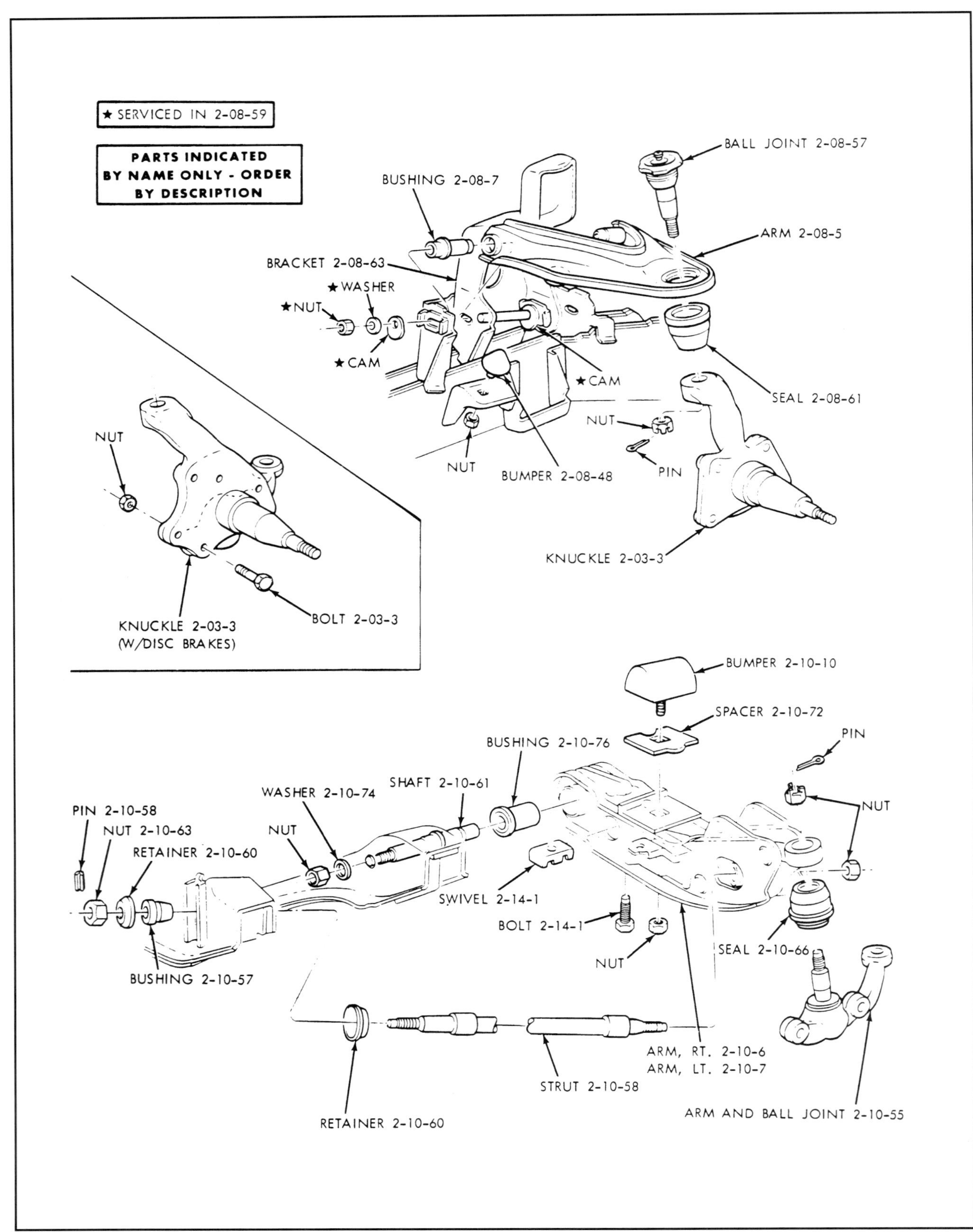

A front suspension typical of 1967-1969 models. A 1970-1974 suspension shown here.

use an epoxy-based paint; this paint is extremely durable and can be washed. Be sure to mask everything, as this paint has more overspray than other types of paint. If you are painting with the K-member still in the car, instead of masking the entire car, place a generous coat of wax on the body and all other areas you don't want painted. Leave this coat of wax on while you are painting. The overspray will land on the wax and it can be easily buffed away.

The third cross-member supported the transmission, and the same rear member was used to support all transmission types. However, the A-bodied cars (1967-1969) *did* use a different rear member than the E-bodies (1970-1974). This member should also be painted semi-gloss black..

Front Suspension

All models covered in this guide used a system of upper and lower control arms sprung by torsion bars. Upper control arms were changed only once, with the redesign in 1970, and the suspension type does not affect their usage.

Lower control arms can be confusing. All 1967-1969 A-bodies used the same set of lower arms all three years, with or without a front sway bar. But with the 1970-1974 E-bodies, two different sets of lower arms were used. Those with a front sway bar use a different set of lower arms than did a model without a front sway bar. A sway bar became standard in 1973 models, meaning there was only one set of lower control arms.

The sway bar was available as part of three packages: the Trailer package, the Rally suspension, and the Formula S package. A sway bar was standard with the so-called Musclecars, a group that includes the Cuda, Challenger R/T, Challenger Rally, AAR Cuda, Challenger T/A, and the 1967-1969 Barracudas with 340-ci or 383-ci engines.

Torsion bars acted as springs and handled the load. Cars with a performance suspension came with larger-diameter torsion bars. The larger the diameter, the

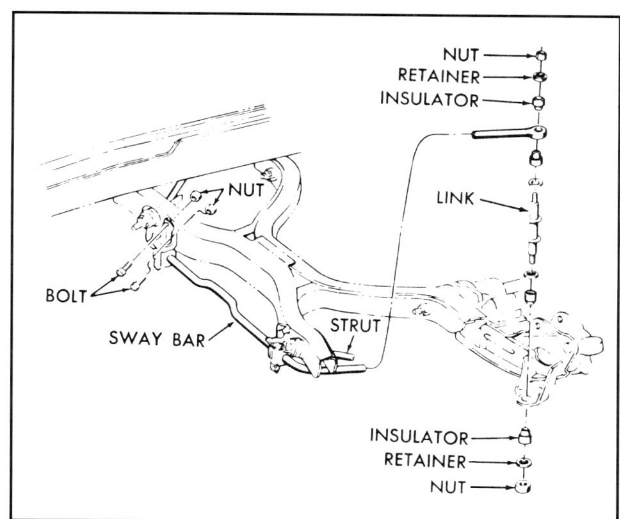

A 1967-1969 front sway bar.

higher the rating and the harsher the ride, but the car handled better. Torsion bars can be identified by the last three digits of their part number stamped in the anchoring end of the bar.

There has been confusion regarding the correct finish for suspension components. Some feel the control arms were left as unpainted steel, while others feel they were painted semi-gloss black. Both are correct, as the finish was dependent on what type of paint the part vendor had available at the time. Note that most of the pre-1970 cars have the natural finish, while the 1971 and later cars' suspensions are painted semi-gloss black. The natural look is actually an unpainted part dipped into Cosmoline, a chemical that is an anticorrosive agent used to prevent parts from rusting on the parts shelf. Cosmoline gave the parts a dull silver appearance with a slight yellow-gold tint. This look can be duplicated by first painting the parts stainless steel, then giving them a light transparent coat of gold paint. Originally the gold tint would quickly wear off, usually within the first year

Front Control Arms

Model Year	Upper Arms		Lower Arms	
	Driver	Passenger	Driver	Passenger
1967 A-body	2071453	2071452	2535365	2535364
1968-1969 A-body	2071457	2071456	2535365	2535364
1970-1972 E-body	1857857	1857856	2535879*	2535878*
1973-1974 E-body	1857857	1857856	3402935	3402934

* = Without sway bar; ** = With sway bar.

of driving, thus creating the illusion of unpainted parts. The best bet for restoration purposes is the other finish, semi-gloss black, as most components were painted this color. Use an epoxy paint for long-lasting results. Bolt heads that secure the lower control arms to the front subframe should have an unpainted appearance.

Sway bars were usually painted semi-gloss black; however, some have been found that were left unfinished. As for torsion bars, they, too, were usually painted semi-gloss black, along with color-coded stripes that were used to identify them. These stripes are about 1/2 inch wide and are located 10 inches from the anchoring end of the bar. The bar on the driver's side will have two stripes; the second stripe is about 2 inches above the first stripe and is also used for identification.

1967-1974 Torsion Bar Identification

STANDARD SUSPENSION

Engine	Model Year	Diameter	Length	ID Number	Color Code
225-ci six-cyl.	1967-1969	.83	35.8	888 Right 889 Left	Yellow
225-ci six-cyl.	1970-1972	.86	41	774 Right 775 Left	Orange
273-ci V-8	1967	.85	35.8	890 Right 891 Left	Olive
318-ci V-8	1968-1969	.87	35.8	892 Right 893 Left	Blue
318-ci V-8	1970	.88	41	776 Right 777 Left	Green
318-ci V-8	1971-1974	.86	41	774 Right 775 Left	Orange
340-ci	1968-1969	.87	35.8	892 Right 893 Left	Blue
340-ci	1970-1971	.90	41	778 Right 779 Left	Silver
340-ci	1972-1973	.86	41	774 Right 775 Left	Orange
360-ci	1974	.86	41	774 Right 775 Left	Orange
383-ci	1967-1969	.89	35.8	984 Right 985 Left	White
383-ci 2-bbl	1970-1971	.86	41	774 Right 775 Left	Orange
383-ci 4-bbl	1970-1971	.90	41	778 Right 779 Left	Silver
426 Hemi	1970-1971	.92	41	780 Right 781 Left	Brown
440-ci	1969	.89	35.8	984 Right 985 Left	White
440-ci	1970	.92	41	780 Right 781 Left	Brown
440-ci	1971	.90	41	778 Right 779 Left	Silver

1967-1974 Torsion Bar Identification

HEAVY-DUTY SUSPENSION

Engine	Model Year	Diameter	Length	ID Number	Color Code
225/273	1967-1969	.87	35.8	892 Right	Blue
				893 Left	Blue
318-ci	1970-1974	.90	41	778 Right	Silver
				779 Left	Silver
340-ci	1968-1971	Same as standard suspension			
340-ci	1972-1973	.90	41	778 Right	Silver
				779 Left	
360-ci	1974	.90	41	778 Right	Silver
				779 Left	
383-ci	1967-1969	Same as standard suspension			
383-ci 2-bbl	1970-1971	.90	41	778 Right	Silver
				779 Left	
383-ci 4-bbl	1970-1971	Same as standard suspension			
426-ci	1970-1971	Same as standard suspension			
440-ci	1969-1971	Same as standard suspension			

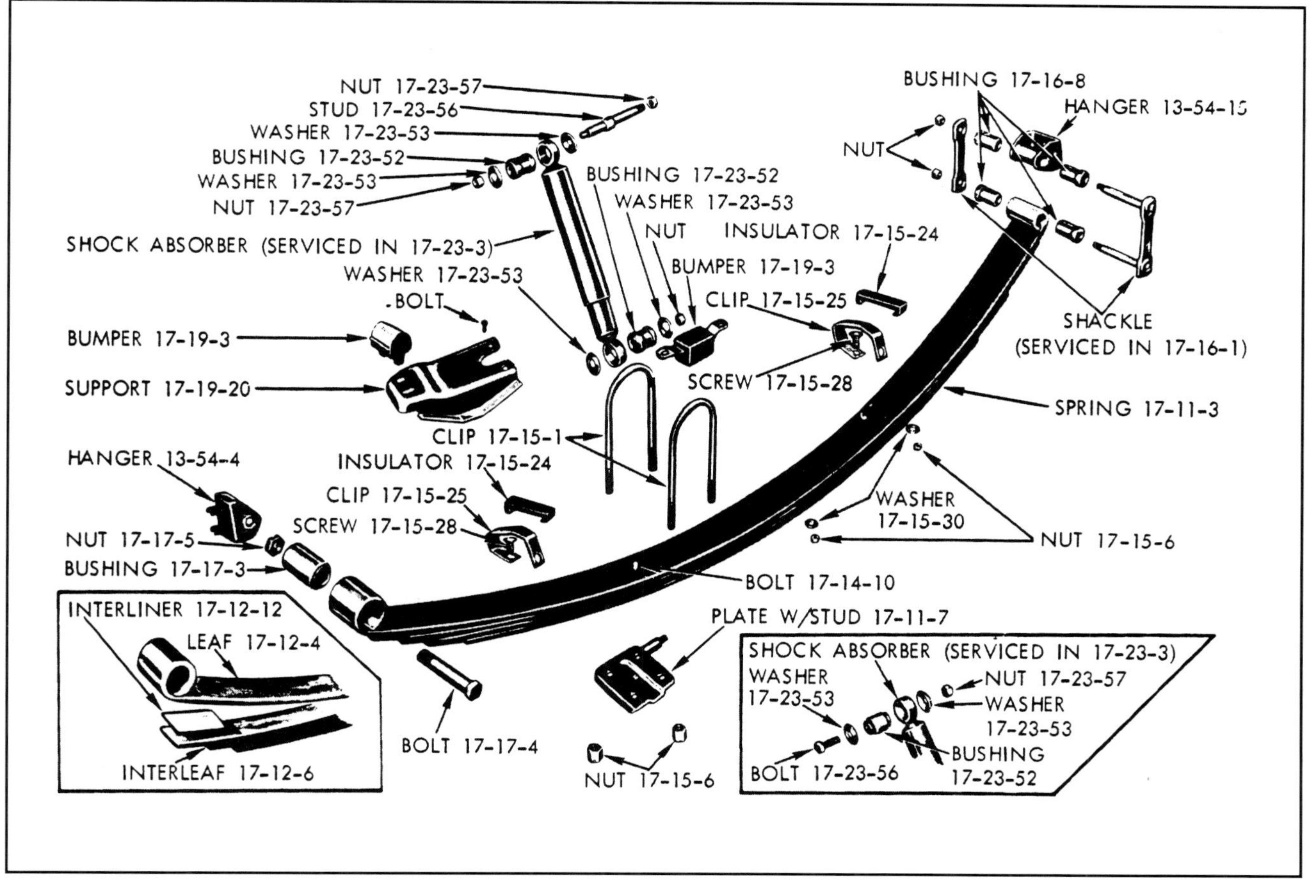

An example of a typical rear suspension.

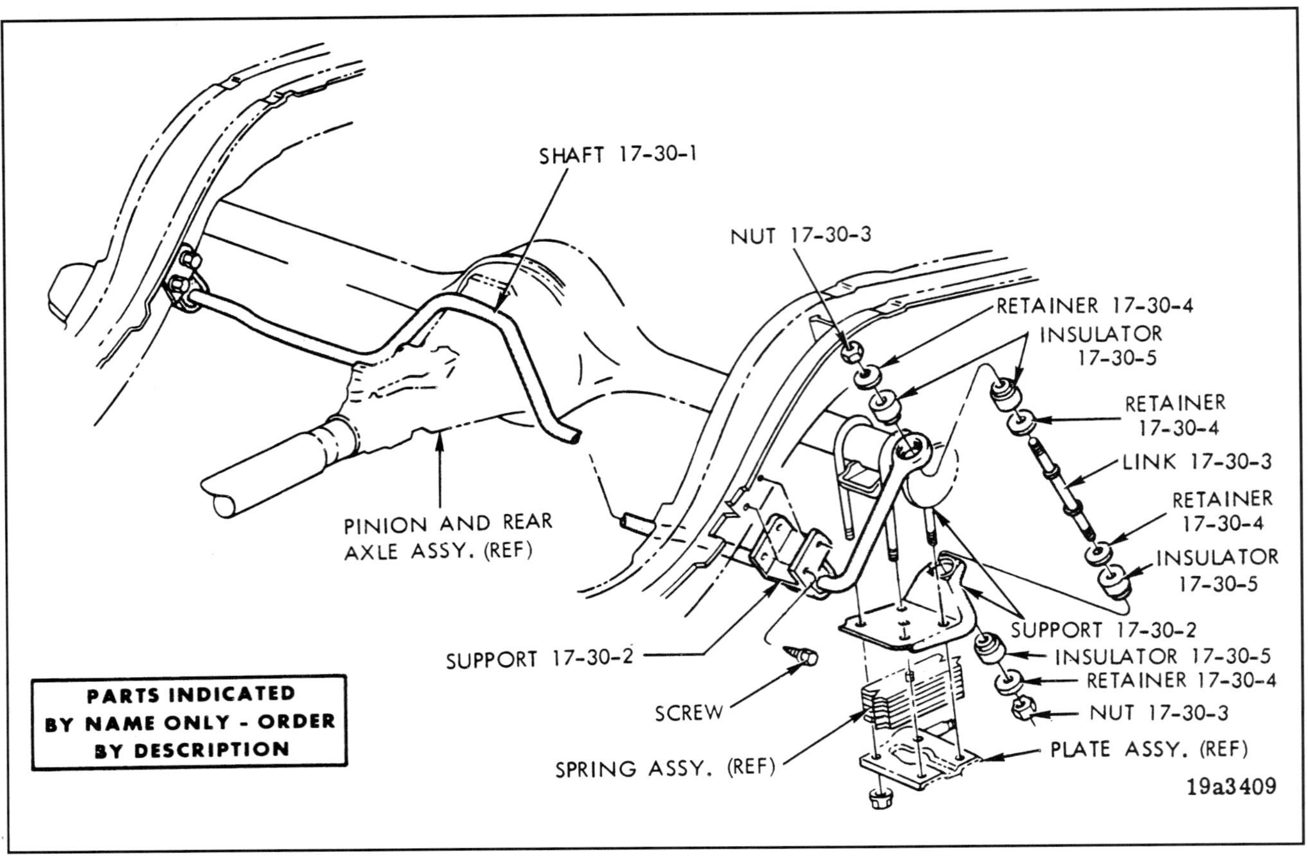

A rear sway bar for late-1970 to 1974 models.

1967-1974 SWAY BAR IDENTIFICATION

	Year(s)	Diameter	Part Number
A-Body			
	1967	.88	2462838
	1968-1969	.88	2535533
E-Body			
	1970-1974	.92	2835862
	Trans-Am	94x	2948723

Rear Suspension

The rear suspension was sprung with semi-elliptical multileaf rear springs. Those models with a performance or heavy-duty suspension had more leaves, or the individual leaves were stiffer (higher-rated). The Trans-Am models used four and a half leaves, just like the standard E-body suspension, but each leaf was high-rated and they were arched, giving the car a 1 3/4-inch ride height increase at the rear. This gave it a race car stance, plus provided clearance for the tailpipes on the side of the car. Do not use the standard-style spring on this model.

As stated previously, all 1970-1974 models used rear springs with four and a half leaves—with one exception. The 1970-1971 models with either the 440-ci or 426-ci Hemi powerplants used five and a half leaves on each side.

Springs usually are painted semi-gloss black, but some, especially the 1967-1969 models, may have an unpainted finish. The unpainted finish can be duplicated by painting the leaves stainless steel. What about color codes, those dabs of paint applied to various points on the car at the factory for quality control? It is common practice to apply dozens of these marks to the undercarriage. But studies of untouched original cars reveal that these marks were not that widely used. Not every part and bolt on every car was checked by an inspector, only random parts on random cars were selected to be inspected.

Only careful cleaning will reveal the codes; if you find them, note their location and their color, then reapply them. A Polaroid camera works excellently for noting the location, but write down the color, as film has a way of changing tints sometimes. Don't be alarmed if you

1967-1974 Barracuda and Challenger Rear Leaf Springs

Model Year(s)	Type of Suspension	Engine	Number of Leaves
1967-1969	Standard	225-ci six-cyl.	5
1967-1969	Heavy-Duty	225-ci six-cyl.	6
1970-1972	Std./Heavy-Duty	225-ci six-cyl.	4 1/2**
1967	Standard	273-ci 2-bbl	4 1/2
1967	Heavy-Duty	273-ci 2-bbl	6
1967	Standard	273-ci 4-bbl	6
1968-1969	Standard	318-ci V-8	4 1/2
1968-1969	Heavy-Duty	318-ci V-8	6
1970-1974	Std./Heavy-Duty	318-ci V-8	4 1/2**
1968-1969	Standard	340-ci V-8	6
1970-1973	Std./Heavy-Duty	340-ci V-8	4 1/2** #
1974	Std./Heavy-Duty	360-ci V-8	4 1/2**
1967-1969	Standard	383-ci V-8	6
1970-1971	Standard	383-ci 2-bbl V-8	4 1/2**
1970-1971	Standard	383-ci 4-bbl V-8	4 1/2 ^
1969	Standard	440-ci	6
1970-1971	Standard	426-ci or 440-ci	5 1/2

** = Heavy-Duty suspension used same number of leaves but is stiffer;
# = Models with 340-ci 3x2-bbl used special springs;
^ = Heavy-Duty suspension standard.

don't find any paint marks; it simply means that your car was one of those not checked.

Rear Sway Bar

One complaint that road testers had with the early 1970 Barracuda was the severe rear plow during hard cornering. Chrysler tightened the rear suspension with the addition of a rear antisway bar that was introduced after the first of the year. The rear sway bar became part of the Rally suspension in 1971 models and continued through to the end of the 1974 models. The bar should be painted semi-gloss black. Note that on all AAR and T/A models, the rear sway bar was standard equipment.

Shock Absorbers

Both front and rear heavy-duty shocks were part of the Formula S package. In 1969, the shocks were given new part numbers, and six-cylinder-equipped and 318-ci V-8-equipped cars used the same shocks. Heavy-duty shocks, both front and rear, were mandatory if the 340-, 383-, or 440-ci powerplants were ordered.

For 1970, models with a six-cylinder engine or two-barrel V-8 powerplant used a different set of shocks than those models with a four-barrel or multiple carburetors. In 1971, the part numbers were changed from the previous year, but those with a six-cylinder or two-barrel still used a different set of shocks than the high-performance models. The 1972-1973 models used the same shocks despite engine size, which were the same shocks used on

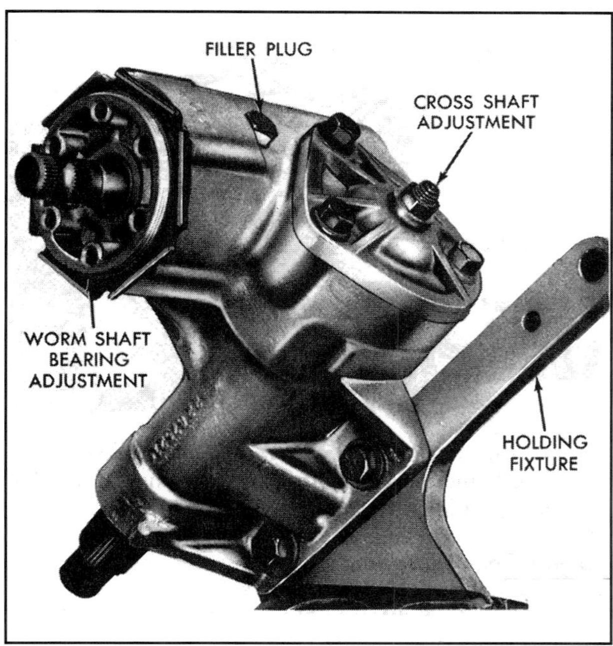

A manual steering gearbox.

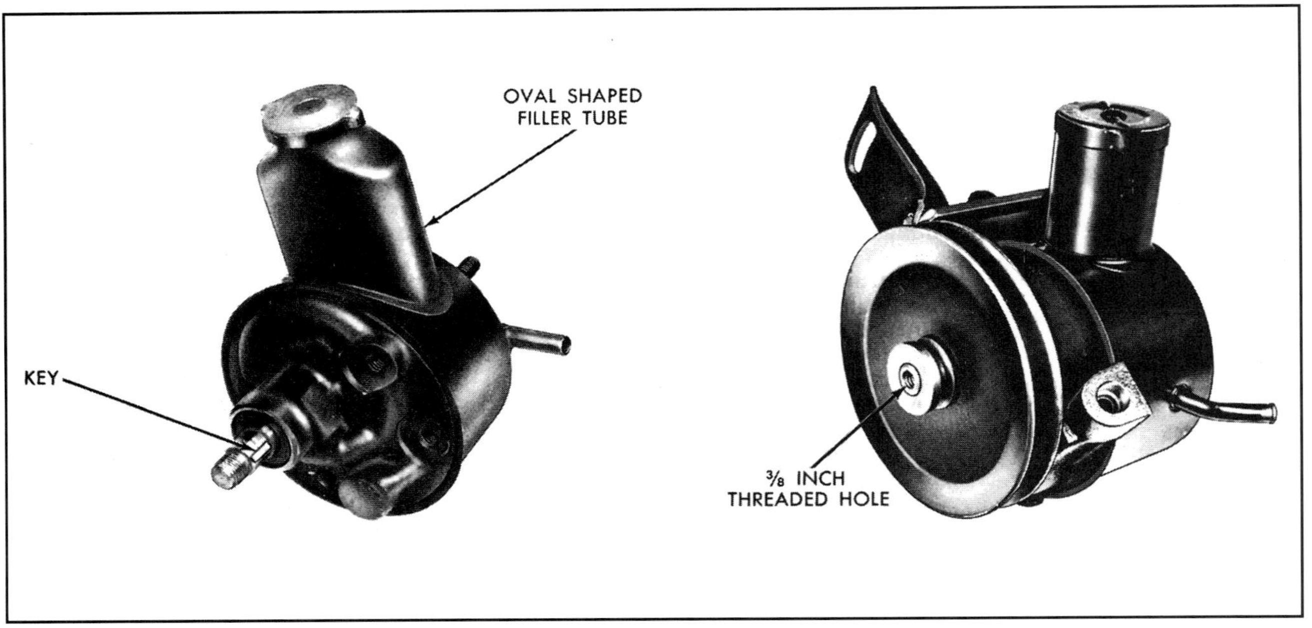

On the right is a typical thread hole-type power steering pump. On the left is a typical key slot-type power steering pump.

1971 models with a six-cylinder or two-barrel V-8 powerplant. Shock assemblies were usually painted gloss black except the mounting plates, which were unpainted. Note that careful cleaning on the end of the shock's eye bolt may reveal an inspector's mark.

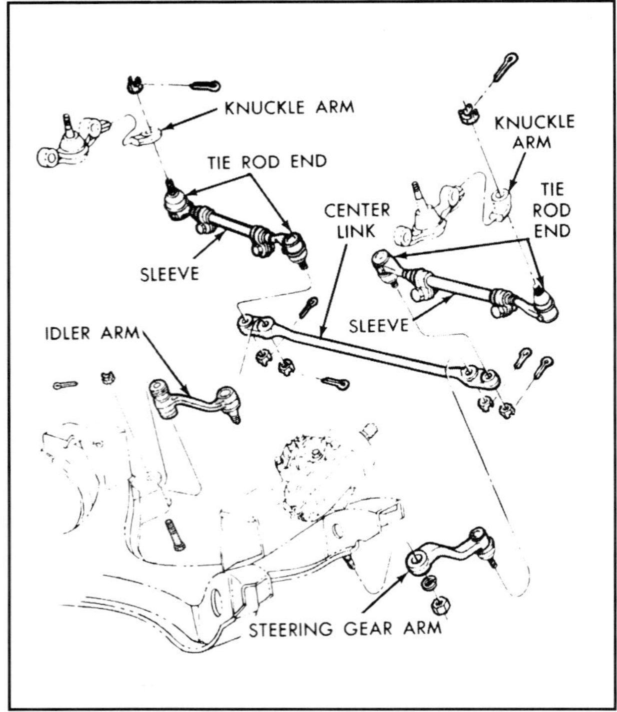

A breakdown of the steering linkage.

Steering Systems

Manual steering with a 24:1 ratio was standard in all models all eight years—except for those exported to England, where power steering was part of the package. A quick-ratio manual steering gearbox, with a 16:1 ratio, was optional on the 1967-1969 models but was not recommended with the 383-ci engine. Power steering was optional for all models and engine sizes, except the 1967-1968 cars with a 383-ci engine and the 1969 440-ci V-8.

Power steering gearboxes used hydraulic fluid fed by a pump. Several different pumps were used. The 1967-1968 models used the 0.96-ci displacement pump; it can be recognized by its 4 5/8-inch inside-diameter reservoir. Beginning in 1969, the selection was increased. The six-cylinder and those with 383-ci engines used a 1.06-ci displacement pump; this pump can be identified by the 3/8-inch diameter threaded hole in the pump shaft. All other V-8s in 1969 used the 0.94-ci displacement pump, which is a Saginaw-built unit and has a key-slotted shaft.

In 1970 those cars with a six-cylinder engine used the same pump as was used in 1969. Trans-Am cars used a special 1.06 displacement pump that was matched to the quick-ratio steering gearbox. It took only about two and a half turns of the steering wheel to go from lock-to-lock. There is a belief that the Trans-Am power steering pump was used on late-1971 to 1974 E-bodies, but this is not true. The late-1971 models with a V-8 did use a similar pump, but the part numbers are different.

In 1972 all pumps were of the key slot-shaft design, but each engine used a different part number. In 1973 and 1974, most models used a pump with a 3/8-inch

1967 Barracuda Power Steering Belts

Engine	*Without A/C*	*Length*	*With A/C*	*Length*
225	1327471	36 1/2	1859297	38 3/8
273	1854895	39	1854895	39

Note: P/S not available with 383-ci engine

1968 Barracuda Power Steering Belts

Engine	*Without A/C*	*Length*	*With A/C*	*Length*
225	1327471	36 1/2	1859297	38 3/8
318/340	1854895	39	1854895	39

Note: P/S not available with 383-ci V-8 engine

1969 Barracuda Power Steering Belts

Engine	*Without A/C*	*Length*	*With A/C*	*Length*
225	1678280	42	2402934	42 1/2
318/340	1678280	42	2402934	42 1/2
383-ci	2951153	43	Option n/a	
440-ci	Option n/a		Option n/a	

1970-1971 Barracuda/Challenger Power Steering Belts

Engine	*Without A/C*	*Length*	*With A/C*	*Length*
225	3512025	40 3/4	Option n/a	
318/340	2951984	42 1/2	2951898*	45 1/2
383/440	3419000	42 1/2	2951202*	44
Hemi	2268386	39 3/8	Option n/a	

* = Engines with multicarburetors not available with air conditioning.

1972 Barracuda/Challenger Power Steering Belts

Engine	*Without A/C*	*Length*	*With A/C*	*Length*
225	3512025	40 3/4	Option n/a	
318/340	2951984	42 1/2	2951898	45 1/2

1973-1974 Barracuda/Challenger Power Steering Belts

Engine	*Without A/C*	*Length*	*With A/C*	*Length*
318/340	2951984	42 1/2	2951898	45 1/2
360*	2951984	42 1/2	2951898	45 1/2

* = 1974 models only.

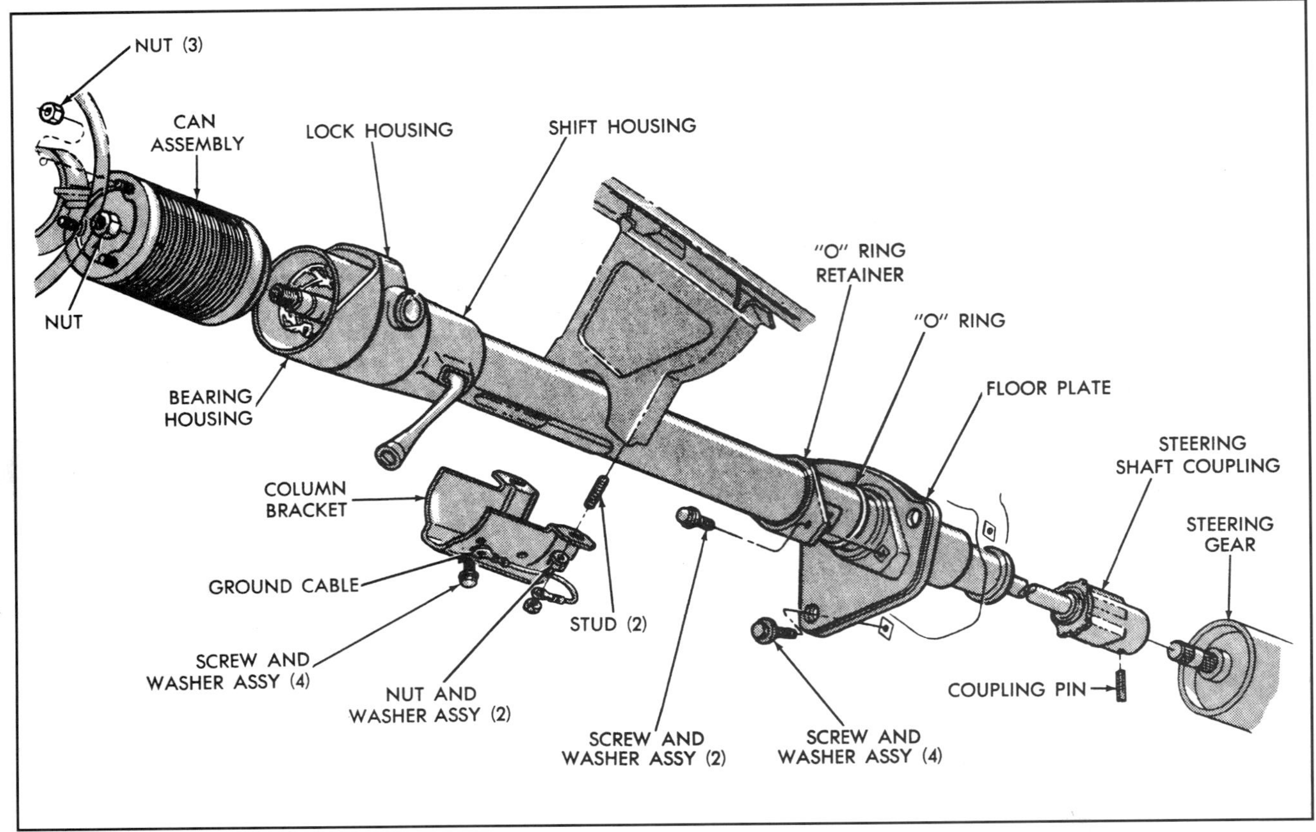

A typical steering column; the 1970-1974 style is shown.

threaded hole in the shaft; this is the same pump used on late-1971 models that many compare to the Trans-Am pump. Some 1973 and 1974 models were equipped with the key slot-type pump used in 1972.

Steering gearboxes should have an unpainted cast finish to them, and the end caps of the gearbox should have a dull aluminum appearance. Sometimes the bolts holding the caps have a flat black appearance. Power steering pumps, whatever type, should have a semi-gloss black finish.

Steering Columns

Beginning with the 1967 models, an energy-absorbing steering column was part of the federally mandated standard safety equipment. Several different columns were used, and those with manual steering used a different shaft than those with power steering. Besides the type of steering, transmission type and shifter location will affect the usage. A tilt steering column became an option beginning with the 1970 models, which also required another set of special columns. Engine size can also affect usage, such as the case of 1967-1969 models with the 383-ci engine. The 1969 Cuda with a 440 used the same column as those with a 383-ci and automatic transmission without power steering.

The steering column jacket was painted to match the interior trim in a flat finish, except white or certain other colors in 1967 to 1969 models. Check the accompanying charts for paint colors. The steering columns on the 1970 models were painted flat black (Ditzler 9324) despite interior trim color. The 1971-1974 models were also painted black, but it was a low-gloss finish listed as Ditzler 9388.

Steering Wheels

Standard in 1967-1968 models was a three-spoke steering wheel with a bright, partial-horn ring. The steering wheel rim was molded in a color that was color-keyed to the interior trim, and the same steering wheel was also available with a full-horn ring as an option. A simulated wood-rim steering wheel was also optional and was included in the "Sports Package" option, which also included the 150 miles per hour speedometer. If your car has the 150 miles per hour speedometer, it will also have the simulated-walnut steering wheel. Because the steering wheel was a separate option, your Barracuda will not necessarily have a

continued on page 71

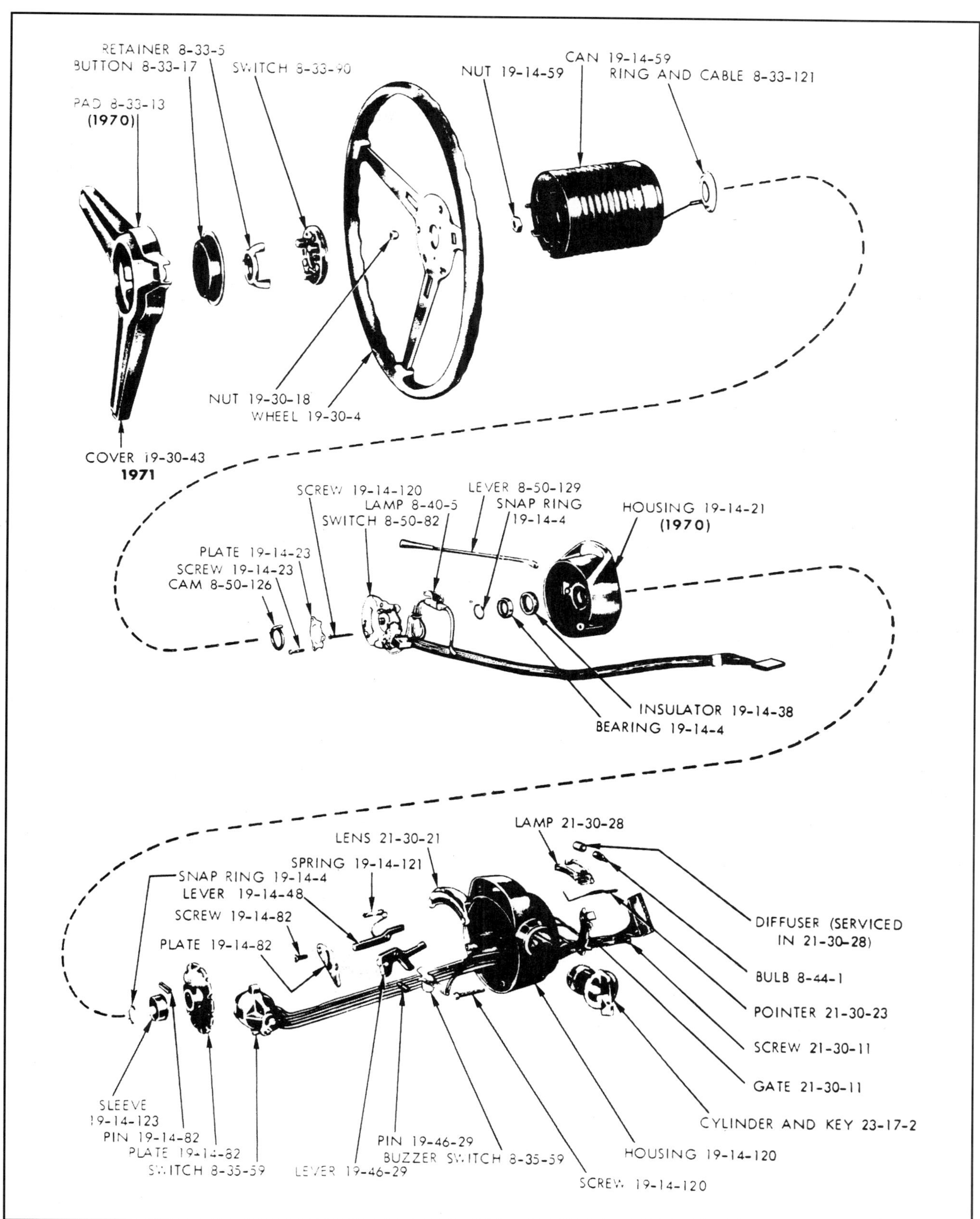

An exploded view of the 1970-1971 steering wheel.

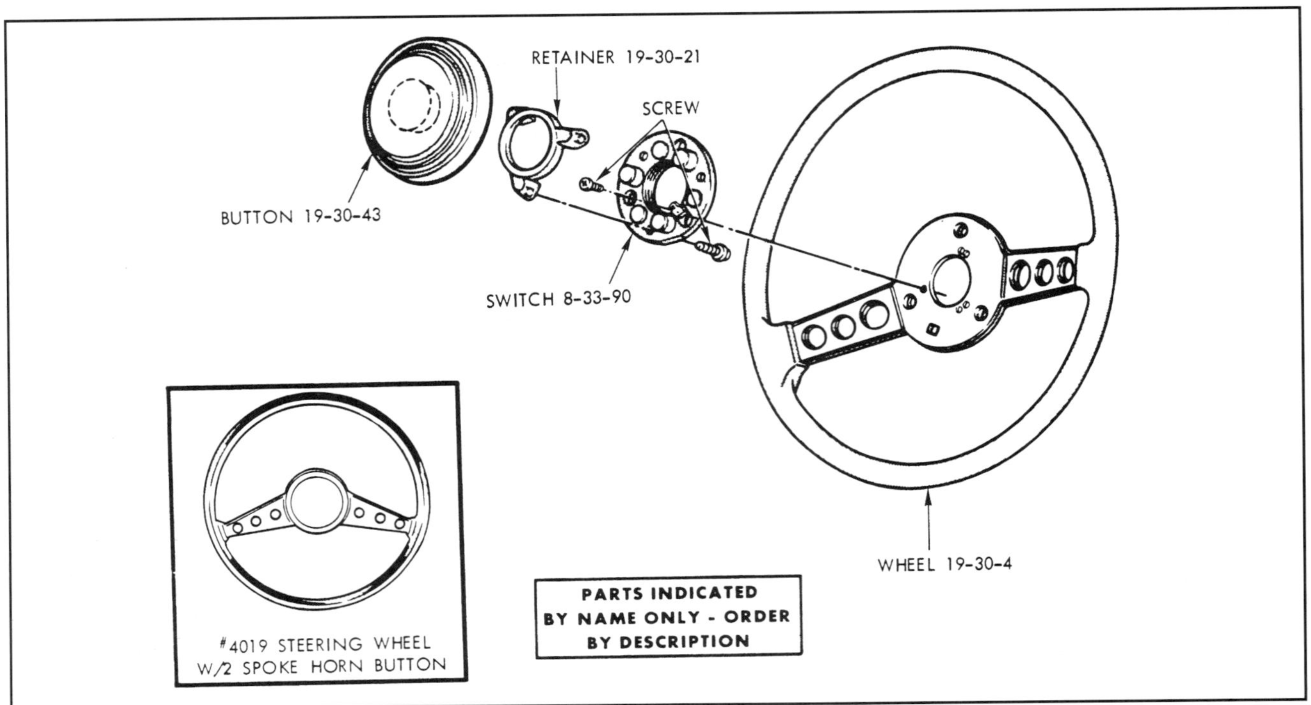

The 1972-1974 Barracuda and Challenger steering wheel.

A typical 1967-1968 standard steering wheel with a partial horn ring.

1967 Barracuda Steering Wheel Colors

Interior Code	Interior Trim	Paint Color Name	Ditzler Code No.
H5B, H6B	Dark Blue	Ensign Blue	13157
H5R, H6R	Dark Red	Derby Red	71390
H5X, H6X	Black	Satin Black	9324
H5T, H6T	Tan	Chestnut	22754
H5K, H6K	Copper	Copper Brown	22755
H5C, H6C	White	Ensign Blue	13157
H5V, H6V	White	Derby Red	71390
H5W, H6W	White	Satin Black	9324

All but Satin Black and Derby Red are metallic.

1968 Barracuda Steering Column Colors

Interior Codes	Trim Color	Paint Name	Ditzler Paint No.
HB5, H6B, D6B	Bright Blue	Baltic Blue 9324	13705
H6F, D6F	Dark Green	Bayou Green 43925	43925
H5X, H6X, D6X	Black	Jewel Black 9324	9324
D6Y	Gold	Laser Gold 23062	23062
H5C, H6C, D6C	White	Baltic Blue 9324	13705
H5W, H6W, D6W	White	Jewel Black 9324	9324
H5D, H6D, D6D	White	Bayou Green 43925	43925
D6E	White	Laser Gold 23062	23062
H5V, H6V, D6V	White	Regatta Red 71688	71688
H6R, D6R	Red	Regatta Red 71688	71688

1969 Barracuda Steering Column Paint Colors

Interior Codes	Trim Color	Paint Name	Ditzler Paint No.
H4B, LB2, G6B	Bright Blue	Baltic Blue	13705
H4X, L2X, H6X, D6X	Black	Jewel Black	9324
H4W, H6W	White	Jewel Black	9324
H4V, H6V	White	Regatta Red	71688
H4C, H6C	White	Baltic Blue	13705
H4F, H6F	White	Bayou Green	43925
L2R, H6R, D6R	Red	Regatta Red	71688
D6U	Tan/black	Jewel Black	9324
D6T, X1T	Tan	Sienna Tan	23076
F6P	(1)	Jewel Black	9324
D6P	Pale yellow and black	Jewel Black	9324
F6J	(2)	Bayou Green	43926
H6G, D6G	Green	Bayou Green	43926

(1) = Yellow-and-black florapattern. (2) = Yellow-and-green florapattern.

1970-1974 E-Body Steering Column Paint Colors			
Model Year	**Interior Color Codes**	**Paint Name**	**Ditzler Paint Number**
1970	All codes	Flat Black	9324
1971-1974	All codes	Black	9388

A typical 1970 standard steering wheel with no horn ring.

Continued from page 66
150 miles per hour speedometer if it has the simulated-walnut steering wheel.

In 1969, the standard steering wheel was a three-spoke unit, with slots in the spokes and a color-keyed leather-like rim and a padded horn button. The full-horn ring remained optional, as did the simulated wood-grain steering wheel. Standard in 1970 models was a wood-grain three-spoke steering wheel with a center color-keyed pad. Some models came with a partial-horn ring, but most used no horn ring. Optional was a tan-and-black wheel, with a color-keyed center horn cap that was held in place with three screws.

In 1971, the style was the same but the textured finish was changed to black coachman grain with a black center shroud. The tan-and-black steering wheel remained optional but now only used a black center cap. Although they are seen on the E-bodies today at car shows, the soft-rim steering wheel was not available on the Barracuda or Challenger models; this wheel was available on the Satellite and Charger models. For 1972 to 1974, only one steering wheel was available, and it was a two-spoke unit with a black rim. Each spoke featured three round holes and the spokes were connected in the center with a black center horn cap. No other wheel was optional, not even the simulated-walnut rim.

A few early 1970 models came with a horn ring.

1967 Steering Wheel Color Usage

Interior Codes	Wheel Color
HB5, H6B, H5C, H6C	Blue
H5K, H6K	Copper
H5R, H6R, H5V, H6V	Red
H5T, H6T	Tan
H5X, H6W, H5W	Black
Note: All codes	Wood grain

1968 Steering Wheel Color Usage

Interior Codes	Wheel Color
H5B, H6B, D6B, H5C, H6C, D6C	Blue
H6F, D6F, H5D, H6W, D6D	Green
H5X, H6X, D6X, H5W, H6W, D6W	Black
H6R, D6R, H5V, H6V	Dark Red
D6Y, D6E	Gold
Note: All codes	Wood grain

1969 Steering Wheel Color Usage

Interior Codes	Wheel Type	Wheel Color
H4B, H4C, H6B, H6C, D6B	Std.	Blue
H4F, F6J, H6F, H6G, D6G, D6J	Both	Green
H4V, H6R, H6V, D6R	Both	Red
H4W, H4X, F6P, H6X, D6P, D6S, D6U, D6X	Both	Black
Note: All codes	Wood grain	Wood Grain

1970 Steering Wheel Horn Cap Color Usage

Interior Codes	Cap Color
P5X9, PRX9, H6X9, P6XW, PRXW, H4XW, H6XW, P6XY, H5X9, P6A8, HRX9, L6XW, L6XW	Black
P6B5, H4B5, H6B5, P6BW, H4BW, H6B5, H6B7, H5B5, H4B5	Brite Blue
P6E4, H6E4, P6EW, H6EW	Red
P6F8, H4F8, H6F8, P6FW, H4FW, H6FW	Dark Green
P6K4, P5K4, H6K4, HRK4	Burnt Orange
P6T5, PRT5, H6T5, H5T5, HRT5	Light Tan

1971 Barracuda/Challenger Horn Cap Color Usage

Interior Code	Horn Cap color
H6X9, H4X9, P6X9, P5X9, H6XW, H4XW, H6XV, H5X9, PRX9, SRX9, H5XV, L6X9, L6XW, H6XW, H5XX, HRX9, H6Y3	Black
H6B5, H4B5, P6B5, L6B7, H6B7	Brite Blue
L6F8, H6F8, H5F8, H4F8, L5FW, P6F8	Green
H6T5, H4T5, P6T5, L6T5, H6T5	Light Tan

1972-1974 Barracuda/Challenger Horn Cap Color Usage

Interior Code	Horn Cap Color
All trim codes	Black

Chapter 4

Transmissions and Drivetrains

Manual Transmissions

Both three-speed and four-speed manual transmissions were available on the Barracudas and Challenger line, and availability of the particular transmission is dependent on the model and the engine size. Manual transmissions from 1968 and later can be identified by the transmission identification number, a 13-digit-and-character code. It is found on a pad just below the centerline of the forward section of the case, on the right-hand side.

This code will begin with a two-letter symbol for the transmission assembly plant. Either PP (New Process) or PK (Kokomo) was used. This is followed by a three-digit code for the type of transmission. Those models with a six-cylinder engine used a 903-type three-speed transmission. Two different three-speeds were used with the 318-ci engines: Early models (1967-1969) used the type 745, while the 1970-1974 models used the type 230.

Only one type of four-speed was available all eight years, and regardless of engine size, all four-speeds were classified as type 833. Several different units were used and those used in high-performance models featured special heavy-duty interior components.

Following the transmission-type code will be a four-digit date code; this is the same date code used on the engine block, so it's the sequential number of that day's production. Beginning in 1968, the car's VIN, or the last eight digits after 1968, were also stamped onto this pad. To have a matching-numbers car, the same last eight digits of the VIN must appear here on the transmission.

A three-speed was standard on all models with six-cylinder engines, the 318-ci, and the 273-ci two-barrel V-8. In 1970, the type 745 was replaced by the tougher 230 design, which allowed it to be used behind more powerful engines. Thus, the 340-ci four-barrel and the 383 four-barrel were now standard with a three-speed man-

IDENTIFICATION PAD

The identification pad location on manual transmissions.

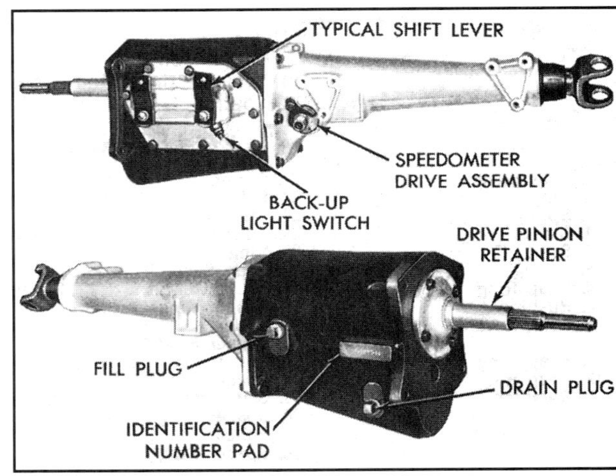

The three-speed type A-230 transmission is cast-iron gray and natural aluminum.

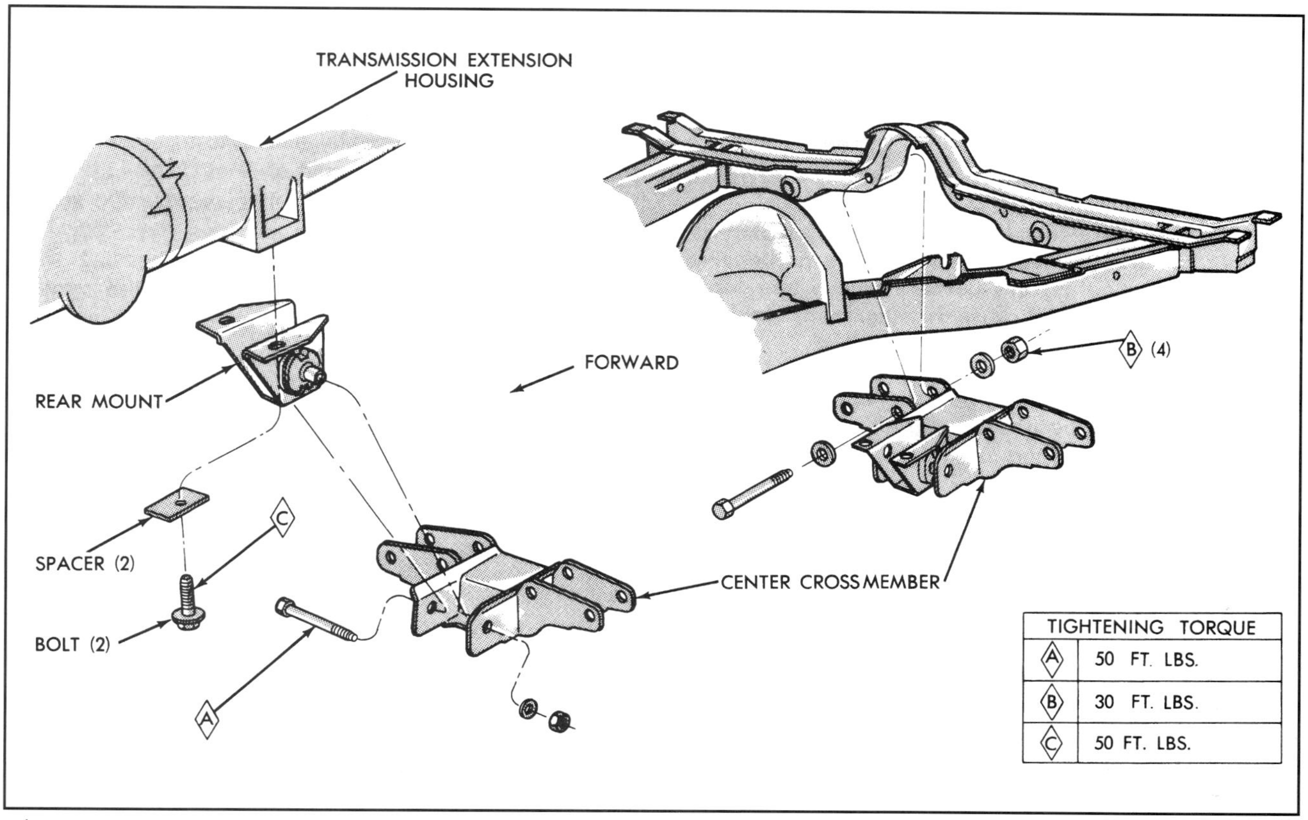

TRANSMISSION EXTENSION HOUSING
FORWARD
REAR MOUNT
SPACER (2)
BOLT (2)
CENTER CROSSMEMBER
A
B (4)
C

TIGHTENING TORQUE	
A	50 FT. LBS.
B	30 FT. LBS.
C	50 FT. LBS.

A late-1971 to 1974 manual transmission mounting. The rear mount is gloss black except with Hemis, where it is painted bright yellow.

TRANSMISSION EXT. HOUSING
REAR
TAB BENT 90°
SECTION A-A
REAR MOUNT
B (2)
A
BEND TAB TO RETAIN MOUNT
CENTER CROSSMEMBER
C (4)
A

TIGHTENING TORQUE	
A	200 IN. LBS.
B	40 FT. LBS.
C	90 FT. LBS.

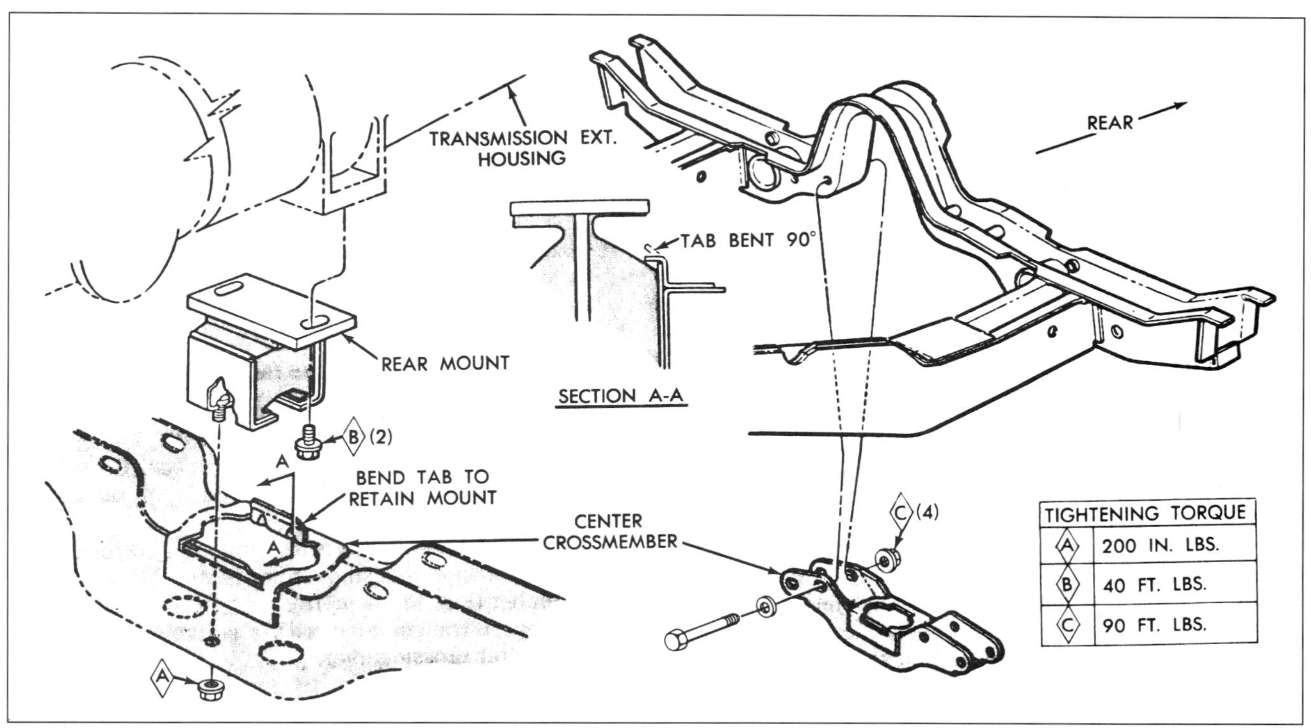

The 1967 to early 1971-style manual transmission mounting.

A 1970-1974 rear transmission support. *Year One*

ual transmission. Before 1970, only a four-speed or automatic transmission was available with these powerplants. A manual transmission was not available with the 383-ci two-barrel V-8 in 1970 or 1971, as an automatic transmission was standard. When the 340-ci engine was phased out of production at the end of the 1973 model year, a three-speed manual transmission remained standard with the 360-ci engine in 1974 models.

Four-speed manual transmissions were a no-cost option for models with the 1967 273-ci four-barrel, the 1968-1969 340-ci four-barrel, the 1967-1969 383-ci four-barrel, and the 1970-1971 440-ci four-barrel and 3x2-barrel. It was standard on the 1970 Trans-Am cars and the 1970-1971 Hemi cars.

A four-speed was an extra-cost option with these powerplants and models: the 1967 273-ci two-barrel; 1968-1969 318-ci; 1970-1971 383-ci four-barrel; 1970-1973 340-ci four-barrel; and the 1974 360-ci four-barrel. It also found its way onto six-cylinder-equipped cars, but only on those exported overseas.

The type-745 transmission should have a cast-iron gray finish, and the type-230 should have a dark gray forward section and an aluminum-colored tail shaft. The four-speed is all aluminum, so to duplicate the original fresh-cast finish, paint it with a flat-gloss aluminum paint. There may be a three-digit ID number code painted on the side of the housing which is visible only by careful cleaning. These numbers were usually done in either yellow, light blue, or light green paint. A chart has been provided for you to repaint these codes. A white cross may also be found on the housing; this is an inspector's mark.

Gearshifts

The 1967-1969 Barracudas with a three-speed manual transmission used a bright-plated column-mounted

Transmission ID Code Numbers

			Engine Displacement				
Year	**Trans. Type**	**273-ci**	**318-ci**	**340-ci**	**383-ci**	**440-ci**	**Hemi**
1967	4-speed	395	n/a	n/a	041	n/a	n/a
1968	4-speed	n/a	041	041	041	n/a	046
1969	4-speed	n/a	602	602	602	n/a	n/a
1970	3-speed	n/a	687	765	690		
	4-speed	n/a	696	696	675	n/a	n/a
				789#		677	677
1971	3-speed	n/a	687	830	825	n/a	n/a
	4-speed	n/a	757	757	825	755	755
1972	3-speed	n/a			n/a	n/a	n/a
	4-speed		757	757	n/a	n/a	n/a
1973	3-speed	n/a			n/a	n/a	n/a
	4-speed	n/a	804	804	n/a	n/a	n/a
1974	3-speed	n/a			n/a	n/a	n/a
	4-speed	n/a	416	416 **	n/a	n/a	n/a

** = 360-ci V-8 in 1974.

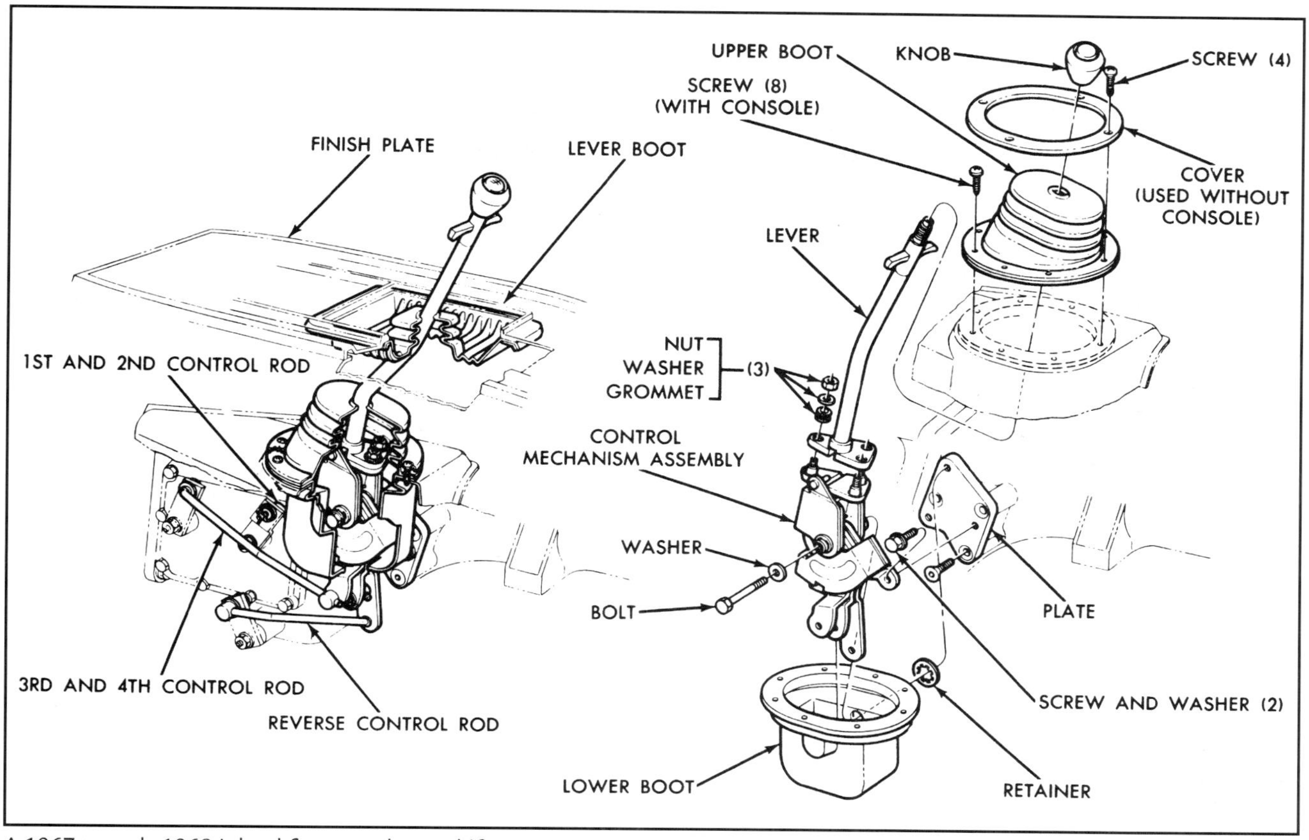

UPPER BOOT
KNOB
SCREW (4)
SCREW (8)
(WITH CONSOLE)
FINISH PLATE
LEVER BOOT
COVER
(USED WITHOUT
CONSOLE)
LEVER
1ST AND 2ND CONTROL ROD
NUT
WASHER
GROMMET
(3)
CONTROL
MECHANISM ASSEMBLY
WASHER
BOLT
PLATE
3RD AND 4TH CONTROL ROD
REVERSE CONTROL ROD
SCREW AND WASHER (2)
LOWER BOOT
RETAINER

A 1967 to early 1968 Inland four-speed gear shift.

CONSOLE
BOOT ASSY.
LEVER ASSY.
NUT
KNOB
SCREW (4)
SCREW (4)
KNOB
NUT
LEVER
CONTROL
MECHANISM
ASSY.
COVER (USED
WITHOUT CONSOLE)
BOOT ASSY.
SCREW (8)
1ST & 2ND ROD
WASHER (2)
CLIP
3RD & 4TH ROD
WASHER (2)
CLIP
PLATE
SCREW (3)
BOLT
WASHER
SWIVEL
CLIP
(3)
BOLT
WASHER
REVERSE ROD
CLIP

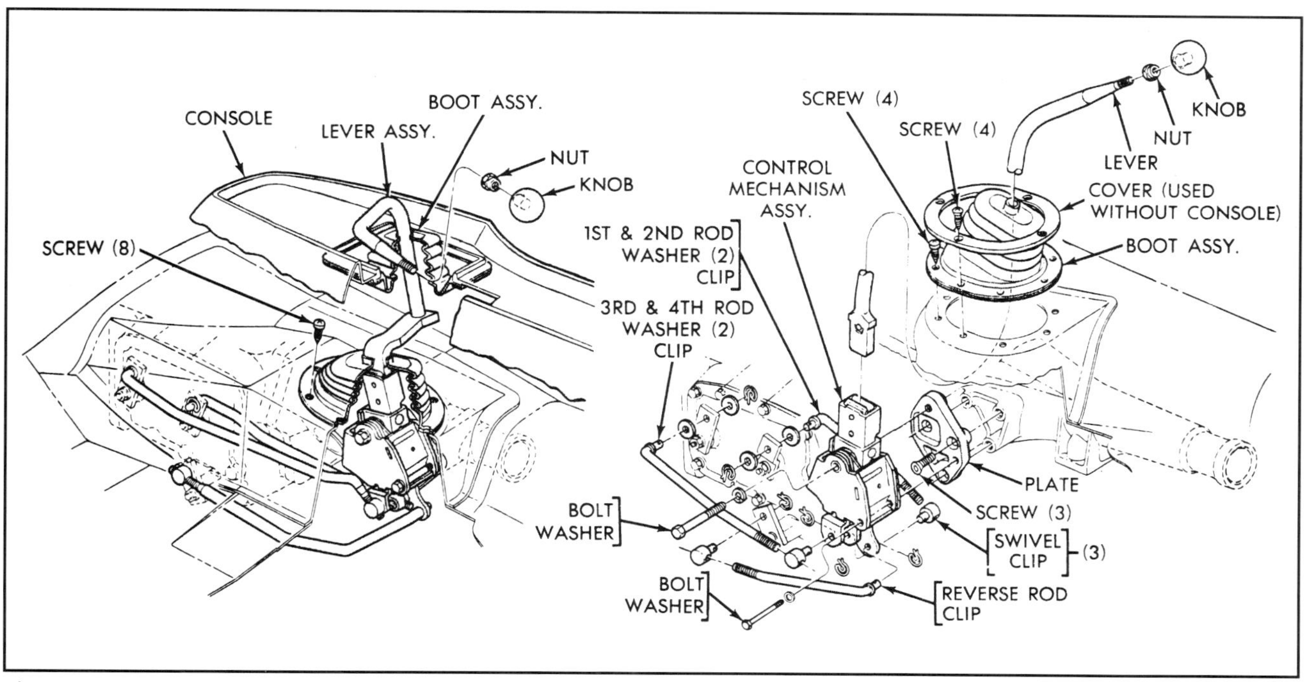

The 1968-1969 Hurst-built four-speed shifter.

shift lever with a black plastic knob; a floor-shifted three-speed was not available. In the 1970-1974 models, only a floor-mounted three-speed shift lever was used. Two different shift lever assemblies were used during this time, with the change occurring midway through the 1971 model year. The upper portion was changed and uses different knobs. The early-style lever used a black knob with a 1.88-inch outside diameter and an inlaid shift pattern. The later-style lever used a 1.81-inch outside diameter knob, and it, too, had an inlaid shift pattern. Although both levers used a 3/8-inch stud, the thread is different so be sure that the proper knob is used. The early style used a 24-thread while the later style used left-hand 16-thread. The thread can be read with a pitch gauge.

All four-speed transmissions used a floor-mounted shift lever, but their design is greatly influenced by model year and console. All 1967 and early 1968 models used an Inland-built shift lever. This lever can be easily recognized by its use of a chrome-plated, T-shaped reverse lock-out trigger. Two different Inland shift levers were used, one with a console and one without a console. The unit used with the console has a more curved design. Both shift levers used a large, black, plastic knob with a white inlaid shift pattern.

Shortly after the release of the 1968 models, the Inland shift lever was replaced with the more-durable Hurst-built unit. Dates of this change vary from factory to factory as on-hand supplies had to be used up. This lever featured a built-in lock-out device and required no release trigger. As with the Inland lever, different Hurst units were used with and without a console. Those with the console are visually different and have a radical double curved-design lever. Both levers used a simulated walnut-grain knob with an inlaid shift pattern.

Only the Hurst shift lever was used in 1969, and models built early used the same set of levers used in the latter part of 1968. Around January 17, 1969, those *without* a console were replaced. The difference is subtle but apparent visually (later versions have less curve in the lever), so the proper shift lever should be used.

Hurst also built the 1970-1974 four-speed shift lever commonly called a "pistol grip" shift due to design of the handle, which felt and visually resembled the grip of a handgun. Unlike the previous years, the same lever was used with or without a console. However, the 1970-1971 models used a different part number than the 1972-1974 models. Both the upper lever and lower mechanism were changed, so the levers will not interchange, yet

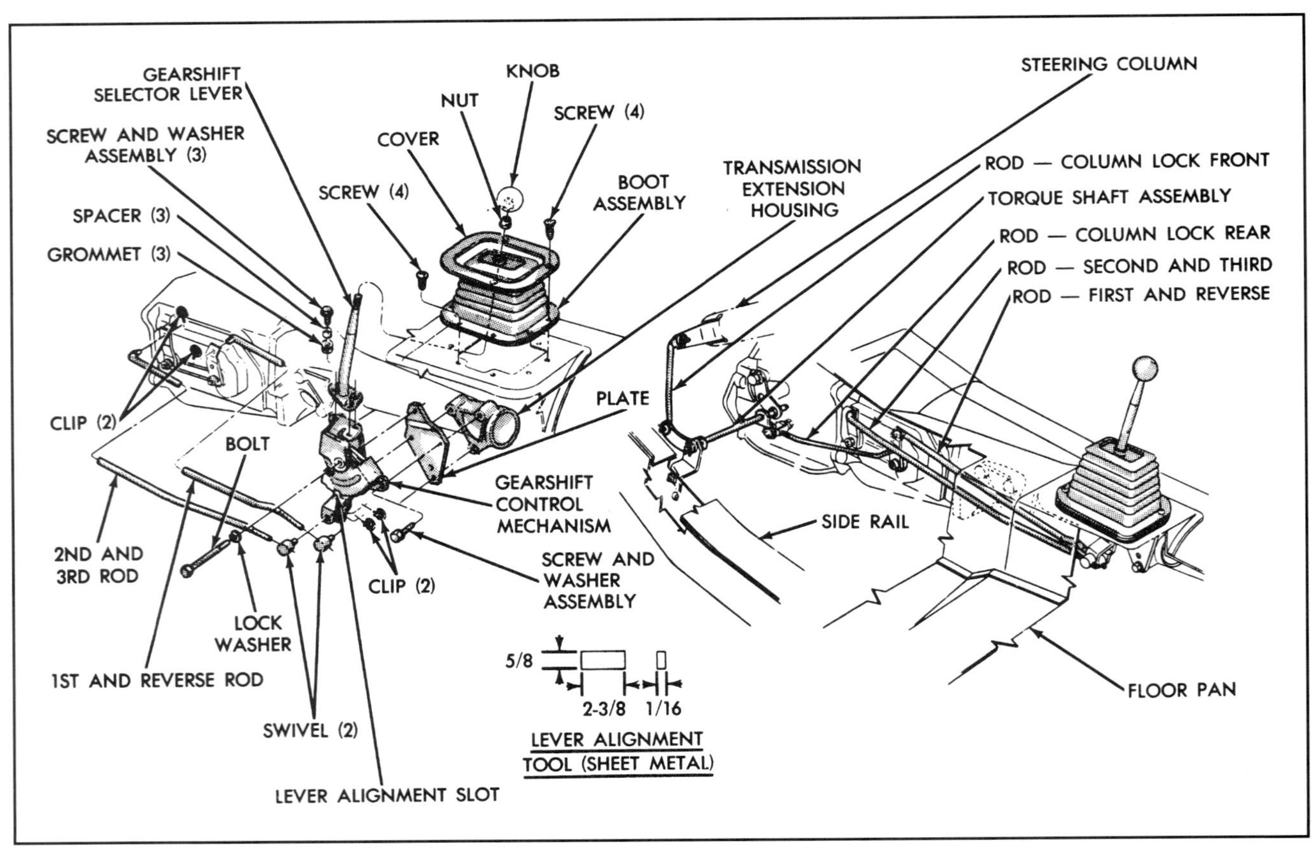

A 1970-1974 three-speed floor shifter.

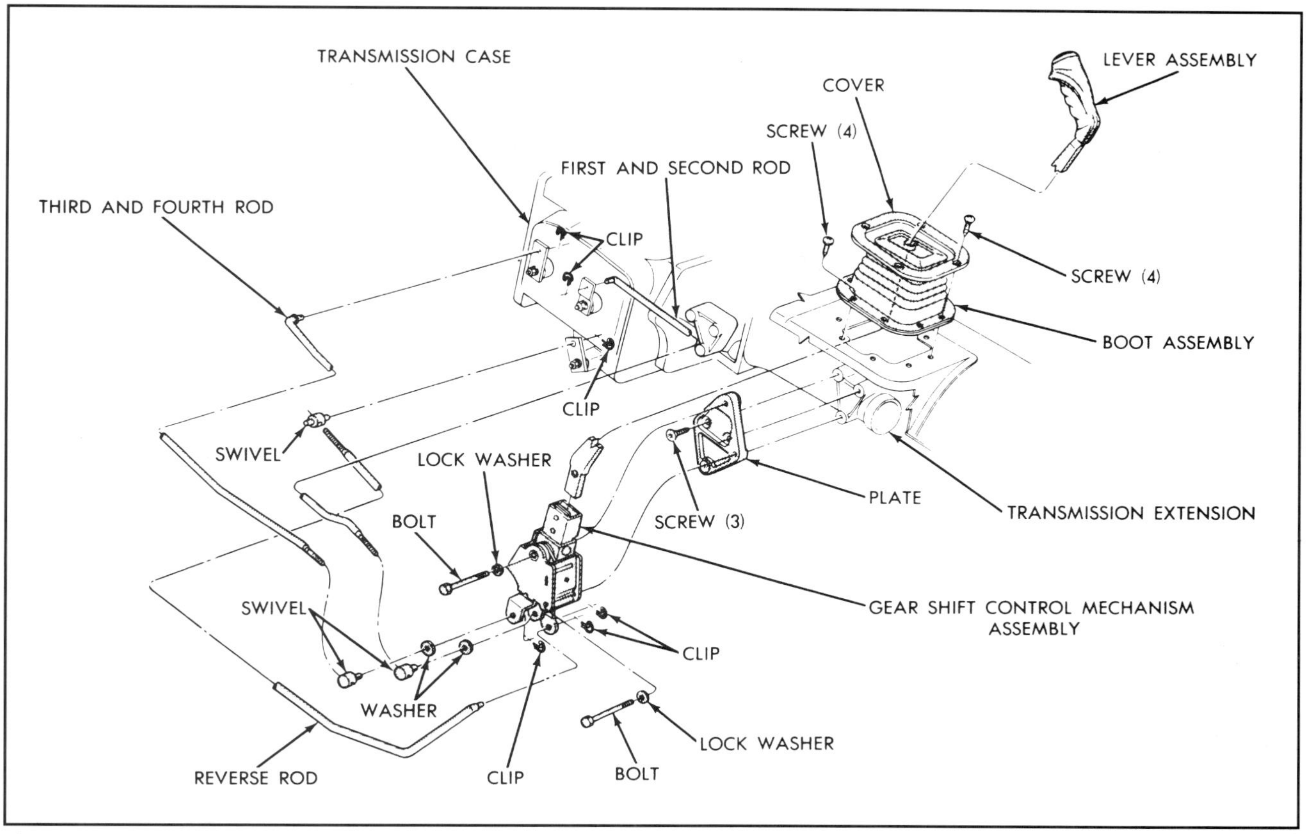

The 1970-1974 Hurst pistol-grip four-speed shifter.

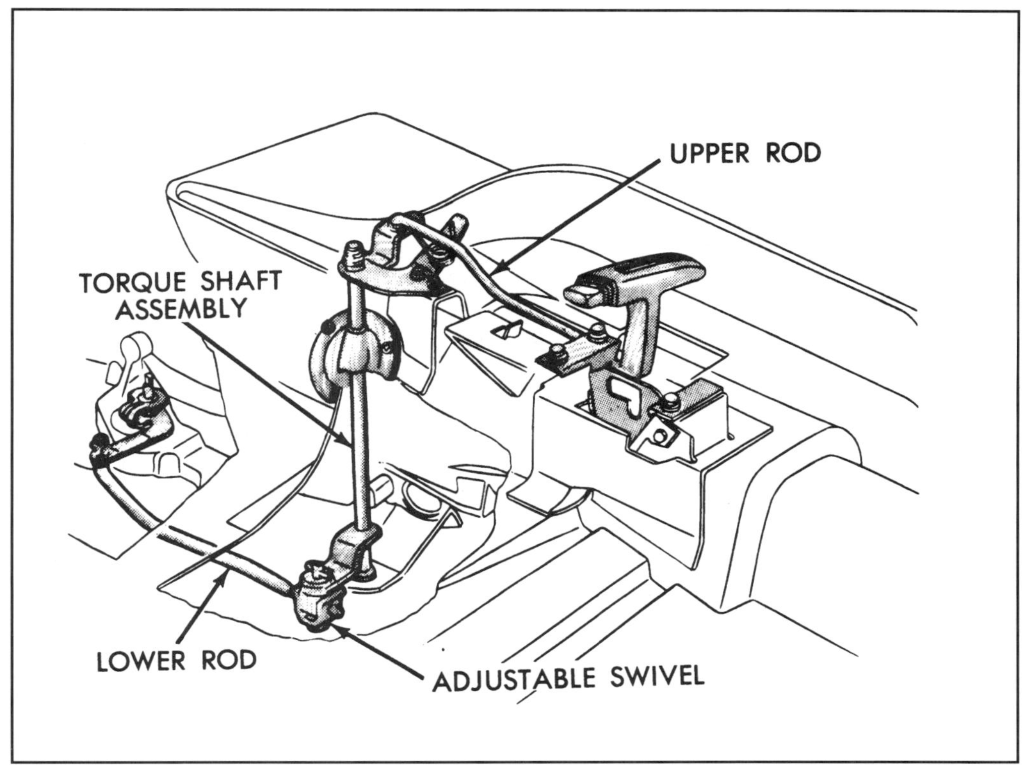

A 1971-1974 automatic floor-shifter linkage.

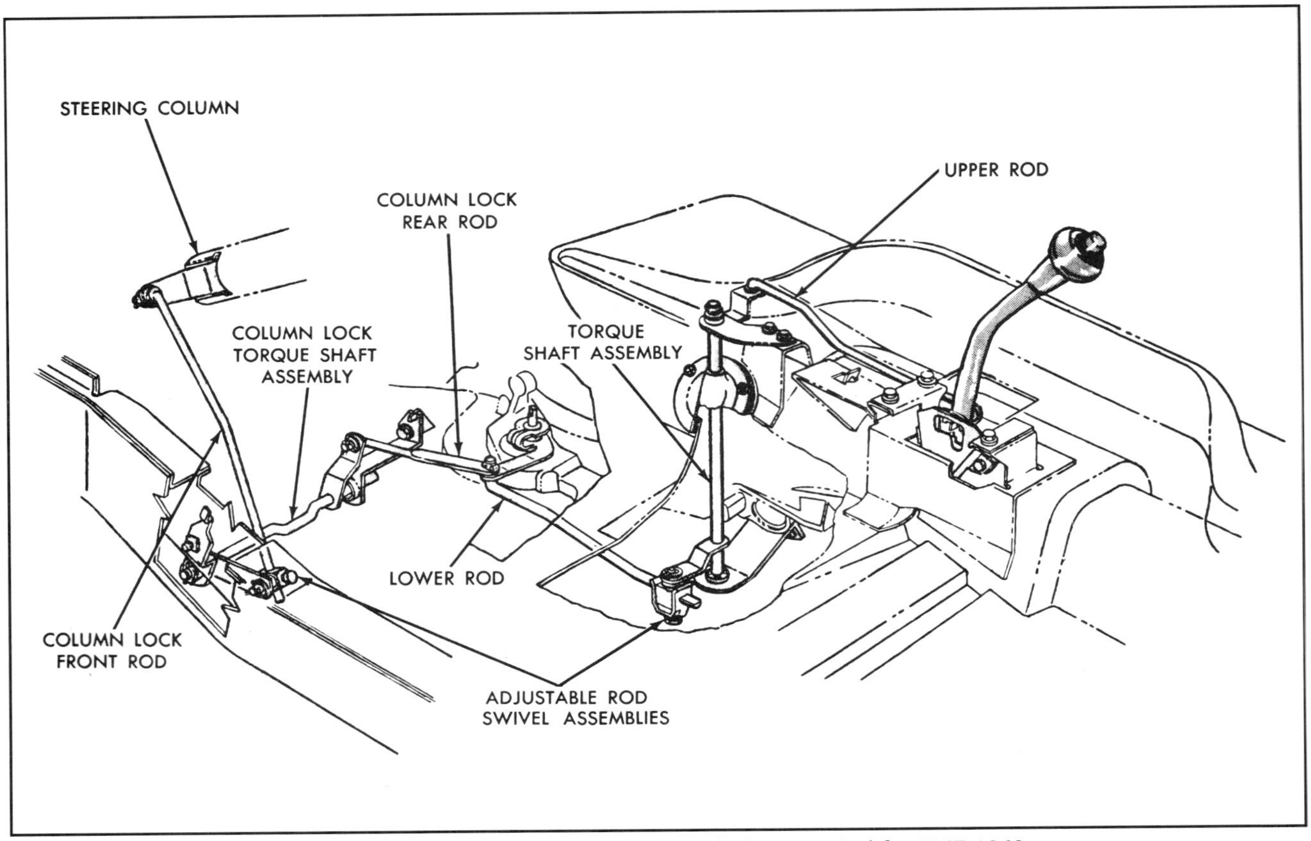

The console automatic floor shifter linkage. A 1970 version is shown, which was typical for 1967-1969.

they used the same simulated walnut grip handles and shift pattern lens.

An oblong-shaped shift boot was used without a console and a square-shaped boot was used with a console in the 1967-1969 models. The Inland lever used a different boot than the Hurst-built unit only when used *without* a console. The same boot was used with a console, regardless of the manufacturer, for all 1967-1969 models. An oblong-shaped shift boot continued to be used on 1970 models without a console. This is the same boot that was used on 1968-1969 Barracudas—with the Hurst shift lever without a console. A square-shaped boot was used on 1971-1974 models with or without a console, but the 1972-1974 models used a different part number. Those with a floor-mounted three-speed used a square-shaped boot all five years. The same boot used with the four-speed was used with the three-speed in 1971, but beginning in 1972, the three-speed used a different boot with more folds.

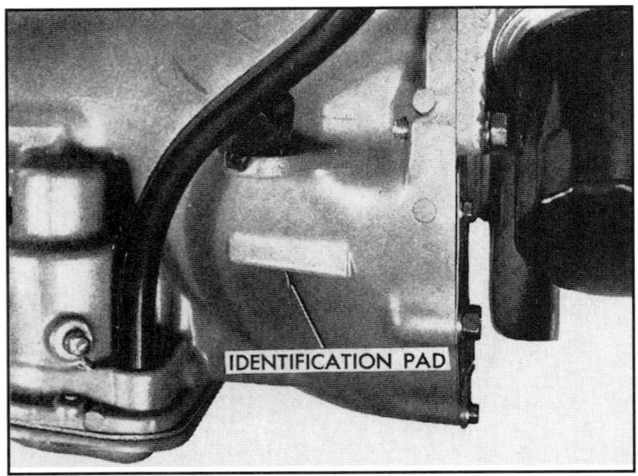

The location of the automatic transmission identification pad.

Automatic Transmissions

Like manual transmissions, 1968-and-later automatic transmissions can also be identified by an identification number. It is stamped just above the oil pan on the left-hand side of the unit. Just as with manual transmissions, it, too, begins with the transmission assembly code (PK for the Kokomo plant). After the PK code is the seven-digit part number, which is followed by the build date. The last four digits are the sequential number of units built that day.

1968 Transmission and Converters ID Numbers

Engine	Trans ID Marks *	ID Part No ˜	Converter Diameter	Stall Speed	Part No.	Notes
225-ci six-cyl.	904 G	2892027	10 3/4	2,100 rpm	2801762	Used up to 2-1-68
225-ci six-cyl.	904 G	2892069	10 3/4	2,100 rpm	2801762	From 2-1-68 to 5-15-68
225-ci six-cyl.	904 G	2892077	10 3/4	2,100 rpm	2801762	After 5-15-68
225-ci six-cyl.	904 G	2892050	10 3/4	2,100 rpm	2801762	Export before 2-1-68
225-ci six-cyl.	904 G	2892070	10 3/4	2,100 rpm	2801762	Export after 2-1-68
318-ci 2-bbl	904 LA	2892029	10 3/4	2,400 rpm	2801762	Before 2-1-68
318-ci 2-bbl	904 LA	2892072	10 3/4	2,400 rpm	2801762	From 2-1-68 to 5-15-68
318-ci 2-bbl	904 LA	2892080	10 3/4	2,400 rpm	2801762	After 5-15-68
340-ci	727 A	2892032	10 3/4	2,500 rpm	2801764	
383-ci	727 B	2892031	10 3/4	2,800 rpm	2801764	
426 Hemi	727 B	2801544	10 3/4		2801766	Drag race only

* = Found on bell housing; ˜ = Found on pan rail.

1969 Transmission Converter ID Numbers

Engine	Trans.ID Marks *	ID Part No.˜	Converter Diameter	Stall Speed	Part No.	Notes
225-ci six-cyl.	904 G	2892078	10 3/4	2,000 rpm	2801762	Export
225-ci six-cyl.	904 G	2892077	10 3/4	2,000 rpm	2801762	USA
318-ci	904 LA	2892080	10 3/4	2,200 rpm	2801762	
340-ci	727 A	2892089	10 3/4	2,400 rpm	2801764	
383-ci	727 B	2892091	10 3/4	2,600 rpm	2801764	
440-ci	727 B	2892093	10 3/4	2,300 rpm	2801764	May have used 383-ci unit also

* = On bell housing; ˜ = On pan rail.

1970 Transmission Converter ID Numbers

Engine	Trans. ID Marks *	Trans. ID No.˜	Converter Diameter	Stall Speed	Part No.	Notes
225-ci six-cyl.	904 G	3410636	11 3/4	2,000 rpm	2801762	Until June 1970
225-ci six-cyl.	904 G	3410777	11 3/4	2,000 rpm	2801762	After June 1970
318-ci	904 LA	3410637	11 3/4	2,200 rpm	2801762	Early type
318-ci	904 LA	3410779	11 3/4	2,200 rpm	2801762	Later type
340-ci	727 A	3410769	10 3/4	2,450 rpm	2801764	4-bbl and 3x2-bbl
383-ci 2-bbl	727 B	3410667	11 3/4	2,100 rpm	(1)	Before 4-27-70
383-ci 2-bbl	727 B	3515815	11 3/4	2,100 rpm	(1)	After 4-27-70
383-ci 4-bbl	727 B	3410668	10 3/4	2,600 rpm	2801764	Before 4-27-70
383-ci 4-bbl	727 B	3515816	10 3/4	2,600 rpm	2801764	After 4-27-70
426 Hemi	727 B	3410671		2,800 rpm	2801766	
440-ci 4-bbl	727 B	3410670	10 3/4	2,300 rpm	3410839	
440-ci 3x2-bbl	727 B	3410672	10 3/4	2,300 rpm	3410839	

Beginning with the 1972 models, the location was the same but the format is changed. The seven-digit part number now begins the identification code. After the part number is a single-letter code that shows the change level; the letter "A" begins the first change, "B" the second and so on.. The last eight digits of the identification number decode the build date and the daily production total. Due to internal differences in transmissions, it is important that the proper part number be used. This is especially true with the high-performance engines.

Automatic transmissions are categorized by family groups. This includes the 904 G group, which is used with six-cylinder-equipped cars, and the 904 LA group, which is used with 273-ci and 318-ci engines. The 727-A group was the heavy-duty unit for small-blocks, and the 727 B was used with big-blocks and Hemis. The group

1971 Transmission Converter ID Numbers

Engine	Trans. ID Marks *	Trans. ID No.˜	Converter Diameter	Stall Speed	Part No.	Notes
225-ci six-cyl.	904 G	3515804	11 3/4	2,000 rpm	2801762	
318-ci	904 LA	3515806	11 3/4	2,200 rpm	2801762	
340-ci 4-bbl	727 A	3515843	10 3/4	2,450 rpm	2801764	
340-ci 3x2-bbl	727 A	3410769	10 3/4	2,450 rpm	2801764	AAR and T/A only
383-ci 2-bbl	727 B	3515850	11 3/4	2,100 rpm	(1)	
383-ci 4-bbl	727 B	3515846	10 3/4	2,600 rpm	2801764	
426 Hemi	727 B	3515849		2,800 rpm	2801766	
440-ci 4-bbl	727 B	3515805	10 3/4	2,300 rpm	3410839	
440-ci 3x2-bbl	727 B	3515850	10 3/4	2,300 rpm	3410839	

* = On bell housing; ˜ = On pan rail.

1972 Transmission Converter ID Numbers

Engine	Trans. ID Marks *	Trans. ID No.˜	Converter Diameter	Stall Speed	Part No.	Notes
225-ci	904 G	3515871	11 3/4	2,000 rpm	2801762	Early
225-ci	904 G	3681061	11 3/4	2,000 rpm	2801762	Late
318-ci	904 LA	3515873	11 3/4	2,200 rpm	2801762	Early type
318-ci	904 LA	3681063	11 3/4	2,200 rpm	2801762	Later type
340-ci 4-bbl	727 A	3515843	10 3/4	2,450 rpm	2801764	Early
340-ci 4-bbl	727 A	3681052	10 3/4	2,450 rpm	2801764	Late

* = On bell housing; ˜ = On pan rail

1973 Transmission Converter ID Numbers

Engine	Trans. ID Marks *	Trans. ID No.˜	Converter Diameter	Stall Speed	Part No.
318-ci	904 LA	3681063	11 3/4	2,200 rpm	2801762
340-ci 4-bbl	727 A	3681052	10 3/4	2,450 rpm	2801764

* = On bell housing; ˜ = On pan rail.

code will be found in raised, 3/8-inch-high letters on the lower left-hand side of the bell housing. Transmissions housings should have a fresh, unfinished aluminum-cast appearance. This can be duplicated by painting it aluminum silver. The pan was left unpainted, which can be duplicated by painting it stainless steel.

Torque converters also differ greatly with the transmission and engine output. Both 11 3/4- and 10 3/4-inch-diameter converters were used, and the latter of these was used with high-performance applications. The converter should have a natural, unpainted appearance.

Shift Levers

A column-mounted, chrome-plated shift lever was standard with all automatic transmissions, except the 1969 models with a 383-ci or 440-ci powerplant; in these models, a floor-mounted shift lever was mandatory. The 1967 column-mounted lever is unique and will fit no other model year. The 1968 and 1969 models had the same lever both years. In 1970, two different column-mounted levers were used. One had a flat-black finish while the other one had a chrome finish; either is correct for 1970 models. In 1971, only a flat-black shift lever was used, but it used a different part number than the unit in 1970. The 1967-1968 models used a chrome plastic knob, and the 1969-1974 models use a knob molded in black plastic.

A 1967 and early 1968 Inland four-speed shift knob. *Year One*

A floor-shifted automatic required the optional console all eight years and was a required option in 1969 models with a 383-ci or 440-ci engine. The 1967 and 1968

1974 Transmission Converter ID Numbers

Engine	Trans. ID Marks *	Trans. ID No.~	Converter Diameter	Stall Speed	Part No.
318-ci	904 LA	3681843	11 3/4	2,200 rpm	2801762
360-ci 4-bbl	727 A	3681863	10 3/4	2,450 rpm	2801764

* = On bell housing; ~ = On pan rail.

Transmission Kick Down Spring Color Code

Model Year	SPRING IDENTIFICATION		
	Number of Coils	Color Code	Part Number
1967-1970	75	See Note 1	See Note 1
1969	36	Green	2946637
1970	20	Green	3418817
1970-1974	36	Green	2946637
1970-1971	19	Black	25636453

Note 1: Four different springs used 75 coils: red with black stripe, 2806463, 1967-1969; orange with red stripe, 2843783, 1967-1969; yellow with red stripe, 2806464, 1970; and white, 2951450, 1970 only.

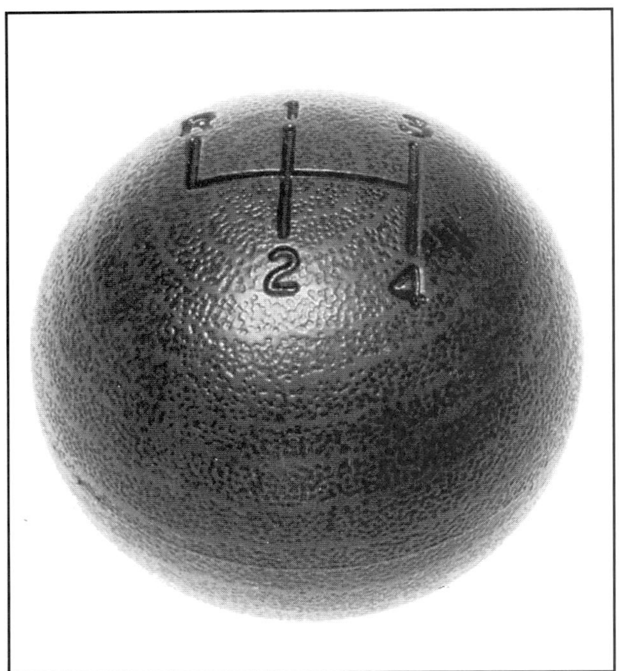

The Hurst-style shift knob. *Year One*

A pistol-grip shifter boot. *Year One*

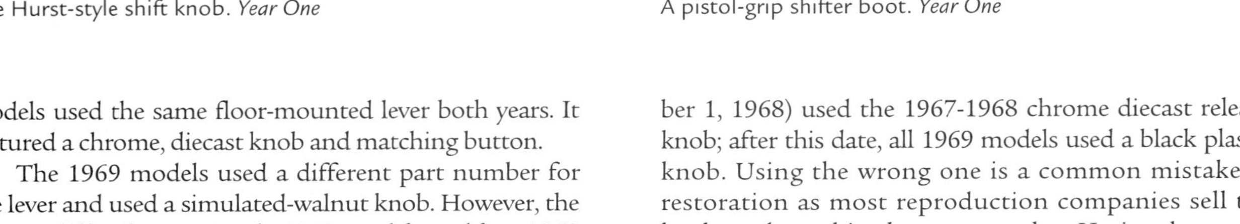
models used the same floor-mounted lever both years. It featured a chrome, diecast knob and matching button.

The 1969 models used a different part number for the lever and used a simulated-walnut knob. However, the button differs between early-1969 models and late-1969 models. Early models (built up until approximately October 1, 1968) used the 1967-1968 chrome diecast release knob; after this date, all 1969 models used a black plastic knob. Using the wrong one is a common mistake in restoration as most reproduction companies sell the knobs and matching buttons together. Having the proper knob can mean additional points at a showing or an

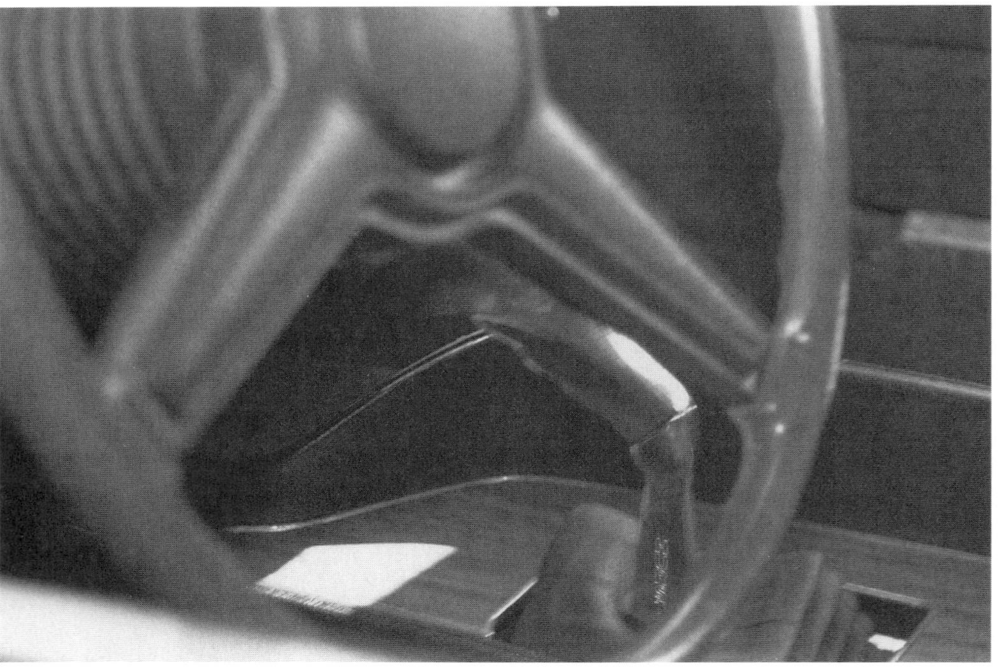
The same shifter was used with or without a console.

event where the judge knows the car well.

The 1970 model used a similar design to the 1969 lever; both used the same walnut knob and black release button, but the shift lever assembly on the 1970 models is straighter. In 1971, the console-mounted lever was again restyled. It was much shorter and supported a black plastic "T" handle with a bright, chrome-plated release button on the side. The same floor-mounted lever was used until the end of the 1974 model year.

The pistol-grip pattern lens. *Year One*

Clutches

Several different clutch discs were used and they vary in diameter from 9 1/4 inches to 11 inches with colored springs for identification. Most models used a Borg & Beck clutch disc, while a few models did use an enclosed unit made by Auburn. The pressure plate was keyed to the disc size and type, and it, too, has color-coded springs. Some pressure plates will have centrifugal assist rollers that can further identify them. Charts have been included here to help you identify the correct disc and pressure plates.

Bell Housing

The bell housing is directly related to engine size and clutch diameter. Housings used with a 10 1/2-inch-diameter clutch disc will have a rounded front pan edge, and the mounting bolt diameter pattern is 15 1/2 inches (outside diameter) from hole to hole. Those used with the larger 11-inch-diameter disc have a flat front pan edge and the mounting bolt diameter pattern measurement will be 15 3/4 inches. Housings used until the 1969 model year were made out of cast-iron, while from

1967 Barracuda Clutch Disc and Pressure Plate ID

Engine	Clutch Disc Springs Number	Color	Disc Diameter	Part No.	Pressure Plate Springs Number	Color	Rollers	Plate Part No.
225-ci	6	Light Blue	9 1/4	2448336	6	4 Pink, 2 White	None	2525464
225-ci	Enclosed	Enclosed	9 1/4	2401121	3	Red stripe	None	2800828
273-ci 2-bbl	Enclosed	Enclosed	9 1/2	2401120	3	White	None	2800827
273-ci 383-ci 4-bbl;	10	5 Green, 5 Tan	10 1/2	2266232	12	6 White, 6 Tan	None	2409688

Enclosed-case Auburn unit; all others are Borg & Beck.

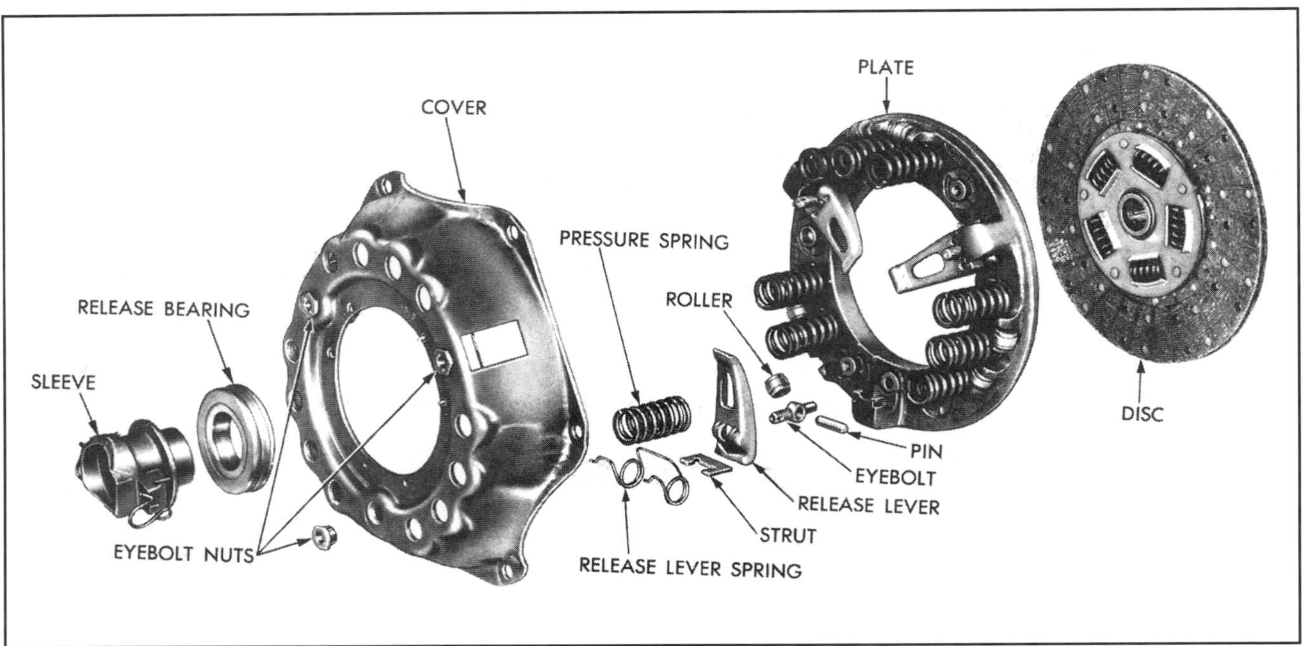

A typical clutch assembly.

1968 Barracuda Clutch Disc and Pressure Plate ID

Engine	Clutch Disc Springs Number	Color	Disc Diameter	Part No.	Pressure Plate Springs Number	Color	Rollers	Plate Part No.
225-ci	6	Light Blue	9 1/4	2448336	6	4 Pink, 2 White	None	2525464
225-ci	Enclosed	Enclosed	9 1/4	2401121	3	Red stripe	None	2800828
318-ci 2-bbl; Heavy-duty on 225-ci	Enclosed	Enclosed	9 1/2	2401120	3	White	None	2800827
340-ci 4-bbl; 383-ci	10	5 Green, 5 Tan	10 1/2	2266232	12	6 White, 6 Tan	None	2409688
426 Hemi	5	Plain	11	2768162	12	9 White, 3 Plain	Three	2768160

Enclosed-case Auburn-built unit.

1969 Barracuda Clutch Disc and Pressure Plate ID

Engine	Clutch Disc Springs Number	Color	Disc Diameter	Part No.	Pressure Plate Springs Number	Color	Rollers	Plate Part No.
225-ci	Enclosed	Enclosed	9 1/4	2401102	3	Red stripe	None	2409692
225-ci Heavy-duty	Enclosed	Enclosed	9 1/2	2401120	3	White	None	2800827
318-ci	10	5 Green, 5 Tan	10 1/2	2266232	9	3 White, 6 Plain	Six	2122255
340-ci 383-ci	10	5 Green, 5 Tan	10 1/2	2266232	12	6 White, 6 Tan	Six	2409688

Enclosed-case is Auburn-built unit.

1970 Barracuda Clutch Disc and Pressure Plate ID

Engine	Clutch Disc Springs Number	Color	Disc Diameter	Part No.	Pressure Plate Springs Number	Color	Rollers	Plate Part No.
225-ci	Enclosed	Enclosed	9 1/4	2448336	3	Red stripe	None	2525464
318-ci	10	5 Green, 5Tan	10 1/2	2266232	9	3 White, 6 Plain	Six	2122255
340-ci	10	5 Green, 5 Tan	10 1/2	2266232	12	6 White, 6 Tan	Six	2409688
383-ci	10	5 Green, 5 Tan	11	3410160	12	6 White, 6 Tan	Six	3410157
426 Hemi	5	Plain	11	3410161	12	9 White, 3 Plain	Three	3410158
440-ci	5	Plain	11	3410161	12	9 White, 3 Plain	Six	3410159

Enclosed-case is Auburn-built unit.

1971 Barracuda and Challenger Clutch Disc and Pressure Plate ID

Engine	Clutch Disc Springs Number	Color	Diameter	Disc Part No.	Pressure Plate Springs Number	Color	Rollers	Plate Part No.
225-ci	Enclosed	Enclosed	9 1/4	2448336	3	Red stripe	None	2525464
318-ci	10	5 Green, 5 Tan	10 1/2	2266232	9	3 White, 6 Plain	Three	3515301
340-ci	10	5 Green, 5 Tan	10 1/2	2266232	12	6 White, 6 Tan	Six	2409688
383-ci	10	5 Green, 5 Tan	11	3410160	12	6 White, 6 Tan	Six	3410157
426 Hemi	5	Plain	11	3410161	12	9 White, 3 Plain	Three	3410158
440-ci	5	Plain	11	3410161	12	9 White, 3 Plain	Six	3410159

Enclosed-case is Auburn unit

1972 Barracuda and Challenger Clutch Disc and Pressure Plate ID

Engine	Clutch Disc Springs Number	Color	Diameter	Disc Part No.	Pressure Plate Springs Number	Color	Rollers	Plate Part No.
225-ci	Enclosed	Enclosed	9 1/4	2448336	3	Red stripe	None	2525464
318-ci	10	5 Green, 5 Tan	10 1/2	2266232	9	3 White, 6 Plain	Three	3515301
340-ci	10	5 Green, 5 Tan	10 1/2	2266232	12	6 White, 6 Tan	Three	3515681

Enclosed-case is Auburn unit.

1973 Barracuda and Challenger Clutch Disc and Pressure Plate ID

Engine	Clutch Disc Springs Number	Color	Diameter	Disc Part No.	Pressure Plate Springs Number	Color	Rollers	Plate Part No.
318-ci	6	Plain	10 1/2	3681630	9	3 White, 6 Black	None	3681615
340-ci	6	Plain	10 1/2	3681630	12	6 White, 6 Tan	Three	3515681

1974 Barracuda and Challenger Clutch Disc and Pressure Plate ID

Engine	Clutch Disc Springs Number	Color	Diameter	Disc Part No.	Pressure Plate Springs Number	Color	Rollers	Plate Part No.
318-ci	6	Plain	10 1/2	3681630	9	3 White, 6 Black	None	3681615
360-ci	10	5 Green, 5 Brown	11	3681630	12	Purple	Three	3743400

1967-1969 A- Body and 1970-1974 E-Body Bell Housings

Model Year	Engines	Material	Clutch Dia.	Trans.	Casting No.
1967-1968	273, 318-ci	Cast	9 1/2	3-speed	2780902
1967	273-ci	Cast	9 1/2	4-speed	2806081
1968	318, 340-ci	Cast	10 1/2	4-speed	
1969-1971	318, 340-ci	Aluminum	10 1/2	4-speed	2892482
1970-1971	383, 440-ci, Hemi	Aluminum	11	4-speed	2892513
1972-1973	318, 340-ci	Aluminum	10 1/2	4-speed	3515734
1974	318-ci	Aluminum	10 1/2	4-speed	3743859
1974	360-ci	Aluminum	11	4-speed	3743859
1967-1969	383-ci	Cast	10 1/2	4-speed	

Note: Hemi and those with 440-ci bell housing will have 4 3/4-inch diameter front bearing; all others will have 4 5/8-inch diameter.

1969 to 1974 the housing was made of aluminum. A casting number will also appear on the bell housing to help further identify it. Housings made of cast-iron should be painted cast-iron gray, and the later units made of aluminum should be painted flat aluminum.

Clutch Pedals

Clutch pedals in the 1967-1969 model years can be confusing as engine size can affect their usage.

In 1967 Barracudas, all models except those with a 383-ci engine used part number 2781145. Those with a 383-ci powerplant used part number 2883457. Oddly enough, all 1968-1969 Barracudas with a V-8 used the 383-ci pedal from 1967, while those with a six-cylinder engine used the other pedal that was used in 1967.

For the 1970 pedal, those models with a six-cylinder engine used part number 3467079, except exports. Six-cylinder models sent overseas and all V-8 models used part number 3467098.

For 1971, the six-cylinder models and V-8s continued to use different pedals. Six-cylinders used part number 3575110, and the V-8s used part number 3557111. These same pedals were used again in 1972 with the same engine restrictions. Due to the deletion of the six-cylinder powerplants in the 1973 model year, only one pedal (part number 3575177) was used both years.

All pedals should be painted semi-gloss black and use a rubber pad. Three different pads were used. The first pad was used from 1967 to 1969, the second pad was used from 1970 to 1972, and the third pad was used in 1973 and 1974 models. A chrome bezel was offered as part of a dress-up package for models up to 1971. After that, no bezel was offered around the clutch pedal in either model, as a separate option or as part of a dress-up package.

Note that the 1967-1969 models used a different bezel than the 1970 and 1971 models. And the bezel was standard in interior dress-up packages and specialty models such as the Gran Coupe and the Challenger S.E.

Driveshafts

Two types of driveshafts were used: The type 7260 can be identified by its 2 1/8-inch yoke, while the type

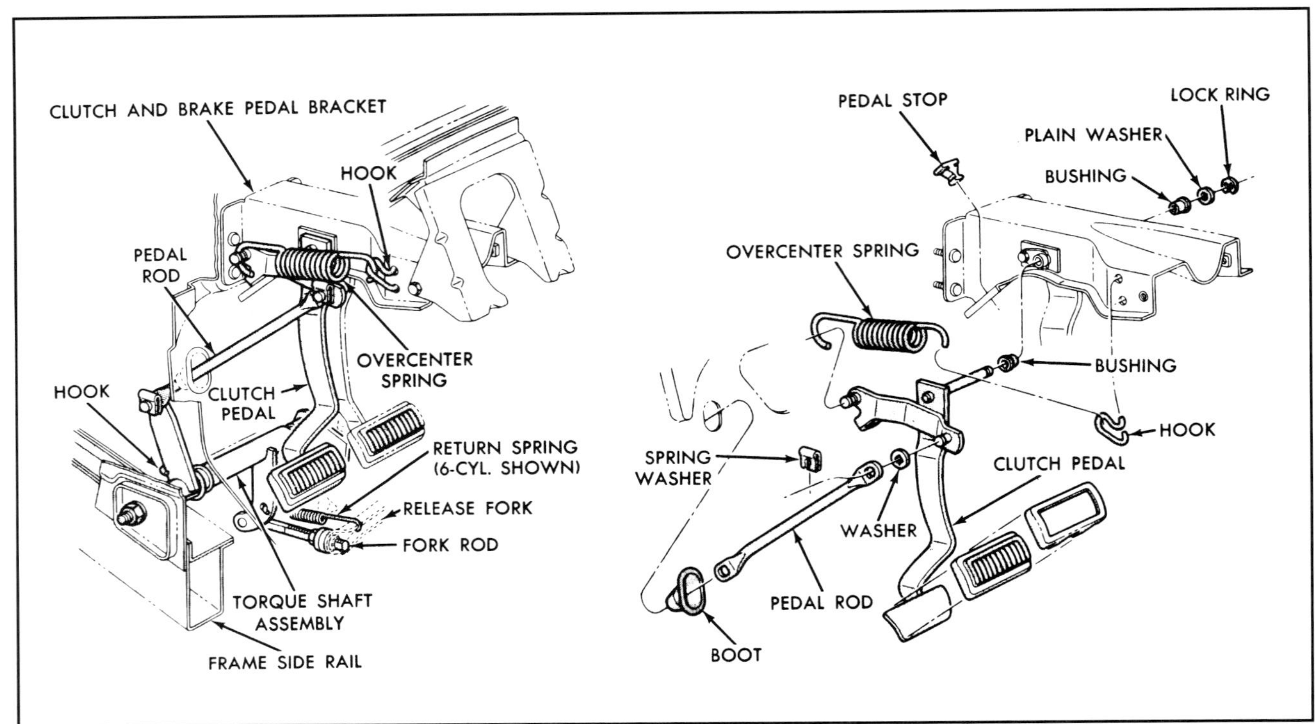

The 1967-1969 clutch pedal and linkage assembly.

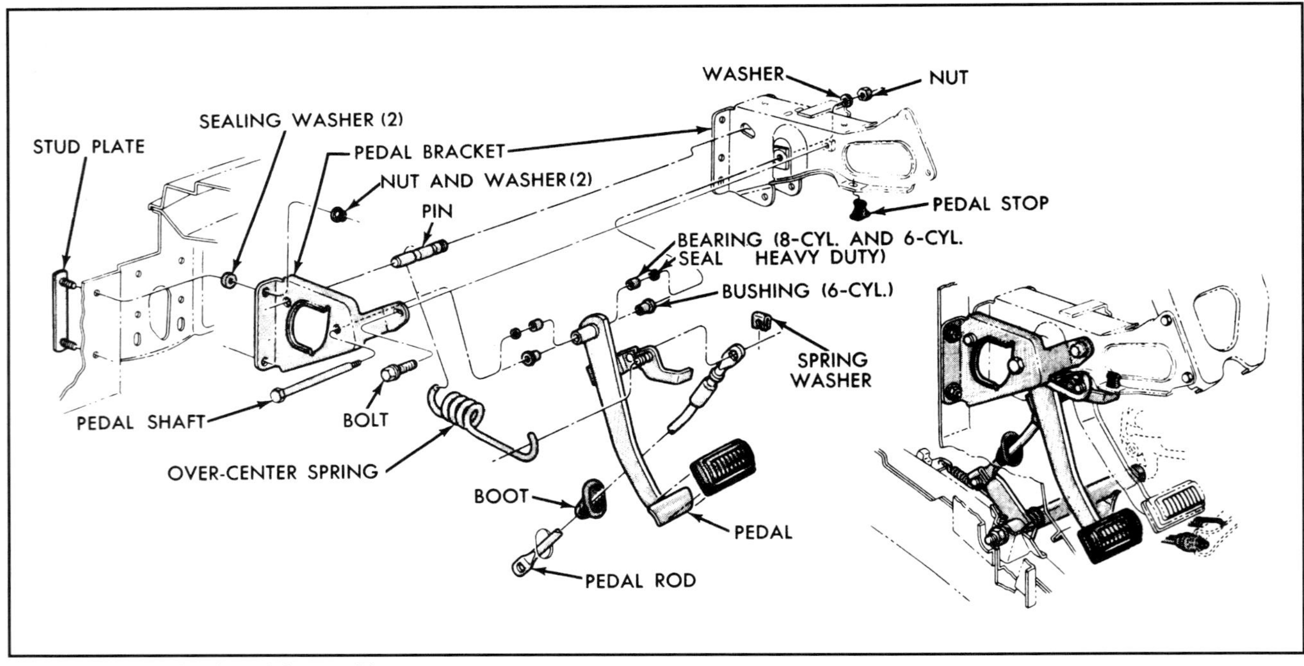

The 1970-1974 clutch pedal assembly.

A 1967-1969 clutch pedal pad. *Year One*

The 1970-1972 clutch pedal pad. *Year One*

7290 has a wider 2 5/8-inch yoke. The latter of these are used with high-performance applications. Driveshafts can also be identified by their length and diameter, with each of these measurements determined by the make, model year, engine, transmission, and rear axle type. Because of the longer wheelbase on Dodges, the driveshafts will not interchange. Driveshafts should be measured from eyelet to eyelet at the eyelet center points.

Hemi engine-equipped cars used a special driveshaft that had nearly prefect balance. Consequently, when the yoke needs to be replaced, the whole shaft must be replaced. Failure to do so will result in an unbalanced driveshaft that can cause damage to your rear axle and transmission case.

Driveshafts should be finished in a stainless steel color, but some were painted semi-gloss black. The rear yoke should be painted cast-iron gray to duplicate the fresh-cast appearance. An inspector's mark of a white "X" may be found on the shaft. At the factory the driveshaft was installed before the undercoating was applied, so it is common that overspray did find its way onto the shaft. It is acceptable to imitate the factory look, but it can look unprofessional on a fully restored show car.

Rear Axles: Identification

Three different axles were used; they are listed and identified by the diameter of the ring gear. The following diameters were used: 7 1/4 inches, 8 3/4 inches, and 9 3/4 inches—the latter of which is known as the Dana 60 axle.

The 7 1/4-inch axle was used under models equipped with a six-cylinder engine or a two-barrel V-8 up to the 1972 model year. The 7 1/4-inch axle is easily identified by its oddly shaped nine-bolt cover and was a general-use axle; it should not be considered for high-performance use.

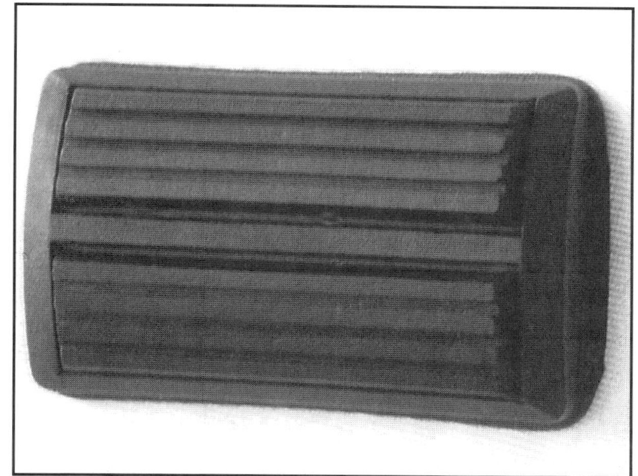

A 1973-1974 clutch pedal pad.

The most common type of axle used was the 8 3/4-inch axle, commonly called a "banjo axle" because of its smooth, one-piece design with a weld on the center hump. This axle was the only performance option available for the 1967-1969 Barracudas, with one exception—the 1968 Hurst-built Hemi Cuda with a four-speed transmission that used a special 9 3/4-inch axle. It was also the only axle available for the 1972-1974 models, regardless of the engine size.

Banjo axles have a removable carrier which will have a casting number on it. This number is useful because three different diameter pinion shafts were used with the 8 3/4-inch axle. Those models with the type 7260 driveshaft used the 1 3/8-inch diameter pinion,

continued on page 97

1967 Barracuda Driveshafts

Type	Engine	Trans.	Axle Type	Ratios	Driveshaft Specs. Length	Dia.	Part No.
7260	225-ci	All	7 1/4	2.93, 3.55, 3.91	51.61	2 3/4	2660702
7260	225-ci	All	7 1/4	2.76, 3.23	51.61	2 3/4	2533192
7260	273-ci	3-speed or Auto	7 1/4	2.93 3.23	51.61	2 3/4	2660702
7290	273-ci	All	8 3/4	All	49.58	2 3/4	2781952
7290	383-ci	4-speed	8 3/4	All	48.60	2 3/4	2852206
7290	383-ci	Auto	8 3/4	All	44.88	3	2852216

1968 Barracuda Driveshafts

Type	Engine	Trans.	Axle Type	Ratios	Driveshaft Specs. Length	Dia.	Part No.
7260	225-ci	All	7 1/4	3.55 3.91	51.43	2 3/4	2533192
7260	225-ci	All	7 1/4	3.23	51.43	3	2852231
7260	225-ci Export	4-speexd	7 1/4	All	51.12	2 3/4	2660682
7290	318, 340, 383-ci	4-speed	8 3/4	All	48.60	2 3/4	2852206
7290	340, 383-ci	Auto	8 3/4	All	44.88	3	2852216
7290	318-ci	Auto	8 3/4	All	49.27	3	2781952

1969 Barracuda Driveshafts

Type	Engine	Trans.	Axle Type	Ratios	Driveshaft Specs. Length	Dia.	Part No.
7260	225-ci	3-speed	7 1/4	3.55	51.43	2 3/4	2660702
7260	225-ci	3-speed	7 1/4	Except 3.55	51.43	3	2852231
7260	225-ci Export	4-speed	7 1/4	All	51.12	2 3/4	2660682
7260	318-ci	Auto	8 3/4	2.76	49.27	2 3/4	2781952
7290	318-ci	Auto	8 3/4	2.76	49.27	2 3/4	2883608
7290	340,383; 440-ci	Auto	8 3/4	3.23 3.55	44.88	3	2852216
7290	318,340, 383-ci	4-speed	8 3/4	All	48.60	3	2852206

1970 Barracuda Driveshafts

Type	Engine	Trans.	Axle Type	Ratios	Driveshaft Specs. Length	Dia.	Part No.
7260	225, 318-ci	Auto	7 1/4	2.76, 3.23	50.18	3 1/4	2883766
7260	225-ci	Manual	7 1/4	3.23	46.06	3 1/4	2883772
7260	318-ci	Auto	8 3/4	3.23	47.95	3 1/4	2883768
7290	318-ci	Manual	8 3/4	3.23	43.85	3 1/4	2883769
7290	383-ci , 2-bbl	All	8 3/4	2.76, 3.23	43.85	3 1/4	2883769
7290	340, 383-ci 4-bbl	All	8 3/4	All	43.60	3 1/4	2883636
7290	440,426-ci	Auto	8 3/4	All	43.60	3 1/4	2883636
7290	440,426-ci	All	9 3/4	All	42.60	3 1/4	n/a

1970 Challenger Driveshafts

Type	Engine	Trans.	Axle Type	Ratios	Driveshaft Specs. Length	Dia.	Part No.
7260	225, 318-ci	Auto	7-1/4	2.76, 3.23	52.08	3 1/4	3578778
7260	225-ci	Manual	7-1/4	3.23	48.06	3 1/4	2883763
7260	318-ci	Auto	8-3/4	3.23	49.95	3 1/4	2883779
7290	318-ci	Manual	8 3/4	3.23	45.85	3 1/4	2883782
7290	383-ci, 2-bbl	All	8 3/4	2.76, 3.23	45.85	3 1/4	2883782
7290	340, 383-ci 4-bbl	All	8 3/4	All	45.60	3 1/4	2883656
7290	440, 426-ci	Auto	8 3/4	All	43.60	3 1/4	2883656
7290	440, 426-ci	All	9 3/4	All	42.60	3 1/4	n/a

1971 Barracuda Driveshafts

Type	Engine	Trans.	Axle Type	Ratios	Driveshaft Specs. Length	Dia.	Part No.
7260	225, 318-ci	Auto	7 1/4	2.76, 3.23	49.89	3 1/4	2996146
7260	225-ci	Manual	7 1/4	3.23	46.06	3 1/4	2883772
7260	318-ci	Auto	8 3/4	3.23	47.95	3 1/4	2883768
7290	318-ci	Manual	8 3/4	3.23	43.79	3 1/4	2996134
7290	383-ci 2-bbl	Auto	8 3/4	2.76, 3.23	43.79	3 1/4	2996134
7290	340, 383-ci 4-bbl	All	8 3/4	All	43.60	3 1/4	2883636
7290	440, 426-ci	Auto	8 3/4	All	43.60	3 1/4	2883636
7290	440, 426-ci	All	9 3/4	All	42.60	3 1/4	n/a

1971 Challenger Driveshafts

Type	Engine	Trans.	Axle Type	Ratios	Driveshaft Specs. Length	Dia.	Part No.
7260	225, 318-ci	Auto	7 1/4	2.76, 3.23	52.08	3 1/4	3578778
7260	225-ci	Manual	7 1/4	3.23	48.06	3 1/4	3578763
7260	225, 318-ci	Auto	8 3/4	3.23	49.89	3 1/4	2996146
7290	318-ci	Manual	8 3/4	3.23	45.60	3 1/4	2883656
7290	383 2-bbl	All	8 3/4	2.76, 3.23	45.85	3 1/4	2883782
7290	340, 383 4-bbl	All	8 3/4	All	45.60	3 1/4	2883656
7290	440, 426	Auto	8 3/4	All	43.60	3 1/4	2883656
7290	440, 426	All	9 3/4	All	42.60	3 1/4	n/a

1972 Barracuda Driveshafts

Type	Engine	Trans.	Axle Type	Ratios	Driveshaft Specs. Length	Dia.	Part No.
7260	225, 318-ci	Auto	8 3/4*	All	47.95	3 1/4	288376
7260	225, 318-ci	Auto	8 3/4	All	47.89	3 1/4	2996138
7260	340-ci	All	8 3/4	All	43.79	3 1/4	2996134
7290	318, 340-ci	Manual	8 3/4	All	43.60	3 1/4	2883636

* = Small sliding spline.

1972 Challenger Driveshafts

Type	Engine	Trans.	Axle Type	Ratios	Driveshaft Specs. Length	Dia.	Part No.
7260	225, 318-ci	Auto	8 3/4*	All	49.95	3 1/4	2883779
7260	225, 318-ci	Auto	8 3/4	All	49.89	3 1/4	2996146
7260	225, 318-ci	Manual	8 3/4	All	45.79	3 1/4	2996142
7260	340-ci	All	8 3/4	All	45.79	3 1/4	2996142
7290	340-ci	Auto	8 3/4	All	45.60	3 1/4	2883656
7290	All	Manual	8 3/4	All	45.60	3 1/4	2883656

* = Small sliding spline.

1973 Barracuda Driveshafts

Type	Engine	Trans.	Axle Type	Ratios	Driveshaft Specs. Length	Dia.	Part No.
7260	318-ci	Auto	8 3/4	All	47.89*	3 1/4*	2883758
7260	318-ci	Auto	8 3/4	All	47.40**	3**	3578138
7260	All	All	8 3/4	All	43.79	3 1/4	2996134

* = Before October 1,1972; ** = After October 1,1972.

1973 Challenger Driveshafts

Type	Engine	Trans.	Axle Type	Ratios	Driveshaft Specs. Length	Dia.	Part No.
7260	318-ci	Auto	8 3/4	All	49.89*	3 1/4*	2996146
7260	318-ci	Auto	8 3/4	All	49.40**	3**	3578146
7260	318-ci	Manual	8 3/4	All	45.79	3 1/4	2996142
7260	340-ci	All	8 3/4	All	45.79	3 1/4	2996142

* = Before October 1,1972; ** = After October 1,1972.

1974 Barracuda Driveshafts

Type	Engine	Trans.	Axle Type	Ratios	Driveshaft Specs. Length	Dia.	Part No.
7260	318-ci	Auto	8 3/4	All	47.40	3	3578138
7260	All	All	8 3/4	All	43.79	3 1/4	2996134

1974 Challenger Driveshafts

Type	Engine	Trans.	Axle Type	Ratios	Driveshaft Specs. Length	Dia.	Part No.
7260	All	Auto	8 3/4	All	49.40	3	3578146
7260	All	Manual	8 3/4	All	45.79	3 1/4	2996142

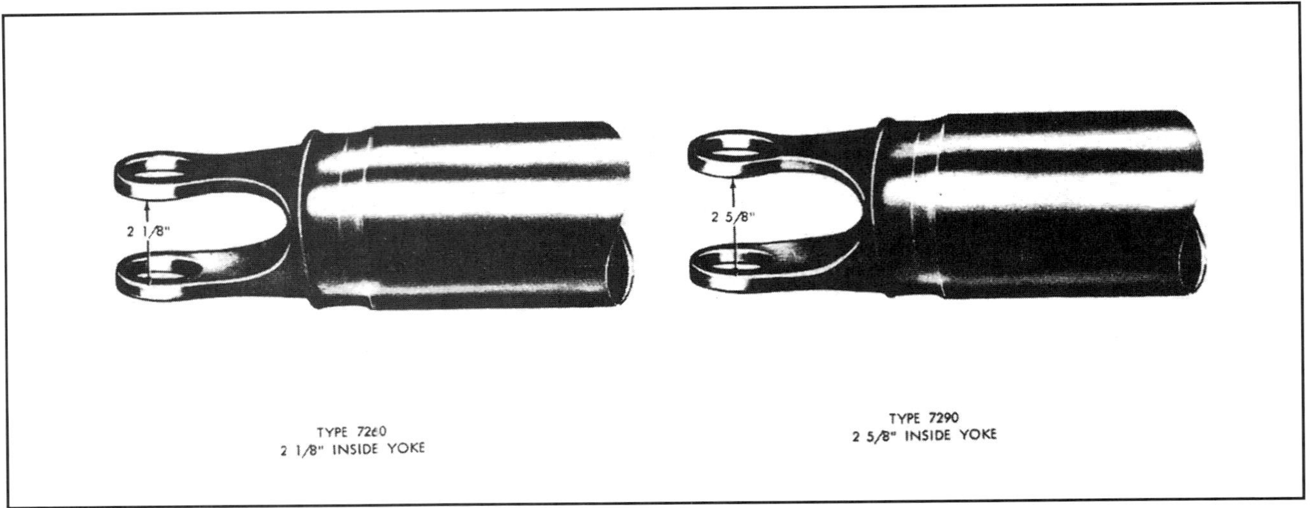

Propeller shaft identification can be determined by the inside measurement of the yoke area. The Type 7260 shaft has a 2 1/8-inch gap to its yoke, while the Type 7290 shaft has a 2 5/8-inch yoke gap.

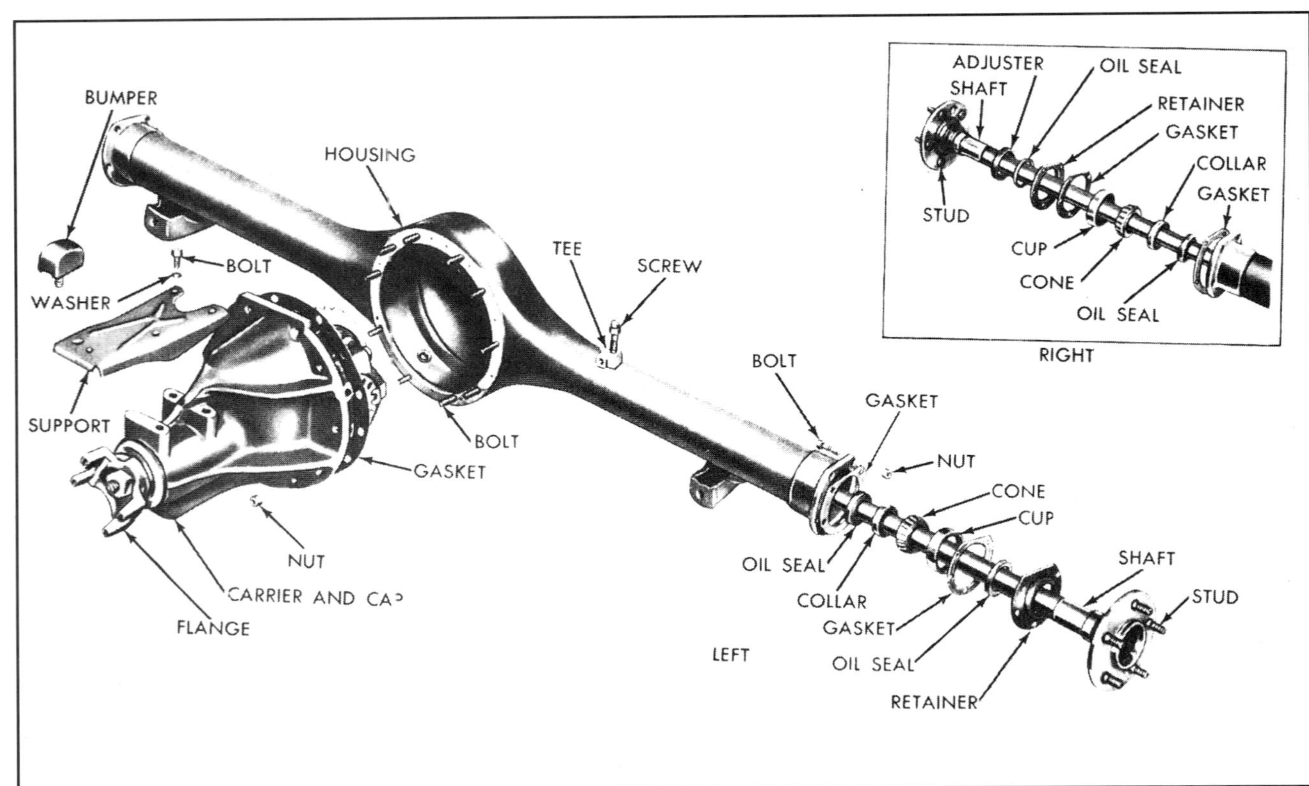

A detailed view of the 8 3/4-inch rear axle assembly.

Continued from page 91

while the 7290-type driveshaft used the larger 1 3/4-inch diameter or the 1 7/8-inch tapered pinion shaft. The casting number will be embossed 2 inches below the yoke on the left-hand side of the carrier. Those with the smaller pinion used casting number 2070741, while the larger pinions used casting number 2070742 for 1967-1968. In 1969 the pinion tapered and the casting number was changed to 2881489, which was used until the end of the 1974 model year.

The 9 3/4-inch axle saw very limited use, as it was only standard when the 426 Hemi and a four-speed manual transmission were both ordered. It was, however, included in an axle package for the 440-ci engine or the Hemi with automatic transmission. The Dana 60 axle was not used under the 1967-1969 Barracuda except on the 1968 Hurst Hemi Cuda with a four-speed transmission. The 9 3/4-inch axle can be quickly identified by its hexagon-shaped cover held on with 10 bolts.

Semi-gloss black epoxy paint should be used to paint the axle regardless of the type. After careful cleaning, you may find three digits in yellow paint on the axle tube on the driver's side. These numbers were the last three digits of the part number of the axle assembly. These numbers will not be found on the 9 3/4-inch axle; instead they used a white tape with the part number in red ink wrapped around the axle tube on the driver's side.

For 1967-1968 axles with the Sure-Grip option, a tag that reads "Use Limited Slip Differential Lube Only" will be attached to the cover of the carrier. On the 8 3/4-inch axle, the tag can be found at the 11 o'clock position, and the ratio code tag will be found at the 1 o'clock position. On all other axles, the lube tag will be found at the 5 o'clock position and the ratio tag is at the 7 o'clock position. The 1969 models and some early 1970 models with the Sure Grip differential will have a dab of orange paint around the filler plug. On late-1970 to 1974 models, the orange paint is dabbed just below the ratio code tag.

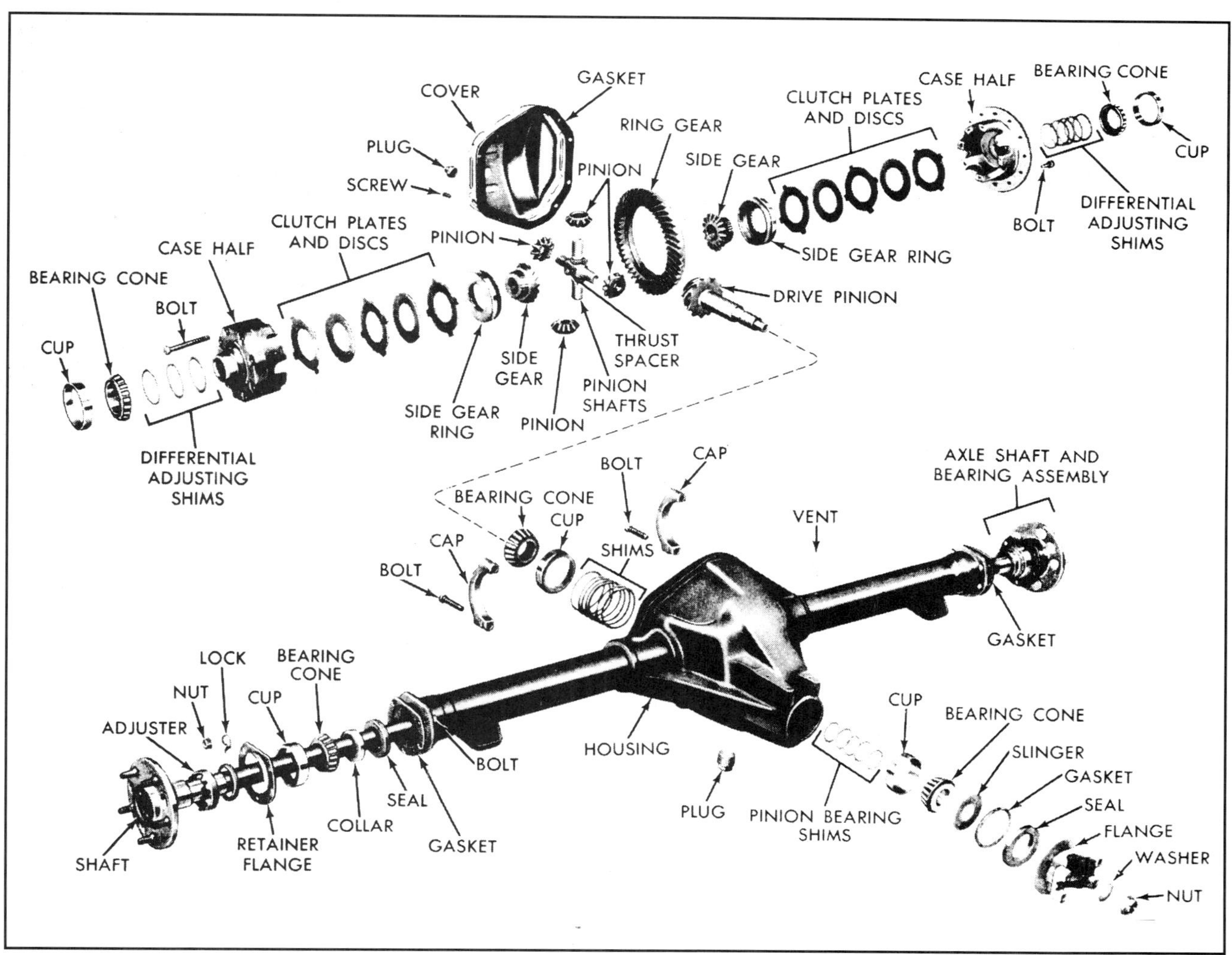

A detailed view of the 9 3/4-inch rear axle assembly.

Chapter 5

Brakes

Except those 1967 and 1968 models exported to England, all 1967-1969 Barracudas were standard with nonpower front and rear drum brakes. Cars with six-cylinder engines used 9-inch-diameter drums, while those with V-8s used 10-inch drums. Those exported to England were equipped with front disc brakes. Nonpower front drum brakes were also standard on all 1970 and 1971 models; however, two different systems were used. Those models with six-cylinder engines, the 318-ci or the 383-ci two-barrel came standard with 10-inch drum brakes, while those models with a four-barrel or multiple carburetors were standard with 11-inch drum brakes front and rear.

The 11-inch drums, known as heavy-duty brakes, were optional on the cars with a two-barrel V-8 powerplant only as a separate option or as part of the towing package. Heavy-duty brakes were not available with a six-cylinder powerplant, nor were the 11-inch drum brakes available on 1967-1969 models.

Front disc brakes were optional since 1967 on all models, except the 1969 Barracuda with a 440-ci engine, where this option was not available. Nonpower front

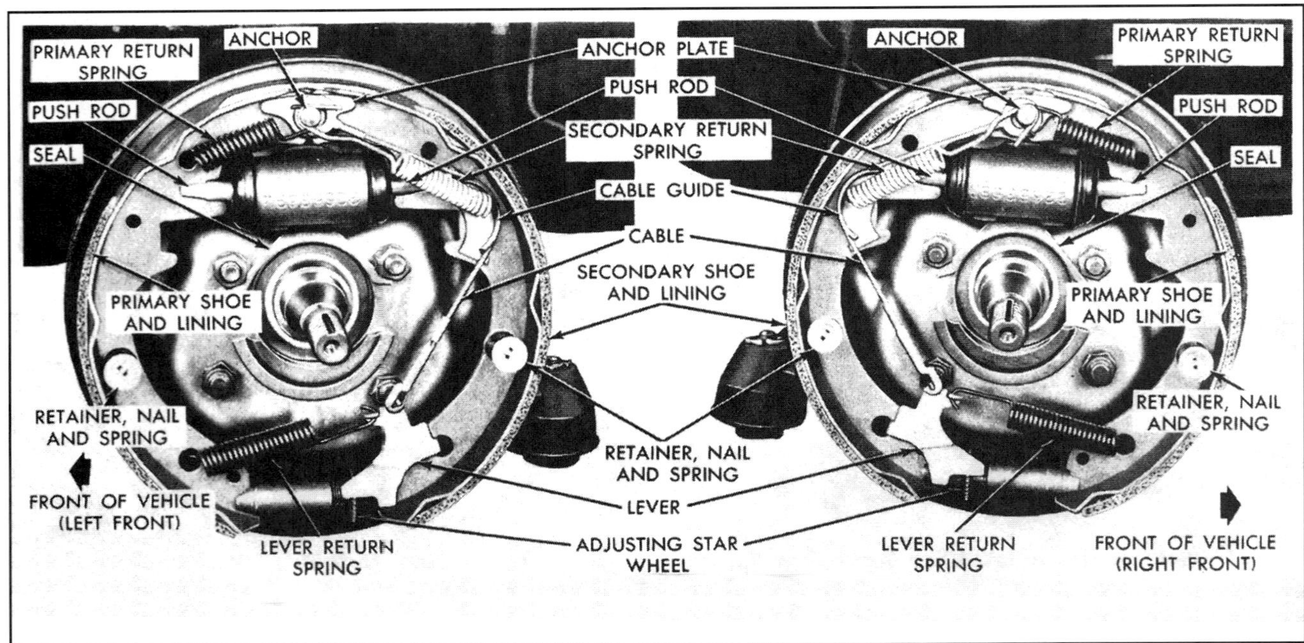

A detailed view of the front brake assembly.

A typical 1967-1969 master cylinder with drum brakes.

disc brakes became standard equipment for all 1973 models. Those with a 340-ci engine and all 1974 cars with a 360-ci engine were mandatory with power-assisted front disc brakes. When front disc brakes were ordered on a 1970-1971 model, on which 11-inch drum brakes were standard, the rear drums were reduced to 10 inches in diameter. No cars were built with front disc brakes and 11-inch rear drum brakes.

Master Cylinders

All 1967-1974 models used a tandem-brake master cylinder. While drum diameter does not affect the master cylinder, the brake type in use does have an affect. Those with drum brakes and those with disc brakes used two different master cylinders, and the two will not interchange. They are also visually different.

From 1967 to 1970, all master cylinders used a 1-inch-diameter piston, while the 1971-1972 models used a 1 1/32-inch bore. In 1973, two different master cylinders were used; those without power-assisted disc brakes used a master cylinder with a 1-inch bore, while those with power-assisted disc brakes used a cylinder with a 1 1/32-inch bore. These two master cylinders were used again in 1974 models with the same restrictions.

Master cylinders used on drum brakes were usually left unpainted. To duplicate the fresh-cast appearance, paint the assembly cast-iron gray. The cover and hold-down clamp on 1967-1970 models with drum brakes should have a cadmium gold appearance. On models with disc brakes, the master assembly was usually painted semi-gloss black—both the body and cover. Most master cylinders on 1971-1974 models were painted semi-gloss black regardless of the brake type. Master cylinders were finished by the brake vendor, not the Chrysler assembly plant. Thus, there are differences in the finish, so it is possible that some master cylinders used with drum brakes were painted semi-gloss black, or a master cylinder used with disc brakes was left unfinished.

Power Brake Unit

Only the Midland-Ross-manufactured booster

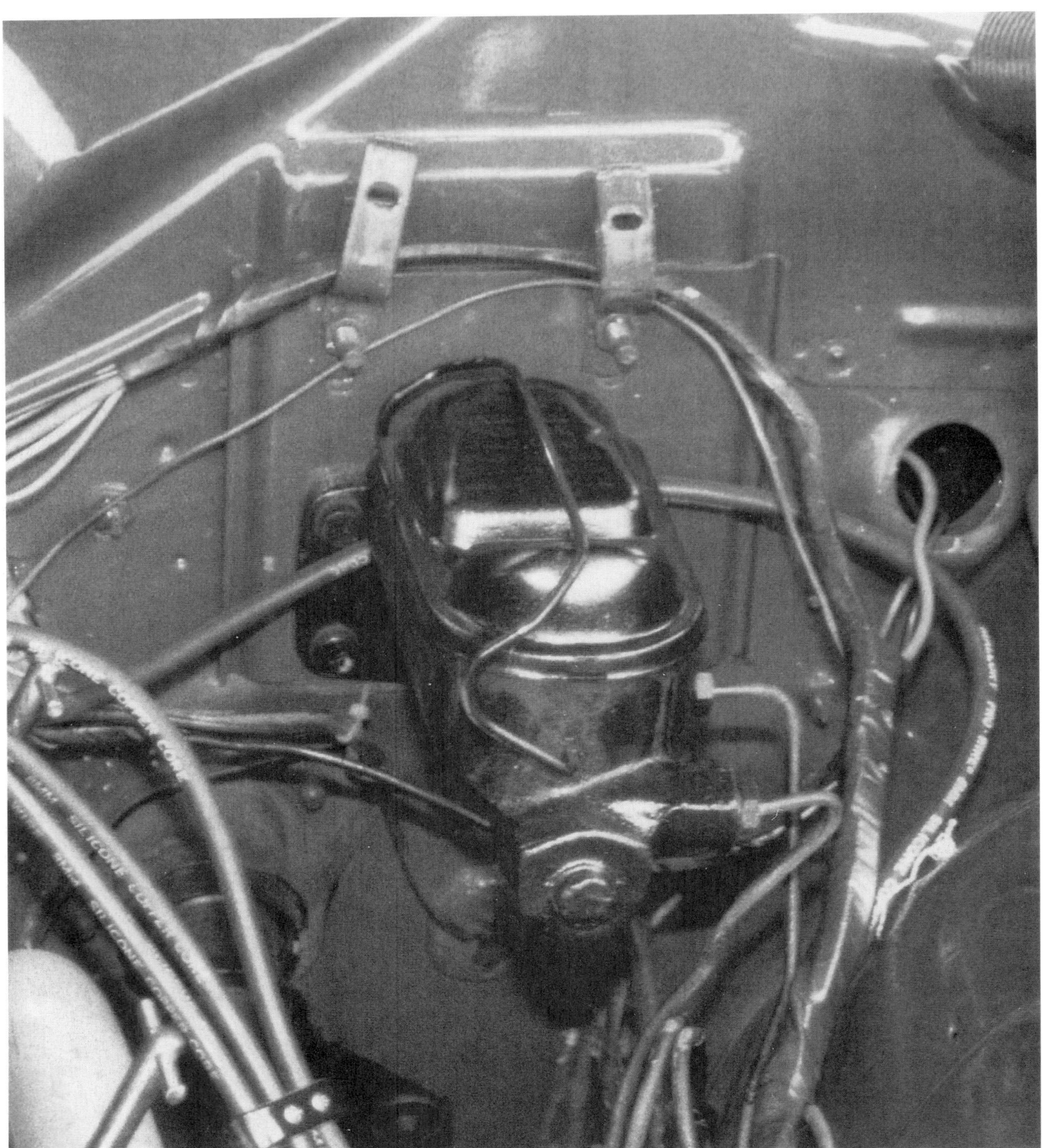

A disc brake master cylinder for a system that is not power-assisted.

chamber was used in 1967-1969 models. The same chamber was used with drum or disc brakes. The 1967-1968 unit is stamped 2881536, while the 1969 unit is listed as 2944006.

In 1970, a host of different chambers were used. Some were made by Midland-Ross; others were made by the Bendix Corporation. The two can be identified by their design: the Midland-Ross unit uses a clamp to hold the two halves together, while the Bendix can be identified by the notched outer edges of the two housing halves. Unlike previous years, those with disc brakes and those with drum brakes used two different housings. Another important note is that on 1971 models with drum brakes, those with 10-inch drums used a different chamber than those with the larger 11-inch brakes.

Hemi-equipped models and the Trans-Am models used specially modified chambers with a tandem diaphragm; a standard booster chamber will not correctly

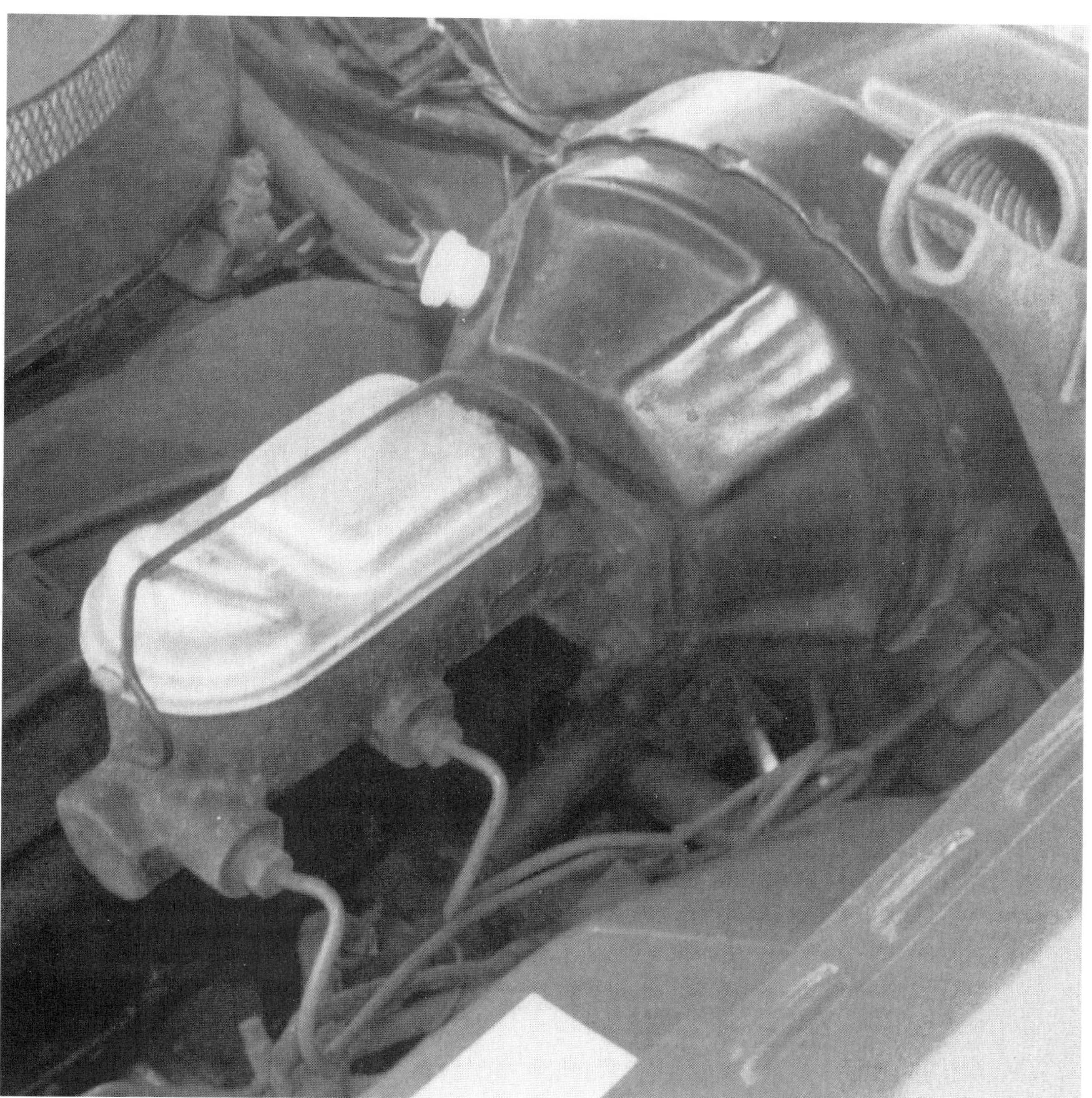

Hemi-equipped cars used a special booster chamber.

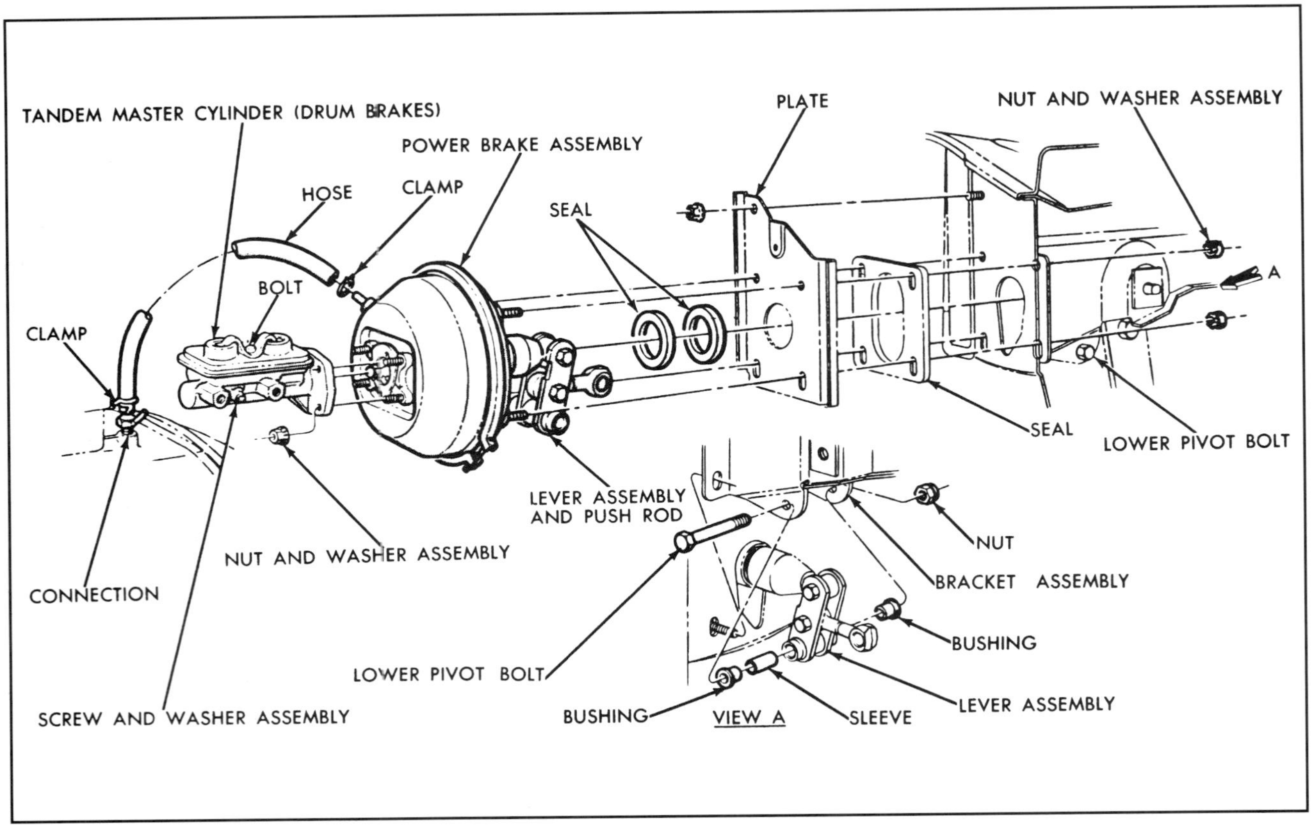

TANDEM MASTER CYLINDER (DRUM BRAKES)
POWER BRAKE ASSEMBLY
PLATE
NUT AND WASHER ASSEMBLY
HOSE
CLAMP
SEAL
BOLT
CLAMP
A
SEAL
LOWER PIVOT BOLT
LEVER ASSEMBLY
AND PUSH ROD
NUT
NUT AND WASHER ASSEMBLY
BRACKET ASSEMBLY
CONNECTION
BUSHING
LOWER PIVOT BOLT
SCREW AND WASHER ASSEMBLY
BUSHING
VIEW A
SLEEVE
LEVER ASSEMBLY

A typical Midland Ross booster chamber.

CONNECTOR
HOSE
CLAMP (2)
NUT AND WASHER
ASSEMBLY
PLATE
GASKET
POWER BRAKE
UNIT ASSEMBLY
CLIP
GASKET
BOLT
ACTUATOR
NUT AND WASHER
ASSEMBLY (4)
NUT AND WASHER ASSEMBLY
SCREW AND WASHER ASSEMBLY
TANDEM MASTER CYLINDER
(DRUM BRAKE)

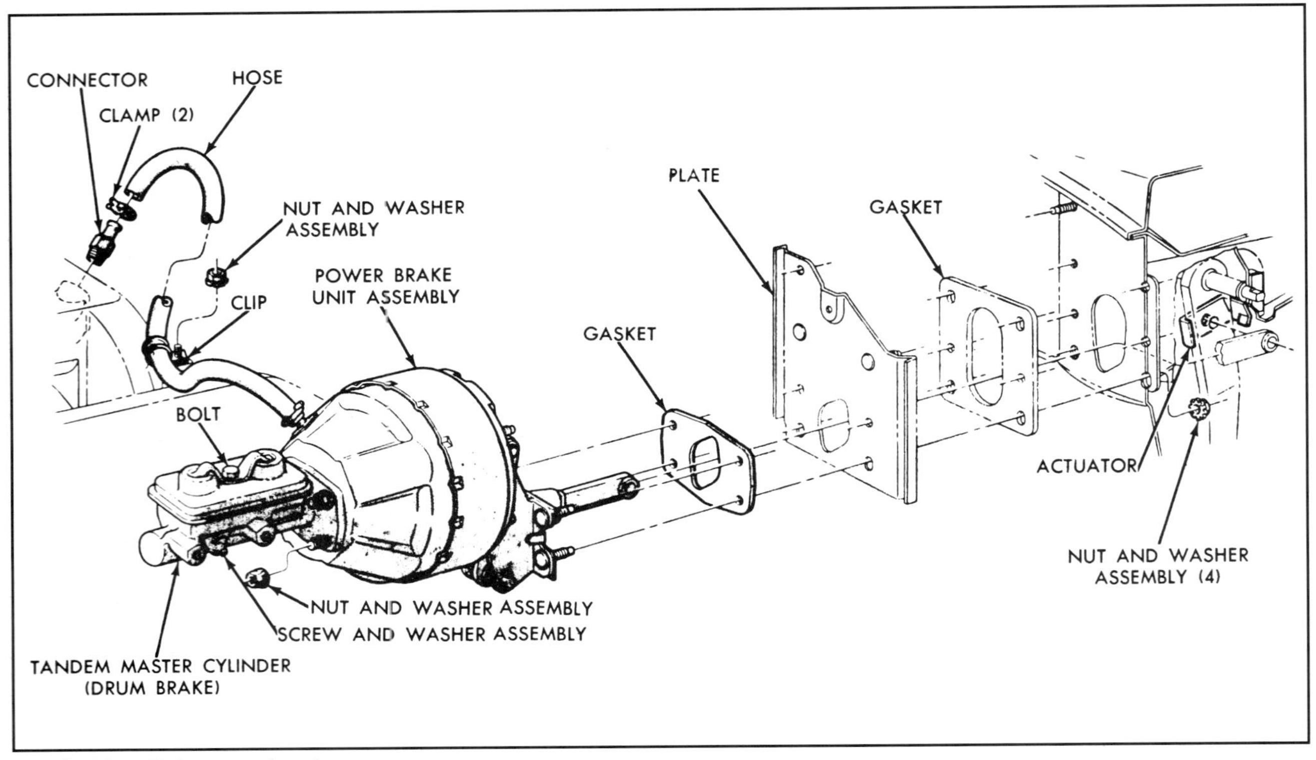

A typical Bendix booster chamber.

fit these models. As stated earlier, drum brakes were deleted in 1973 when front disc brakes became standard. Thus only one booster chamber was used, and it continued over into the 1974 model year unchanged. Models with a 340-ci, 360-ci, or a 318-ci engine with air conditioning were mandatory with power disc brakes.

Finishing for booster chambers can be more confusing than it is for the master cylinders. As with the master cylinders, finishing of booster chambers was done by the parts vendor. Midland-Ross-built units were usually left unpainted, and this look can be reproduced by painting the unit cadmium gold. Most Bendix-built units were painted semi-gloss black.

When you carefully clean the chamber you may find a dab of paint on top of the chamber or over the check valve; these are inspector marks. Just as with other components, not every chamber was checked, only random cars. So it is possible that your booster chamber will not have an inspector's mark. Although it is long gone by now or faded, a decal with an ID number is used on the Bendix-built chambers. In 1970 and 1971 models, the background was white with the number 45 in black. On 1972 and later models, the decal has a white background with red and blue numbers. This number will be the last two digits of the part number that can be found on the build sheet. Booster chambers used a black-colored plastic check valve. A rubber hose was routed from this valve to a provision on the engine. A spring ring wire clamp was used on each end of this hose.

Brake Drums

As mentioned above, brake drums came in three diameters, and the size depended mainly on the size of the engine and the model year. Two different materials were used in manufacturing 9-inch brake drums for the 1967-1969 models: cast-iron and steel. Brake drums made by Motor Wheel were steel-encased, while those made by Kelsey-Hayes were made out of cast-iron. All

1967-1974 Barracuda and Challenger Power Booster Chambers

Disc Brakes

Model Year	Engine	Drum Size	Part No.
1967-1968	All	All	2881536
1969	All	All	2994406
1970	Except Hemi or 340-ci 3x2-bbl	10 inches	3420987
1970	Hemi	10 inches	2944486
1970	340-ci 3x2-bbl	10 inches	3461118
1971	Hemi	10 inches	3579272
1972	All	10 inches	3579272
1973-74	All	10 inches	3580225

Drum Brakes

Model Year	Engine	Drum Size	Part No.
1967-1968	All	All	2881536
1969	All	All	2994406
1970	Except Hemi	All	2944489
1970	Hemi	11 inches	2944309
1971	Except Hemi	10 inches	3461287
1971	Except Hemi	11 inches	3579272
1971	Hemi	11 inches	3461300
1972	All	10 inches	3461360 #

= Field-installed unit.

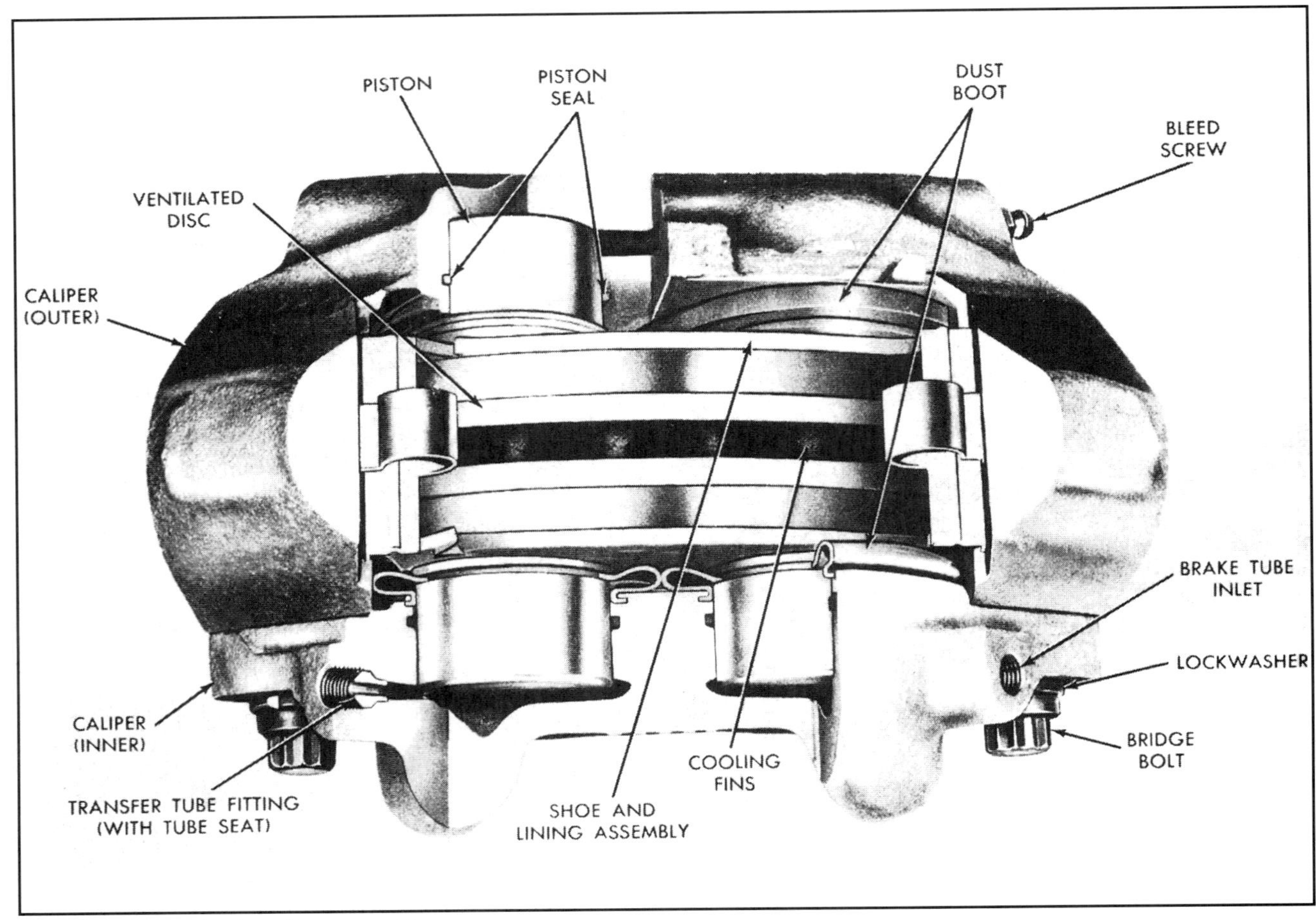

A 1967-1969 disc brake caliper assembly.

rear drums were encased steel and were made by Motor Wheel. The drum made by Motor Wheel will be stamped "MW"; those made by Budd bear the letter "B"; and on those made by Kelsey-Hayes, the letters "KH" will be stamped on the drum.

All V-8-equipped 1967-1969 Barracudas used the 10-inch drums made by Motor Wheel that can be identified by the "MW" stamp. In 1970, Kelsey-Hayes built both the 10- and 11-inch drums, and as in previous years, the front drums were unique to each side. In 1971, the front drums were restyled so they would fit either side, and two different manufactures were used. As mentioned above, Motor Wheel stamped its pieces "MW," and Kelsey-Hayes stamped its parts "KH." For 1973-1974 models, front disc brakes were standard, and only 10-inch rear drums built by Kelsey-Hayes were used. Brake drums were left unfinished, and to duplicate the look of fresh-cast steel, paint the drums stainless steel in a flat finish. For those few 9-inch drums that were made of cast-iron, paint the drums cast-iron gray to reproduce the factory look.

Backing plates were used behind each drum. The backing plates are matched to the drum size. The A-bodies (1967-1969) used a different set than those used on the E-bodies (1970-1974), even though both used 10-inch brakes. The rear axle type will also affect the usage of the rear backing plates in the A-bodies. Those with a 7-1/4-inch axle used a different set of backing plates than those cars with an 8-3/4-inch axle, even though both used 10-inch drums. Backing plates were left unpainted, which can be duplicated by painting them stainless steel. Some, especially those on 1972-1974 models, were painted semi-gloss black; either finish is correct.

Rotors

The 1967-1969 Barracudas used a 11.04-inch-diameter cast-iron rotor, ventilated for better cooling. The E-bodies used two different diameters: The 1970-1972 models used a 11-3/4-inch rotor, while the 1973 and 1974 models used a larger 11.98-inch-diameter rotor. Both were made out of cast-iron and ventilated.

As with drum brakes, 1967-1970 rotors were unique to each side, while beginning in 1971 the rotors were restyled to fit either side. All rotors should have a natural

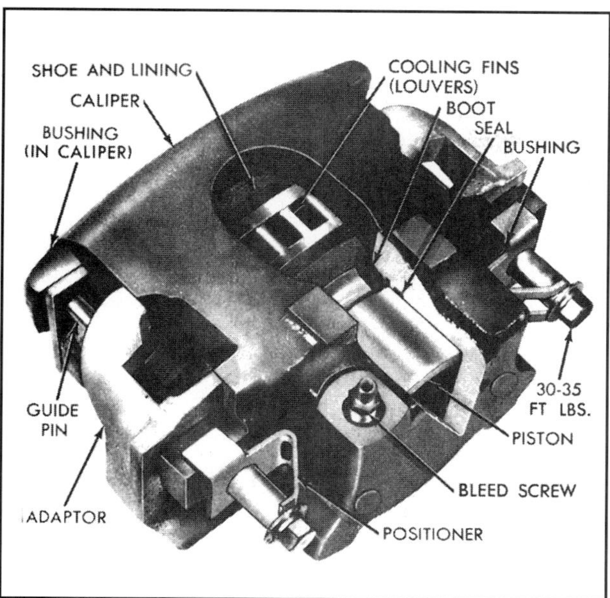

The 1970-1974 floating type of disc brake caliper.

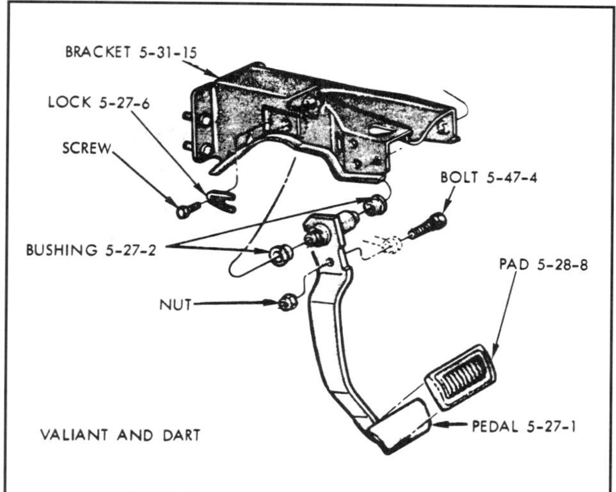

The brake pedal linkage used in 1967-1969 is shown here.

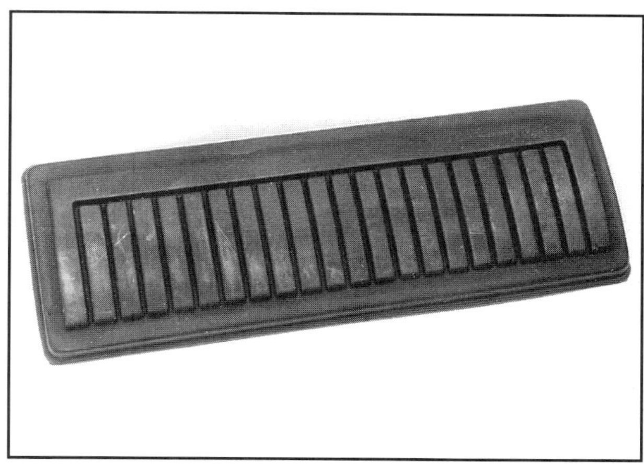
A 1967-1969 brake-pedal pad. *Year One*

cast-iron appearance on the hub. The portion gripped by the caliper should have a bright and smooth finish.

Calipers

From 1967 to 1969, the Barracuda used a fixed, four-position caliper, and three different housings were used. All 1967 and early 1968 models used part numbers 2881588 for the right-hand side and 2881589 for the left-hand side. Those made after November 1, 1967, used part numbers 2925160 (right) and 2925161 (left) until the end of the 1968 model year. All 1969s used part numbers 2925220 (right) and 2925221 (left).

The E-bodies used a floating single-piston caliper design made by Kelsey-Hayes. Three different housings were used: Those in 1970 models used part numbers 2944712 (right) and 2944713 (left); both the 1971 and 1972 models used the same calipers, listed as part numbers 3461964 (right) and 3461965 (left); and the 1973 and 1974 models used part numbers 3580852 (right) and 3580353 (left). All calipers were made of cast-iron and should have an unpainted finish; this can be achieved by painting them cast-iron gray. The holding bolts should have a dull metallic appearance.

Brake Pedals and Pads

Three different pedals were used with the 1967-1969 Barracudas. Those with a three-speed manual transmission used a different pedal than those with a four-speed transmission. Those with an automatic transmission used a physically different pedal with a much larger pedal face. Although three different pedals were used, only two pads were used, one for a manual transmission and the other for automatic-equipped cars. A trim bezel was placed around the pad if the interior decor group package was ordered.

The transmission type continued to affect the usage of the brake pedal for the 1970-1974 E-bodies. Those used in 1970 are unique and are used in no other model or year. Pedal part numbers were changed for 1971 models; they continued to be used into the 1972 model year and will not correctly fit 1970 models. Pedals were changed again in 1973, continuing over into the 1974 models.

Although the pedals changed between the 1970-1972 models, they used the same pedal pads. These pads, however, are different than those used in earlier models. The pad design was again changed for the 1973 model year and continued into 1974 models. A trim bezel was part of the Gran Coupe and Challenger S.E. models in 1970 and 1971 only. No bezel was available for the 1972-1974 models as part of a package or a separate option.

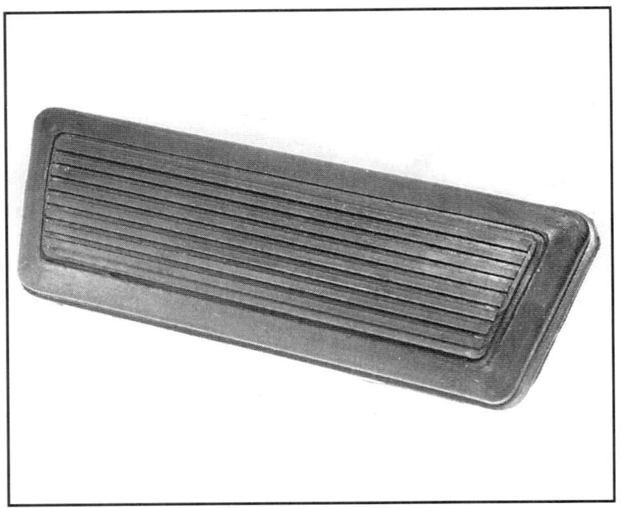

A 1970-1972 brake-pedal pad. *Year One*

A 1970-1972 parking brake-pedal pad. *Year One*

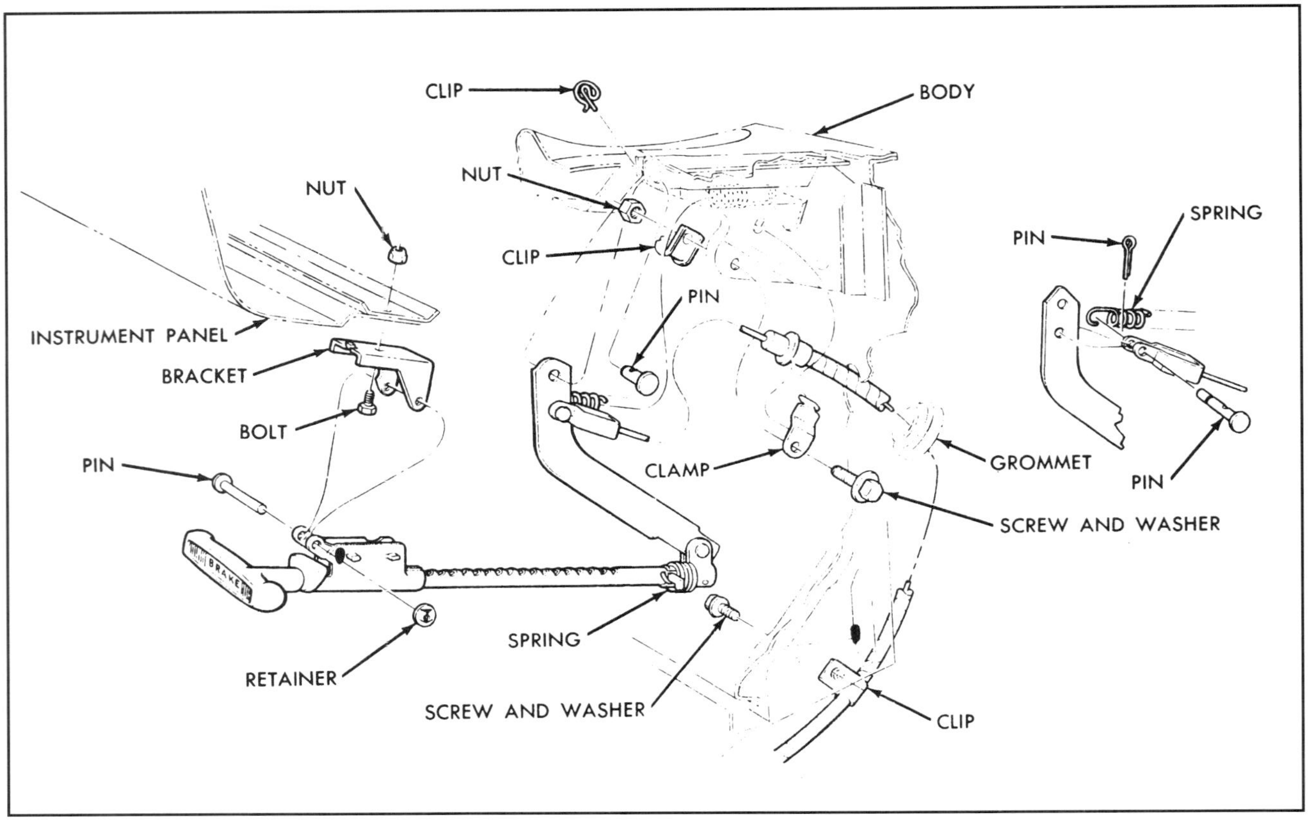

The 1967-1969 parking brake.

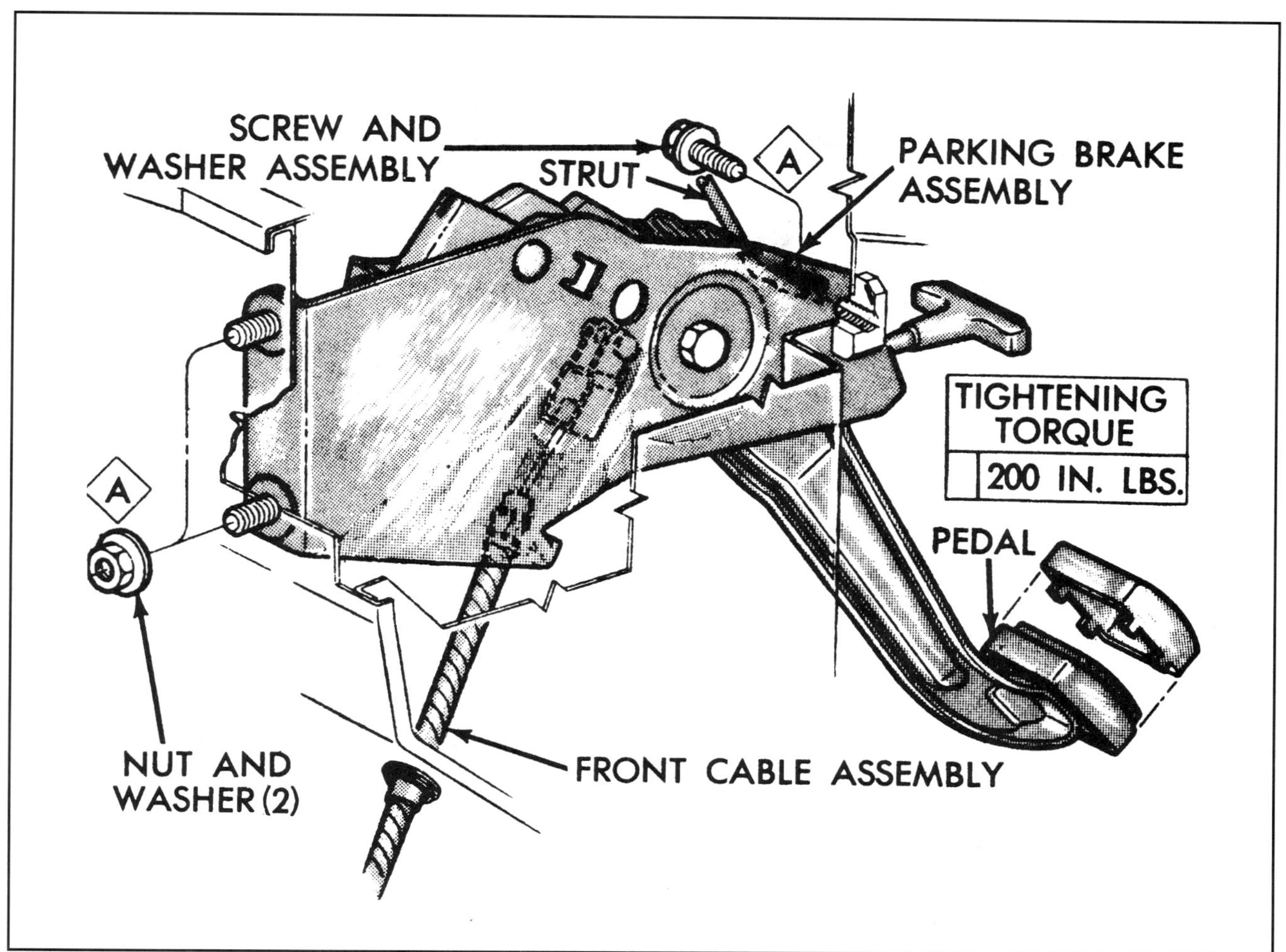

The 1970-1974 parking brake.

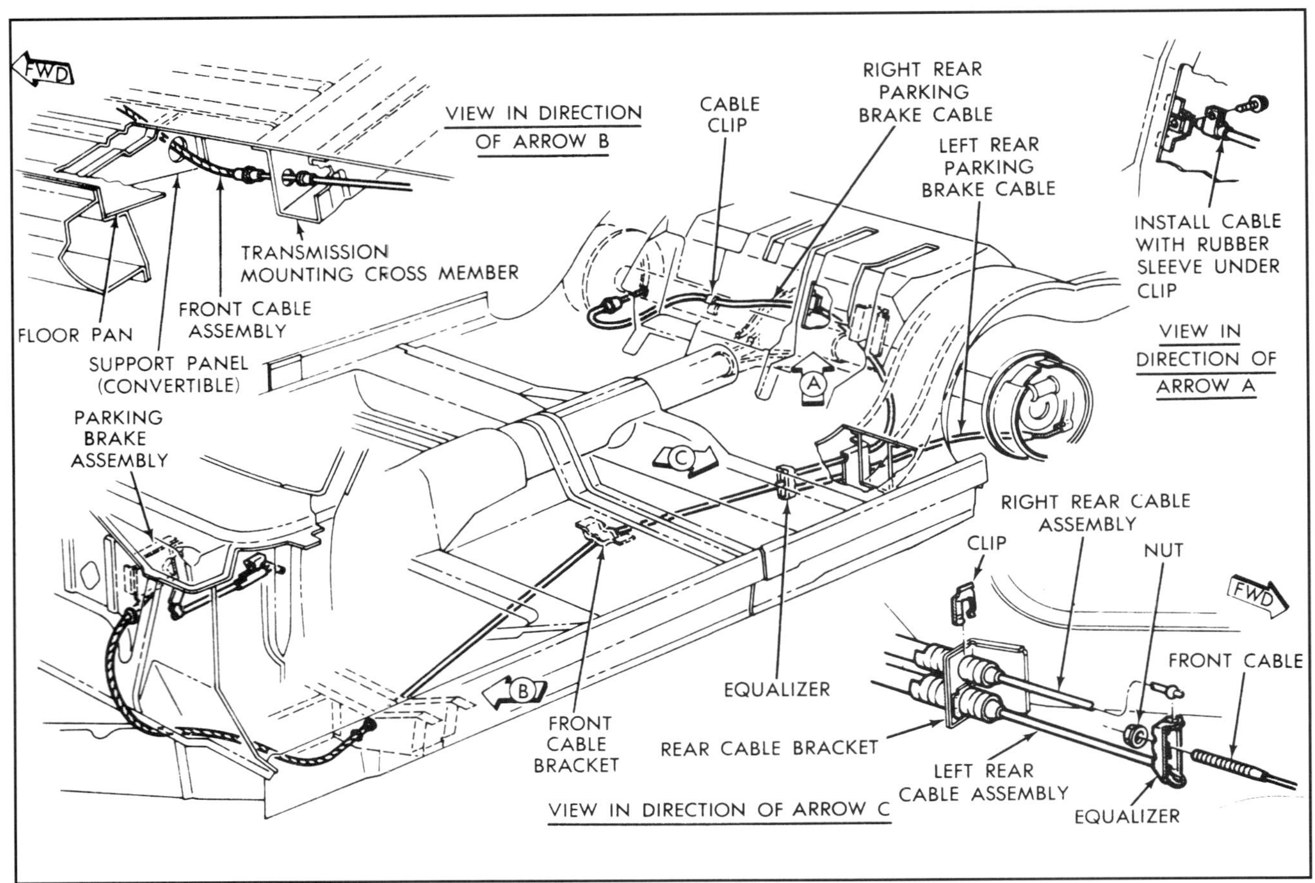

The 1967-1969 parking brake cable routing.

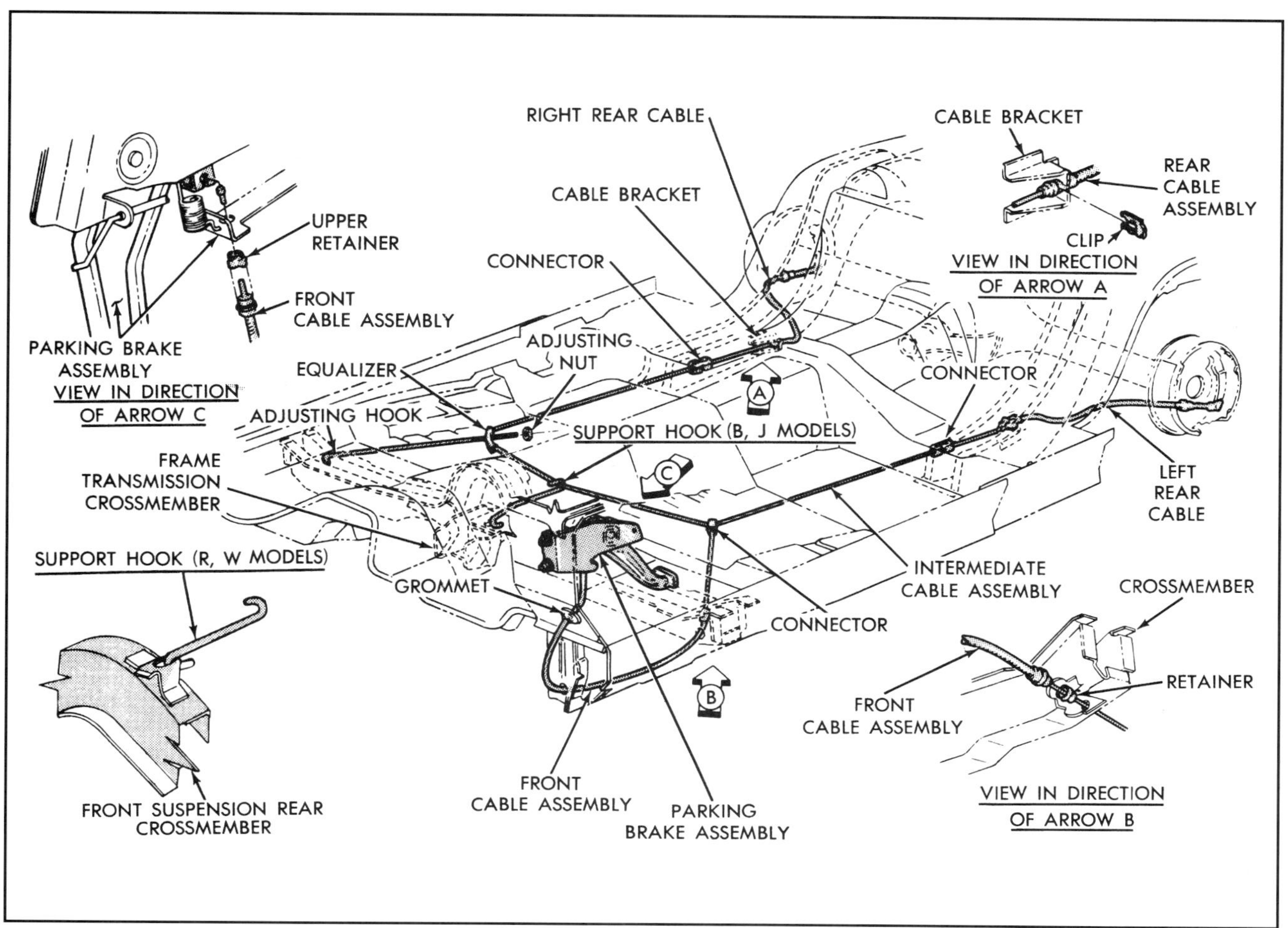

The 1970-1974 parking brake cable routing.

Chapter 6

Wheels, Wheel Covers, and Tires

Standard Wheels

Stamped-steel 14x4 1/2-inch wheels were standard on all 1967-1969 Barracudas except those with a four-barrel carburetor. Those models with a 340-ci, 383-ci, or 440-ci were standard with 14x5 1/2-inch stamped-steel wheels. The 14x5 1/2-inch wheels were optional on the other Barracudas. Stamped-steel wheels were painted the same color as the lower exterior of the car.

Stamped-steel wheels were also standard on all 1970-1974 models. Those models with a six-cylinder engine or the 318-ci V-8 used 14x5-inch wheels. When equipped with the 383-ci or 440-ci engine, 14x6-inch stamped-steel wheels were standard. Stamped-steel 15x7-inch wheels were optional on all 1970-1971 cars with a big-block and standard on cars with a 340-ci or 426 Hemi engine. Standard wheels on 1972-1973 models with a 340-ci engine measured 14x5 1/2 inches, and they were optional with all other engines. In 1974, standard wheels for cars with a 360-ci engine measured 14x5 1/2 inches, which were again optional on cars with a 318-ci engine. In all years, a matching spare wheel of the same size was used.

Before early 1971, the wheels were painted the same color as the body. Beginning in early March 1971, the wheels, when equipped with hubcaps, were instead painted gloss black.

Standard lug nuts all eight years will have a fresh cast-steel appearance. This can be duplicated by painting the nuts stainless steel. Up to and including the 1970 model year, left-hand thread lugs were used on the

The date code is stamped on the wheel near the valve stem.

The Magnum 500 road wheel was used from 1970-1974.

1970-1974 E-Body Standard Stamped-Steel Wheel ID Numbers

Model Year	Wheel Size Number	Identification
1970-1971	14x5.00	3420976
1972-1974	14x5.00	3621952
1970-1971	14x5.50	3420977
1972-1974	14x5.50	3621953
1970-1971	14x6.00	3420978
1970-1971	15x7.00	2944450
1972-1974	15x7.00	3580070 (spare tire only)

driver's side, and right-hand thread lugs were used on the passenger's side. Thus, the lugs or nuts will not swap sides. Beginning with the 1971 models, all lugs on both sides of the car used right-hand thread lugs and nuts.

On 1967-1969 models, the wheel diameter and date code is stamped into the wheel near the valve stem. The date code will begin with the code for the wheel manufacturer, followed by the year code. Below this is the wheel's stamping date. For example, the code "KH8 10 11" would decipher this way: Kelsey-Hayes (KH), 1968 (8), September (10), 11 (11), which would mean this was for a 1969 model. Wheels with a date stamped after July are usually for the next model year. On 1970 and later models, the part number is stamped into the wheel near the valve stem—along with the Chrysler pentastar logo—instead of the date code. A chart of wheel part numbers is provided here to help identify the correct wheels.

Styled Wheels

No styled wheel option was offered on the 1967-1969 Barracuda. It was not until the introduction of the E-Bodies in 1970 that styled wheels appeared. Optional wheels on all cars with a six-cylinder engine or 318-ci engine in 1970 and 1971 were 14x5-inch five-spoke Magnum 500-style wheels listed as part number 2944474.

Slotted Rally wheels were available for all models. Those with a six-cylinder engine or a 318-ci engine used 14x5 1/2-inch wheels listed as part number 2944252. All others used 15x7-inch slotted wheels, listed as part number 2944390, was which not available on cars with a six-cylinder engine or single two-barrel carburetors.

When styled wheels were ordered, the spare tire usually is a standard stamped-steel wheel of compatible size. For those cars with the Magnum 500-style wheels, a stamped-steel 14x5 1/2-inch wheel painted gloss black was used as a spare, while the 14x5 1/2-inch slotted Rally wheels used a space saver tire (part number 2944395). The exception to the rule is those models with the 15x7-inch Rally wheels, for which a matching styled wheel was used as the spare tire.

Both the 14-inch and the 15-inch slotted Rally wheels were painted Argent Silver and used a center hub painted light gray. In 1970, the hub was listed as part number 3461066, and in 1971 it was changed to

An example of the 15x7-inch Rally wheels.

part number 3461352. The 1971 part is darker gray than the one used on 1970 models. A bright chrome trim ring was used on both the Magnum 500 wheel and the 14-inch Rally wheel in both years. The 15-inch wheels used a different trim ring each year; 1970 models used a polished trim ring, while the 1971 models used a brushed aluminum ring. A 1970-style trim ring on a 1971 model is considered incorrect. It is possible a few models built in early 1971 could have used the polished ring.

The 14x5 1/2-inch Magnum 500-style road wheel was still optional for all models from 1972 to 1974 and was listed as part number 3580059 all three years. Slotted 14x 5 1/2-inch Rally wheels were also optional and used part number 3580058. Both the Magnum and the Rally wheels used a bright trim ring. Rally wheels measuring

The standard hub cap on 1970-1971 Barracuda.

15x7 inches are listed as being available for 1972 models as a dealer-installed option only. A 340-ci engine and the Rally suspension package had to be ordered from the factory. Proof of this requires a paper statement by the dealer dated before the original customer took delivery of the car. No trim ring was used on the 15-inch wheels.

The center hub for the slotted Rally wheels was also restyled for 1972 and became more pronounced and brightly plated. Only four styled wheels were used with either option, and a plain, stamped-steel wheel of the same size was used as the spare. The part number for the spare wheel was the same as the standard stamped wheel. The spare was painted gloss black.

Hub Caps and Wheel Covers

Standard on all 1967-1968 Barracudas, except the 1967 fastback models, was a hubcap listed as part number 2823001 that features the Plymouth logo in the center. Standard on the 1967 fastback and optional on all

The 28-hole optional wheel used on 1970-1972 Barracuda.

other 1967 body styles was the simulated mag-style cover. This cover, listed as part number 2823010, features six simulated slots and the Plymouth logo in a large center dome. This cover was again used in 1968 and 1969 but was now optional on all body styles. Part number 2823010 was a factory-issued option, and it should not be confused with the dealer-installed simulated mag-wheel cover, which is listed as part number 2808487. The dealer-installed cover featured a five-spoke design, with five bright-plated simulated lug nuts around a center dome with the Plymouth crest. The dealer-installed cover was available on all 1967-1969 Barracudas.

Optional for 1967-1969 models was the bolt-on cover. This five-slot cover was listed as part number 2823014 and is easily recognizable by five holes drilled into the center depression that allowed the cover to be directly bolted onto the wheel. Like the other covers, it, too, had the Plymouth logo in the center dome.

In 1968, the simulated-wire wheel cover became available. This cover, part number 2881787, was dominated by

The 1970-1971 simulated-wire wheel cover.

several wire spokes and a round center dome with the Plymouth logo. This cover continued into the 1969 model year unchanged.

The standard hubcap in 1969 was listed as part number 2944088, and the Plymouth name is imprinted on it. As stated previously, some covers available for 1969 models were carried over from the 1968 model year. A new option was the deep-dished cover. Listed as part number 2944165, it featured 30 blades that rose up in the center to house a center dome, and a decal

A deep-dish wheel cover for a 1970 Challenger.

that read "Plymouth Division" was used on the center dome. This option was available only if the D70- or E70-series tires were ordered. Due to its design, this cover will not fit cars with 14x4 1/2-inch wheels; 14x5 1/2-wheels are essential.

Standard on all 1970-1971 Barracudas was a bright-plated hubcap (part number 2944088) with the words "Plymouth Division" in black lettering. A trim ring was available as an option around the standard hubcap for 1971 models only. It was the same trim ring used on the styled wheels described above, so all 15-inch wheels used a brushed aluminum trim ring and all 14-inch wheels used a chrome trim ring. A stainless steel hubcap (part number 2944089) was standard on the 1970-1971 Challenger, and it featured the Dodge tri-star logo in the center. As with the Barracuda models, a trim ring was optional with the hubcaps in 1971.

Both models were available with a 14-inch simulated-wire wheel cover (listed as part number 2944400). It featured a center dome with no model logo. No 15-inch simulated-wire cover was offered, but the 14-inch cover did continue over into the 1971 model year. Barracudas were optional with a Deluxe wheel cover. This cover looks like a large pie pan with 28 holes drilled in the outer edge of it. In the center it read "Plymouth Division." This cover remained optional until the end of the 1972 model year. It was available only for those models with 14-inch wheels and was mostly used on base Barracuda and Gran Coupe models.

Another cover was added in 1971, one so rare that in some books about the Barracuda it is not even mentioned. It is listed as part number 3461401 and looks like a stainless disc with nine holes drilled in a-circle. It was available with 14-inch wheels in 1971 only. It is possible

The space saver spare tire was used with some styled wheels.

that a few Cudas with a 383-ci or 440-ci engine were installed with these covers, but no Hemi or 340-ci equipped Cudas were installed with these covers because they were not offered for 15-inch wheels.

Challengers in 1970 were available with three different wheel covers: the wire wheel cover described above, the deep-dish cover, and its replacement. The first deep-dish cover, part number 2944441, featured a five-spoke design. Each spoke was separated by multiple ridges, and in the center was a red color appliqué with the tri-star Dodge emblem and the words "Dodge Division" printed on it. Around June 10, 1970, part number 2944433 took this cover's place. The second cover featured six slots with a depressed center dome with the Challenger name done in script. In 1971 the wire wheel cover remained optional, as did the late-style deep-dish wheel cover. All covers were for 14-inch wheels only.

For 1972, Barracudas came standard with a stainless steel hubcap (part number 3461450) which used no name or logo. The Challengers came standard with the same hubcap as they did in previous years. The 28-hole wheel cover was the only optional wheel cover available for the Barracuda in 1972. Only one wheel cover was optional on the Challenger, and it featured a large center with the Dodge name imprinted on it and was surrounded by 33 small spokes. Early models, those built

1967 Barracuda Tires

Engine	Standard	With A/C	With Disc Brakes	A/C and Disc Brakes	Optional Upgrade	Brand***
225-ci	6.95x14	6.95x14*	6.95x14	6.95x14#	D70x14 D70x14**	(6.95x14) Goodyear Power Cushion
273-ci	6.95x14	D70x14	6.95x14# D70x14**	D70x14	D70x14	
383-ci	D70x14	n/a	E70x14	n/a	None	(D70x14) Firestone Wide 1 Ovals

*** = Recommendation of standard tire, other brands could have been used;
* = 8-ply tires on convertible; # = Hardtop or fastback; ** = Convertible only.
D70x14 available as either as Red Streak or whitewall tires.

MODEL	TIRE PRESSURES (COLD)				VEHICLE FULL RATED LOAD — LBS.
	FOR ALL LOADS UP TO FULL RATED		PERMISSIBLE FOR 4 PASS. OR LESS		
	FRONT	REAR	FRONT	REAR	
FASTBACK	28	30	24	26	950
	SEE OWNER'S MANUAL				BX-29

A 1967 Barracuda fastback tire-pressure decal. It was affixed to the B-body striker post on the driver's side.

MODEL	TIRE PRESSURE (COLD)				VEHICLE FULL RATED LOAD — LBS.
	FOR ALL LOADS UP TO FULL RATED		PERMISSIBLE FOR 5 PASS. OR LESS		
	FRONT	REAR	FRONT	REAR	
SEDANS, H.T.	30	30	24	24	1100
CONVERTIBLE	26	26	24	24	1100
	SEE OWNER'S MANUAL				VL

A 1967 Barracuda tire-pressure decal for all body styles except the fastback. It was white with a red border and was affixed to the driver's door striker post.

MODEL	TIRE PRESSURE (COLD) PSI				VEHICLE FULL RATED LOAD			
	FOR ALL LOADS UP TO FULL RATED		RECOMMENDED FOR 5 PASS. OR LESS		LBS.	SEATING CAPACITY		
	FRONT	REAR	FRONT	REAR		1st.SEAT	2nd.SEAT	LUGG.COMP.
H.T., FASTBACK & CONV.	30	30	24	24	1100	3 PASS.	3 PASS.	200 LBS.
	SEE OWNERS MANUAL							B

The 1968 Barracuda tire-pressure decal was placed on the driver's door striker post.

up to March 1972, used part number 3461460 and the spokes were painted dark gray. Later models used part number 3580153 and the spokes were chrome-plated. The chrome-plated cover remained optional on the 1973 and 1974 Challengers. A revised cover with 28 holes was available for the 1973 and 1974 Barracudas; it looks like the older cover, but four-circles were stamped into the center of the cover. This cover was listed as part number 3699017 both years.

TIRE PRESSURES PSI (COLD)

MAX. VEHICLE CAP. OR LESS		5 PASS. OR LESS	
FRONT	REAR	FRONT	REAR
30	30	26	26

VEHICLE CAPACITY
MAX. 6 PASS. + 200 LBS.

MAXIMUM VEHICLE CAPACITY		5 PASS. OR LESS
3 PASS.	1ST SEAT	2 PASS.
3 PASS.	2ND SEAT	3 PASS.
200 LBS.	LUGG. COMP.	0
1100 LBS.	TOTAL	750 LBS.

MINIMUM TIRE SIZE

D70—14 4 PLY RATING

SEE OWNER'S MANUAL FOR ADD. DATA

PRINTED IN U.S.A. 34004 76

The 1969 Barracuda tire-pressure decal was attached to the driver's door striker post. This version was used with a car equipped with a 340-ci engine.

Tires

Original tire size can be affected by many different factors, including engine size and options like air conditioning or disc brakes. Many different brands of tires were used, and the brand used may differ from factory to factory. Original sizes are listed here, and the brand names listed are meant only as a guide, as they were the most popular. When Red Streak tires were standard, whitewall tires of the same size were available as a no-cost option.

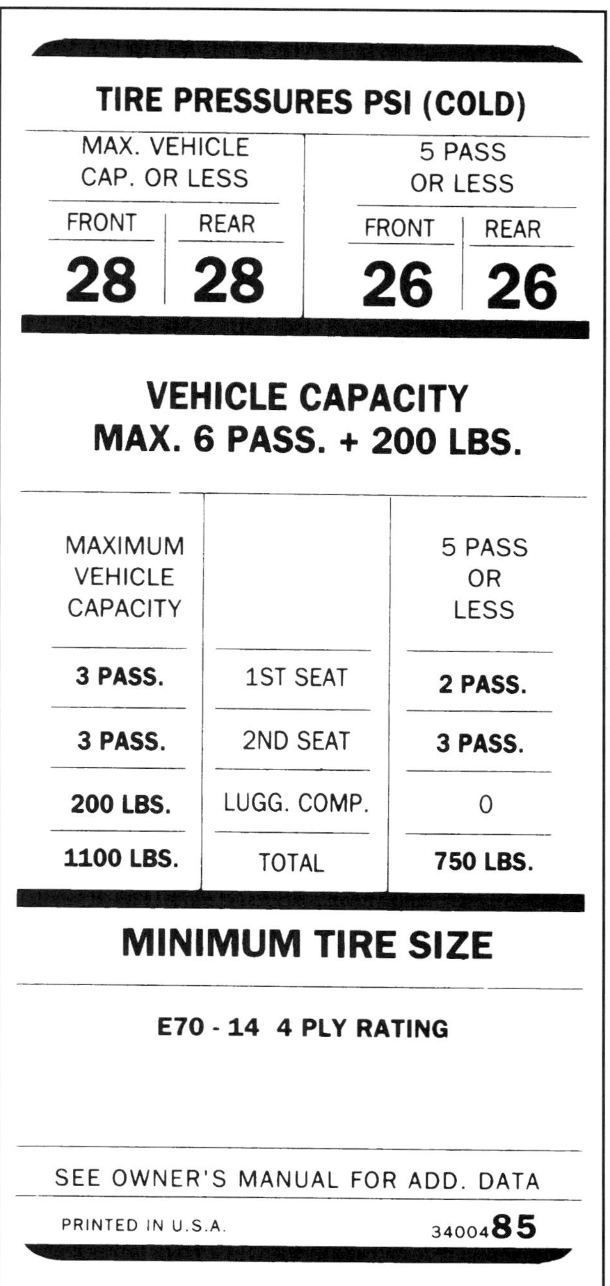

TIRE PRESSURES PSI (COLD)

MAX. VEHICLE CAP. OR LESS		5 PASS OR LESS	
FRONT	REAR	FRONT	REAR
28	28	26	26

VEHICLE CAPACITY
MAX. 6 PASS. + 200 LBS.

MAXIMUM VEHICLE CAPACITY		5 PASS OR LESS
3 PASS.	1ST SEAT	**2 PASS.**
3 PASS.	2ND SEAT	**3 PASS.**
200 LBS.	LUGG. COMP.	0
1100 LBS.	TOTAL	**750 LBS.**

MINIMUM TIRE SIZE

E70 - 14 4 PLY RATING

SEE OWNER'S MANUAL FOR ADD. DATA

PRINTED IN U.S.A. 34004**85**

This 1969 Barracuda tire-pressure decal for E70x14 tires attached to the driver's door striker post.

TIRE PRESSURES PSI(COLD)

FOR ALL LOADS UP TO AND INCL.
MAXIMUM VEHICLE CAPACITY

FRONT	REAR
25	28

MAXIMUM
VEHICLE CAPACITY
4 PASSENGERS + 200 LBS.

1ST SEAT	2 PASSENGERS
2ND SEAT	2 PASSENGERS
LUGG. COMP.	200 LBS.
TOTAL	800 LBS.

MINIMUM TIRE SIZE

F70 x 14 LOAD RANGE B

SEE OWNER'S MANUAL FOR ADD. DATA

PRINTED IN U.S.A. 3402062

This 1970 E-body tire-pressure decal for cars with F70x14 tires and no air conditioning was placed on the driver's door striker post.

TIRE PRESSURES PSI (COLD)

MAX. VEHICLE CAP. OR LESS		3 PASS. OR LESS	
FRONT	REAR	FRONT	REAR
28	32	26	28

VEHICLE CAPACITY
4 PASSENGERS + 200 LBS.

MAXIMUM VEHICLE CAPACITY		3 PASS. OR LESS
2 PASS.	1ST SEAT	2 PASS.
2 PASS.	2ND SEAT	1 PASS.
200 LBS.	LUGG. COMP.	0
800 LBS.	TOTAL	450 LBS.

MINIMUM TIRE SIZE

E60 X 15 LOAD RANGE B

SEE OWNER'S MANUAL FOR ADD. DATA

PRINTED IN U.S.A. 3402059

This 1970 E-body tire-pressure decal was used with E-70x15 tires.

1968 Barracuda Tires

Engine	Standard	With A/C	With Disc Brakes	A/C and Disc Brakes	Optional Upgrade	Brand***
225-ci	6.95x14	6.95x14*	6.95x14	6.95x14# D70x14**	D70x14 E70x14 +	(6.95x14) Good year Power Cushion
318-ci	6.95x14	D70x14	6.95x14# D70x14**	D70x14	D70x14 E70x14+	(D70x14) Firestone Wide Oval
340-ci	E70x14	E70x14	E70x14	E70x14	None	(E70x14) Goodyear Polyglas
383-ci	E70x14	n/a	E70x14	n/a	None	(E70x14) Goodyear Polyglas

*** = Recommendation of standard tire, other brands could have been used;
* = 8-ply tires on convertible; # = Hardtop or fastback; ** = Convertible only;
+ = Only if heavy-duty suspension is also ordered; D70x14 available in blackwalls or whitewalls.
E70x14 Red Streak or whitewall standard at no cost.

1969 Barracuda Tires

Engine	Standard	With A/C	With Disc Brakes	A/C and Disc Brakes	Optional Upgrade	Brand***
225-ci	6.95x14	6.95x14*	6.95x14	6.95x14# D70x14**	D70x14	(6.95x14) Goodyear Power Cushion
318-ci	6.95x14	D70x14	6.95x14# D70x14**	D70x14	D70x14	(D70x14) Firestone Wide Oval
340-ci	E70x14	E70x14	E70x14	E70x14	None	(E70x14) Goodyear Polyglas
383-ci	E70x14	n/a	E70x14	n/a	None	(E70x14) Goodyear Polyglas
440-ci	E70x14	n/a	n/a	n/a	None	(E70x14) Goodyear Polyglas

*** = Recommendation of standard tire, other brands could have been used;
* = 8-ply tires on convertible; # = Hardtop or fastback; ** = Convertible only; # = Hardtop or fastback; ** = Convertible only.

TIRE PRESSURES PSI(COLD)

MAX. VEHICLE CAP. OR LESS		3 PASS. OR LESS	
FRONT	REAR	FRONT	REAR
28	32	24	28

VEHICLE CAPACITY
4 PASS. + 200 LBS.

MAXIMUM VEHICLE CAPACITY		3 PASS. OR LESS
2 PASS.	1ST SEAT	2 PASS.
2 PASS.	2ND SEAT	1 PASS.
200 LBS.	LUGG. COMP.	0
800 LBS.	TOTAL	450 LBS.

MINIMUM TIRE SIZE

F60·x 15 LOAD RANGE B

SEE OWNER'S MANUAL FOR ADD. DATA

RINTED IN U.S.A. 3402064

This 1970 Hemi E-body tire-pressure decal was placed on the driver's door striker post.

TIRE PRESSURES PSI(COLD)

FOR ALL LOADS UP TO AND INCL MAXIMUM VEHICLE CAPACITY

FRONT	REAR
24	28

MAXIMUM VEHICLE CAPACITY
4 PASSENGERS + 200 LBS.

1ST SEAT	2 PASSENGERS
2ND SEAT	2 PASSENGERS
LUGG. COMP.	200 LBS.
TOTAL	800 LBS.

MINIMUM TIRE SIZE

E60 x 15 - FRONT ONLY
G60 x 15 - REAR ONLY
ALL TIRES LOAD RANGE B
DO NOT INSTALL TIRES
OTHER THAN SPECIFIED

SEE OWNER'S MANUAL FOR ADD. DATA

PRINTED IN U.S.A. 3402098

This 1970 Trans Am tire-pressure decal was placed on the driver's door striker post.

1970 Barracuda and Challenger Tires

Engine	Standard	With A/C	With Disc Brakes	A/C and Disc Brakes	Optional Upgrade	Brand***
225/318-ci	E78x14	E78x14	E78x14	E78x14	F78x14 F70x14	(E78x14) Goodyear
340-ci 4-bbl 426 Hemi	E60x15	E60x15	E60x15	E60x15	None	(E60x15) Goodyear Polyglas GT
383/440-ci	F70x14	F70x14	F70x14	F70x14	E60x15	(F70x14) Goodyear Polyglas GT
340-ci 3x2-bbl	E60x15 * G60x15 **	n/a	E60x15* G60x15**	n/a	None	Goodyear Polyglas GT

* = Front tires; ** = Rear tires; *** = Recommendation only; other brands could have been used.

1971 Barracuda and Challenger Tires

Engine	Standard	With A/C	With Disc Brakes	A/C and Disc Brakes	Optional Upgrade	Brand***
225/318-ci	D78x14	D78x14	D78x14	D78x14	E78x14 F78x14 F70x14#	(D78x14) Goodyear
426 Hemi	E60x15	E60x15	F60x15	E60x15	None	(E60x15) Goodyear Polyglas GT
340-ci 4-bbl 383/440-ci	F70x14	F70x14	F70x14	F70x14	E60x15+	(F70x14) Goodyear Polyglas GT
340-ci 3x2-bbl	E60x15 * G60x15 **	n/a	E60x15* G60x15**	n/a	None	Goodyear Polyglas GT

= Available only if heavy-duty suspension is also ordered; + = Only if disc or heavy-duty brakes are also ordered;
* = Front tires; ** = Rear tires; *** = Recommendation only, other brands could have been used.

1972 Barracuda and Challenger Tires

Engine	Standard	With A/C	With Disc Brakes	A/C and Disc Brakes	Optional Upgrade	Brand***
225-ci	7.35x14	F78x14	F78x14	F78x14	F78x14 F70x14#	(7.35x14) Firestone
318-ci	F78x14	F78x14	F78x14	F78x14	F70x14#	(F70x14) Goodyear
340-ci	F70x14	F70x14	F70x14	F70x14	E60x15+	(F70x14) Goodyear Polyglas GT

= Only if heavy-duty suspension is also ordered; + = Only power front disc brakes are ordered, dealer-installed;
*** = Recommendation only, other brands could have been used.

1973 Barracuda and Challenger Tires

Engine	Standard	With A/C	With Disc Brakes	A/C and Disc Brakes	Optional Upgrade	Brand***
318-ci	7.35x14	F78x14	F78x14	F78x14	F78x14 F70x14#	(7.35x14) Firestone
340-ci	F78x14^ F70x14**	F78x14^ F70x14**	78x14^ F70x14**	F78x14^ F70x14**	F70x14#	(F78x14) Goodyear

^ = On Barracuda or Challenger models only; ** = On Cuda or Rally models;
# = Only if heavy-duty suspension is also ordered; *** = Recommendation only, other brands could have been used.

1974 Barracuda and Challenger Tires

Engine	Standard	With A/C	With Disc Brakes	A/C and Disc Brakes	Optional Upgrade	Brand***
318-ci	7.35x14	F78x14	F78x14	F78x14	F78x14 FR78x14* F70x14#	(F70x14) Goodyear
340-ci	FR78x14 ^ F70x14**	FR78x14^ F70x14**	FR78x14^ F70x14**	FR78x1 F70x14**	4F70x14#	(FR78x14) Goodyear Radial

* = Standard on Cuda models with 318-ci; ^ = On Barracuda or Challenger models only;
** = On Cuda or Rally models; # = Only if heavy-duty suspension is also ordered;
*** = Recommendation only, other brands could have been used.

Chapter 7

Exterior Sheet Metal

Exterior Finish

All models covered in this guide were originally finished in acrylic enamel. For the correct finish, which is also the easiest, refinish in Ditzler acrylic enamel. For a more dazzling shine, opt for acrylic lacquer. Note that lacquer is more expensive and harder to apply as the old finish will have to be either stripped off or a top-quality sealer will have to be applied over it before

1967 Exterior Paint Colors

Paint Code	Color Name	Chrysler No.	Ditzler Acrylic Enamel	DuPont Acrylic Lacquer
AA1	Silver Metallic (Met.)	AAY2A4	32398	4656L
BB1	Black	TAY1X9	9300*; 9000#	99L
CC1	Medium Blue Met.	CAY2B7	13159	4797L
DD1	Light Blue Met.	BAY2B4	13043	4758L
EE1	Dark Blue Met.	BAY2B9	13040	4757LH
881	Bright Blue Met.	CAY2B6	13336	4812L
FF1	Light Green Met.	CAY2F4	43547	4801L
GG1	Dark Green Met.	CAY2F9	43540	4800L
HH1	Dark Copper Met.	CAY2K8	22659	4807LH
KK1	Light Turquoise Met.	CAY2Q4	13195	4799L
LL1	Dark Turquoise Met.	CAY2Q8	13214	4798L
MM1	Turbine Bronze Met.	BAY2K6	60492	4761LH
PP1	Bright Red	BAY1H6	71483	4770LH
QQ1	Dark Red	CAY2R7	71552	4810LM
RR1	Yellow	CAY2M4	50731	4698L
SS1	Soft Yellow	CAY1Y1	81539	4764L
TT1	Medium Copper Met.	CAY2K4	22706	4808L
WW1	White	VAY1W1	8362	4559L
YY1	Tan Met.	CAY2T4	22700	4805L
ZZ1	Gold Met.	CAY2Y4	22715	4802L
661	Mauve Met.			4809D

* = Early models; # = Late-models; change occurred around September 1,1966.

1968 Exterior Paint Colors

Paint Code	Color Name	Chrysler No.	Ditzler Acrylic Enamel	DuPont Acrylic Lacquer
AA1	Buffed Silver Met.	DAY2A4	8588	5859L
BB1	Black	DAY2X9	9000	99L
EE1	Midnight Blue Met.	DAY2B8	13372	4880LH
FF1	Mist Green Met.	DAY2F3	43646	4881L
GG1	Forest Green Met.	DAY2F9	43649	4883L
JJ1	Ember Gold Met.	DAY2Y5	22807	4889L
LL1	Surf Turquoise Met.	DAY2Q7	13371	4884LH
MM1	Turbine Bronze Met.	BAY2K6	60492	4872LM
PP1	Matador Red		71483	4770LH
QQ1	Electric Blue Met.	DAY2B5	13354	4861LH
RR1	Burgundy Met.	DAY2R8	50749	4885LM
SS1	Sunfire Yellow	DAY1Y2	81574	4887L
TT1	Avocado Green Met.	DAY2F6	43647	4882L
UU1	Frost Blue Met.	DAY2B4	13445	4890L
WW1	White		81574	4887L
XX1	Satin Beige	AAY1L1	22441	4953L
YY1	Sierra Tan Met.	DAY2T6	22855	4891L
221	Hawaiian Blue		4958A**	4958L

** = DuPont acrylic enamel number.

1969 Exterior Paint Colors

Paint Code	Color Name	Chrysler No.	Ditzler Acrylic Enamel	DuPont Acrylic Lacquer
A4	Silver Met.	AY2EA4	2016	4979L
B3	Ice Blue Met.	AY2EB3	2018	4981L
B5	Blue Fire Met	AY2EB5	2019	4982L
B7	Jamaica Blue Met.	AYE2B7	2020	4983L
F3	Frost Green Met.	AYE2F3	2023	4986L
F5	Limelight Met.	AY2EF5	2024	4887L
F8	Ivy Green Met.	AY2EF8	43786	4988L
L1	Sand Pebble Beige	AY2EL1	22542	4998L
Q5	Seafoam Turquoise Met.	AY2EQ5	13534	4960L
R6	Scorch Red	AY2ER6	2029	4992LM
R4	Barracuda Orange		4959AH**	4959LH
T3	Honey Bronze Met.	AY2ET3	2030	4993L
T5	Bronze Fire Met.	AY2ET5	2031	4994LH
T7	Saddler Bronze Met.	AY1ET7	2032	4995LH
W1	Alpine White	AY1EW1	81574	4887L
X9	Black Velvet	AY1TX9	9300	88L
Y21	Sunfire Yellow	AY1DY2	81574	4887L
Y3	Yellow Gold	AY1DY3	81575	4888L
Y4	Spanish Gold Met.	AY2EY4	2034	4997L

** = DuPont acrylic enamel code.

you apply the fresh lacquer. Otherwise, the new paint will not bond to the car. The choice is yours. Acrylic enamel is correct, but the shine of acrylic lacquer is more likely to impress the average car show judge, except those at concours showings who will deduct points for having the wrong finish.

Do not change the color, as color codes are clearly listed on the fender tag. On the 1967-1968 models, the paint code is on the bottom line under the heading PNT, which stands for paint. On the 1969-1974 models, the paint code will begin the second line from the bottom. Two-tone cars will use two different paint codes, the first code for the roof color and the second for the body. Note that on 1971-1974 models the roof color begins the third line from the bottom, and the code for the body color still begins the second line. Listed in the charts are the paint codes with the original paint numbers for the correct Ditzler acrylic enamel. Paint numbers for DuPont's acrylic lacquer finishes in the same colors are also listed for reference.

1970 Exterior Paint Colors

Paint Code	Color Name	Chrysler No.	Ditzler Acrylic Enamel	DuPont Acrylic Lacquer
A4	Silver Poly	AY2EA4	2016	4979L
B3	Light Blue Poly	AY2EB3	2018	4981L
B5	Bright Blue Poly	AY2EB5	2019	4982L
B7	Dark Blue Poly	AYE2B7	2020	4983L
C7	Plum Crazy	AY2EB7	2210	5182LM
E5	Rally Red	AY2FE5	2136	5092LM
F4	Lime Green Met.	AYE2F4	2133	5085L
F8	Ivy Green Met.	AY2EF8	43786	4988L
J5	Sub Lime	AY1FJ5	2128	5181L
K2	Vitamin C Orange	AY2FK2	2201	5065LH
K3	Burnt Orange	AY2FK3	2135	5087LM
K5	Deep Burnt Orange	AY2FK5	2135	5088LM
L1	Sand Pebble Beige	AY2EL1	22542	4998L
P6	Frosted Teal	AY2FP6	2132	5084L
R6	Scorch Red	AY2ER6	2029	4992LM
T3	Sahara Tan	AY2ET3	2031	5089L
T6	Burnt Tan	AY2FT6	2131	5089L
V2	Hemi Orange	AY1EV2	2186	5067LH
W1	Alpine White	AY1EW1	81574	4887L
X9	Black Velvet	AY1TX9	9300	88L
Y1	Top Banana	AY1DY1	2211	5180L
Y2	Sunfire Yellow		4887A**#	5077LH#
Y3	Yellow Gold	AY1DY3	81575	5308LH
Y4	Citron Mist	AY2FY4	2117	5086L
Y6	Citron Gold	AY2FY6	2102	5077LH

Note: Some color names differ between the makes although the codes are the same. For example, Y1 is Top Banana on a Challenger and Lemon Twist on a Barracuda. Refer to the paint code in the proper year for your refinishing needs.
** = DuPont acrylic enamel code; # = Not available on Challenger.

1971 Exterior Paint Colors

Paint Code	Color Name	Chrysler No.	Ditzler Acrylic Enamel	DuPont Acrylic Lacquer
A4	Gunmetal Gray	AY2GA4	2014	5245L
B2	Light Blue Pcly	AY2GB3	2304	5246L
B5	True Blue Poly	AY2GB5	2306	5251L
B7	Evening Blue Poly	AYEGB7	2306	5249L
C7	Plum Crazy	AY2EB7	2210	5182LM
E5	Rally Red	AY2FE5	2136	5092LM
F3	Amber Sherwood	AY2GF3	2316	5254L
F7	Ivy Green Met.	AY2GF7	2317	5255L
J6	Sassy Green	AY2GJ6	2319	5127L
K6	Autumn Bronze	AY2GK6	2312	5257LH
K3	Burnt Orange	AY2FK3	2135	5087LM
L5	Bahama Yellcw	AY1EL5	2325	5257LM
T2	Tunisian Tan	AY2GT2	2313	5259L
V2	Hemi Orange	AY1EV2	2186	5067LH
W3	Sno-White	AY1GW3	2300	5262L
X9	Black Velvet	AY1TX9	9300	99L
Y1	Top Banana	AY1FY1	2211	5180L
Y3	Citron Yella	AY1FY3	2320	5308LH
Y8	Gold Leaf	AY2G48	2307	5309LH
Y9	Tawny Gold	AY2GY9	2311	5266 L

Note: Some color names differ between the makes although the codes are the same. For example Y1 is Top Banana on a Challenger and Lemon Twist on a Barracuda. Refer to the paint code in the proper year for your refinishing needs.

1972 Exterior Paint Colors

Paint Code	Color Name	Chrysler No.	Ditzler Acrylic Enamel	DuPont Acrylic Lacquer
A4	Winchester Gray	AY2GA4	2314	5245L
B1	Blue Sky	AY1HB1	2424	5411L
B3	Basin Street Blue	AY1TB3	2423	5351L
B5	True Blue	AY2GB5	2306	5251L ^
E5	Red	AY1FE5	2136	5929L
F7	Sherwood Green	AY2GF7	2317	5255L
F3	Amber Sherwood	AY2GF3	2316	5254L
T6	Mojave Tan	AY2HT6	2426	5421L
T8	Chestnut	AY2HT8	2425	5422L
V2	Hemi Orange	AY2EV2	2186	5967L
W1	Spinnaker White	AY1EW1	2033	4996L
X9	Formal Black	AY1TX9	9300	99L
Y1	Lemon Twist	AY1FY1	2211	5180L
Y4	Honeydew	AY2GY4	2310	5236L
Y8	Gold Leaf Poly	AY2GY8	2307	5309L
Y9	Tawny Gold	AY2GY9	2311	5266L

1973 Exterior Paint Colors

Paint Code	Color Name	Chrysler No.	Ditzler Acrylic Enamel	DuPont Acrylic Lacquer
A5	Dark Silver	AY70JA5	2513	5542L
B1	Light Blue	AY69HB1	2424	5411L
B3	Super Blue		2423	5351L
B5	Bright Blue	AY70GB5	2306	5574L
E5	Bright Red	AY69FE5	2136	5092LM
F1	Pale Green	AY69JF1	2515	5544L
F3	Light Green	AY70GF3	2316	5555LH
F8	Dark Green	AY70JF8	2514	5547LH
L4	Parchment	AY69HL4	2427	5415L
K6	Autumn Bronze	AY70GK6	2312	5257LM
V2	Tor Red	AY1EV2	2186	5067LH
W1	Eggshell	AY69EW1	2033	4996L
X9	Black	AY69TX9	9300	99A
Y1	Top Banana	AY69FY1	2211	5180L
Y3	Honey Gold	AY69JY3	2517	5422L
Y6	Golden Haze	AY70JY6	2509	5548LH
Y9	Dark Gold	AY70Y9	2510	5551LH

1974 Exterior Paint Colors

Paint Code	Color Name	Chrysler No.	Ditzler Acrylic Enamel	DuPont Acrylic Lacquer
B1	Light Blue	AY69KB1	2626	4285L
B5	Lucerne Blue	AY70KB5	2627	4285LH
E5	Bright Red	AY69FE5	2136	5092L
E7	Burnished Red	AY70GE7	2321	
G2	Frosty Green	AY69KG2	2629	42860LH
G8	Deep Sherwood	AY70KG8	2631	42861LH
J6	Avocado Gold	AY70KJ6	2632	42862LH
L4*	Parchment	AY69HL4	2427	5415L
L8	Dark Moonstone	AY70KL8	2633	42863L
T5	Sienna	AY70KT5	2534	4264L
T9	Dark Chestnut	AY70KT9	2590	42865LM
W1	Eggshell	AY69EW1	2033	4996L
X9	Black	AY69TX9	9300	99A
Y4	Golden Fawn	AY69KY4	2635	5410L
Y5	Yellow Blaze	AY69KY5	2636	42867LM
Y6	Golden Haze	AY70JY6	2509	42867LM
Y9	Dark Gold	AY70Y9	2510	5551LH

* = Not used on Barracudas; some color names may differ between Dodge and Plymouth. Always refer to the code, not the name.

The 1967-1969 Barracudas used a spilt-type grille. A 1967 model is shown. *Chrysler Historical Photo*

Grilles

All 1967 Barracuda models used the same set of grilles. Listed as part numbers 2785424 (right) and 2785425 (left), it was two separate units, one mounted on each side of the front divider bar. The grilles featured cross-hatched inserts painted dark gray and the frame was painted flat silver. Front turn lamps were housed in the grille and had the appearance of road lamps.

The grille-insert design was changed for 1968 models, and the pattern was of several rows of inverted, vee'd blades. The grille assembly was again a two-part design listed as part numbers 2786548 (right) and 2786549 (left). The textured plastic units were painted flat black on the inner edges of each blade. As in 1967, the front turn lamps were housed in the grille and the frame was painted flat silver.

For 1969, the inserts used a fine cross-hatch pattern. According to Chrysler, two different grilles were used. Those without the Cuda or Formula S package used part numbers 2998196 (right) and 2998197 (left) and the inserts were painted dark gray. Cudas or those with the Formula S package used part numbers 2998198 (right) and 2998199 (left) and the inserts were painted flat black.

In 1970, the all-new Barracuda continued to use the twin-grille theme, but the grille was a one-piece design. The divider bar that was part of the car's sheet metal in 1967-1969 was now part of the plastic grille and featured gill-like slots on the sides. The turn lamps were mounted in the upper frame of the grille.

The grille insert featured a large cross-hatch pattern that was painted flat black. On all models but the AAR, the frame was painted silver; on the AAR model the frame was painted flat black. Cuda models used molding trim on the grille. These moldings added a horizontal bar across each insert, and this molding was painted flat red. The Plymouth nameplate (part number 2998282) was used on the left-hand side of the grilles on all models.

In 1970, Dodge introduced the Challenger, and its grille design was a single-piece design with a small cross-hatch pattern that was painted flat black. On the

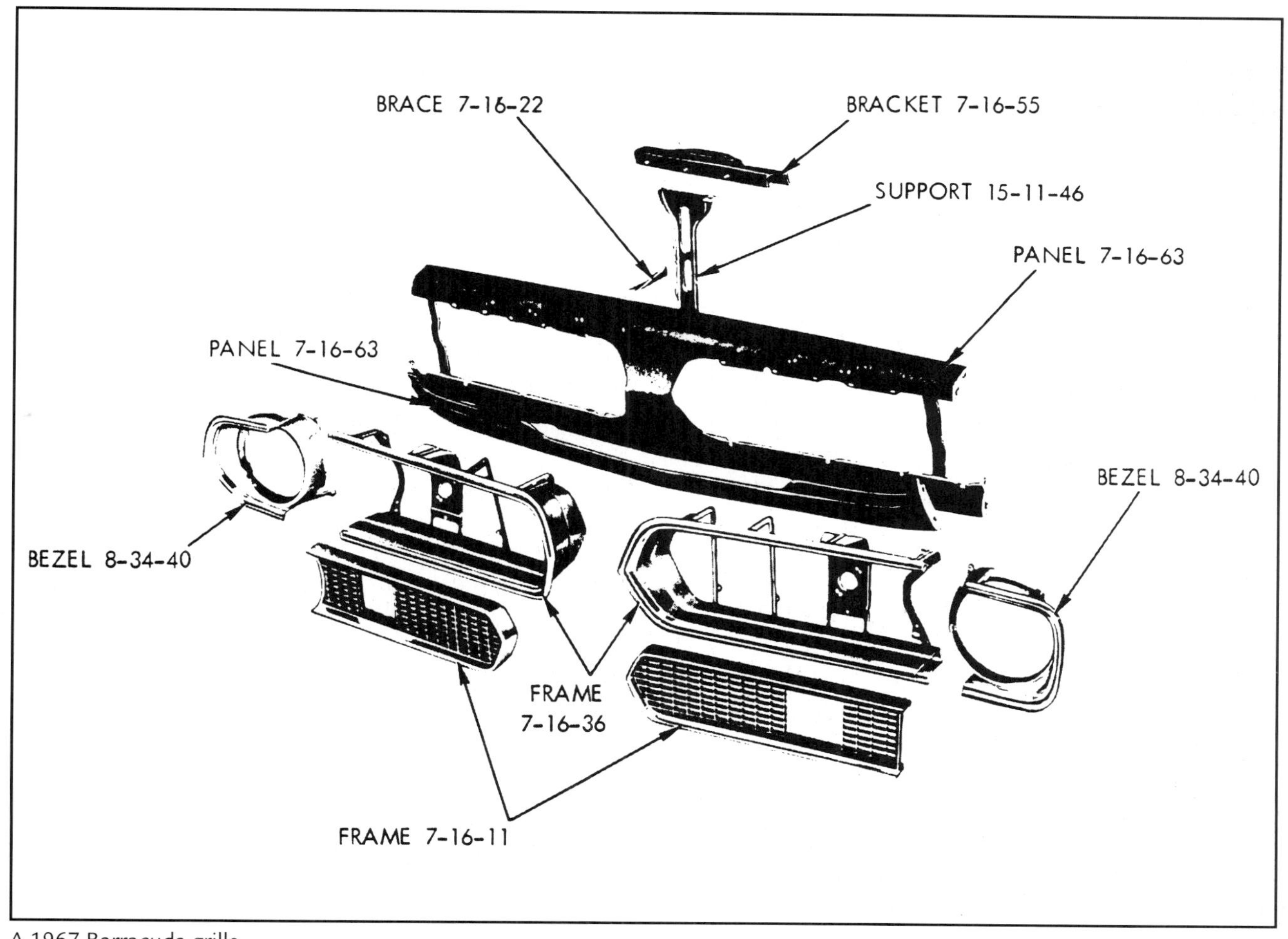

A 1967 Barracuda grille.

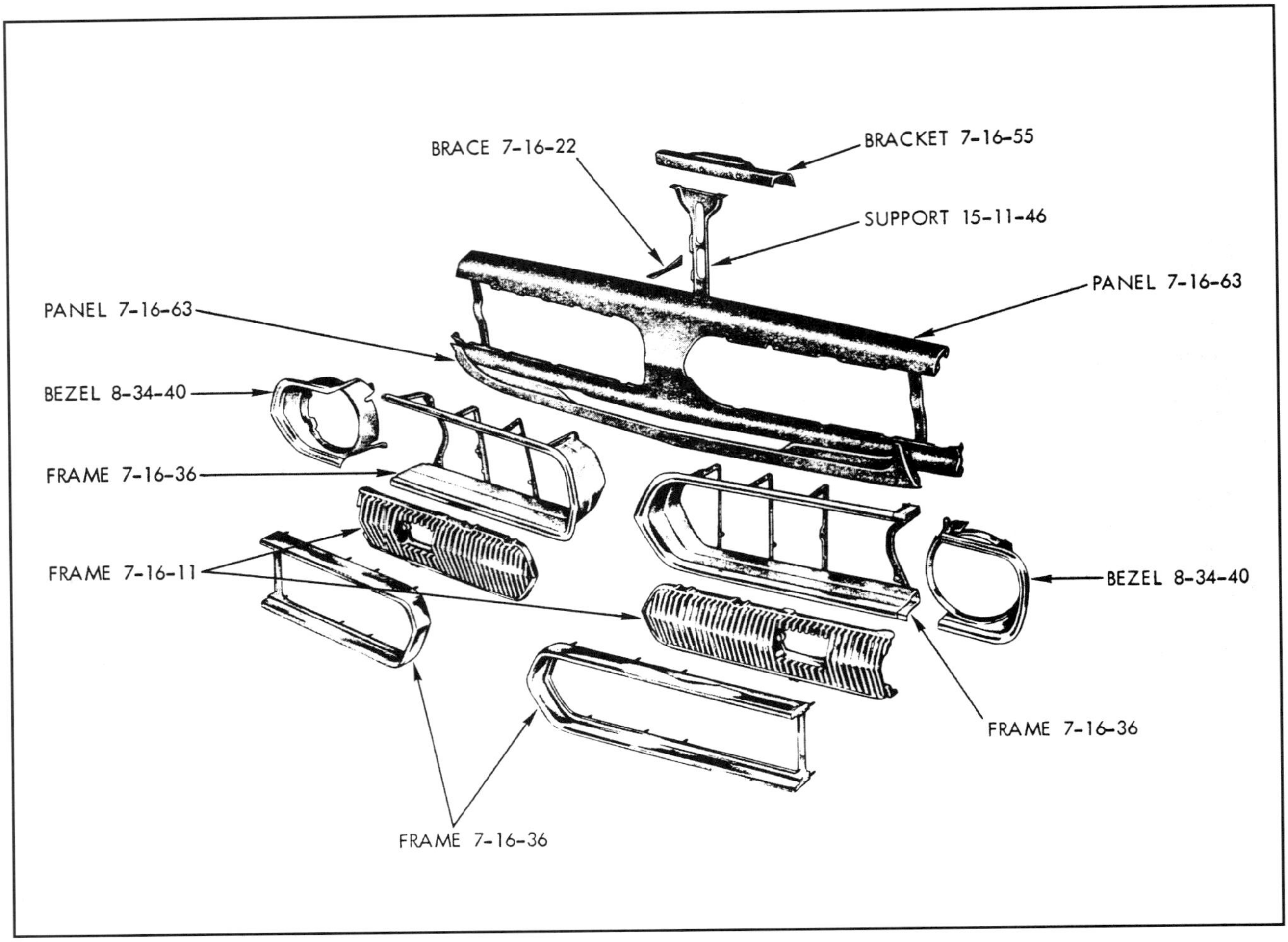
BRACE 7-16-22
BRACKET 7-16-55
SUPPORT 15-11-46
PANEL 7-16-63
PANEL 7-16-63
BEZEL 8-34-40
FRAME 7-16-36
FRAME 7-16-11
BEZEL 8-34-40
FRAME 7-16-36
FRAME 7-16-36

The 1968 Barracuda grille.

Challenger

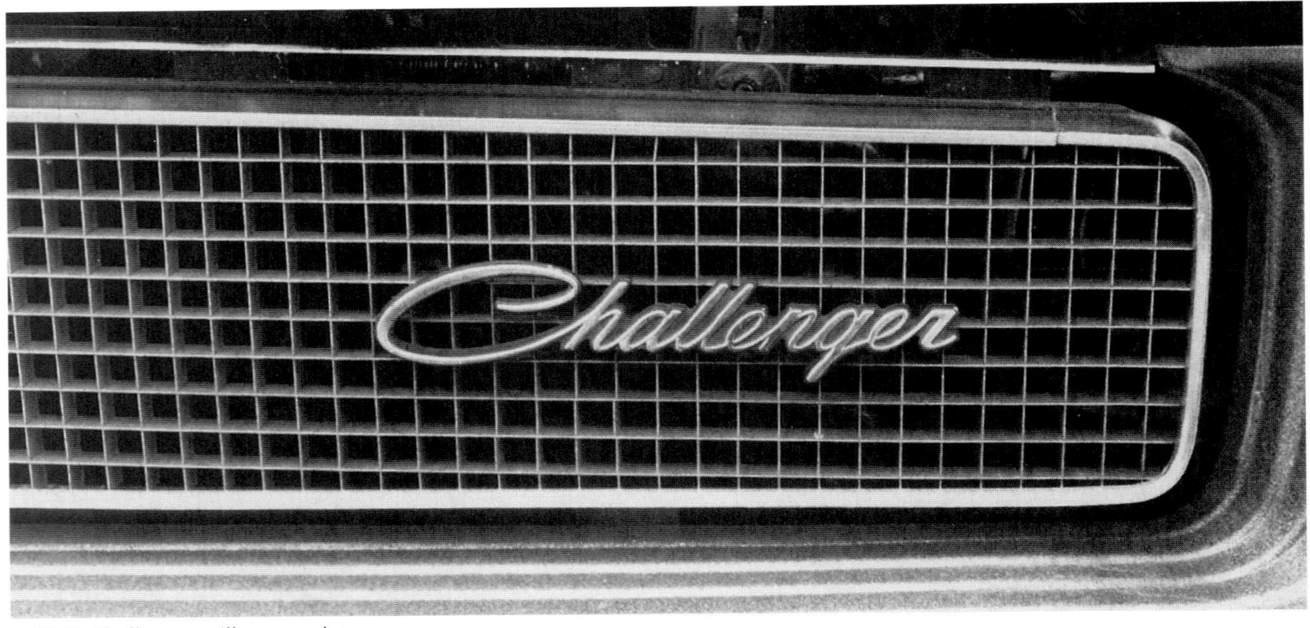

A 1970 Challenger grille nameplate.

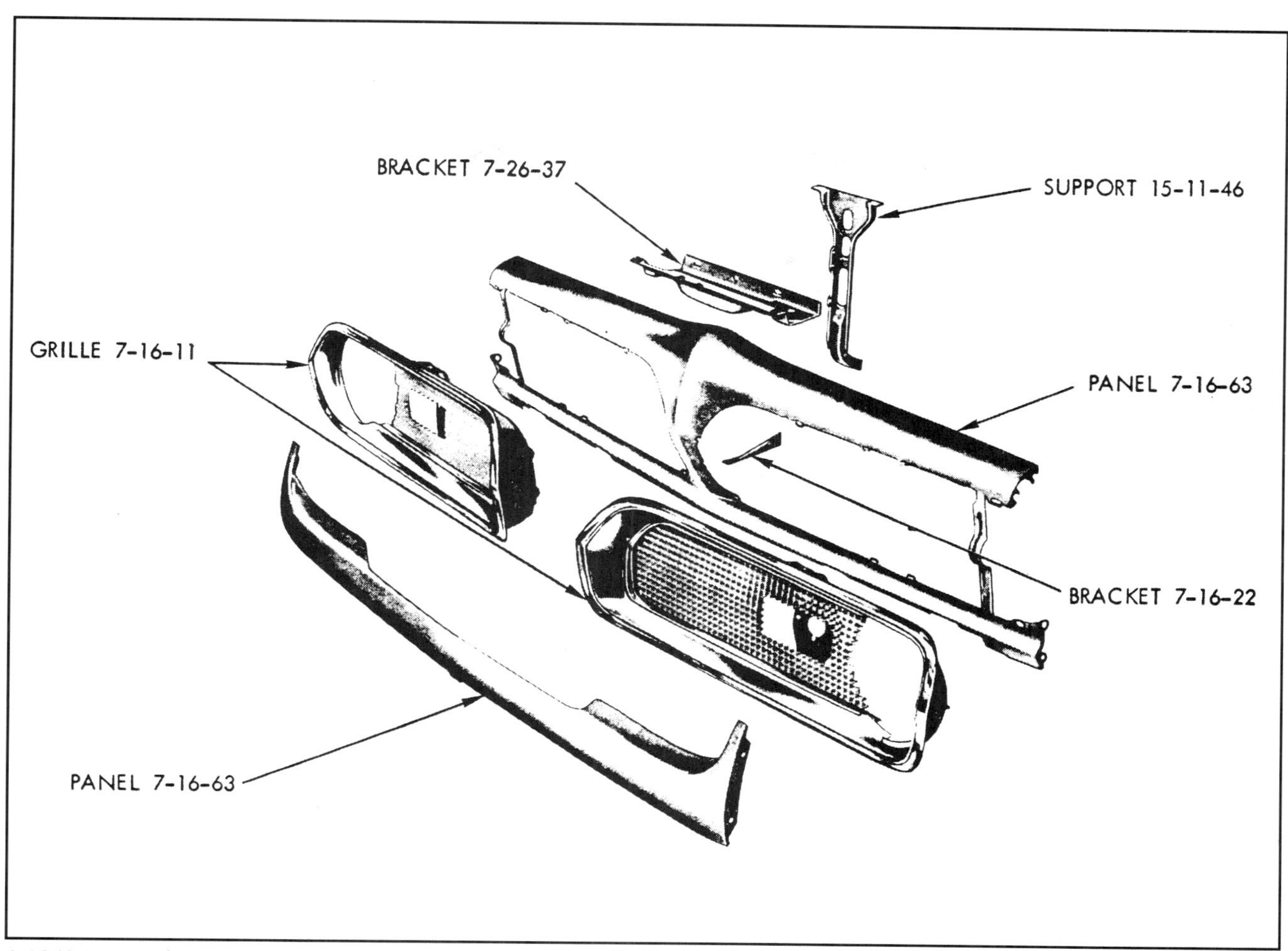

A 1969 Barracuda grille.

base Challenger, the frame was painted dark gray and on the R/T and the T/A models, the frame was painted flat black. The Challenger nameplate (part number 2998546) was mounted on the left-hand side of the grille. On Challenger R/Ts, a red-and-black inlaid R/T emblem (part number 2998547) was used with the Challenger nameplate. Most factory photos of the Challenger T/A show that no nameplate of any kind was used on the grille.

The twin-venturi grille design that graced the Barracuda since 1967 was abandoned on the 1971 Barracudas for a multiple-venturi design. The grille layout now consisted of inserts of thin horizontal blades housed in a frame of six backward-D-shaped vents. All Barracuda models came standard with a grille painted Argent Silver, including the inserts. Colored-keyed grilles were available as optional equipment on Cuda models only in these colors: Avocado (FJ6),- Citron Yella (GY3), Crazy Plum (FC7), Snow White (GW3), Tor-Red (EV2), Bright Blue (GB5), Sherwood Green Metallic (GF7), Autumn Bronze Metallic (GK6), and Rally Red (FE5). Up to build date August 8, 1970, on a Cuda ordered in these colors, the colored grille was standard; after this date it was optional. Only the frame of the grille was painted, and the inserts remained dark gray.

The Challenger picked up the twin-venturi grille design which consisted of two deep inset air scoops. Models without the Rally instrument cluster and without the Shaker Hood used a grille that was painted Argent Silver. All R/Ts and those base Challenger models with the Rally cluster and Shaker Hood used a grille that was painted dark gray. Moldings traced around the outer edges of each venturi on both grilles and the Dodge nameplate (part number 3443554) were used and mounted in the left-hand-side insert. The lone T/A model that was built used a flat black grille with black trim moldings and no Dodge nameplate.

The Barracuda returned to the twin-grille design with single headlamps for the 1972 model. The grille was dominated by a louvered center divider bar, and the inserts of the grille were thin, flat, horizontal slats. Only one grille was used with all Barracuda and Cuda models, and the frame was painted Argent Silver and the inserts were painted flat black.

In 1973 and 1974, the part number was changed to 3672673, but the design and style were the same as in 1972 models.

Unlike the Barracuda, two different grilles continued to be used on 1972 Challenger models. Base Challengers used one and the Challenger Rally, which took the R/T's place, used the other. Both grilles used an insert made of a large cross-hatch pattern. On base models, the insert is painted silver-gray; on Rally models it is painted flat black. A bright molding traced around the outer edge of the grille and the Challenger nameplate (part number 3573505) was mounted on the left-hand side of the grille in both models. This same set of grilles was used again in 1973 and 1974 models with the same restrictions.

Hoods and Header Panels

Only one hood was used on all 1967 Barracudas. It was predrilled to accept black-accented simulated hood vents (part numbers 2582860, right, and 2582861, left). The vents were held on with 16 nuts and seals, and a welt was placed under each vent to prevent water from entering the engine compartment. The Barracuda symbol (a fish in a-circle) was mounted on the front edge of the hood in the center. This emblem was listed as part number 2784610 and was held on with one nut.

Hinges are unique to each side and will not swap places. They used coil hood springs. Hood hinges, hinge springs, and the hood pop-up spring should be painted the same color as the hood. The hood striker should have a unpainted appearance, and the catch should have an unpainted steel appearance, as should the hood latch. The hood release was located at the front of the hood, and it, too, was left unpainted. The look can be duplicated by painting it stainless steel.

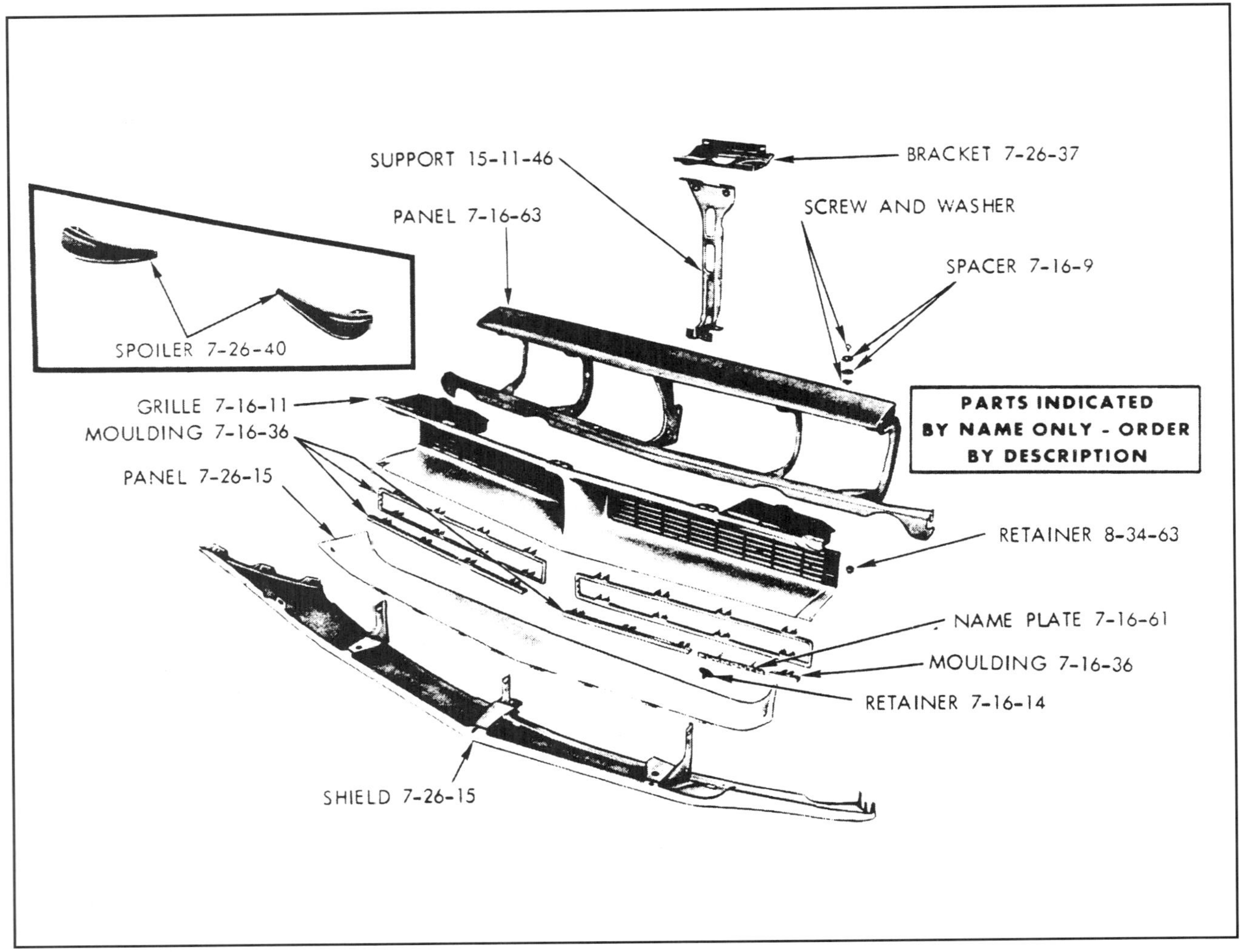

An example of the 1970 Barracuda grille.

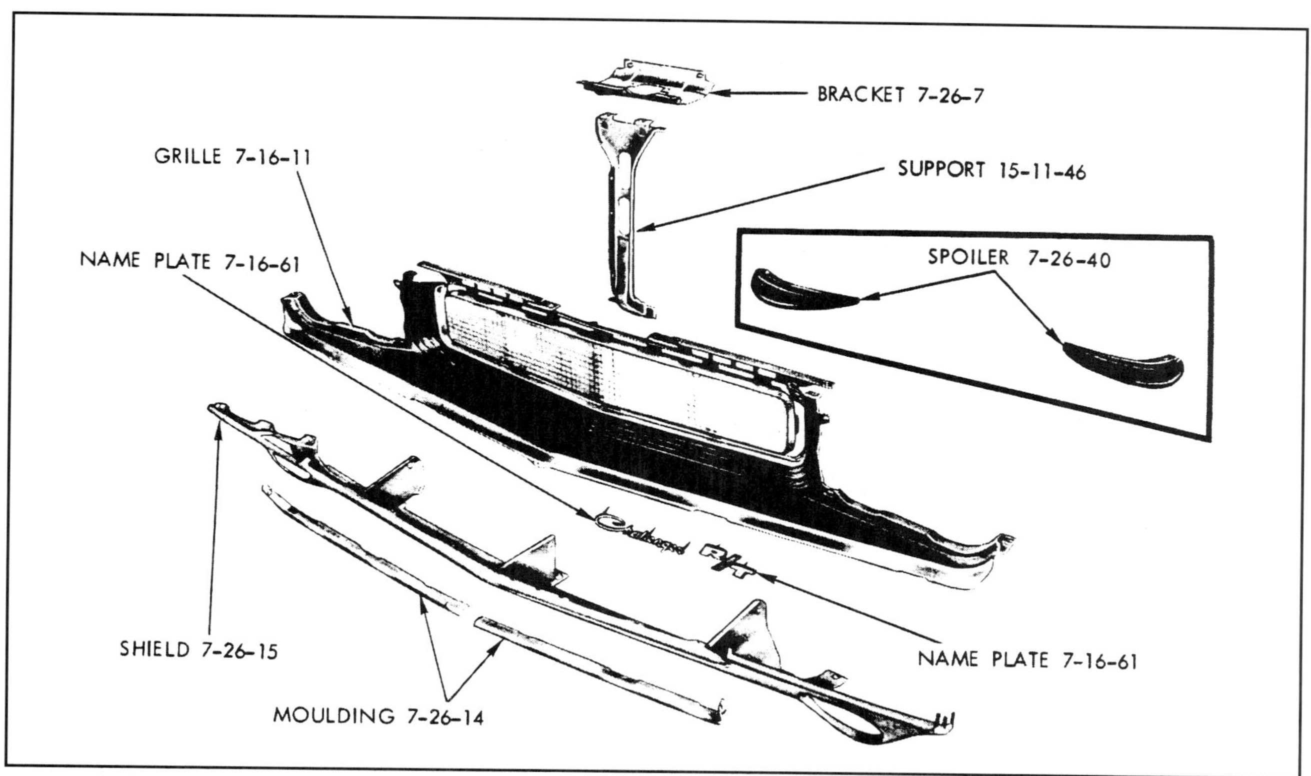

A 1970 Challenger grille.

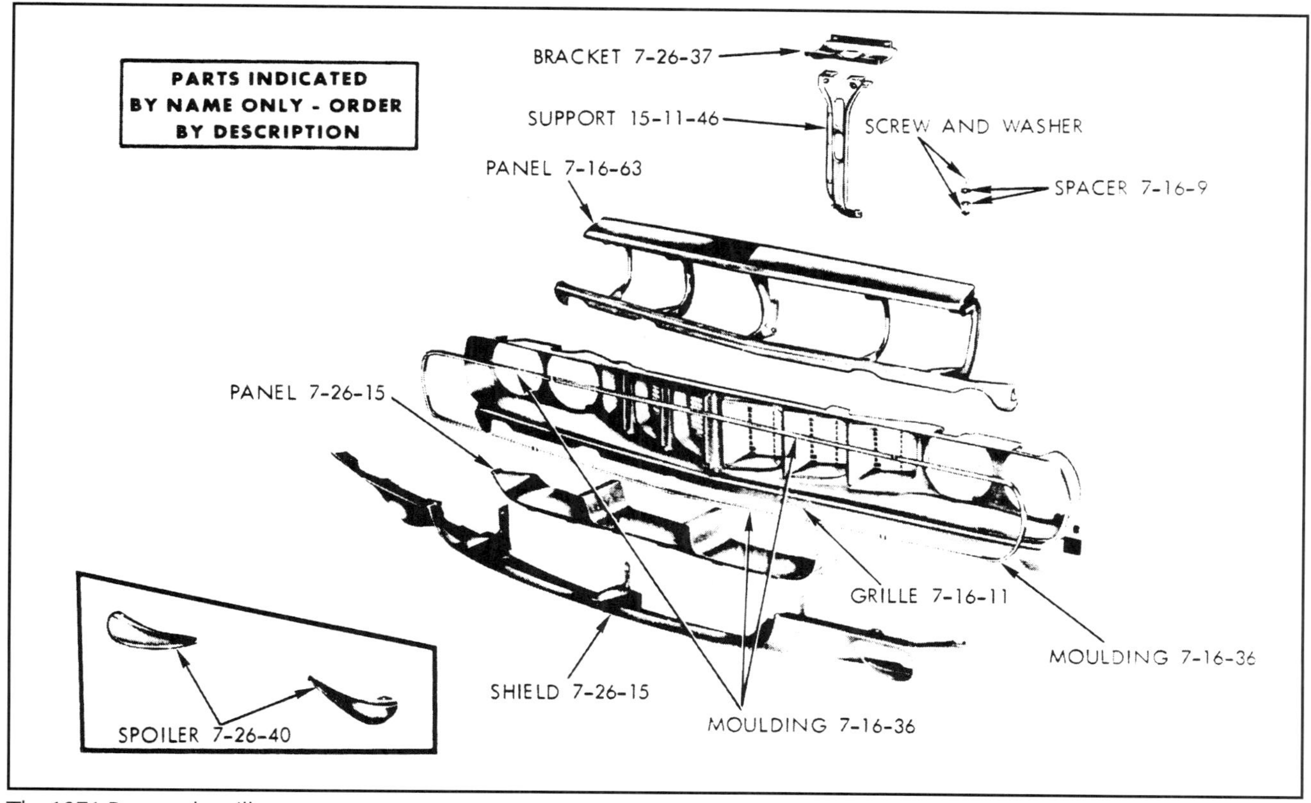

The 1971 Barracuda grille.

A body colored grille was optional on some 1971 Barracudas.

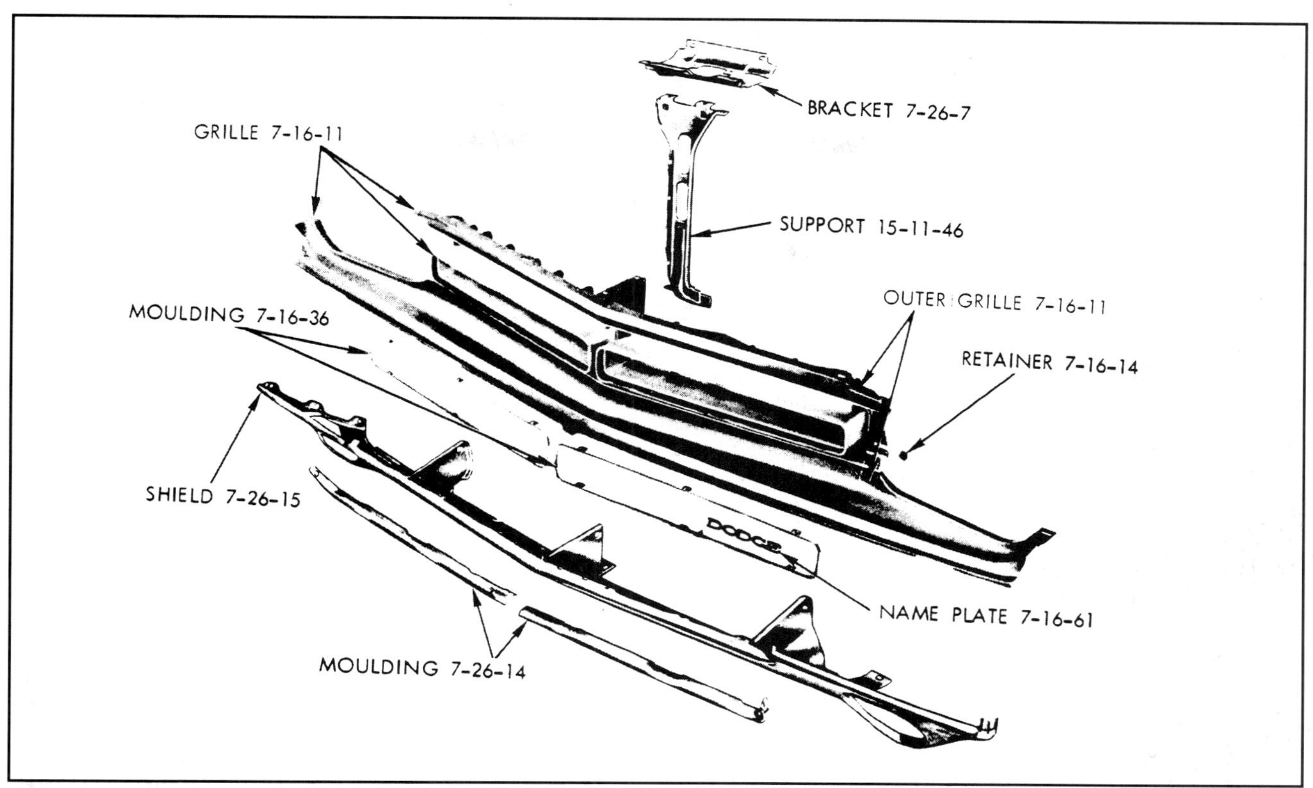

An example of the 1971 Challenger grille.

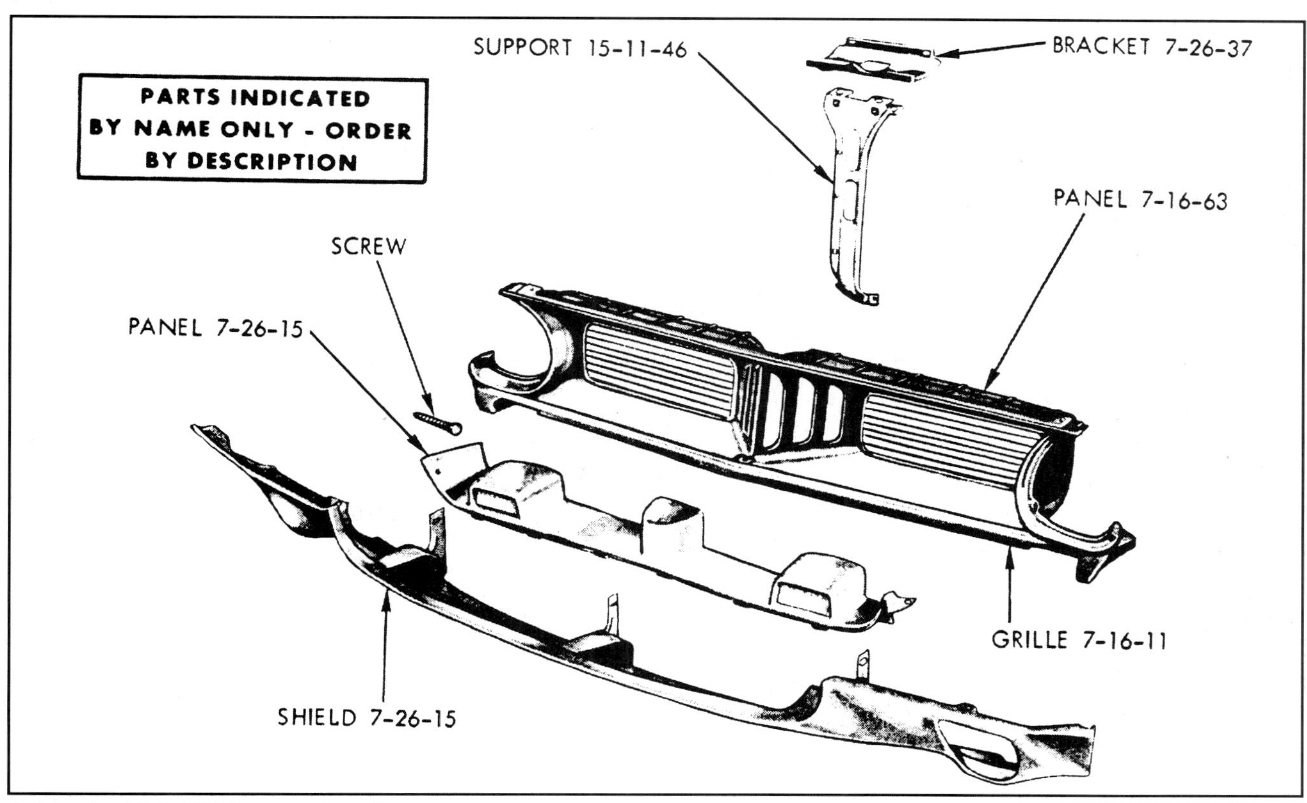

A view of a 1972-1974 Barracuda grille.

On the header panel, the Plymouth name was spelled out in individual bright-plated letters: P-2582767; L-2582768; Y-2582769; M-2582770; O-2582771; U-2582772; T-2582773; and H-2582774. Some letters were held on with a single nut while others were held on with two nuts.

1968 Hoods

Although they look similar and used the same hinges, springs, and pop-up spring, the 1968 Barracuda hood is different from the 1967 hood. It used a different part number and a new safety catch and latch. Simulated hood vents continued to be used, but they were completely restyled. When used with six-cylinder or 318-ci engines, vents with these part numbers—2786642, right, and 2785643, left—were installed. These vents have no engine callouts. If the 340-ci engine was ordered, then special vents were used that had callouts that read "340-S" inlaid in red on a black background. These vents were listed as part numbers 2786640 (right) and 2786641 (left). With the 383-ci engine, the vents read "383-S," and they were listed as part numbers 2785746 (right) and 2785747 (left).

Another carry-over from the 1967 model was the fish emblem at the front of the hood, and it used the same part number. When option code 355 ("Light Package") was ordered, a set of hood-mounted turn indicators were mounted on the front edge of the hood. The Plymouth nameplate was now a single emblem listed as part number 2785791 positioned on the left-hand side of the front header panel.

The Hurst-built 1968 Hemi Barracuda used a special fiberglass lift-off hood with a large center Ram Charger-type hood scoop. Hinges, the safety catch latch, and hood pop-up spring were all removed and the hood was held in place with four NASCAR-style hood-down pins. The hood scoop had a wide-mouth design that required two support posts to keep it from collapsing under full throttle. No Barracuda fish emblem was used on this hood, but the Plymouth nameplate was used on the header panel.

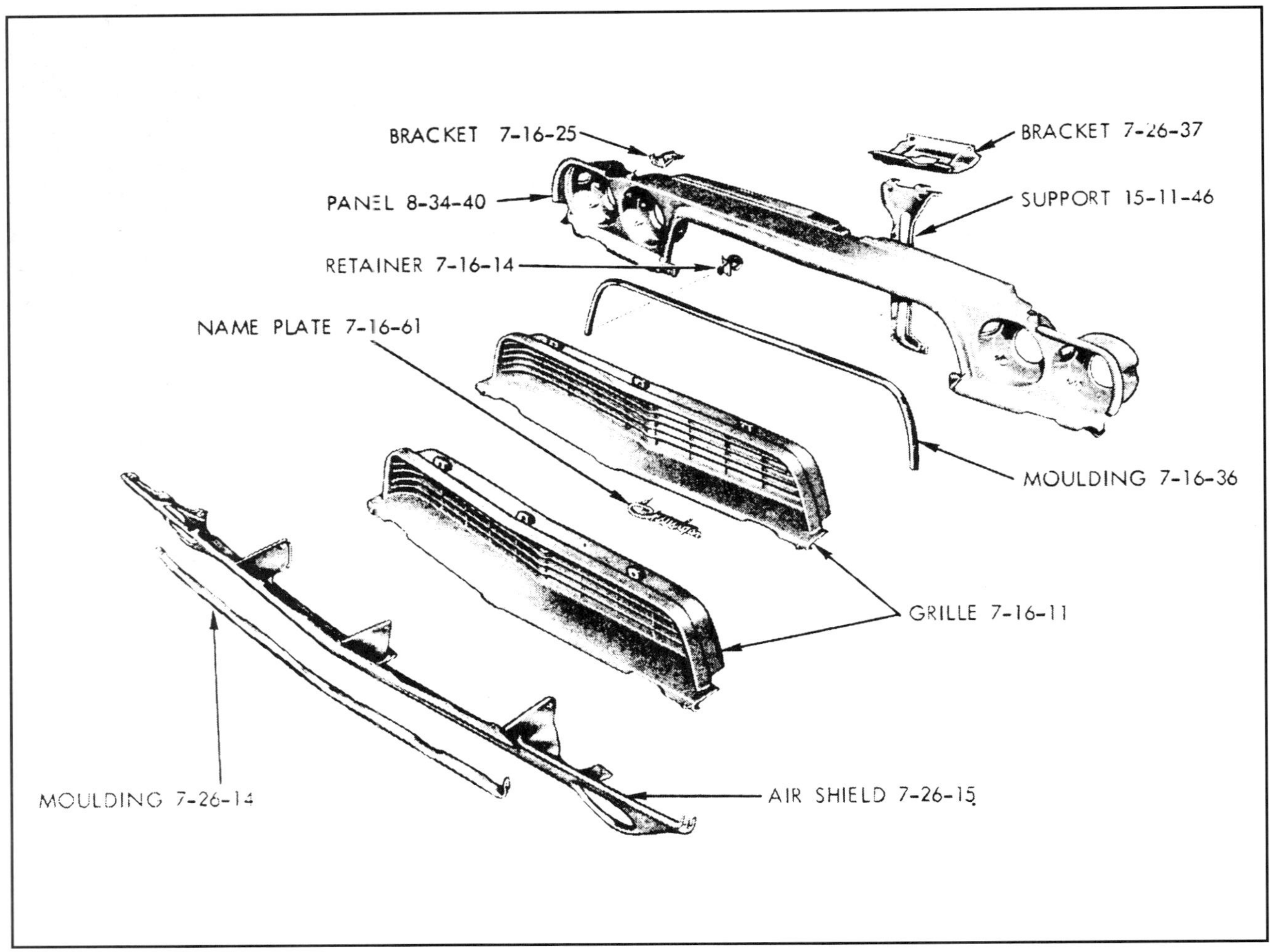

The 1972-1974 Challenger grille.

A 1968 Barracuda hood with the Formula S package. *Chrysler Historical Photo*

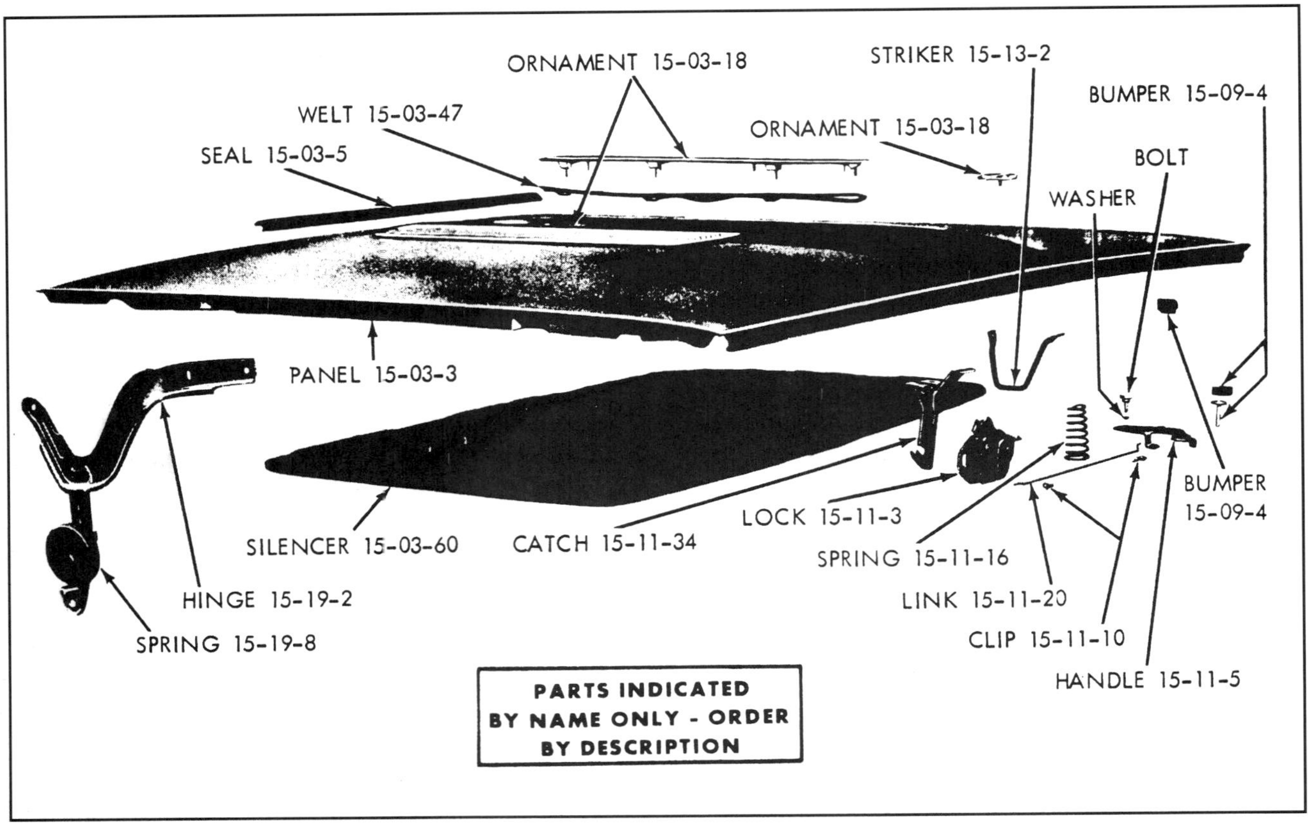

ORNAMENT 15-03-18
STRIKER 15-13-2
BUMPER 15-09-4
WELT 15-03-47
ORNAMENT 15-03-18
SEAL 15-03-5
BOLT
WASHER
PANEL 15-03-3
BUMPER 15-09-4
LOCK 15-11-3
SILENCER 15-03-60
CATCH 15-11-34
SPRING 15-11-16
HINGE 15-19-2
LINK 15-11-20
CLIP 15-11-10
SPRING 15-19-8
HANDLE 15-11-5

PARTS INDICATED BY NAME ONLY - ORDER BY DESCRIPTION

A 1967 Barracuda hood, which was typical of 1968-1969 hood styles.

A 1969 Barracuda fastback with the Cuda 383 package. *Chrysler Historical Photo*

1969 Hoods

In 1969, the simulated hood vents were abandoned for a clean, flat hood. This hood was used on all models, including those with the Cuda package. When the Cuda option packages A56 (Cuda 340) or A57 (Cuda 383) were marked off, two tiny hood scoops were installed at the back of the hood. Each scoop requires four holes to be drilled into the standard hood. No holes were cut into the hood, so the scoops were nonfunctional. Also included in these packages were black tape stripes that were routed under the scoops, not over them. The scoops themselves were painted flat black to match the stripe. All Cuda 440 models feature these scoops and stripes.

The hood hinges were the same parts that were used in the two previous years, as were the springs. Hinges and hood springs were painted the same color as the hood, but a dab of red paint was used on the springs for identification. Also the same as in previous years were the hood striker and hood pop-up spring. The hood release latch was completely redesigned, and the release lever hung down behind the grille. The latch was unpainted and the handle itself was painted flat black. To duplicate the fresh factory look of the latch, paint it stainless steel. No fish emblem was used on the front of this hood, but front turn-signal lamps were still part of the light package now listed as A01 on the option sheets. A Plymouth nameplate was in the same location that it was in in 1968 and used the same part number.

1970 Hoods

Several hoods were used in 1970, and each model used one of four different hoods. Base Barracudas (B-H) and the Gran Coupe (B-P) models used a flat steel hood listed as part number 2934856, which used no nameplates or trim. Cuda models (B-S) used a hood with twin molded-in, simulated air scoops. This hood was listed as part number 3417069. On the outboard sides of each scoop engine were callout badges with the Cuda nameplate. The numbers and lettering were inlaid in red, and the following emblems were used: Cuda 383, 2998796; Cuda 440, 2998797; Cuda 440-6, 2998798; Cuda 340, 3443159; and Hemi Cuda, 3462269.

The Cuda hood became an option on base Barracudas and Gran Coupe models after November 25, 1969. It was called the Performance Hood (J54), and to get this option, both the J54 and the hood hold-down pin (option J45) had to be checked off. If the 340-ci engine

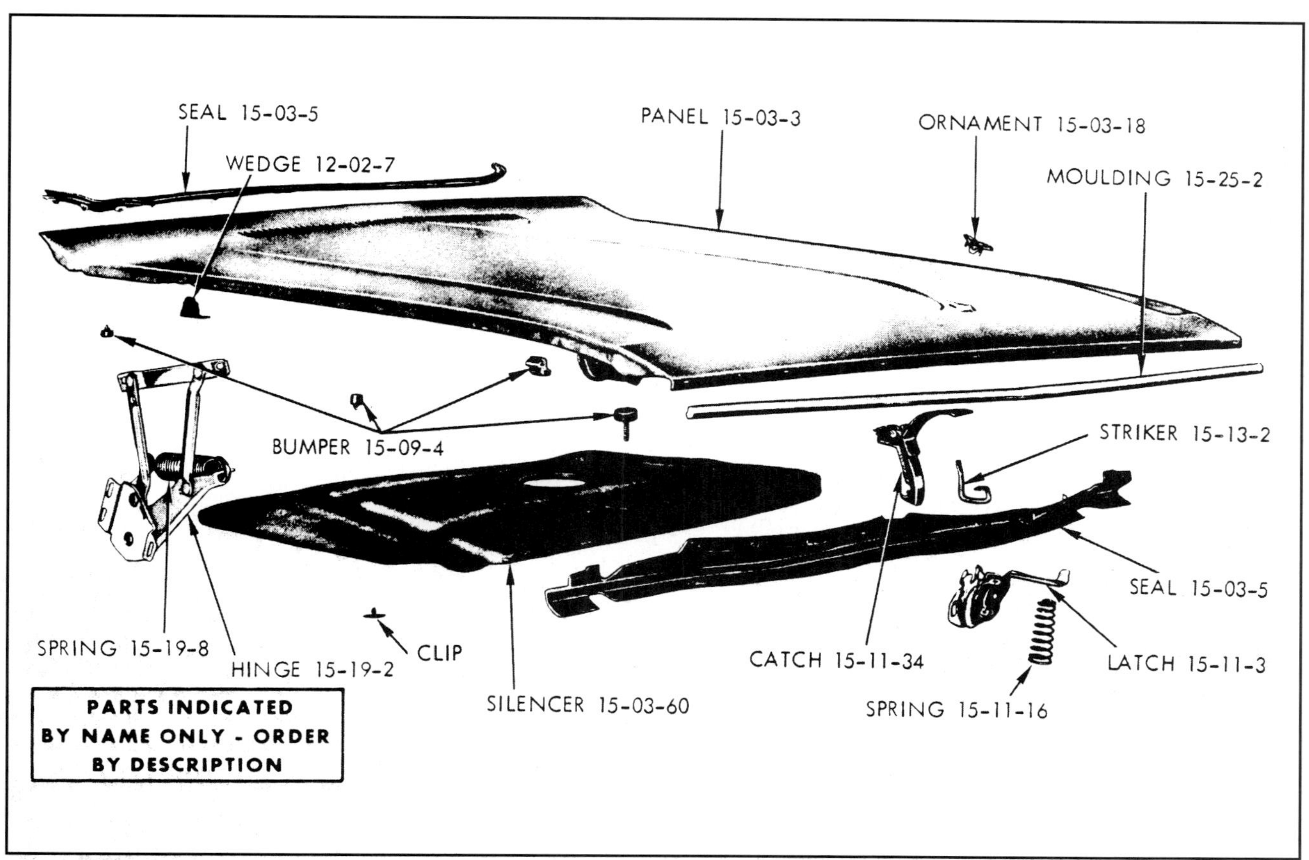

A look at the 1970-1974 Challenger hood, which was typical of Barracuda hood styles.

was also checked off, then callouts that read "340 Four Barrel" (part number 3577361) were used. Use of the "Cuda 340" callouts on a Barracuda or Gran Coupe would be incorrect.

The Fresh Air Hood option (N96), commonly called the Shaker Hood, was listed as part number 2998805 and was an extra-cost option for cars with a 340-ci, 383-ci, or 440-ci engine, and was standard on Cudas with a 426-ci Hemi. It was used with Hemi cars and those models with the 440 3x2-barrel powerplant all year.

Beginning on July 29, 1969, the Shaker Hood became available with the 340-ci, 383-ci (335 horse power), and the 440-ci four-barrel engines, including the 340-ci base Barracudas and Gran Coupes. But this was the case only until December 12, 1969, when orders of Shaker Hoods with the 340-ci engines were unexpectedly halted.

The Fresh Air hood has a hole cut out in the center, and the air cleaner assembly will stick up through this opening. The top of the air cleaner was designed as twin air scoops that vibrated with the engine, thus giving the hood its nickname. Engine callouts were placed on each side of the scoop. The same emblems used on the standard Cuda hood were used on the sides of the Shaker Hood scoops, with the exception of the 340-ci. Those used on the performance hood that read "Cuda 340" are not the same callouts used on the Shaker Hood. On the Shaker Hood, part number 3462271 was used, although it still read "Cuda 340." The two are not the same length and will not interchange. Hood hold-down pins were included when this hood was ordered.

A fourth fiberglass hood was used only on the AAR Cuda. This hood was made of fiberglass and listed as

A hood with no air scoops was standard on all 1970-1974 Barracuda models. *Chrysler Historical Photo*

Cuda models came standard with twin simulated air scoops. *Chrysler Historical Photo*

The Shaker Hood is a desirable performance option. *Chrysler Historical Photo*

part number 3443686. It was painted flat black and featured a functional, molded-in air scoop. NASCAR-type hold-down pins were used at the front end of the hood. The latch and pop-up spring were eliminated with the AAR hood, which also required special low-tension hood springs.

With the new design, all hood components were also restyled. The hinges were listed as part numbers 2945842 (right) and 2945843 (left) for all hoods. However, hood springs were different for various hoods. The standard flat hood and the performance (Cuda) hood used the same set of springs listed as part number 3586088, which fits either side. The Shaker Hood and the AAR Cuda hood required the use of lower-tension springs to avoid damaging the hood. Each used a different set of springs, as the Shaker Hood used part number 3586092, while the AAR used extra-low-tension springs listed as part number 3586515. The hood latch was unpainted and listed as part number 2990676. The latch handle was also unique for this year, it should have a cast-steel appearance. Paint the striker (part number 2486697), hinges, and springs (including the pop-up spring) the same color as the hood.

Four hoods were also used on the Challenger models. Base Challenger models used the flat steel hood (part number 2934850). This hood used the Dodge tri-star emblem (part number 2449932) and a bright molding at the front edge. The Challenger R/T models used a hood (part number 3417066) with a raised center dome with twin simulated air scoops. On the sides of these scoops were the engine callouts that were inlaid in red. The following were used: Hemi, 2998800; 383 Magnum, 2998801; 440 Magnum, 2998802; 440 Six Pack, 2998804; and 340 Four Barrel, 3443247.

The same molding used on the stock flat hood was also used on this hood. However, the tri-star emblem was not used; instead the Dodge name was spelled out in single-block lettering. The following letters were used: D, 2579655; O, 2998231; G, 2579657; and E, 2579658. Unlike on the Barracuda, the base Challenger was not available with this hood as an option.

The Shaker Hood option was also available on Challenger R/Ts, only it was listed as part number 3443271 and was available for all engines with a four-barrel or multiple carburetors all year long. Unlike Cudas, Challenger R/Ts with a Hemi did not have this as their standard hood, so it is correct to find this car without a Shaker Hood or the N96 code on the fender tag. The Dodge name was spelled out across the hood like the standard R/T, and this hood also used the same molding. Engine callouts were positioned along the sides of the scoop assembly. The callouts were the same as those used on the standard R/T hood, except for the 426 Hemi. This model used special emblems that are unique to each side and will not fit the standard hood nor swap sides. These callouts were listed as part numbers 3462489 (left) and 3462490 (right). Hood hold-down pins were included with this hood.

The Challenger T/A models used a fiberglass hood (part number 3443685) with a molded-in scoop with a center divider bar. The hood was painted flat black and held in place at the front with two NASCAR-style hood hold-down pins. No nameplate was used on this hood and it required a special edge molding listed as part number 3420000.

All 1970 Challenger hoods used the same set of hinges as those used on the Barracudas, but those with the Shaker Hood or the fiberglass hood used low-tension

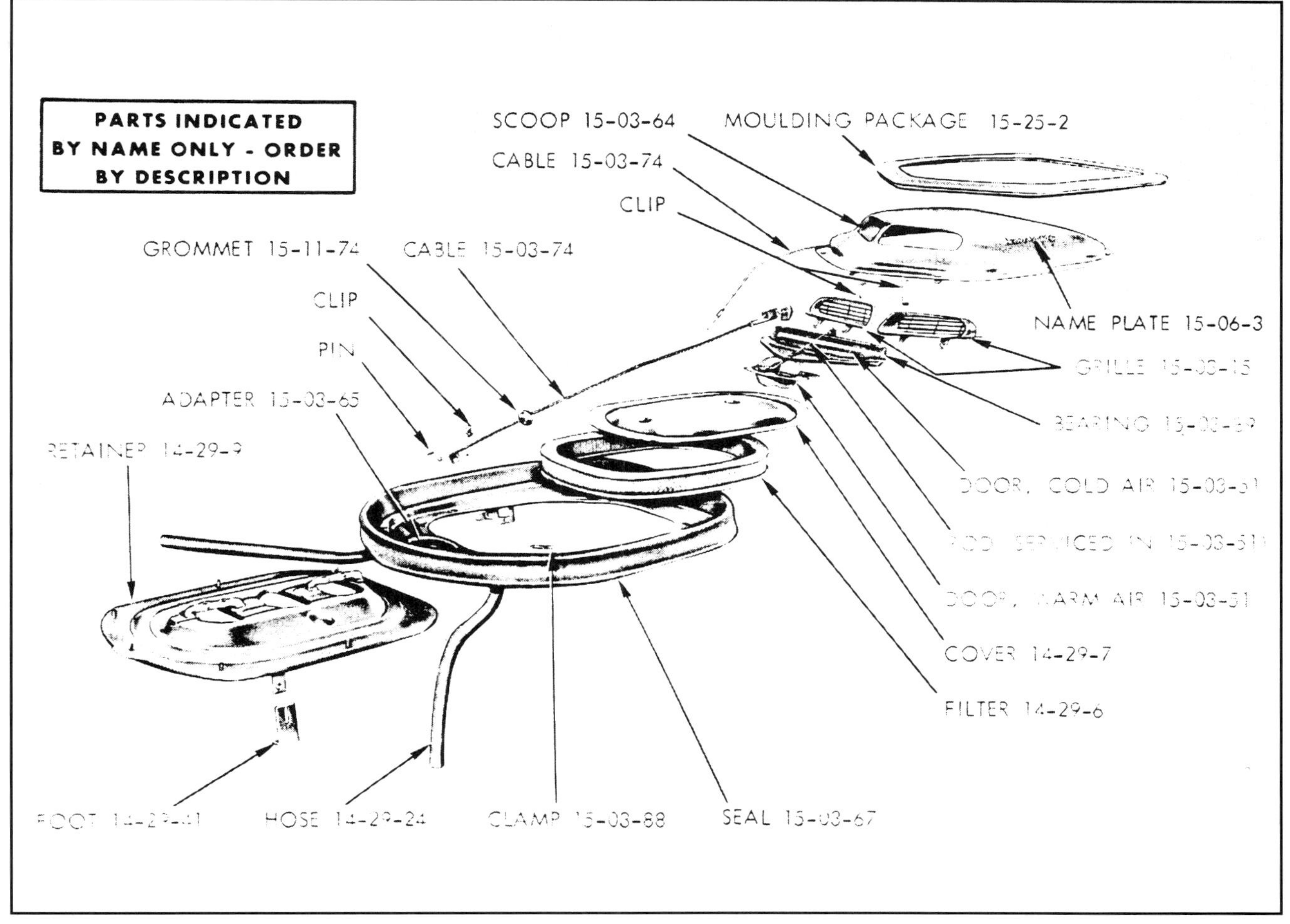

The Shaker air cleaner assembly.

The Shaker Hood requires special bacges in some cases.

springs. The Challenger's Shaker Hood used the same hood springs used on Barracudas with the Shaker Hood, but the T/A model used a different spring (listed as part number 3586214) than those used on the AAR Cuda. Using the improper hood springs could cause damage to the hood. Hood hinges and hood springs were painted the same color as the car, except on the T/A models, where hinges and springs were painted flat black.

The latch assembly for the 1970 Challenger should be left unpainted, an effect that can be duplicated by painting them stainless steel. The latch was listed as part number 2999081. The catch should have an unpainted cast-steel appearance, and it is listed as part number 2999078. The hood pop-up spring is the same unit used in the Barracudas, and it was painted the same color as the hood. The T/A model did not use a latch, catch, or hood pop-up spring.

1971 Hoods

For 1971, the Barracuda used three different hoods. The Cuda used the same hood it used in 1970, but the base Barracuda and Gran Coupe Barracuda used a new hood. Still a flat steel hood, it was now listed as part number 3417996; this hood featured the Plymouth nameplate (part number 2998042) at the front left-hand edge. This emblem was originally held on with three nuts.

The Cuda hood was still optional on base Barracudas and Gran Coupe models and used the same part number and engine callouts as the year before with one exception, the deletion of the "Cuda 440" nameplate. This callout was deleted as the engine was no longer available. The Plymouth nameplate was also used at the front of this hood; it was positioned just below the hood hold-down pin on the left-hand side. Since inventory was to be used up, it is possible that some early-built models may have not received the Plymouth nameplate.

The Shaker Hood was now listed as part number 3443797, and it still featured a hole cut-out in the center for the air cleaner scoop assembly. The same emblems used in 1970 on this scoop were used again in 1971, except for the deletion of the "Cuda 440" nameplate. Like the year before, this hood came standard with hood hold-down pins, and like all other 1971 hoods, it used the Plymouth nameplate at the left front edge. This option was also available on base Barracuda and Gran Coupe models with a 340-ci or 383-ci engine only. When used on these models with a 340-ci engine, the callouts on the side of the scoop read "340 Four Barrel," and this emblem used the same part number it used in 1970.

There is confusion about which callout was used on the sides of the scoop when the 383-ci engine was ordered in a base Barracuda or Gran Coupe model. There were no

383 Four Barrel nameplates available, so most used the Cuda 383 nameplate though they were not true Cuda models. Though available as an over-the-counter part, the AAR Cuda hood was not installed on a production 1971 car from the factory.

Hood hinge springs used the same part numbers with the same restrictions they used in 1970, but the hinges themselves were given new part numbers and were now listed as 3548890 (right) and 3548891 (left). Also changed was the hood latch (part number 2935373) which was restyled to fit both the Barracuda and Challenger lines; it still had an unpainted appearance. The hood pop-up spring and catch were the same parts used in 1970 models.

Not one hood was carried over from 1970 to the 1971 Challenger line. The base Challenger with a 318-ci or 383-ci two-barrel used the standard flat steel hood, which was now listed as part number 3611342. The Dodge tri-star emblem was used at the front of the hood and it used the same part number as in the previous year. The molding at the back of the hood was the same as that used in 1970, but a different molding (part number 3620475) was used at the front of the hood.

All Challengers, including base models, ordered with an engine with a four-barrel or multiple carburetors came standard with the dome hood with the twin simulated air scoops, commonly called an R/T hood. Listed as part number 3482618, the R/T hood used no emblems, except

The 1970 AAR Cuda hood was made of fiberglass.

The fiberglass Challenger T/A hood was used on Challengers ordered with the Shaker Hood option when supplies of the latter ran out. *Chrysler Historical Photo*

the engine callouts on the sides of the scoops. Callouts were the same units used on 1970 models with the exception of the deletion of the 440 Magnum. When the domed hood was installed on a true R/T model, an "R/T" decal in black or white outline lettering was used on the front edge in the center of the hood. The white decal was used on dark-colored cars and the black decal was used on light-colored cars. This hood used the same front and rear moldings as those used on the flat steel hood.

The Shaker Hood was also given a new part number of 3443880, and it was available on any model with a four-barrel or multiple carburetors. Engine callouts were placed on the sides of the air scoop and these callouts used the same part numbers as those used in 1970, except for the deletion of the 440 Six Pack nameplate. This powerplant was still available in the Challenger R/T model, but the 440 callout, listed as part numbers 3462491 (left) and 3462492 (right), was used instead of the "440 Six Pack" on the Shaker Hood.

The Shaker Hood saw limited production, as only 224 models were so equipped. Of these, only 11 were convertibles and 72 were on base Challengers. The hood used the same moldings used on the other two hoods in 1970. The Dodge tri-star emblem was used at the front of this hood, and hood hold-down pins were included. The R/T decal was deleted when ordered with the Shaker Hood option. It is rumored that one 1971 Challenger T/A was built. Its location today is unknown, but it used the same fiberglass hood as was used in 1970. The same hinge, hood springs, striker, and latch used in 1971 Barracudas found their way into the Challengers. However, the safety catch (part number 3508320) is unique to the Challenger line. Finishing is the same as in 1970 models.

1972 Hoods

For 1972 Barracudas, only two hoods were used, as the Shaker Hood was canceled at the end of the 1971 model year. The standard flat hood (part number 3417996) and the Cuda hood (part number 3417997) with two simulated air scoops remained available. As in the previous years, the Cuda hood was optional on the base Barracuda. The Plymouth nameplate (part number 2998042) was used at the front left-hand side of both

continued on page 152

Challenger R/T and Rally models had this style of hood as standard equipment. *Chrysler Historical Photo*

This shows the 1971-1974 Barracuda's hood use of the Plymouth nameplate.

A 1970 Challenger hood latch.

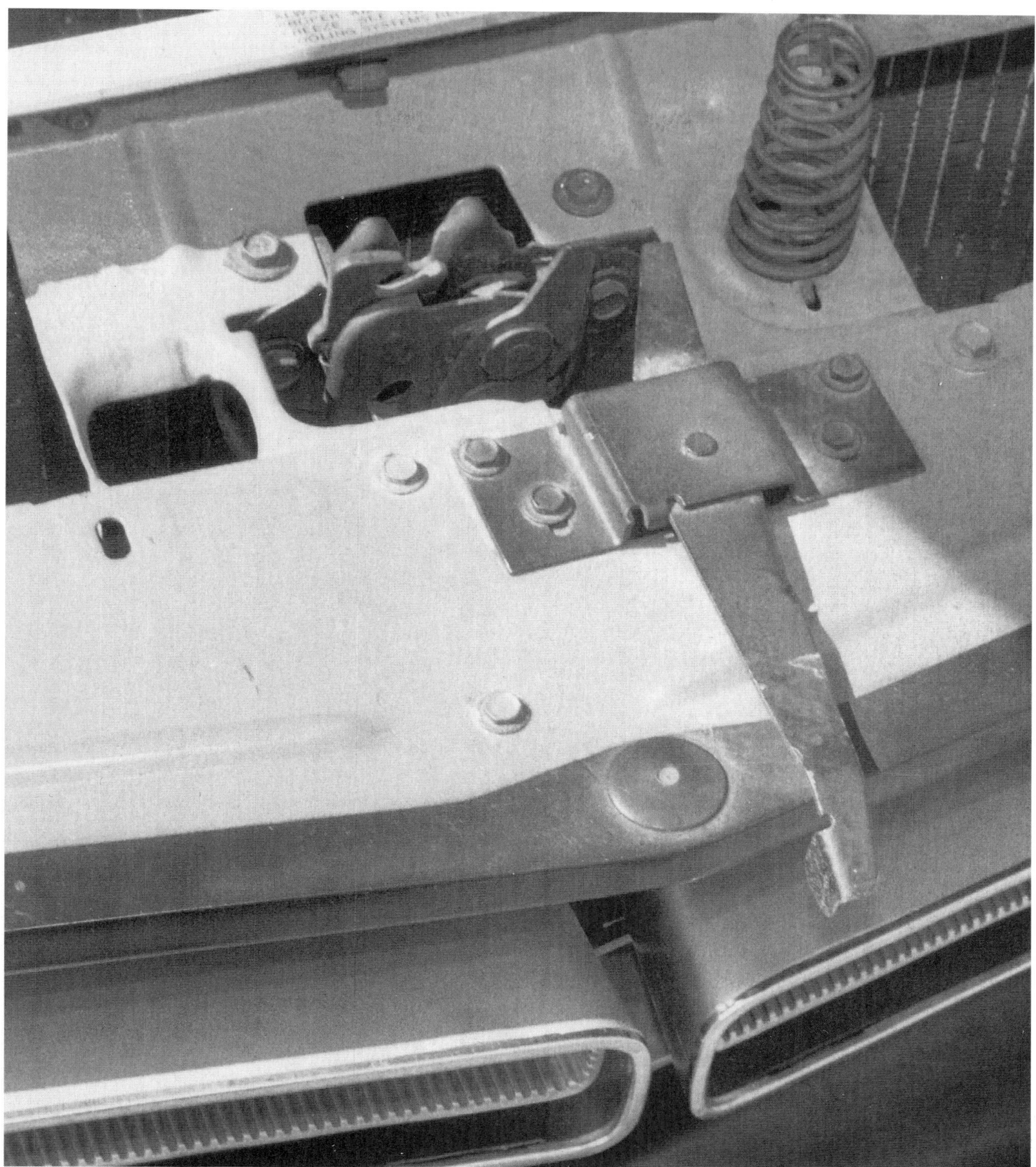
The 1971 Challenger hood latch.

Continued from page 148
hoods. On the Cuda hood, engine callouts were placed on each side of the scoops. Only two were used: on true Cuda models (BS23), the emblem read "Cuda 340" and was listed as part number 3443159. On the base Barracuda model with a 340-ci engine, the callout read "340 Four Barrel" and was listed as part number 3443247.

The Shaker Hood was also dropped from the Challenger's option list, as was the Challenger R/T name. The R/T model was now given the name Rally. Base Challengers with the six-cylinder engine or 318-ci engine used a flat steel hood listed as part number 3611378. All Rally models and all Challengers with a 340-ci engine used a domed hood with simulated twin air scoops that looked just like those used in 1970 and 1971. The Dodge name was spelled at the front of the hood in the center in individual letters; the following letters were used: D, 2579655; O, 2998231; G, 2579657; and E, 2579658. A body color molding, part number 3683011, was used at the front edge of the hood. The molding came in primer and had to be painted to match the car. Only one engine callout was used on the performance hood, and it read "340 Four Barrel" and was listed as part number 3443247.

Hood hinges were restyled and given part numbers 3548888 (right) and 3548889 (left) and fit both Barracuda and Challenger lines. However, the hood springs are different between the lines. Barracudas used part number 3586088 while the Challengers used 3586092. Two different latches were used, and their use was dependent on the

Engine call-outs used on Challengers with a 340-ci engine and the performance hood.

The engine call-out used with a 383-ci engine on 1970-1971 Challengers.

This shows the engine call-out used on Cuda models with the 340-ci engine. Barracudas with the 340-ci engine used a different nameplate.

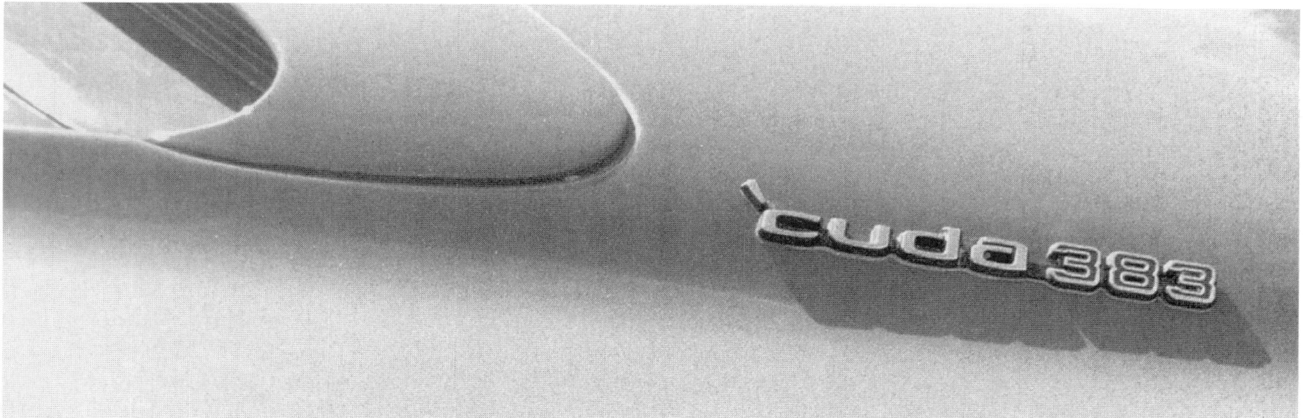

The standard engine call-out on a 1970-1971 Cuda.

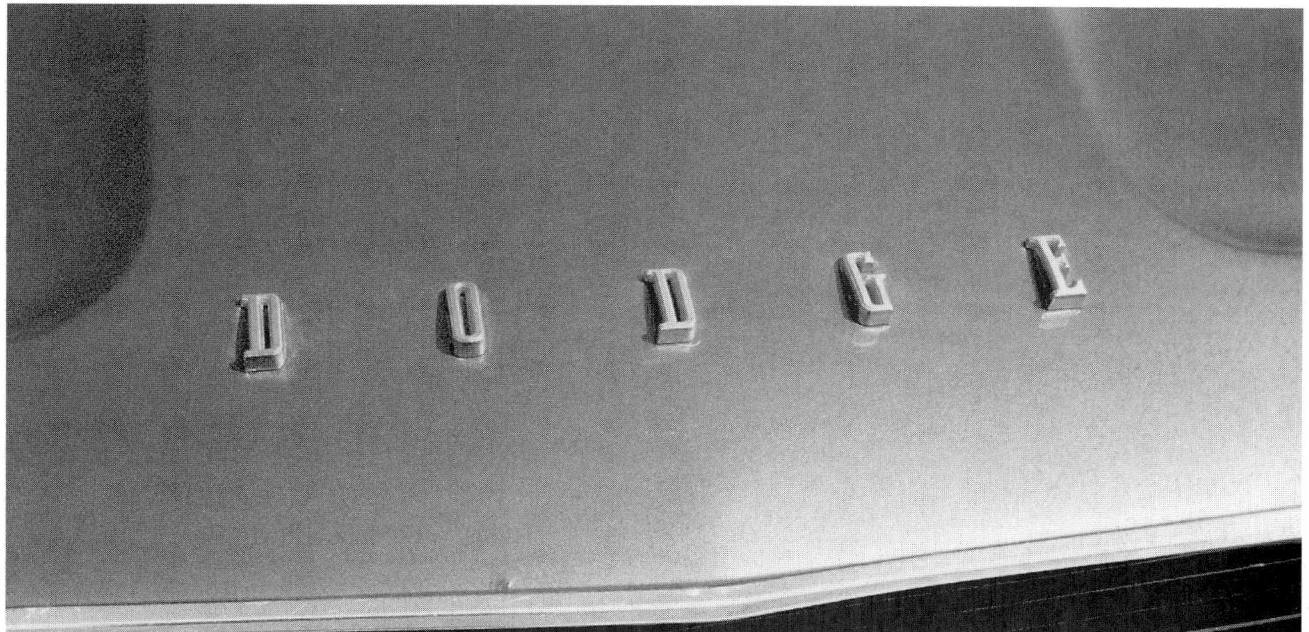

The Dodge name is spelled out across the center of the Challenger R/T's hood.

1967 and 1968 Barracudas with the Formula S package used this fender badge. *Year One*

type of hood release. Those with the hood release handle at the front of the car used part number 2935373, while those with option J52 Inside Hood Release used part number 3670108. This option used a bright T-shaped handle with the words "Hood Release" inlaid in black inside the car. It was mounted under the instrument panel just to the left of the driver. As in the years before, the safety catch did differ between Dodge and Plymouth. Challengers used part number 3508320 while Barracudas used 2945845. Finishing is the same as in previous years.

1973 and 1974 Hoods

The same hoods used on 1972 Barracuda models were used on the 1973 and again on the 1974 models with the same restriction in usage. For 1973, the hood used the same nameplates as it used in 1972, and in 1974 the 340 engine callout was replaced by a callout that read "360 Four Barrel" (part number 3691468) if installed on a standard Barracuda. On the Cuda model the part number was 3691470 and read "Cuda 360."

Challengers in 1973 and 1974 also used the same hoods as in 1972 with the same restrictions. The Dodge

The 1971 Challenger R/T used a decal for its logo on the hood.

A 1967 Barracuda with the 273-ci 4-barrel used this nameplate on the front fender. *Year One*

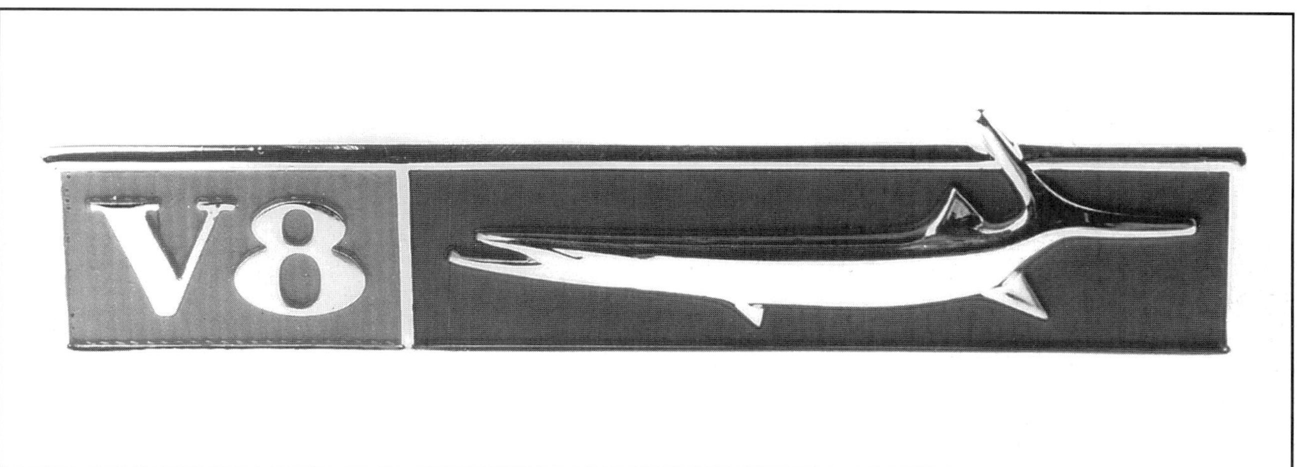

A 1968 273-ci V-8 was identified by this front fender badge. *Year One*

The 1969 Barracuda with the Formula S package used unique call-outs. Those for a 340-ci engine are shown. *Year One*

name was again spelled at the front of both hoods both years, but the lettering was changed. Now the following parts were used: D, 3749006; O, 3749007; G, 3749008; and E, 3749009. The use of 1972-style lettering is not considered correct on 1973 and 1974 models. Also changed was the front molding, which was now listed as part number 3683011. The same callouts used in 1972 were used again in 1973, but in 1974 the "340 Four Barrel" was replaced with a nameplate that read "360 Four Barrel," which was listed as part number 3691468. Hinges were restyled for 1973 models and were listed as part numbers 3582926 (right) and 3582927 (left), and these hinges were used again in 1974. While the hinges changed, the springs did not, and they continued to use the same part numbers used in the 1972 models; hood catches were also the same.

Three different hood latches were used in 1973 models. Those with the hood latch at the front of the car used part number 369862 for both years and both models. However, the Challenger and Barracuda used different release handles. Those 1973 models with an inside hood release built up to June 1973 used part number 3670058, while those built after that date and all 1974 models with this option used part number 3760631. All finishing of components is the same as in 1970.

1970-1971 Gran Coupe Barracudas used this front fender nameplate. *Year One*

Front Fender

The 1967 Barracuda front fender has no turn signal lamps or reflectors. At the front of the forward section

The 1967 and 1970-1971 Barracudas with the 383-ci four-barrel V-8 used this call-out on the fenders. *Year One*

1970-1972 Barracuda script. *Year One*

of the fenders the Barracuda script nameplate, part number 2582878, was used on all body styles and all package options. Behind and just below the script is a small emblem shaped like a fish. This emblem is unique to each side and will not swap positions; they were listed as part numbers 2785320 (right) and 2785321 (left). The fish emblem was used with all applications.

On the rear portion of the front fender in 1967, several different emblems were used, their selection depending on engine size and package options. Those with the Formula S package used a special badge listed as part number 2579443. It was mounted below the beltline and behind the front wheelhouse opening. Those without the Formula S package but with the 273-ci two-barrel V-8 used a V-8 badge listed as part number 2579612. Those with 273-ci four-barrel V-8 used the "Commando V-8" emblem listed as part number 2579613. Those few Barracudas built with the 383-ci used a "383 4-Barrel" medallion listed as part number 2579804. Bright wheel-lip moldings were standard equipment on all Barracuda models and body styles. Part numbers were listed as 2807876 (right) and 2807877 (left), and they were held in place with Phillips-head screws.

The 1968 fender used an amber side-mounted turn signal. More about this lamp can be found in the electrical chapter of this book (chapter 9). Wheel-lip moldings were again standard for all models. They were the same moldings used in 1967, and again they are held on with eight Phillips-head screws. The Barracuda script was moved from the front to behind the front wheelwell opening and was mounted on the beltline. Two different scripts were used: one, listed as part number 2786559, was inlaid in black, while the other, part number 2898939, was solid chrome. There is no explanation regarding why there were two different nameplates.

Just below the script is the engine callout. Those with a six-cylinder used a fish emblem, part number 2785320 (right) and 2785321 (left). These are the same emblems used on the 1967 model. If a V-8 engine was ordered, then an emblem with a fish and a V-8 was used.

The 1970 Challenger with a 318-ci used this set of badges on the fenders.

The 1970 Challenger R/T front fender nameplates.

This callout was deleted if the Formula S package was ordered. When this package was ordered, the Formula S badge, part number 2579443, was used instead in the same location.

Rectangular-shaped, amber-colored signal reflectors were used on the 1969 front fenders. The Barracuda script, now listed as part number 2901852, was solid chrome and was repositioned to the same place it was in 1967. If the six-cylinder, 318-ci, or 440-ci engine was used, then fish-shaped emblems, part numbers 2963656 (right) and 2963657 (left), were used just below and to the far edge of the script. The fish emblems were not used on cars with the 340-ci or 383-ci powerplants.

When the Formula S package was ordered, one of two medallions was used. Those with a 340-ci engine used part number 2901859, which read "340-S," which was inlaid in red. When the 383-ci engine was checked with the Formula S package, then part number 2901858 was used. It read "383-S," and it, too, was inlaid in red. The Formula S was not available with the 440-ci engine, so no 440-S nameplates were used.

If the Cuda package was ordered, the Barracuda script was still used but the engine ID badges were not. Instead, black decals were used on the rear portion of the front fenders just below the belt and behind the wheelwell opening. Two separate decals were used with each package. The decals consisted of the word "'Cuda" (part number 3444983), and below this was the engine callout, of which three were used: 340, 2964914; 383, 2964916; and 440, 2964915. Also part of the Cuda package were black tape stripes. For more information about the stripes, see "Sport Stripes" in this chapter.

Two different sets of fenders were used on 1970 Barracudas. All but those with a 340-ci Hemi or those with the optional F60x15 series tires use the same fenders. Those with the large tires required special fenders with extra-large wheelwells and special wheel-lip openings that provided clearance for the tires. Note that regular fenders *cannot be used* with the F60x15 tires, or tire damage will result.

The Barracuda script, part number 2786559, was used on the rear section of the front fender just below

1971 Cuda models used special louvers on the front fenders.

the waistline of base Barracuda and Gran Coupe models only. When the 383-ci two-barrel engine was ordered on the base Barracuda, a "383" medallion, part number 2949240, was placed just below the Barracuda script on the front fender. When the 383-ci four-barrel (330-horsepower) engine was ordered on the base Barracuda, then the emblem, part number 2579804, that read "383 Four Barrel" was used. These callouts were not used on the Gran Coupe models.

Gran Coupe models used a special Gran Coupe badge listed as part number 3504075 under the Barracuda script with all engines. On Cuda models no nameplate whatsoever was used on the front fenders. Wheelwell lip moldings were standard and were listed as part numbers 3419702 (right) and 3419703 (left); each molding was held on with nine Phillips-head screws for all models.

Challengers used three different sets of fenders. Like Barracudas, those with F60x15 tires required special fenders. While the AAR Cuda used the same set of fenders used on Cudas with a 340-ci engine, the Challenger T/A model used a unique set of fenders. Those from a regular Challenger or one with F60x15 tires will not fit the T/A model, as it used a special radius in the wheel opening and no chrome wheelwell molding was used.

The Challenger script, part number 3444938, was used on the rear of the front fenders just above the beltline of all models except the T/A model. If the 318-ci engine was ordered, then a "V-8" emblem, part number 2579748, was positioned below the script and below the beltline on the car. If the 383-ci four-barrel (330-horsepower) was ordered on the base Challenger or Challenger S.E. models, then an emblem, part number 3504233, that read "383 4-bbl" was used instead of the V-8 medallion.

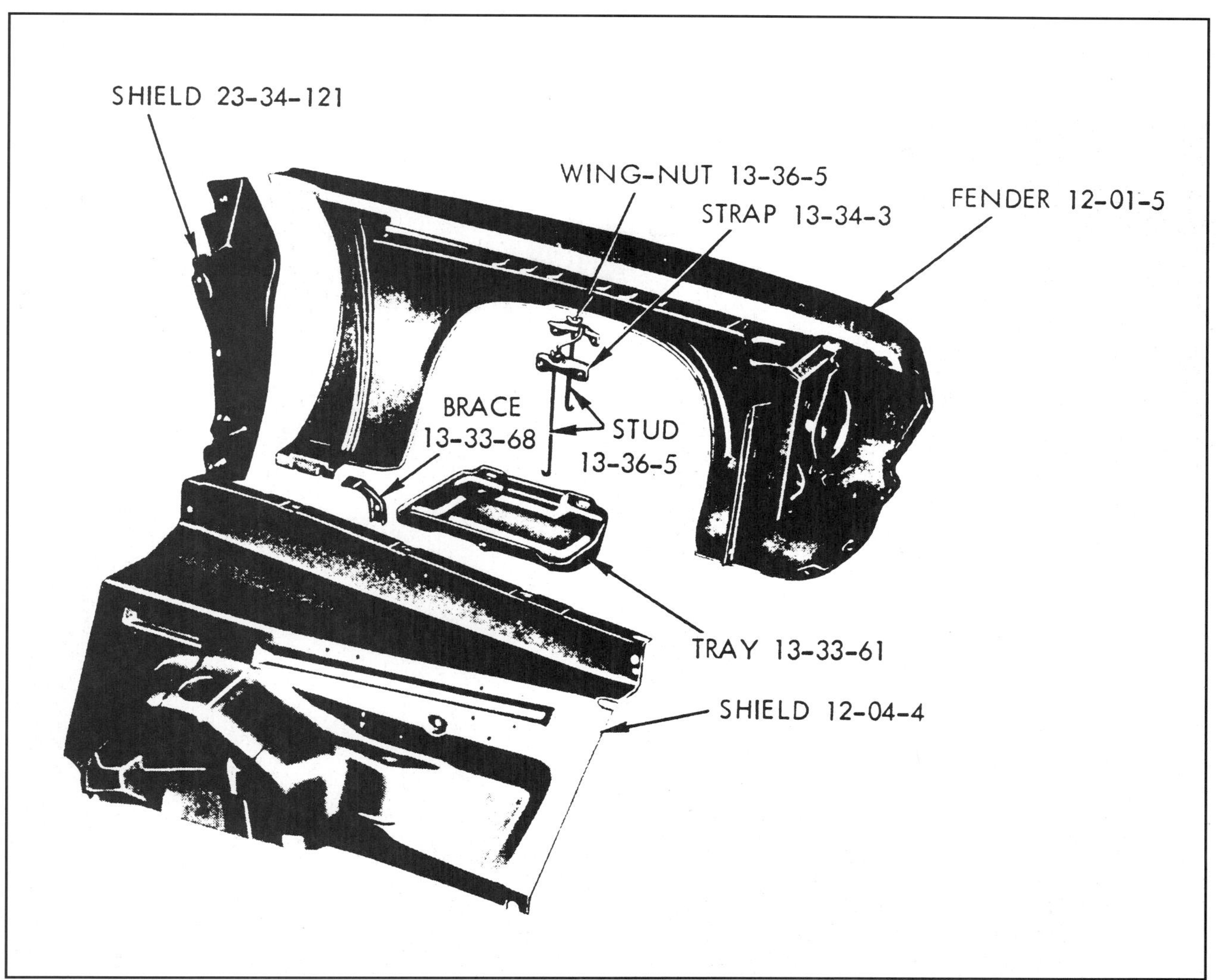

A 1967 Barracuda front fender, which was typical of 1968-1969 front fenders.

Challenger R/T models used a red-and-black "R/T" nameplate, part number 3445223, positioned below the Challenger nameplate on the front fenders.

The Challenger T/A model used no script or engine emblems. Instead, the "T/A" name was part of a black decal stripe that was positioned just above the waistline of the car. The logo will appear on the rear portion of the fenders. Also on the rear of the front fenders and below the waistline is a decal that read "340 Six Pack," with the letters also done in black.

Just as in 1970, those 1971 Barracudas with the F60x15-inch tires used special front fenders. This year the Cuda models used different fenders than those of a base Barracuda or Gran Coupe model. Cudas with F60x15-inch tires also required special fenders different from those Cudas with smaller tires. The difference is that the Cuda models have provisions for four simulated air vents; these vents were listed as part number 3505460 and were held in place with two nuts apiece.

The only emblem used on the front fenders of the base Barracuda was when it was ordered with a 383-ci engine, and then a "383" callout, part number 2949240, was used. No emblems at all were used on the Cuda models. All Barracuda and Cuda models came standard with wheel-lip moldings that were the same parts used in 1970.

Like the Barracuda, the 1971 Challenger with F60x15 tires required special fenders. But unlike the Cuda, the Challenger R/T did not require a unique set of front fenders. The Challenger nameplate, part number 3444938, was positioned on the rear portion of the front fenders just below the car's beltline on all models. Base Challenger models with a 383-ci four-barrel powerplant used an engine callout badge, part number 3505444, just below the Challenger name; this callout was not used on R/T models even when equipped with the 383-ci four-barrel powerplant. Wheelwell moldings were still standard and used the same part numbers used in 1970. The 1971 Challenger T/A used the same stripes and decals it used in 1970.

For 1972, all Barracuda models used the same fender, and no nameplate or engine callouts were used with either the base Barracuda or the Cuda model. Challengers received new fenders and one set fit all models,

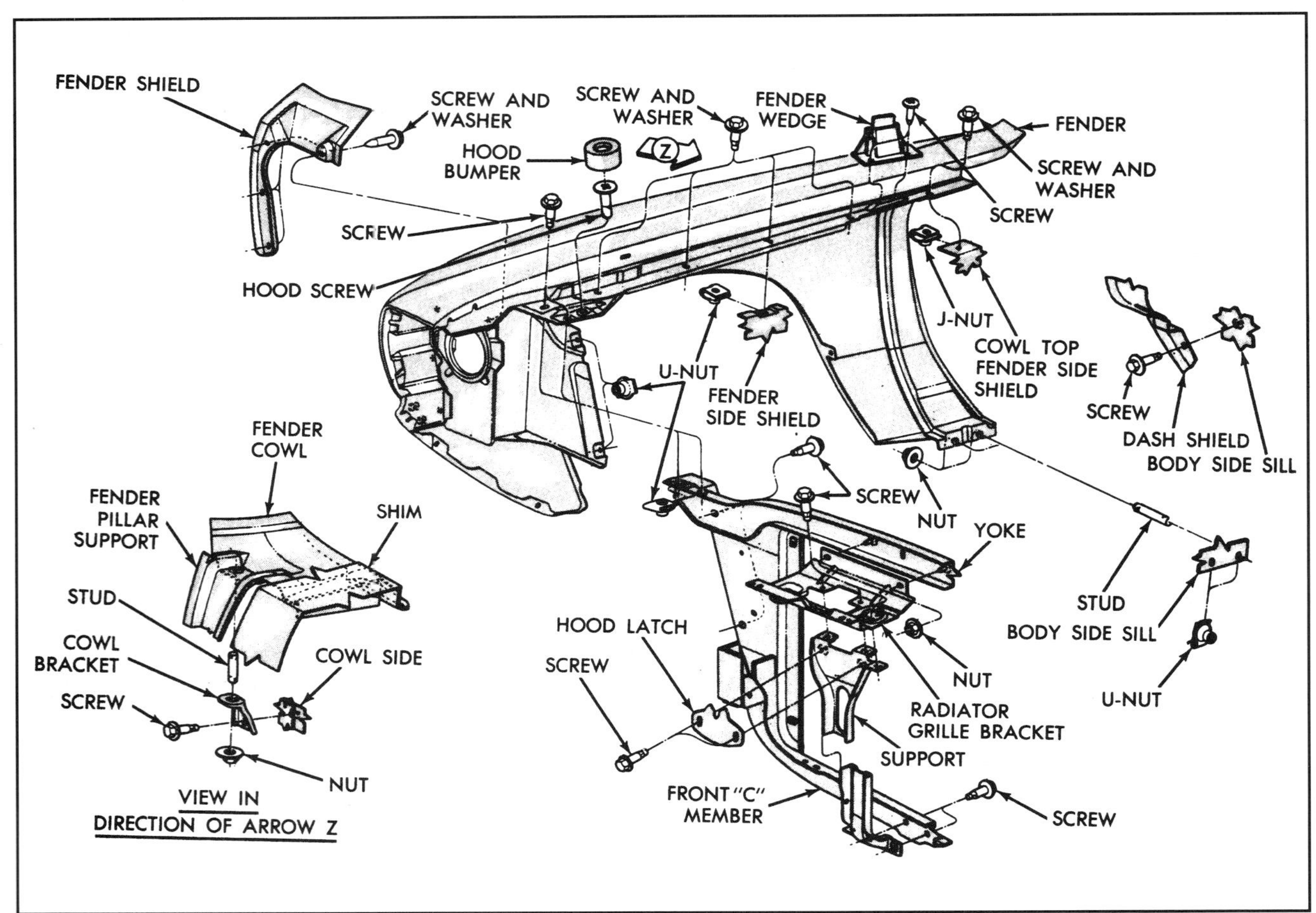

The Challenger front fender was also typical of Barracuda fenders.

including the Rally model. The Rally model featured simulated air scoops on the rear portion of the fender below the beltline. These scoops, part numbers 3613190 (right) and 3613191 (left), bolted onto the production fenders, and side stripes completed the look. No nameplate was used on the front fender of either model.

Again in 1973 and 1974, all Barracuda models used the same fenders used in 1972; the same goes for the 1973-1974 Challengers, which used the same fenders used in 1972. No nameplate was used on the front fenders of either of the models. The Challenger Rally model still used the simulated air scoop, which used the same part number as in 1972.

Doors and Door Handles

All 1967 Barracudas used the same door shells. Bright-plated exterior door handles with black push knobs were used. The interior door handles were pedal-shaped and mounted next to the armrests. The inner door locking knob was color-keyed to the interior trim. No emblems were placed on the doors in 1967.

The 1968 door shell was restyled and will not correctly fit 1967 models because the side rearview mirror is positioned farther back than in 1967. One door fit all body styles and continued to use bright-plated exterior door handles, but this year both black and die-cast push knobs were used. The inner door handles were still of

1970-1974 Cuda models used an ID badge on the inner door panels. *Year One*

1970-1971 Gran Coupe models used this inner-door script. *Year One*

1967 Interior Door Locking Knob Color Usage

Interior Trim Code	Knob Color	Part Number
HB5, H6B, H5C, H6C	Dark Blue	4346BB9
H5T, H6T	Light Tan	4346CT4
H5K, H6K	Copper	4346CK4
H5R, H6R, H5V, H6V	Dark Red	4346BR7
H5X, H6X, H5W, H6W	Black	4346BX9

1968 Interior Door Locking Knob Color Usage

Interior Trim Code	Knob Color	Part Number
H5B, H6B, D6B, H5C, H6C, D6C	Medium Blue	4346DB4
H6F, D6F, H5D, D5D, H6D, D6D	Yellow Green	4346BF9
H5X, H6X, D6X	Black	4364BX9
H6R, D6R, H5V, H6V, D6V	Dark Red	4364DR8
D6Y, D6E	Medium Gold	4364DY5
H5W, H6W, D6W	White	4346DW1

the pedal design but they used different part numbers and will not fit 1967 models. As in 1967, the inner door locking knobs were color-keyed to the interior trim and no emblems were used on the outside of the doors.

Door shells were again restyled in 1969 and will not correctly fit earlier models because the position of the interior locking knob was moved forward. Bright exterior door handles were used with all body styles. Fastbacks used only black plastic push buttons while the coupe and convertible used either the black plastic or diecast buttons. Interior door handles were the same units used on 1968 models. Color-keyed locking knobs were replaced by a chrome knob, part number 3419209, with all interior trims. No exterior door emblems were used.

In 1970, the doors were restyled and all body styles used the same door shell. However, the Barracuda and Challenger doors will not interchange, as the Challenger's door is wider. Both models also used flush-mounted exterior door handles. As with doors, each model used different handles from 1970 to early 1973, and the two will not interchange. After November 15, 1972, both the Barracuda and Challenger used the same door handles, and they will interchange but not fit earlier models. Doors were changed each year except a few early 1973 models, which used the 1972 doors, and the 1974 models, which used the late-1973 door. The change occurred in the 1973 model year with the addition of an impact bar on November 15, 1972.

Inner-door handles were recessed in the armrest of both models, but they differed between the makes. One set was used per model for the entire five-year run. Challengers used part numbers 3454170 (passenger side) and 3454171 (driver's side) while Barracudas used part numbers 3454842 (passenger side) and 3454843 (driver's side).

Both E-bodies used a special interior locking knob, part number 2999950, that was unlike any other Chrysler product. The knob was shaped like a lever and mounted in the armrest all five years. No exterior door emblems were used on 1970 models, but on the 1971 base Barracuda and Gran Coupe models, a small "Barracuda" nameplate, part number 3505456, was used on the outside of the door. It was mounted high above the car's beltline at the front edge of the door, in front of and below the mirrorline. On the 1971 Grand Coupe models, a medallion, part number 3505457, followed the Barracuda nameplate.

Base 1972 Barracudas continued to use the same "Barracuda" nameplate they used in 1971. It still was located on the front of the door, but it was now mounted lower, on the same level as the exterior door handle. No nameplate was used on the doors of the

1973-1974 Barracuda models and the Gran Coupe model was canceled at the end of 1971. No nameplates were used on the doors of Cuda (BS23) or Challenger models throughout the five-year run.

Quarter-Panels

In 1967 no side-turn lamps were used on the quarter-panel and each body style used a different panel. On the left-hand side, a hinged pop-open-type gas cap listed as part number 2823339 was used on all body styles. No nameplates were used on the panel of any model. For 1968, all body styles used a round-shaped side-mounted parking lamp. Again each body style used a different panel, and as in 1967, a pop-open pit stop-type gas cap was used on the driver's side quarter-panel. No nameplates were used with any body styles.

Panels were again restyled in 1969 and each body style used a different panel. Side-marker lamps were replaced by rectangular-shaped reflectors; the reflector was listed as part number 2930746. On the driver's side a new pop-open gas cap was used. It was listed as part number 2925878 and has the word "Fuel" imprinted on the cap. Use of this cap on 1967 or 1968 models would be considered incorrect. No nameplates were used on the quarter-panels.

Unlike the front fenders, no special quarter-panels were used with the F60x15 tires in 1970-1971, but as in previous years, each body style and model used a different set of outer panels. Barracudas no longer used a quarter-panel-mounted gas cap. Instead of that, a screw-on-type cap was located under the rear license plate holder. Challengers did use a quarter-panel-mounted gas cap on the passenger's side. Two different caps were used: the flush-fitting cap that was painted the same color as the body and the flip-top chrome cap with the word "Fuel" imprinted on the cap. No emblems were used on the rear quarter-panels either year on either model.

Panels were redesigned in 1972 and they will not fit earlier models. Only one body style was available

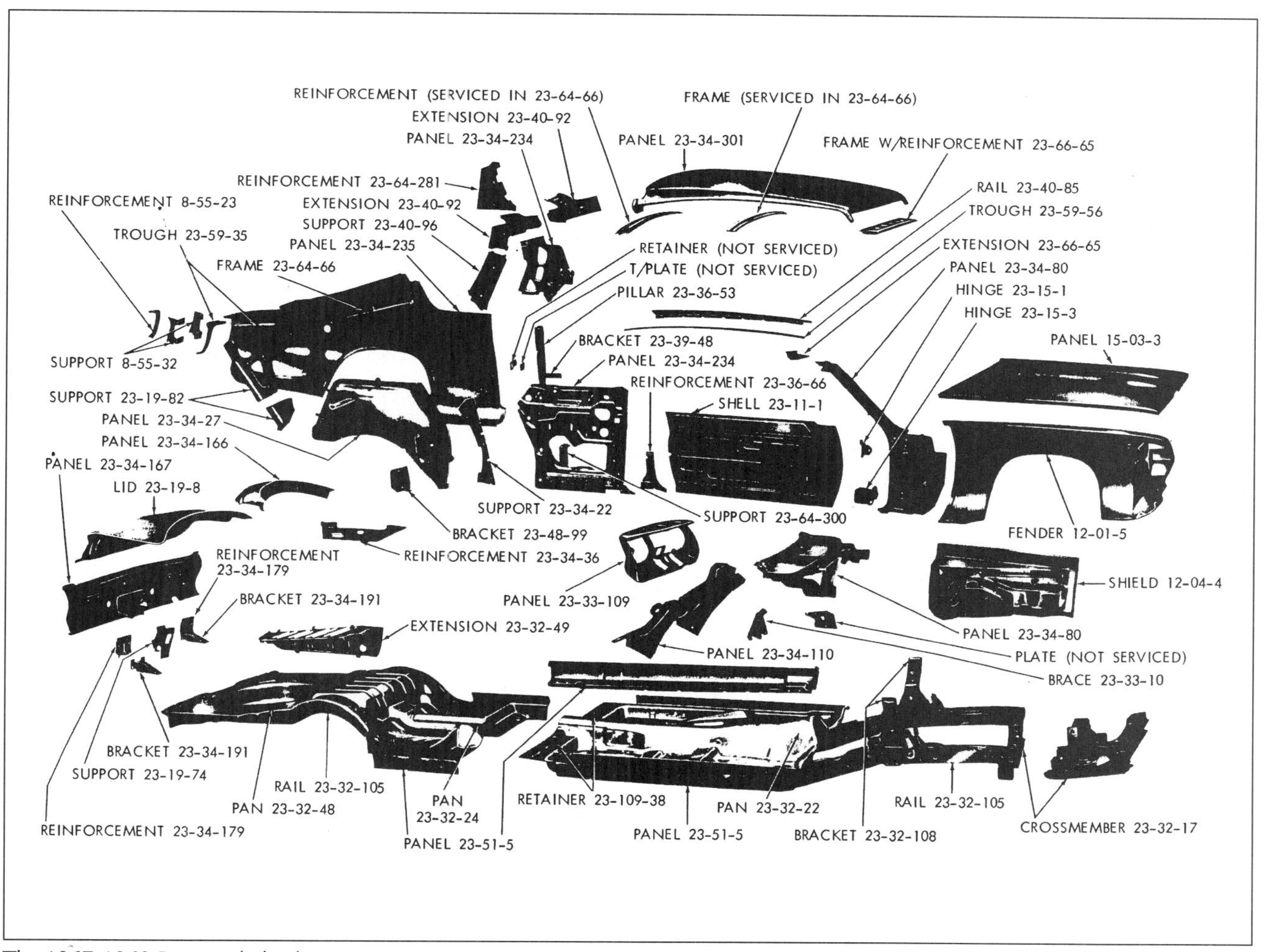

The 1967-1969 Barracuda body.

(two-door hardtop), but the Challenger used a different panel than the Barracuda. Challengers continued to use a quarter-panel-mounted gas cap on the passenger's side. A body color gas cap was still used but a chrome flip-top cap, listed as part number 3549089, was also used. On Barracuda and Cuda models, no quarter-panel emblems were used. On the Challenger and Challenger Rally, the Challenger script nameplate, part number 3505446, was used.

Panels were again restyled in 1973 for both models. Again only a two-door hardtop was available in either model. Challenger models continued to use both the body-colored and chrome-plated gas caps they used in 1972. The Challenger script also continued to be used on the rear quarter-panels, but the emblem was redesigned and given part number 3444938. No nameplates were used on true Cuda models either year on the rear quarter-panels, but the base Barracuda did use the Barracuda nameplate, part number 3505456, on the rear quarter-panels both years.

Rear Deck Lid and Tail End Panel

The 1967 two-door hardtop and convertible both used the same deck lid. However, the fastback used a special deck lid, and a lid from any other body style will not fit. The Barracuda logo (a fish in a-circle), part number 2784610, was used on top of the deck lid in the center near the rear edge on all body styles. A finish panel was mounted across the face of the deck lid, and all body styles used the same panel, listed as part number 2840342. The Barracuda script was placed on the panel on the far right-hand side.

Trunk hinges were also different between the fastback and other body styles and they will not interchange. Hinges should be painted the same color as the deck lid. Torsion bars differed between hardtops and convertibles. Those

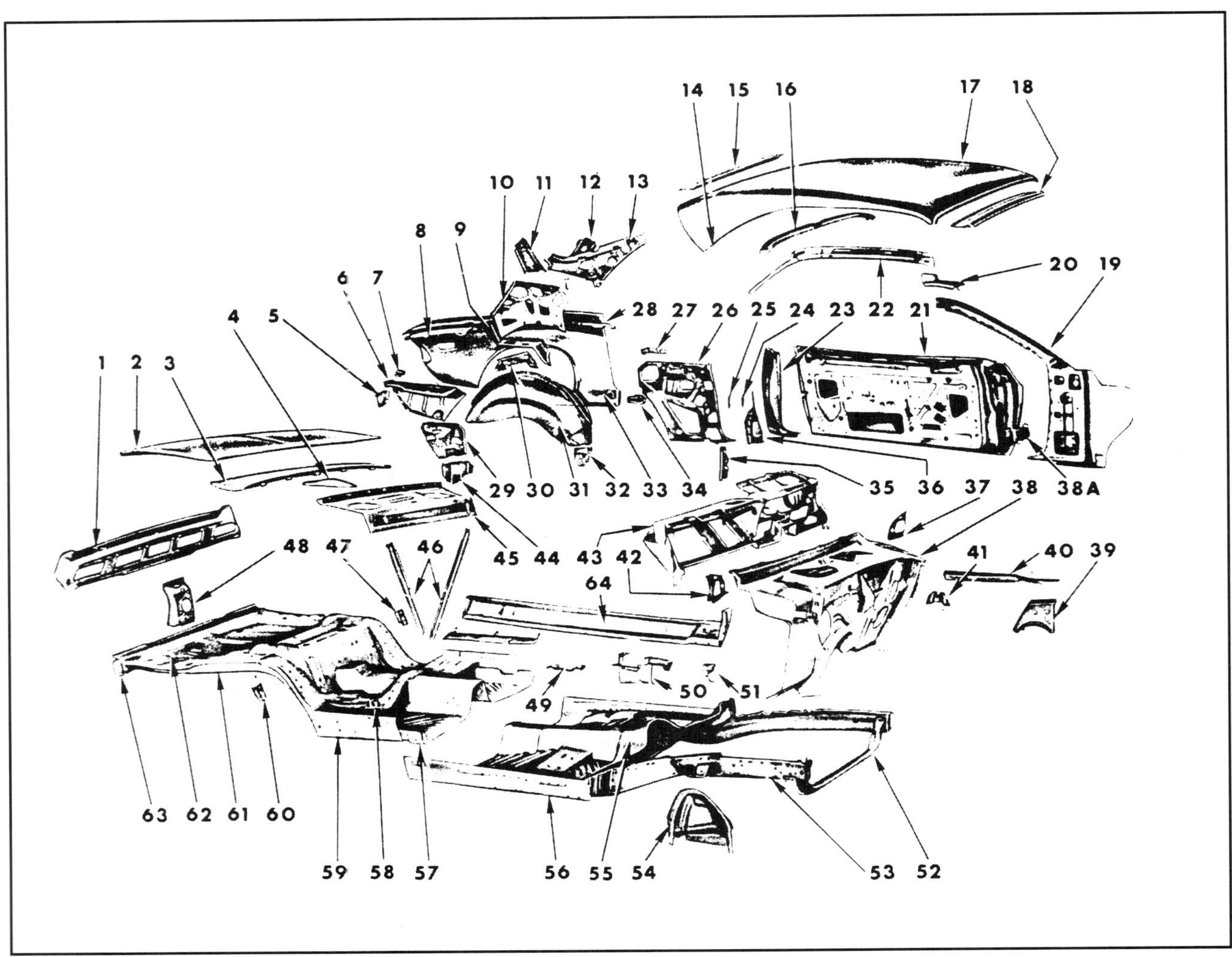

Above and opposite
The 1970-1974 E-body sheet metal.

from a hardtop will not fit a convertible even though the deck lid does fit. Torsion bars should also be painted the same color as the deck lid. The deck lid catch, part number 2244149, was mounted in the floor of the trunk, and it, too, should be painted the same color as the deck lid. The latch itself was listed as part number 2167260 and was bolted to the underside of the deck lid. Usually the latch should have an unfinished appearance, but some have been found painted the same color as the deck lid.

As in 1967, the 1968 Barracuda fastback used a special deck lid listed as a different part number. The convertible and hardtop continued to share a deck lid, but it, too, used a different part number than it did in 1967. A two-part finish molding was used on the rear face of the deck lid. It consisted of an upper molding, part number 3004225, and a lower molding, part number 3004236. These moldings wrapped around the tail-lamps, giving the appearance that it circled the rear end

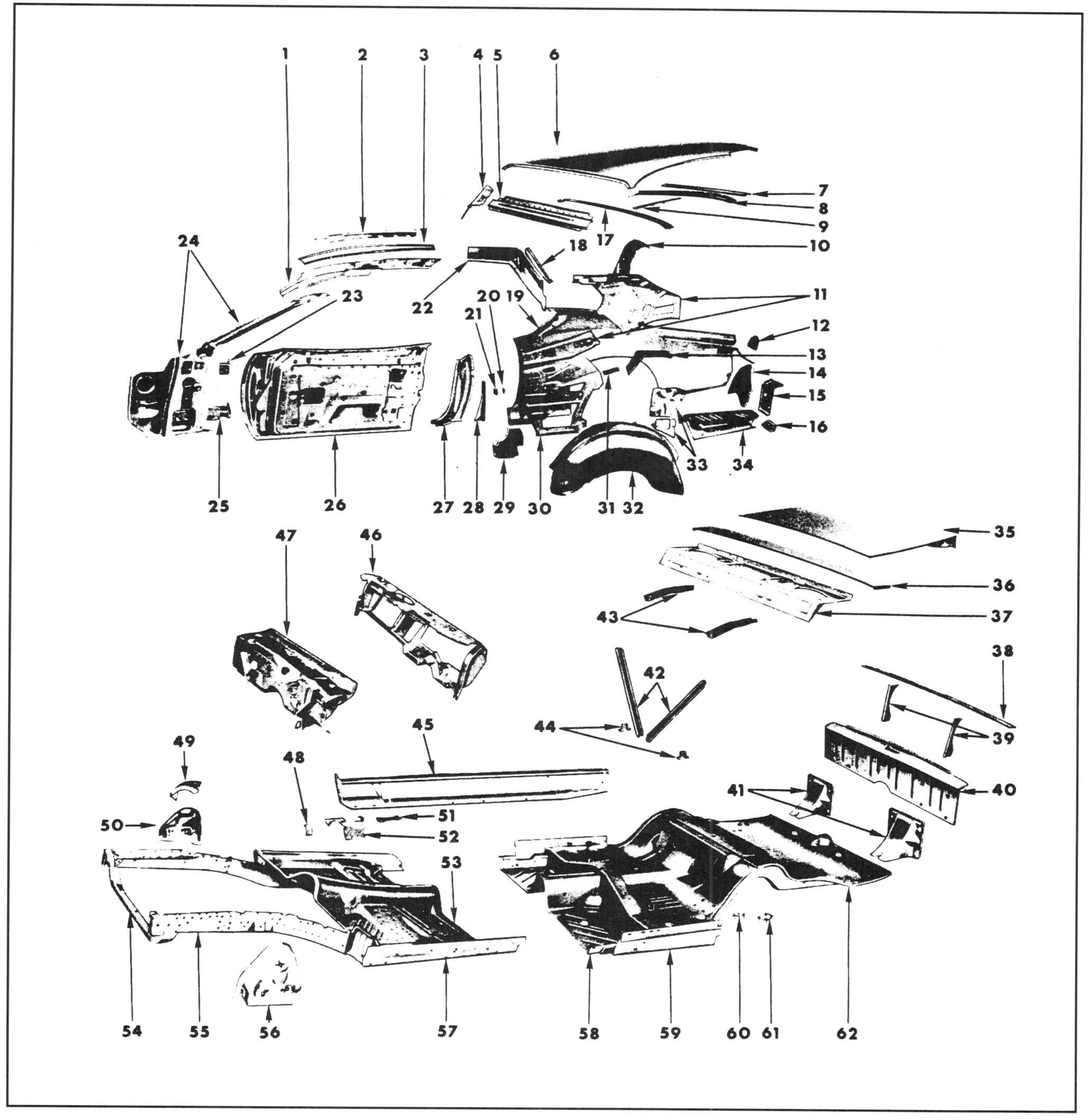

On 1972-1974 Barracudas, the nameplate was on the rear-quarter.

of the car. Reflective tape was also placed across the center face of the deck lid between the moldings. The "Barracuda" nameplate, part number 2840876, was used on the rear face of the deck lid on the right-hand side. In front and just below the nameplate was a fish-shaped emblem listed as part number 2480877. Both the emblems and the moldings were used with all body styles.

The same catch, latch, and torsion bars used in 1967 were used again in 1968, but the hinges were restyled to fit the new deck lid. Those on the hardtop and convertible were designed so that the hinge would fit either side, while those used on the fastback are unique to each side and will not fit other body styles. All finishing is the same as in 1967, including the new hinges.

The 1969 models used the same deck lids, torsion bars, and latch as they did in 1968, but the striker, which was now listed as part number 2244149, was changed. The hardtop and the convertible still used the same

The rear quarter-panel nameplate used on Challengers.

hinges they used in 1968, but the fastback used new hinges. As in 1968, the hinges in the fastback were unique to each side.

A finish panel was placed across the face of the deck lid. Two different panels were used: those without the Formula S package used part number 2902767, which was silver in color; those with the Formula S package used a black panel listed as part number 2902772. Both panels had the Barracuda name spelled out across the center of the panels. Those with the Formula S package also used the Formula S badge on the far lower right-hand-side instead of a fish emblem that was used on the other panel. Those with the Cuda package did not use the black panel; instead, they used the standard silver-finished panel.

Challengers and the Barracuda used different deck lids and they will not interchange. Each model in 1970 used two different lids; the lid used was determined by

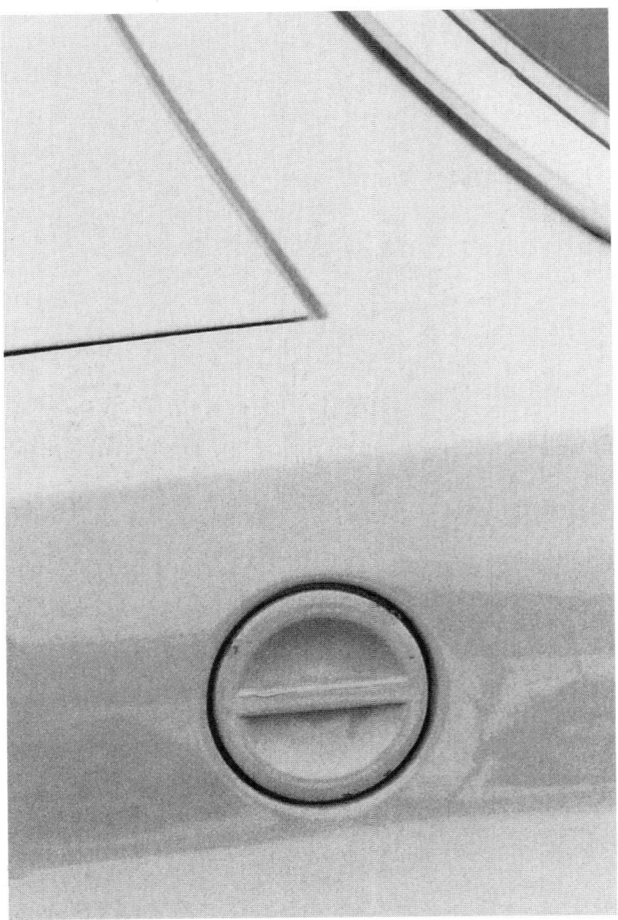

A Challenger body color gas cap.

A Challenger chrome flip-top gas cap.

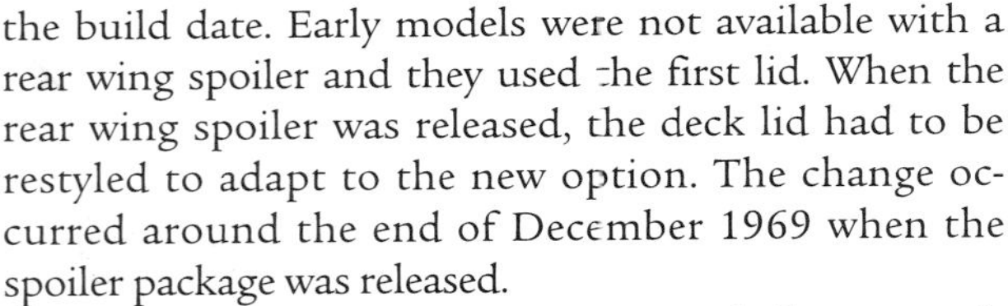

the build date. Early models were not available with a rear wing spoiler and they used the first lid. When the rear wing spoiler was released, the deck lid had to be restyled to adapt to the new option. The change occurred around the end of December 1969 when the spoiler package was released.

The AAR Cuda and the Trans-Am Challenger models came standard with a rear lip-style spoiler. These models did not become available until around the first of March 1970. So all AAR and T/As will have the later-style deck lid. Note that the T/A spoiler was listed as part number 3570371 while the AAR's was listed as 3570369; the two will not interchange.

The deck lid latch and striker arrangement was reshuffled from the 1967-1969 models, with the striker now bolted to the underside of the lid and the latch bolted to the rear inside wall of the trunk. Similarly, the latch now was usually painted and the striker was left unpainted, but some strikers have been found painted the same color as the deck lid. Both the Barracuda and all Challengers used the same set of hinges with all body styles. The torsion rods differed between models and between body styles, as convertibles required stiffer-rated torsion bars to keep the deck lid up when it is open. All finishing is the same as in years before, unless otherwise stated.

A molding, part number 3419701, was used on the deck lid lip of all 1970 Barracuda models. A two-piece molding, part number 3419708, was placed around the rear panel of all models including the AAR Cuda. On base Barracuda and Gran Coupe models, the rear-end panel was painted the same color as the rest of the car. The "Barracuda" nameplate, part number 2786559, was positioned to the right of the license plate holder and to the left of the trunk lock. On Gran Coupe models, a special medallion, part number 3454767, covered over the trunk lock and was used next to the Barracuda name.

On true Cuda models and the AAR model, the rear panel was painted Organosol Black (Ditzler code DDL-9355), and the Cuda nameplate was used instead of the Barracuda script. An important detail in restoration is that the Cuda nameplate was changed around April 1, 1970.

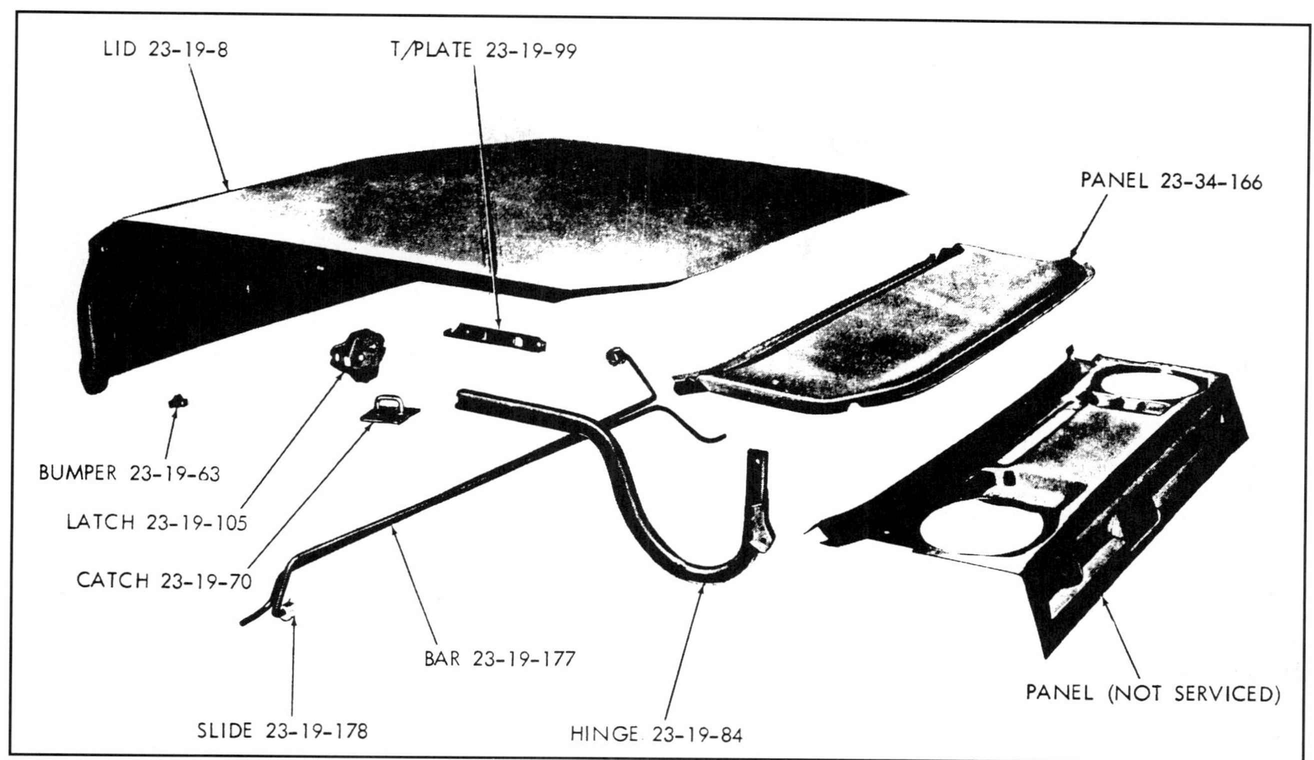

LID 23-19-8
T/PLATE 23-19-99
PANEL 23-34-166
BUMPER 23-19-63
LATCH 23-19-105
CATCH 23-19-70
BAR 23-19-177
SLIDE 23-19-178
HINGE 23-19-84
PANEL (NOT SERVICED)
The 1967-1969 convertible and hardtop deck lid.

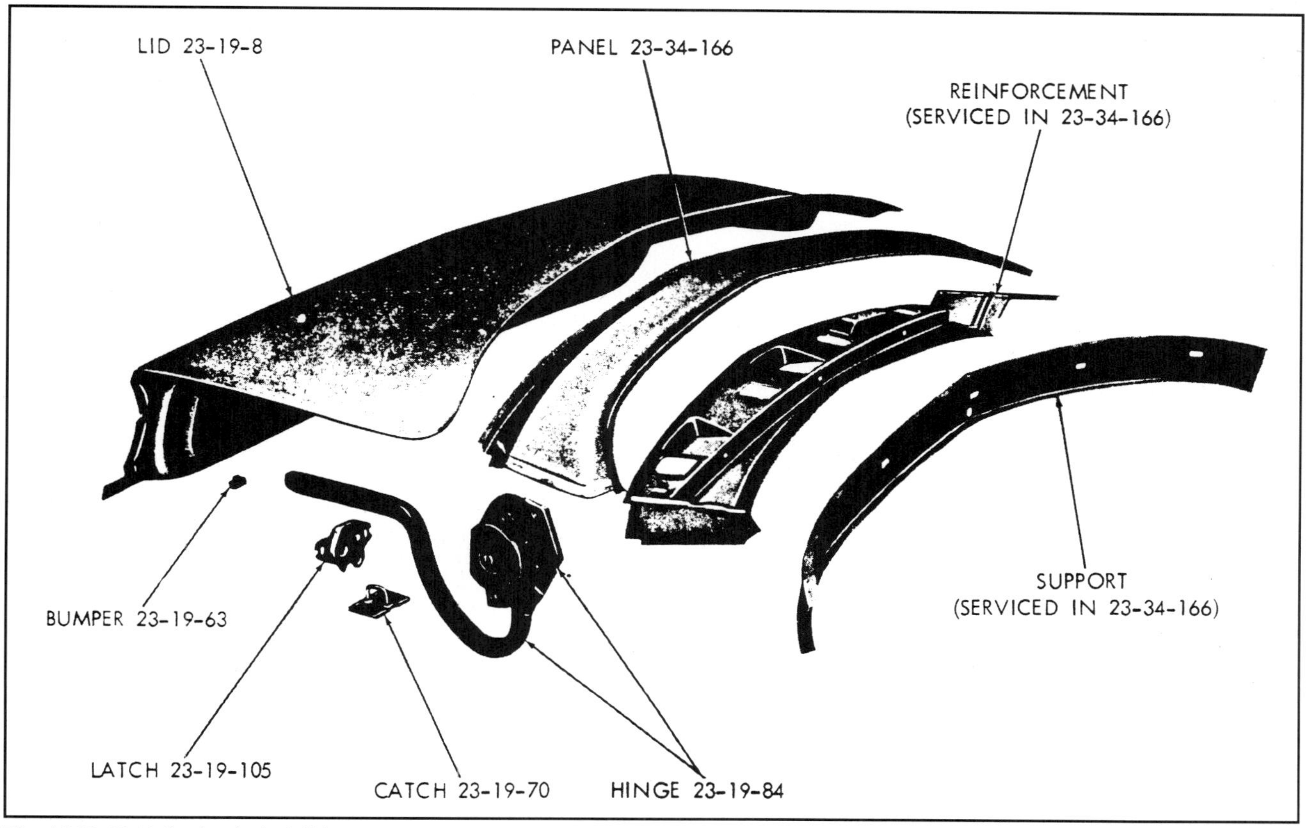

LID 23-19-8
PANEL 23-34-166
REINFORCEMENT
(SERVICED IN 23-34-166)
SUPPORT
(SERVICED IN 23-34-166)
BUMPER 23-19-63
LATCH 23-19-105
CATCH 23-19-70
HINGE 23-19-84
The 1967-1969 fastback deck lid.

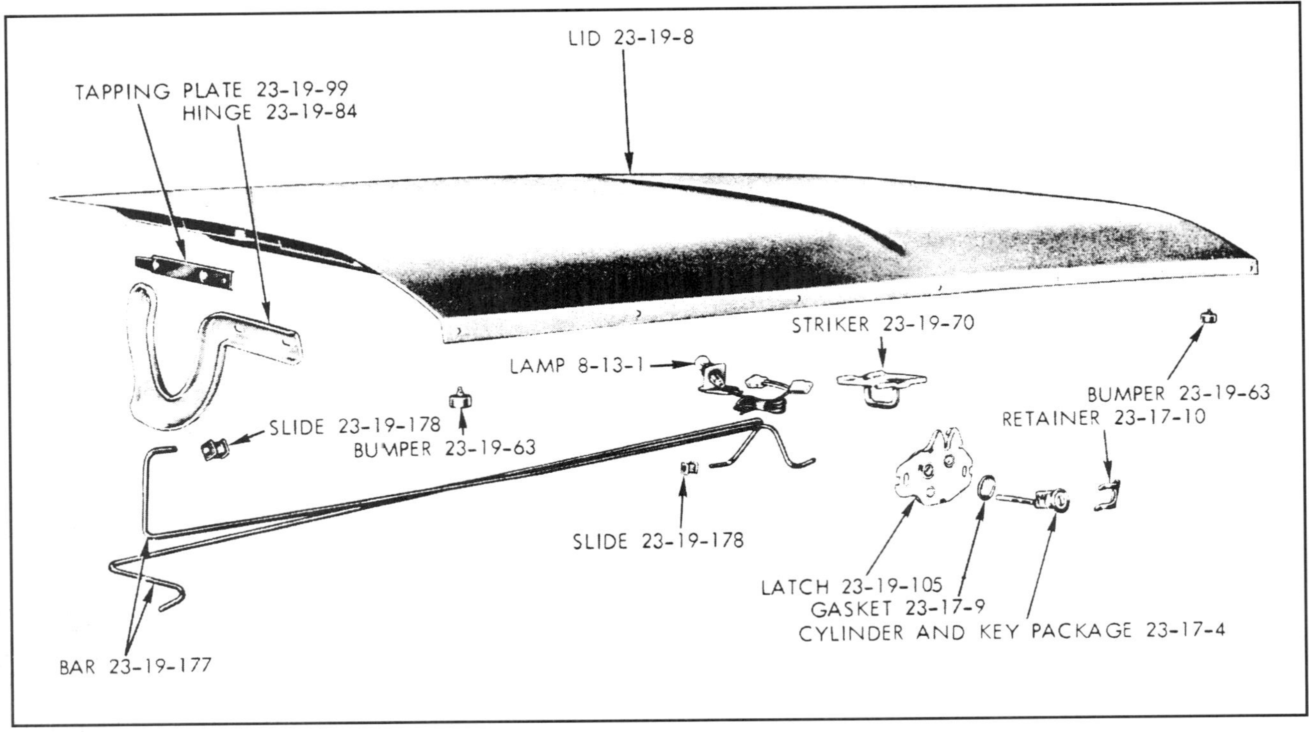

The 1970-1974 E-body deck lid.

Early models used part number 3446960, and after this date part number 3570071 was used. The difference is that the perimeter of the earlier style nameplate is painted Argent Silver, while on the later style it was painted flat black. This probably is the biggest mistake made today in restorations of Barracudas, and even professionals have made this mistake. The later style is the one that most reproduction companies reproduce, as this emblem was also used on 1971 models. If the ad reads for 1970 and 1971 models, it is most likely the later style and would be incorrect for your early-built Cuda. The later style nameplate can be reworked if the edges are carefully repainted a dull silver. Flat aluminum works well.

A molding, part number 3419709, was used on the lip of the deck lid on all Challenger models, including the Challenger T/A model. The molding was extended over to the ends of the quarter-panel, and these moldings were listed as part numbers 3419712 (right) and 3419713 (left). All models except the Challenger T/A used the "Challenger" nameplate, part number 3444938, on top of the deck lid on the lower right-hand corner.

On Challenger R/T models, a small red-and-black "R/T" badge, part number 3445223, was used next to the Challenger script on the deck lid. On the Challenger T/A model, a decal, part number 3612451, that read "Challenger T/A" was positioned on the rear face of the rear spoiler on the far right-hand side. On all Challenger models, the Dodge name was spelled out on the back-up lamp, part number 3420581, mounted in the center of the rear panel between the taillamps.

Deck lids were restyled in 1971 for both models, and as before, Barracuda and Challenger deck lids will not interchange. Hinges were restyled and, as in 1970, they were unique to each side and fit either the Barracuda or Challenger deck lid. Torsion bars were also changed and instead of a two-part design, a solid bar design was used. As with deck lids, each model used a different torsion bar and they will not interchange. Convertibles used a higher-rated bar than those models with a steel roof. The striker and latches were the same parts used in 1970 models. Paint all parts the same as in 1970.

The deck lid of the 1971 Barracuda models, except the Gran Coupe, was clean and free of chrome trim and nameplates. The rear panel also had no chrome trim. Special moldings were used on the Gran Coupe model only, and these moldings were on the rear lip of the deck lid and extended over on to the rear edges of the quarter-panels. Moldings were also used around the rear panel, part number 3419708, which included the upper and lower molding. It was used in either position, and end caps, part numbers 3419704 (right) and 3419705 (left), were used.

The rear panel on the base Barracuda was painted the same color as the lower portion of the car. On Cudas, the rear panel was painted flat black, the same shade used on 1970 Cuda models. The tail-end panel of Gran Coupe models this year was painted Medium Argent Silver, Ditzler code DNA-8575. The model name was in the same position it was in 1970, but used different part numbers. Base Barracudas and Gran Coupe models used the "Barracuda" nameplate, now listed as part number 3505456, and below this is another nameplate that read "By Plymouth" (part number 3570075).

On Cuda models the nameplate was the same part used on the late 1970 models, and the "By Plymouth" nameplate was also placed under this emblem. On Gran Coupe models, a medallion covers the trunk lock, and it, too, used the same part number used on the 1970 models.

Proper trim usage on the tail end of the 1971 Challenger can be confusing, as there were two different sets of moldings and two different rear taillamp panels. On base models without the high-performance engine (340-ci or 383-ci four-barrel), the panel was painted Argent Silver and used bright moldings. Challenger R/Ts or base models with high-performance engines used a black panel and black-accented moldings. The Challenger script nameplate was now positioned on the rear panel between the taillamp, and the Dodge nameplate, part number 2965502, was placed on top of the deck lid on the far right-hand corner of all models. Except the T/A model, which used the same decal on the spoiler it had used in 1970.

The same deck lids, hinges, striker, and latch used on 1971 models were used again on 1972 models. Barracudas continued to use the same torsion bar, but Challengers used a new two-piece bar. Moldings were used around the rear lip of the deck lid and the rear edges of the quarter-panels of all 1972 Barracuda models. The

Barracudas with dual exhaust outlets required a special rear pan.

1971 Challenger Rear Panel Moldings

	Rear Panel	Deck Lid Molding	Outer Moldings	
			Right	Left
Without Black	3570512	3579590	3579592	3579593
With Black	3570513	3579591	3579594	3579595

A Challenger rear pan with dual exhaust.

The position of the Cuda nameplate was revised in 1972 and remained there until the end of 1974.

deck lid lip molding was listed as part number 3419701, and the outer edge moldings used part numbers 3419706 (right) and 3419707 (left). The part numbers may sound familiar because the upper molding was used on 1970 models and the outer moldings were used on 1971 Gran Coupe models.

The rear panel of base Barracuda models was painted the same color as the rest of the car, while the rear panel of Cuda models was painted flat black. The model nameplates were the same part numbers as in 1971, but they were repositioned to the left of the license plate holder, instead of the right as in 1970 and 1971. The "By Plymouth" badge continued to be used under the Barracuda or Cuda nameplates, but the part number was changed to 3569542.

All Challengers used the bright moldings used in 1971, even when they were used on the Rally model that featured a blacked-out rear-end panel. (See listings above for part numbers.) No nameplate was used on the deck lid, and the Challenger script in the center of the rear

Gran Coupe models used this emblem over the trunk lock. *Year One*

On the 1970 Challenger R/T, the nameplate was positioned on the deck lid.

panel was replaced with the Dodge name spelled out in bright capital lettering. The following letters were used: D, 3612986; O, 3612987; G, 3612988; and E, 3612989. The letters have an adhesive backing.

Most of the components used in 1972 models were used again in 1973 and 1974 models, but there were subtle changes. The trunk latch in both models changed in 1973, and again each make used a different latch, and those in the Barracuda are unique to that model. The latch used in the Challenger can also be found in Darts and Duster. Even though the latch changed, the striker remained the same as in previous years. All moldings, nameplates, and color applications also remained the same.

Other Medallions and Emblems

A bronze-colored pentastar, part number 2785540, was used on the lower rear portion of the right front fender of all 1967-1971 models, no matter whether they were from Dodge or Plymouth. The only other place emblems were used was on the rear roof sail panel of the 1970 Challenger S.E. model. Here a special medallion, part number 3446801, was used on each side. This is limited to the 1970 package only, and those models with the formal roof package in 1971 did not use a medallion on the roof.

Vinyl Tops

In 1967, a black or white vinyl roof was available as an option for the two-door hardtop only. Bright moldings were used around the vinyl top as decoration. Special drip rails, part numbers 2840976 (right) and 2840977 (left), were used above the doors; these moldings are not the same parts that were used without a vinyl top. Quarter-belt moldings were listed as part numbers 2809696 (right) and 2809697 (left) and wrapped around the roof sail panels.

For 1968, vinyl top color choices were expanded to include black, Antique White, and Antique Green for the two-door hardtop model only. There is no color restriction with the white or black vinyl top. But when the green vinyl top was ordered, it was available only with the following: the Forest Green interior trim (H6F, D6F); the white-and-green interior (H5D, H6D, D6D); a green or gold exterior with a black interior (H5X, H6X, D6X); a white-and-black interior (H5W, H6W, D6W); or the white-and-green interior with a white or black exterior. Trim moldings used the same part numbers used the year before.

In 1969, color choices and body style availability were increased. The fastback was now available with the vinyl top along with the two-door hardtop. Color choices now included black, white, green, tan, and the wild-colored "Mod Top."

The 1970-1971 Cuda rear-end nameplate placement.

Applications of the green and tan tops were restricted by interior and exterior colors. The green top was available with green exteriors with all interior trim colors. It was also available on cars painted white or bronze with a black, black-and-white, or green interior. The tan top was available on cars painted bronze with all interior trim colors, and for all cars painted white with a black or white-and-black interior, or with any exterior color with a tan, tan-and-green, or the tan-and-black interior.

On September 9,1968, Plymouth proudly claimed itself to be a flower child by making the Mod Top Floral Vinyl Roof available for the Barracuda. It featured a wild pattern of bright yellow and gold flowers with tints of green on a black background. This top was ordered with one of the floral interior trims. The wild-colored top was a turn-off to buyers at the time, and the Mod Top today is one of the rarest options installed on the Barracuda. Many feel that this design was never released on the fastback, but the 1969 master parts catalog shows it as being available.

Moldings used on the two-door hardtop are the same parts used in the years before, but those on the fastback require special moldings. The vinyl top on the fastback did not cover the entire roof and sail panels as it did on the two-door hardtop. Instead, it covered only the center of the roof, from the edge of the windshield to the edge of the rear window. The drip rails were the same as those without a vinyl top because the vinyl covering did not come all the way down to the doors. The covering began and stopped at the point where the corners of the rear window moldings meet with the roof. Special moldings, part numbers 3419120 (right) and 3419121 (left), were routed up and over the roof along the edge of the vinyl covering.

In 1970, the color choices were black, white, green, or Gator Grain. The last of these is a greenish-tan color with a grain that resembles the skin of an alligator, thus the name. The Challenger used the same colors, but late in the year the Dodge Deputy model was released and it used a special white vinyl top. This is not the same white vinyl top used on other models; it is brighter. To hide modifications done to the rear window, all Challenger S.E. models were standard with a vinyl roof.

Moldings were restyled to fit the new roofline, and due to a longer roofline on the Dodge, those moldings from a Barracuda will not fit a Challenger, and vice versa. Drip rails were the same with or without a vinyl roof. Quarter belt moldings that ran under the rear window and wrapped around the sail panels were used only with the vinyl roof or two-tone paint. Barracudas used part numbers 3419782 (right) and 3419783 (left), while Challengers used part numbers 2954408 (right) and 2954409 (left), except the Challenger S.E. This model required special moldings, listed as part numbers 3514058 (right) and 3514059 (left). Besides being different in size, the moldings on the S.E. models used only 14 retainers, while the standard roof molding used 28 retainers. Moldings on Barracudas also use 14 retainers, but they will still not interchange with those on a Challenger S.E. model.

The same color choices were used in 1971, except the Gator Grain was deleted and the color gold was added. All coverings in 1971 used Boar Grain vinyl. Moldings were the same for all models except those Challengers with the formal roof package. This year, part numbers 3620506 (right) and 3620507 (left) were used, and these moldings will not fit 1970 models.

Color choices in 1972 were black, white, or green. The gold roof was not available for either model this year, but would be available again on 1973 and 1974 models. Challenger models used a roof with wide-spaced seams. The seams were located just over the doors and ran down the sail panels, while the Barracudas used a covering with the narrower space seams. The seams were positioned farther inward toward the center of the roof, and the seams only ran from the windshield to the rear window. A change in the grain came in late-1973 models. The date varies with the models and the color. See below for the dates.

In 1970, the Dodge nameplate was part of the back-up lamp.

Since the Challenger was the more popular of the two models and more Challengers came with vinyl tops than the Barracuda, it is possible that the factory could have run short of true Challenger vinyl tops. Some Challengers have been seen using the narrow-seam Barracuda-style vinyl; this is especially true of cars built near the end of the week or month when supplies ran short.

Determining whether your car came with a vinyl top or if it is the correct color is possible with information found on the fender tag of 1969 and later models. The code for the vinyl top option is found on the tag next to the paint code (1969-1970 models) or above the paint code (1971-1974). Vinyl top option codes are listed below.

Convertible Top

A power-operated folding top was standard on all 1967-1969 Barracuda convertibles. It was available in

Date of Vinyl Top Design Change

Barracuda

Color	Date Changed
White	10-1-1972
Black	10-1-1972
Gold	11-1-1972
Green	11-1-1972

Challenger

Color	Date Changed
Green	11-1-1972
White	9-1-1972
Black	9-1-1972
Gold	11-1-1972

The "Mod Top" that was offered in 1969. *Chrysler Historical Photo*

Vinyl Top Color Codes

Color	Code	Years Used
Black	V1X	1969-1974
White	V1W	1969-1974
Gold	V1Y	1971, 1973-1974
Green	V1F	1969-1974
Tan	V1T	1969
Mod Top	V1P	1969
Gator Grain	V1G	1970

either green, white, or black in 1967 and 1968. As with a green vinyl top, there were restrictions on the choice of exterior colors and interior trims that could be ordered with a green folding top; the restrictions are the same as with the vinyl top. Due to these restrictions, the green top was dropped for the 1969 models, and only a white or a black top remained. In 1970 and 1971, both models came standard with a manually operated folding top. Color choices were limited to white or black.

A motor, part number 2573838, with a reservoir and pump (part number 2573847) feed hydraulic fluid to lift cylinders (part number 2603753) that raise and lower the folding top. The convertible top frame should be painted Jewel Black in a semi-gloss finish using Ditzler code 9293, except the header panel. The motor and the pump assembly should be painted semi-gloss black. The header panel was painted to match the interior trim; see below for details. The lifts should have an unpainted appearance, which can be duplicated by painting the cylinders light gray.

The convertible top switch for 1967-1969 models is listed as part number 2820408, and it was mounted on the right-hand side of the driver between the glovebox door and the-cigarette lighter. A plate marked "up and down" was used over the switch. As stated above, beginning in 1970, both the Barracuda and the Challenger convertible models were standard with a manually operated convertible top. This required special lift cylinders. Listed as part number 3504648, they were used only in 1970 and 1971 E-bodies without a power-operated convertible top. They can be easily recognized by their lack of provisions for hydraulic lines. The finish is the same as the 1967-1969 cylinders described above.

A 1972 Barracuda with the vinyl top. *Chrysler Historical Photo*

1967-1969 Barracuda Convertible Header Paint

Interior trim Codes	Color Name	Ditzler Color Number	Years Used
H6B, D6B, H6C	Thunder Blue Met.	13693	1967-1969
H6X, H6W, D6P, D6U, D6W, D6X	Jewel Black	9000	1967-1969
D6T, H6T	Golden Tan Met.	23086	1967, 1969
D6F	Bayou Green Met.	43926	1969
H6R, D6R, H6V	Rally Red	71685	1967-1969
H6K	Dark Bronze Met.	2032	1967

A Challenger with a vinyl top. Note the seams on the side of the roof. *Chrysler Historical Photo*

A power-operated top was standard on 1967-1969 Barracuda convertibles. A 1968 model is shown here. *Chrysler Historical Photo*

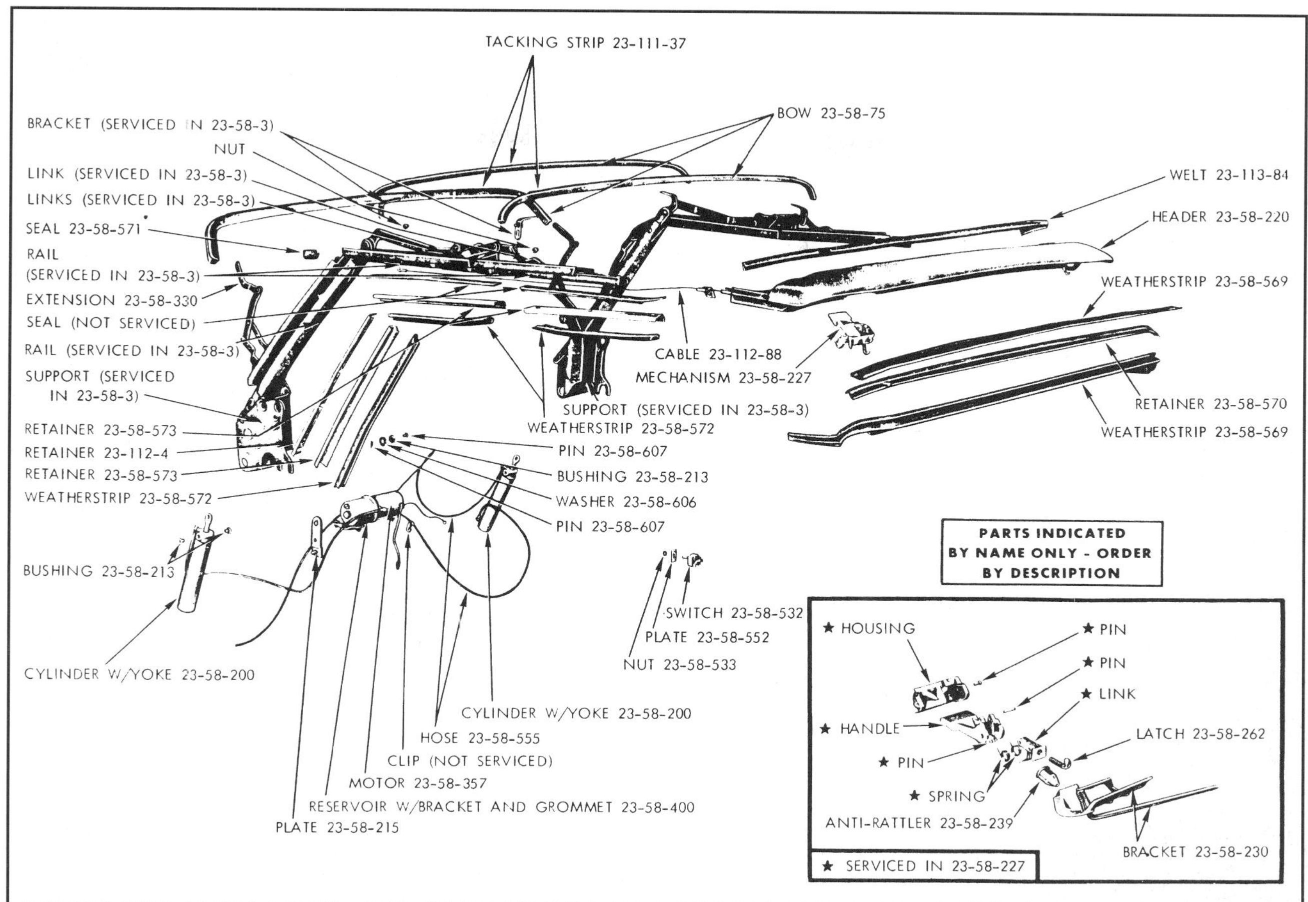

The 1967-1969 folding top.

A power-operated convertible top was optional on both models in 1970 and 1971, with a motor mounted behind the rear seat. The motor and the pump/reservoir were the same units used in earlier convertibles, but the lift cylinders were listed as part number 3505228. All finishing was the same as in 1967-1969, except the header panel, which was painted in a flat finish that matched the instrument panel. See the "Interiors" chapter of this book (chapter 8) for paint code numbers.

The convertible switch was listed as part number 2947406 and was located to the left of the driver just below the headlamp switch. Note that there was a change in the wiring harness that ran from the switch to the motor. All 1970 models and 1971 models built up to January 15, 1971, used part number 2983251, while those few ragtops built after this date used part number 3513720.

Outside Rear View Mirrors

A manually controlled driver's door mirror, part number 2802869, was standard on every 1967-1969 Barracuda model, and a remote-control mirror was optional each year.

In 1967, part number 2802835 was used, and for 1968-1969, the part number was changed to 2935217. Both mirrors have a chrome housing. The control for the remote mirror was mounted inside on the driver's door. A right-hand-mounted outside mirror was not available as a factory option for 1967 models, but became available in 1968. All mirrors used a black 4x3/8-inch gasket.

The chrome-plated nonremote mirror, part number 2999553, was standard on both 1970 E-body models. Most buyers opted for the optional chrome racing mirrors, part number 2999549, or the body-colored racing mirrors. The body-colored mirror, part number 3548053, was originally in primer and was painted to match the car. Both the chrome and body-colored mirrors were remote controlled. A matching right-hand manually adjusted mirror was available as an option. The chrome mirror used part number 3508989 and the body-colored mirror was listed as part number 3508990. The chrome and the body-colored mirrors were available with all exterior colors. However, due to the fact that high-impact colors of Sassy Grass Green (J6) and Moulin

continued on page 185

A 1970 Barracuda convertible. *Chrysler Historical Photo*

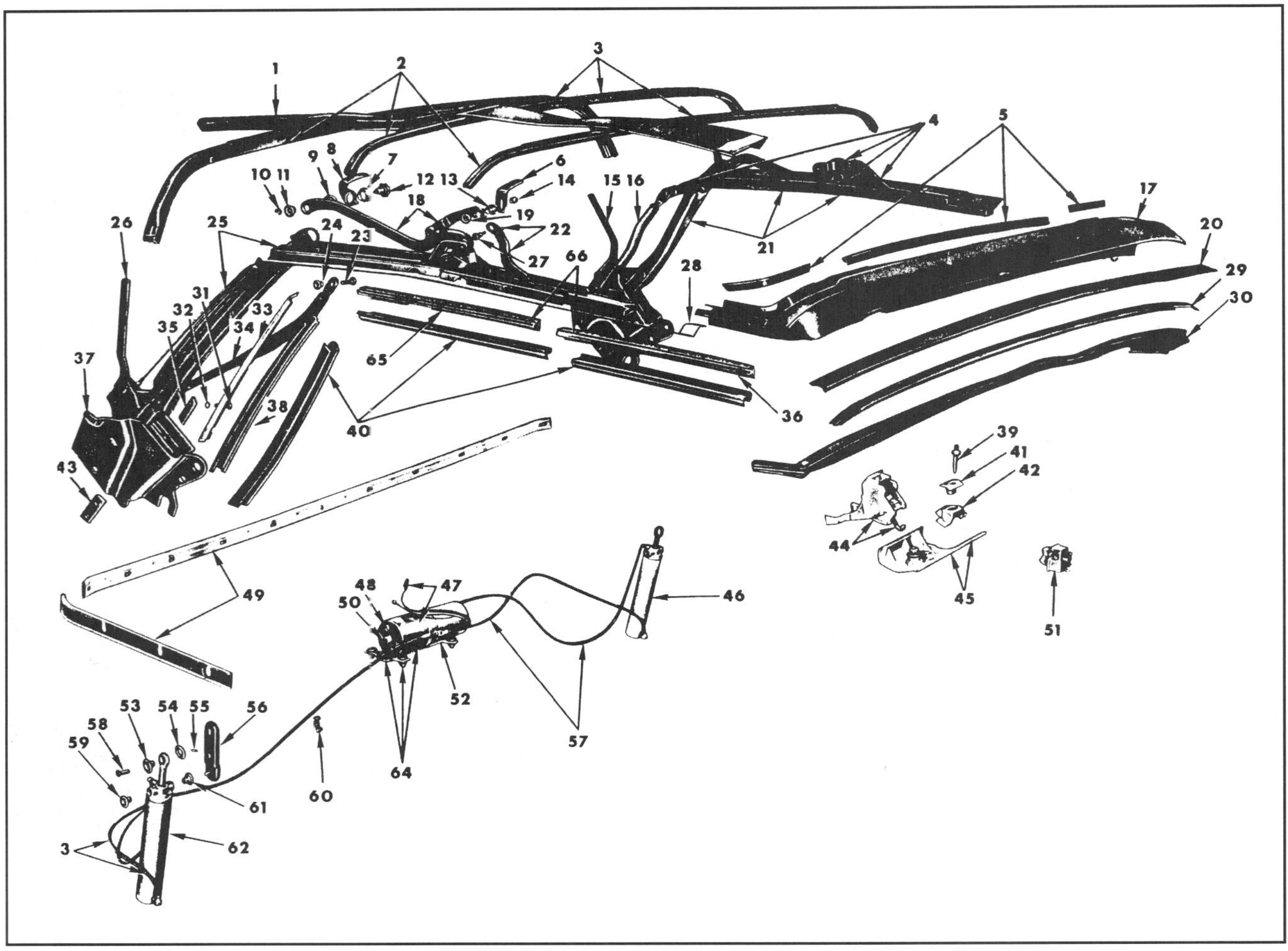

The 1970-1971 folding top.

A 1967 Barracuda two-door hardtop. Note the standard door-mounted side mirror. *Chrysler Historical Photo*

The standard door-mounted mirror on a 1971 Barracuda.

A chrome racing mirror.

continued from page 181
Rouge (FM3) were not available until January, these colors should not appear on a car built early in the run.

A chrome, round-head mirror without remote control, part number 3586645, was standard on the 1971-1974 models. This is not the same unit used on a 1970 model and the two will not interchange, but the 1971-1974 mirror can be found on 1971-1972 Charger models. Optional for both makes in 1971-1972 was either a chrome-plated racing mirror, part number 3586642, or a body-colored racing mirror, part number 3586649. Both mirrors were remote controlled.

Also available was a matching mirror—without remote control—mounted on the passenger's door. The body-colored mirror was listed as part number 3586650 and the chrome racing mirror was part number 3586644. No matching right-hand mirror was available with the standard round-head mirror.

Body color racing mirrors as shown on this car were a popular option. *Chrysler Historical Photo*

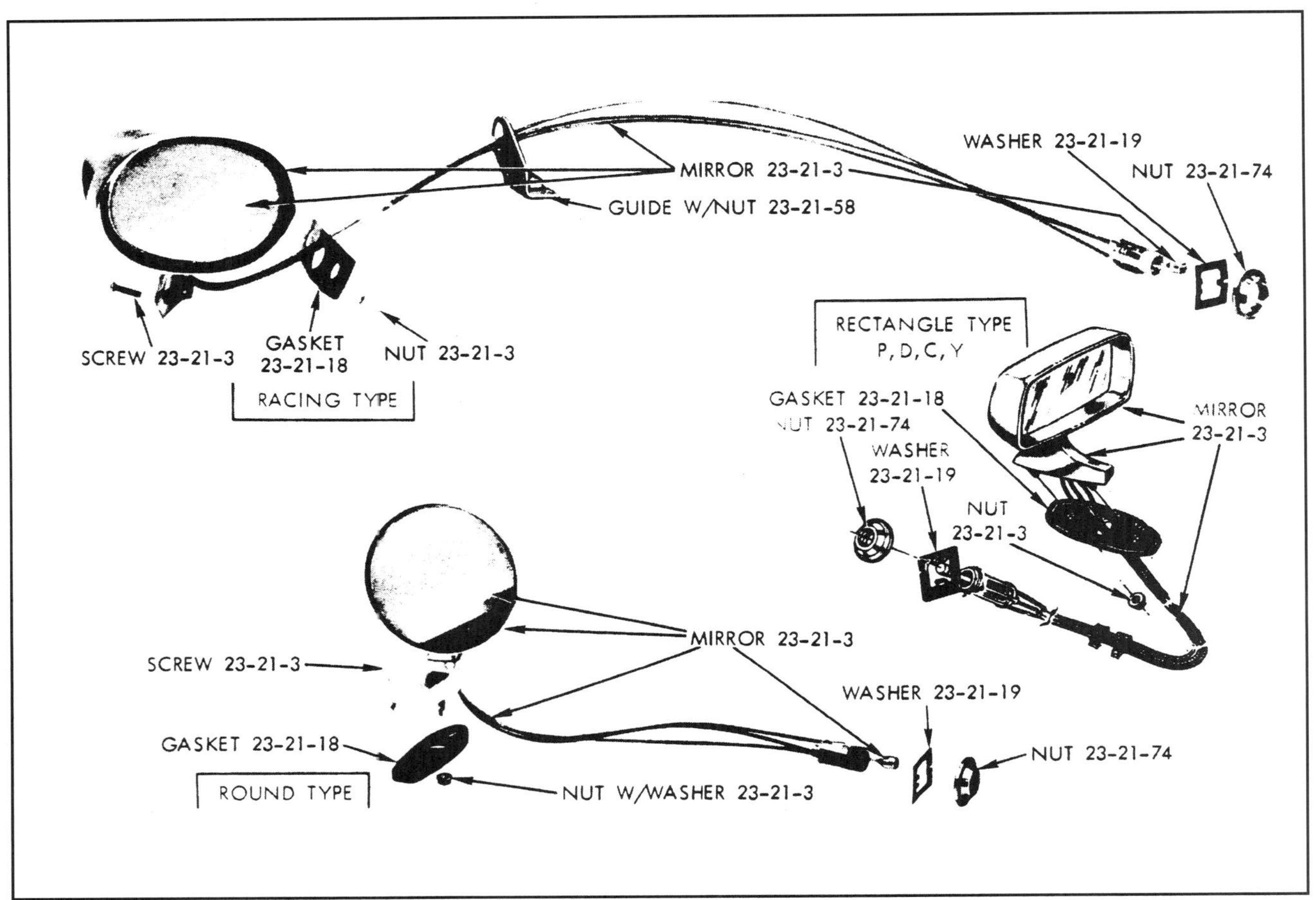

1970-1974 remote mirrors; E-bodies used the top mirror.

The fender tag will tell which mirrors originally came with your car. If your car was built with either the body-colored mirrors or the chrome racing mirrors, the option code will be stamped into the fender tag. If only the driver's-side chrome racing mirror was used, you will find the code G33; if the right-hand chrome racing mirror was installed, then the code G31 was used.

Since body-colored mirrors were installed in pairs, only the code G36 may be found if your car was built with these mirrors. If your 1969 Barracuda was built with the remote-control mirror, then the option code G33 will appear on the tag.

Sport Stripes

In 1967, sport stripes were optional on all Barracuda models and body styles. It consisted of a single stripe that ran down the center of the car from the edge of the front bumper, up the center divider, over the hood, up and over the roof, and down to the rear bumper. If the stripes were ordered on convertibles,

1967 Barracuda Sport Stripes Paint Usage

Stripe Paint Code*	Stripe Color	Ditzler Code
B-	Black	9000
C-	Blue	13074
H-	Red	71498
W-	White	8293

* = First digit in paint code. Example: WB2 is white stripes on a black car.

1968 Sport Stripes

Interior Code	Stripe Color	Stripe Code
H5B, H6B, D6B	Blue	315
H6F, D6F	Green	316
H6R, D6R	Red	312
D6E		White, 313
H5X, H6X, D6X	Black*	311
D6Y, H5W, H6W, D6W	Black or White	311, 313
H5C, H6C, D6C	White or Blue	313, 315
H5V, H6V, D6V	White or Red	313, 312
H5D, H6D, D6D	White or Green	313, 316

* = White stripes were also used with this trim.

The 1969 Cuda package with 383 call-out stripes. *Chrysler Historical Photo*

1969 Accent Stripe Paint

Stripe Color	Ditzler
White	2033
Black	9000
Red	71498
Blue	13074
Green	43870

then stripes were used on the hood and deck only. A thinner stripe bordered the wider center stripe on each side; the thinner stripes are positioned by the letters M and O in the Plymouth name on the header panel. The stripes were color-keyed to the interior, not the exterior. The following colors of stripes were available: white, blue, red, and black. The stripe color can be detected by the first letter in the paint code on the fender tag. For example, the code BA2 would be black stripes on a silver car (A), and the 2 stands for a two-tone finish.

Stripes on the 1968 Barracuda consisted of tape instead of paint. Once again, they were color-keyed to the interior trim. Colors available were white, blue, green, black, and red. The stripes were positioned on the side of the car midway between the beltline and the doorsills. The stripes ran from the rear edge of the front wheelwell molding to the front edge of the rear wheelwell moldings. The pattern consisted of a thin center stripe, bordered on each side by a wider stripe. Note that the stripe originally was a two-piece design, one for the door and one for the quarter-panel.

Four different striping patterns were available on the 1969 Barracudas. The accent stripe was painted on pinstripes that ran from the tip of the fender to the tip of tail, with a gap at each end. They are located on the same plane as the door key lock cylinder. The paints in the chart at left were used.

When the Cuda package was ordered, black tape stripes were positioned on the hood and along the bottom of the car, running from the tip of the front fender to the end of the car. Engine callouts were placed just above the stripe on the rear portion of the front fender. This package originally consisted of 18 individual stripes and decals.

Side stripes were optional with 1970 Challengers.

1969 Cuda Tape Stripes

Stripe	Left	Right
Forward front fender	2965559	2965558
Rear front fender	2965557	2965556
Fender callout (340-ci)	2964914	2964914
Fender callout (383-ci)	2964916	2964916
Fender callout (440-ci)	2964915	2964915
Fender nameplate (Cuda)	3444983	2944983
Door	2965555	2965554
Front-rear quarter	2965551	2965550
Rear-rear quarter	2965553	2965552
Header Panel	2949353	2949352
Hood	2949345	2949344

Wide body side sport stripes were available for all body styles and models in 1969, except those with the Cuda package. The tape stripes were available in three colors, black, white, or red, and were routed just above the beltline. When installed on a six-cylinder or a car with a 318-ci engine, the fender stripe was solid with no engine callout. When ordered with a 340-ci or 383-ci engine, the fender stripe included the engine callout.

If your 1969 Barracuda was ordered with stripes, then the option code for the stripes will appear on the fender tag. The following codes were used for body side stripes: V6W, white stripes; V6X, black stripes; and V6R, red stripes. If the Cuda package was ordered, then either of these codes—A56, Cuda 340, or A57, Cuda 383—will appear on the fender tag. If you're truly lucky, you'll find the code A13, which signifies the 440-ci Cuda conversion. Accent stripes used the following codes: V7B, blue; V7R, red; V7F, green; V7W, white; or V7X, black.

There were four different striping patterns on the 1970 Barracuda models. The only standard stripes were those on the AAR model. This model used a strobe-like flat black stripe that ran from the front fender to the end of the car. As the stripe went back toward the end of the car, the strobes got thinner until they graduated into a decal that read "Cuda AAR" at the end of the quarter-panel. The original stripe came as either a three-piece design (front fender, door, and quarter-panel) or as a solid one-piece stripe that had to be cut to fit the door.

'Hockey Stick' Stripes

The most popular optional stripes were those commonly known as "Hockey Stick" stripes. These stripes began at a point above the door handle, followed the upper body contour line back to the rear of the car, then turned downward and into the engine callout. Only black tape stripes were used, even with black paint. Four different stripes were used, and according to engine displacement, either 340, 383, 440, or Hemi was used. For most of the model year, the Hockey Stick stripes were available only on the Cuda models. After May 1, 1970, the 340 and 383 stripes became optional on the base Barracuda and Gran Coupe models when either of these engines was also selected. The code V6X will appear on your fender tag if your car was ordered with the optional Hockey Stick stripes. Refer to the fifth digit in your VIN to see which stripe was used.

The stripe was originally in two parts: the large quarter-panel portion that also supported the callout and the small portion that crossed over onto the door.

The base Barracuda and Gran Coupe models were also available with narrow bodyside stripes. These tape stripes were available in five colors: black, white, red, blue, or green. The stripes were positioned right along the midline of the car from the tip of the front fender to the tip of rear quarter-panel. They were not available on the Cuda or the AAR models, and they were also not available with colored moldings or the Hockey Stick stripes.

A strobe-like stripe was available for all Barracuda models except the AAR models. The slash marks were thinner at each end and got thicker as they approached the middle of the car. Early models were available only in black or white. After March 9, 1970, chartreuse (light green) and magenta (bright pink) stripes were added. No color restrictions were used with the black or white stripes, but the green and pink stripes had restrictions. The chartreuse was available only on the Sassy Grass Green (FJ6) exterior, and the magenta stripes were used on cars painted Moulin Rouge (FM3). Since these exterior colors were extra-cost colors and were added late (February 6, 1970) in the model year, few cars were built with the pink or green stripes. Some books do not even list these stripes as being available. While the Hockey Stick stripes are the most popular, the strobe side stripes make more of a visual impact.

Like the Hockey Stick stripes, the code for strobe stripes will appear on the fender tag. You'll find the following codes: V4X, black; V4W, white; V4J, chartreuse; and V4M, magenta. The narrow stripes were called accent stripes and will have the following codes: V7X, black; V7W, white; V7B, blue; V7R, red; and V7F, green.

Colored bodyside moldings were available on the base Barracuda or Gran Coupe models only. They came in the same colors as the accent stripes listed above. Bodyside moldings could not be ordered with any stripe package, and like the stripes, an option code will appear on the fender tag. If your car was ordered with this option, one of the following codes will appear on the fender tag: V5X, black; V5W, white; V5B, blue; V5R, red; or V5F, green. Most bodyside moldings were ordered on Gran Coupe models.

Challenger R/Ts in 1970 were standard with bumblebee stripes painted across the rear of the quarter-panels and the deck lid. It consisted of two stripes. The end stripe was 5 1/4 inches wide and a thinner 1/4-inch-wide

The R/T logo was cut into the fender stripes on 1970 R/T models.

inner stripe with a 5/16-inch gap between the wider and thinner stripes. Use acrylic enamel paint for the correct finish. If your car is done in acrylic lacquer, use a good sealer first. At right are the original paints.

A no-cost option for R/T models was the body side tape stripes that had the R/T logo cut into the tape on the front fenders. The tape stripe came in white, black, blue, green, or red all year. After March 11, 1970, chartreuse (light green) and magenta (bright pink) became available. The same color restrictions used on Barracudas were also used on the Challenger models. The side stripes were also available as an extra-cost option on all Challenger models except the T/A models. Though the stripe on the fender has no logo cut into it, it was available in the same colors as those on the R/T models. Bumblebee stripes were not available on base Challengers.

To see whether your Challenger R/T had bumblebee stripes or the longitude stripes, look for the option code on the fender tag. Bumblebee stripes were coded with these codes: V8X, black; V8W, white; V8B, blue; V8F, green; and V8R, red. The code V88 may appear on the fender tag. This code means that the bumblebee stripe was deleted, and no stripe was used.

If the optional bodyside stripes were ordered, then one of the following codes will appear on the fender tag: V6X, black; V6W, white; V6B, blue; V6F, green; V6R, red; V6J, light green; and V6M, pink.

The code V6H on the fender tag indicates the Challenger T/A stripe. This stripe was used only on the

1970 Challenger R/T Bumblebee Stripe Colors

Color	Ditzler Code
White	2033
Black	9000
Bright Red	71498
Bright Blue	13074
Green	43870

The 1970 AAR Cuda strobe side stripes. *Chrysler Historical Photo*

Challenger T/A. It begins at the forward edge of the front fender, and the T/A name was cut into the stripe. The stripe continued over the door and onto the forward portion of the rear quarter-panel. The stripes used on the front fenders and quarter-panels were used with all options, but two different stripes were used on the doors, their use determined by the type of mirror ordered. Those models with chrome or body-colored racing mirrors used a stripe that featured a notch cut into the stripe where the mirror mounts. With the standard mirror, the right-hand door stripe had no notch cut into it. No other stripes were available with this model.

Inspired by the 1968 Road Runner/GTX, the designers of the 1970 Challenger R/T with the standard hood made the performance hood stripe optional. This option was a flat black tape stripe positioned in the

Called "billboard stripes," these str pes cover nearly half of the car.

hood between the hood scoops. This option was not available on the base Challenger or when the Shaker Hood package was ordered. The code V21 will appear on the fender tag if your car was ordered with this option.

"Billboard" Stripes

The most famous stripes and most noticed stripes ever placed on a car were available on the 1971 Cuda. Commonly known as billboard stripes, these stripes covered half of the car. They narrowed as they protruded over on the door, where they ended with the engine callouts. The stripes were available in either black or white. They were originally a two-part design, with the large, wide part that fit over the quarter-panel and the portion with the engine callout placed on the door. The following callouts were used: 340, 383, 440 (used with 440 3x2-barrel only), and Hemi. Some reproductions are of a one-piece design, which are considered incorrect and harder to install. Year One (P.O. Box 129, Tucker, GA 30085) stocks an excellent reproduction of these stripes.

Optional for all 1971 Barracuda models was a combination of bodyside molding and tape stripes. It consisted of colored moldings in either black, gold, or green with matching tape above and below the moldings. Moldings were changed September 1, 1970; early models used moldings that were unique to each side of the car, while the moldings on later built models will fit either side. For correctness, the proper moldings should be used. This option was available on Cuda models but was seldom selected, and it was not available with the billboard stripes.

Twin tape accent stripes were also available for the base Barracuda and Grand Coupe models only. These stripes were available in either white, black, gold, green, or blue. The tape was routed along the top portion of the front fender, back over the door on the same line as the mirror, and curving up at the end on the front portion of

A combination of pinstripes and body side moldings were optional on all 1971 Barracuda and Cuda models. *Chrysler Historical Photo*

Here are the 1971 Challenger side stripes. Note how the R/T logo is cut into the quarter-panel stripe. *Chrysler Historical Photo*

the quarter-panel. On those models with a vinyl top, the stripe butts end with the quarter belt molding used with the top. The original stripe was in three parts: front fender, door, and the quarter-panel. The left-hand door stripe was a two-part design, with one piece running from the door edge to the mirror, and the other running from the rear edge of the mirror to the end of the door. The passenger's door was a solid piece of tape, even when the right-hand mirror was installed.

If your Barracuda or Gran Coupe was equipped with these bodyside stripes, then one of the following codes will appear on the fender tag: V6X, black; V6W, white; V6F, green; or V6Y, gold.

The colored moldings can be identified by these codes on the fender tag: V5X, black; V5B, blue; or V5F, green.

For the billboard stripes, look for one of these two codes on the fender tag: V9X, black stripes, or V9W, white stripes.

Tape stripes were standard on the Challenger R/T and optional on all other models. Two stripes were routed from the front edge of the front fender back over the door. The lower stripe engulfs the exterior door handle and runs over onto the front portion of the quarter-panel. On R/T models, the R/T logo appears and the end of the bottom stripe is cut to fit the "T" in the logo. On other models, no logo is used, and the ends of the stripes are flush.

At the beginning of the year, black, white, orange, and chartreuse stripes were available; shortly after production began, the orange and chartreuse stripes were canceled. The chartreuse stripe was limited to either Dark Green Metallic (GF7), Light Green Metallic (GF3), or Go Green (FJ6) exterior colors only.

Colored bodyside moldings were available on all models only if the side stripes were not ordered. On R/T models the stripes must be deleted, so you'll usually find

Non-R/T's in 1971 used this type of stripe on the rear quarter-panel.

The 1973-1974 Barracuda side-stripe option. *Year One*

the code V98 on the fender tag when this occurs. The moldings came in either black, green, or blue, and they usually—but not always—matched the interior trim. The option code for the stripe or body side molding will appear on the fender tag. The following codes will denote the side stripes: V9X, black; V9W, white; V9F, chartreuse; and V9V, orange.

For the bodyside moldings, the following codes can be found on the fender tag: V5X, black; V9B, blue; and V9F, green.

A black or white tape stripe was optional on all 1972 Barracuda models. It begins at the front fender just above the midline of the car. Then the stripe traces back over the door and door handle to the end of the door, where it turns upward and continues over the quarter-panel. The portion running over the quarter-panel is thinner than that running over the door or front fender. A thin pinstripe traces around the outline of the entire stripe. The stripe was originally one piece and had to be cut to fit.

Multiple strobe-like black stripes were standard on the Challenger Rally models. The decals ran from the simulated air scoop on the front fender to nearly the end of the door. These same tape stripes were also standard on 1973 and 1974 Challenger Rally models.

For 1973 and 1974, side stripes were optional with the Barracuda. Again available in white or black, the bottom of the stripe was routed along on the same line as the exterior door handle, and there is a cut-out in the stripe for the handle. The top of the stripe begins at a rounded point on the front fender and then traces back over the door. It then continues over onto the quarter-

These stripes were standard with the 1972-1974 Challenger Rally. *Chrysler Historical Photo*

panel, where it bends upward slightly and the ends arc to meet the straight bottom portion of the stripe. Base 1973 and 1974 Challengers were optional with accent stripes, and these stripes traced the upper contours of the body and were painted on. The paints in the chart at right were used.

The codes for the stripes on the Barracudas can be found on the fender tag. Strobe stripes can be identified by either of these two codes: V6X, black, or V6W, white. On base Challenger models, the accent stripe will be coded as follows: V7X, black; V7W, white; V7Y, gold; V7F, green; V7B, blue; and V7L, parchment.

1973-1974 Challenger Accent Stripe Colors

Color	Paint Number
White	2033
Black	9000
Light Bright Blue	14016
Medium Gold	23724
Light Green	44647
Parchment	23740

Front Bumpers

The same front bumpers were used on all 1967-1969 Barracudas regardless of body style or model year. Front bumper guards with black rubber cushions were optional for all Barracudas all three years. Like the bumper, the guards and the cushion were not changed and the same part numbers were used all three years. Note that front guards were available only with rear bumper guards for 1967-1969 models, so it is incorrect for a car to have front bumper guards and not have rear bumper guards.

There were nine different bumpers used on 1970 Barracudas. Standard on all models was a chrome bumper, but a body-colored front Elastomeric bumper was available with certain exterior colors. The option used colored high-density urethane foam molded over an unchromed bumper. See the accompanying chart for usage.

Unlike previous years, for 1970 models front bumper guards were available as a separate option and no longer did they have to be ordered with rear guards.

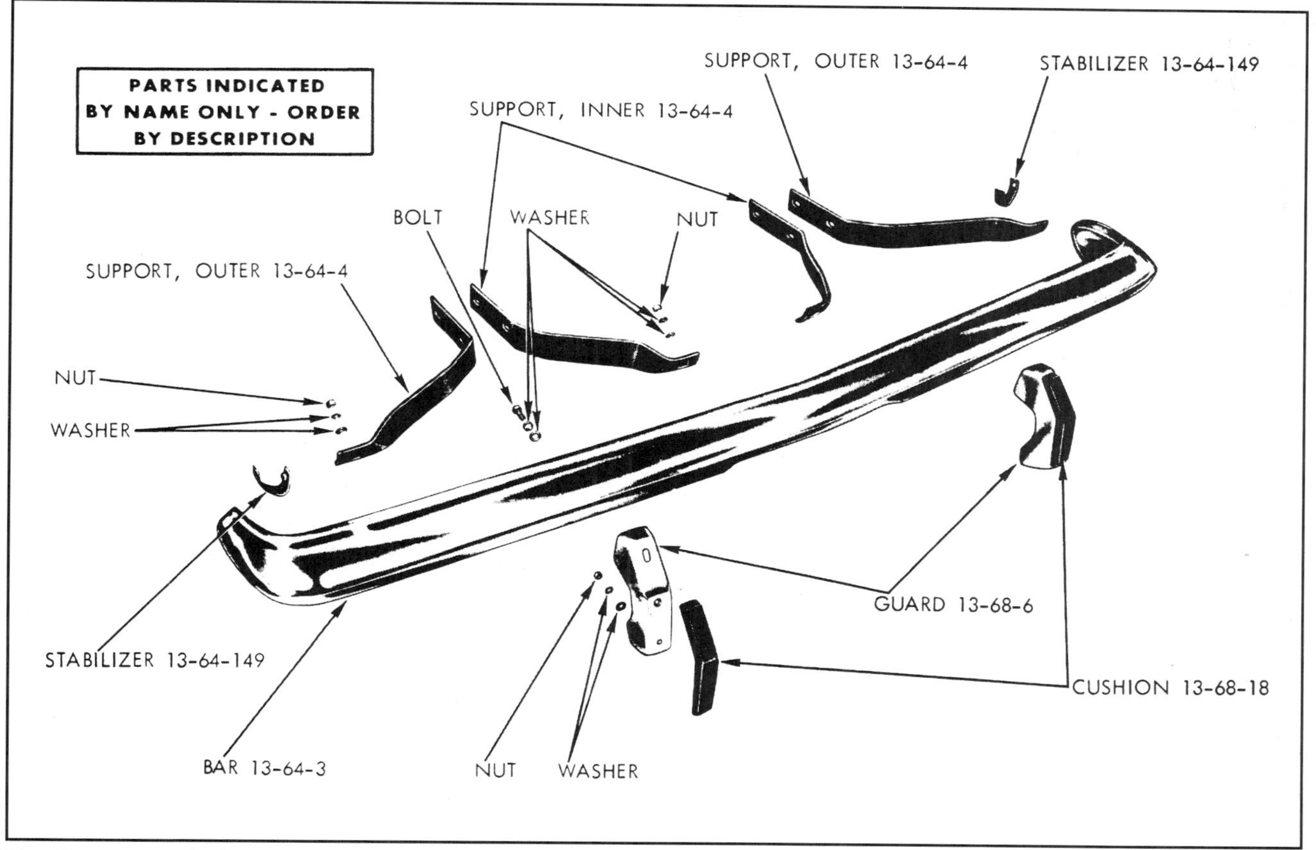

The 1967 Barracuda front bumper was typical of 1968-1969 bumper styles.

1970 Barracuda Colored Front Bumpers		
Exterior Color and Code	**Bumper Color**	**Bumper Part Number**
Blue Fire Met., EB5	Bright Blue Met.	2962275
Rally Red, FE5	Light Bright Red	2962375
Ivy Green Met., EF8	Medium Dark Green Met.	2962377
Deep Burnt Orange, FK5	Medium Burnt Orange	2962378
Alpine White, EW1	White	2962380
Black Velvet, TX9	Black	2962381
In Violet Met., FC7	Purple	2962295
Lemon Twist, FY1	Cadmium Yellow	2962294

However, this year the guards, part numbers 2962288 (right) and 2962289 (left), were available only with the standard chrome bumper. The option code for the colored bumpers can be found on the fender tag. Look for option codes A21 or A22 on your car's fender tag. The latter of these also included a matching rear bumper. To determine whether or not your chrome front bumper had the optional guards, look for the option code M81 or M85. The M85 code also included rear bumper guards.

All Challengers used a chrome front bumper, part number 2962348, all year. A colored front bumper was not an option on the 1970 Challenger line. Front bumper guards with black cushions were optional for all models. Follow the guide provided in the paragraph above to determine if your car has bumper guards or not.

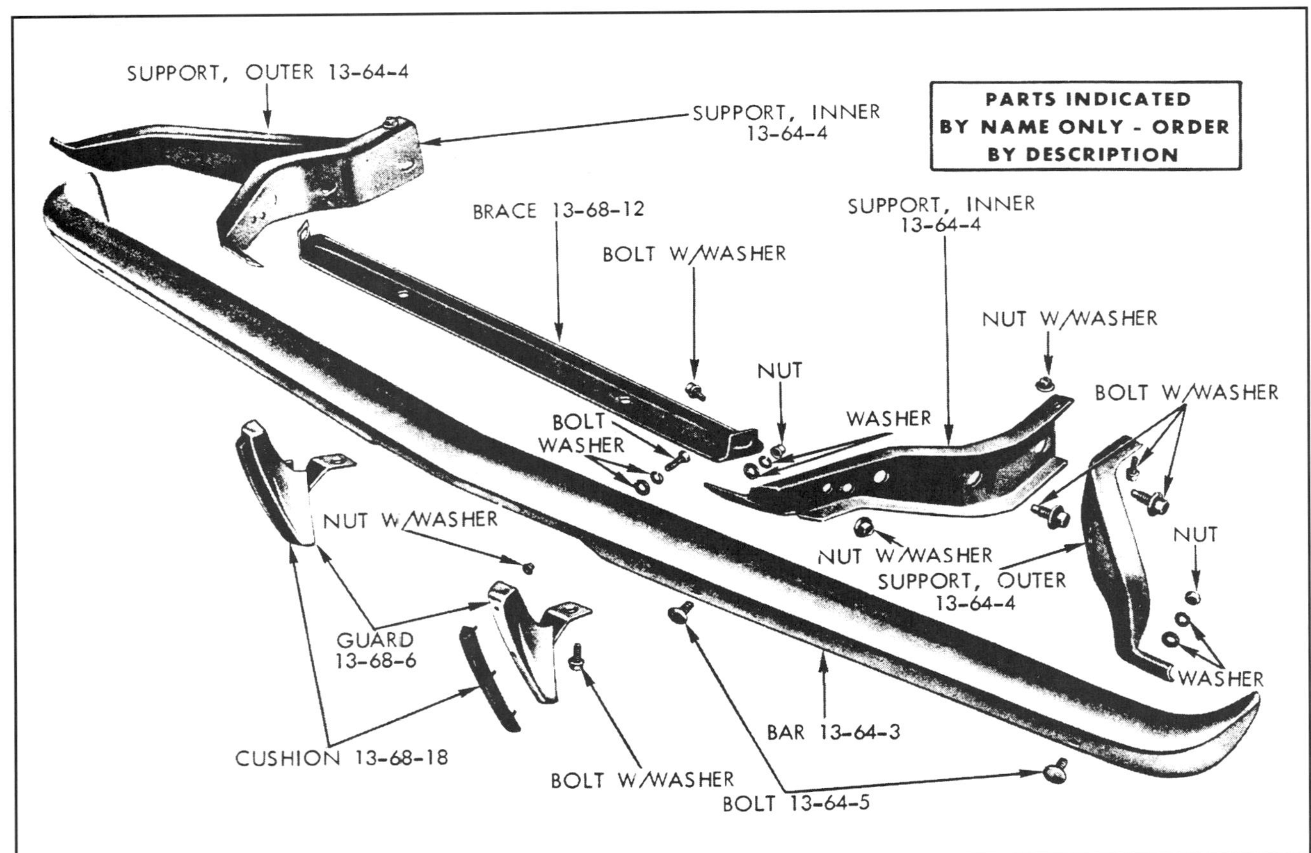

The 1970-1972 Barracuda front bumper.

The front bumper was restyled for the 1971 Barracudas and it will not fit 1970 models. Two chrome bumpers were used, and most models used part number 3464052, but those built after June 1, 1971, used part number 3595035. This is because a federal mandate requiring safety bumpers took effect in June. Since Chrysler built cars into July, the bumper had to be redesigned. This is the same bumper used on all 1972 Barracudas. Colored bumpers again returned as an option, but only six exterior colors were available with this option. Although many believe that a colored grille was a required option with the colored bumper, it was not.

Challengers used three standard chrome bumpers. Early models, those built up to February 1971, used the same front bumper that the 1970 models used. After this date, until June 1971, part number 3595062 was used. Safety measures required another bumper change in June, so from June 1, 1971, until the end of production, part number 3595032 was used. Unlike the Barracuda, the 1972 Challenger did not use this bumper.

Colored Elastomeric front bumpers became optional on the Challenger models in 1971, but only four colors were available with this option: Bright Blue Metallic (GB5); Citron Yella (GY3); Hemi Orange (EV2); and Crazy Plum (FC7). Around April 1971, all painted bumpers except the Citron Yella were canceled. See Barracuda notes above to help you use the fender

1971 Barracuda Colored Front Bumpers

Exterior Color and Code	Color of Bumper	Part Number
True Blue, EB5	Bright Blue Met.	3464250
Sassy Grass Green, FJ6	Avocado	3464875
Citron Yella, CY3	Citron Yella	3464876
In Violet, FC7	Plum	3464877
Tor Red, EV2	Tor Red	3464878
Rally Red, FE5	Red	3464879

Note: Effective April 15, 1971, orders for all Elastomeric bumper groups except CY3 were no longer accepted. Parts remained available and previous orders were filled.

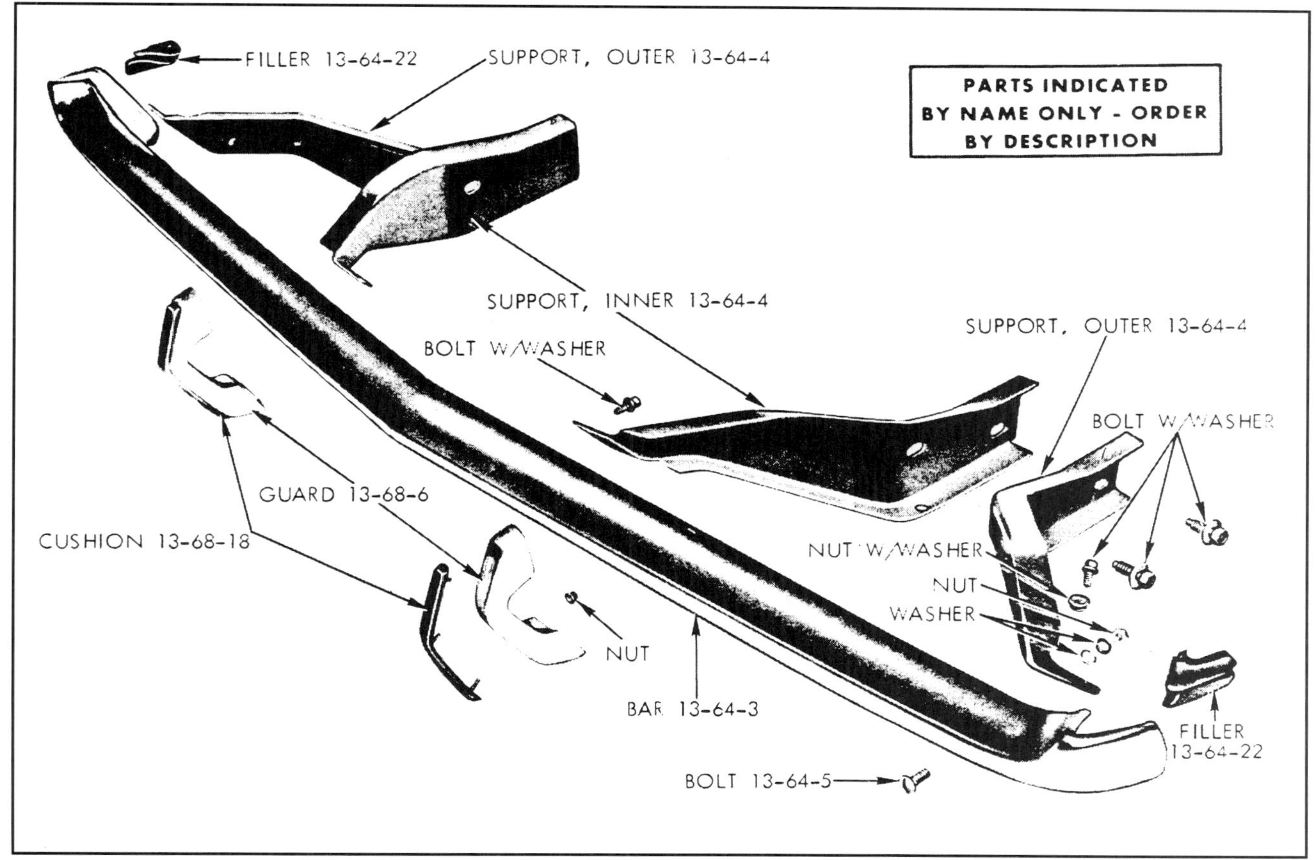

The 1970-1972 Challenger front bumper.

1970 Barracuda Rear Elastomeric Bumpers

Exterior Color and Code	Rear Bumper Color	Bumper Part Number
Blue Fire Met., EB5	Bright Blue Met.	2962390
Rally Red, FE5	Light Bright Red	2961391
Ivy Green Met., EF8	Medium Dark Green Met.	2962392
Deep Burnt Orange, FK5	Medium Burnt Orange	2962393
Alpine White, EW1	White	2962395
Black Velvet, TX9	Black	2962396
In Violet Met., FC7	Purple	2962423
Lemon Twist, FY1	Yellow	2962421
Limelight, FJ5	Light green*	2962422*

* = Available as rear bumper only.

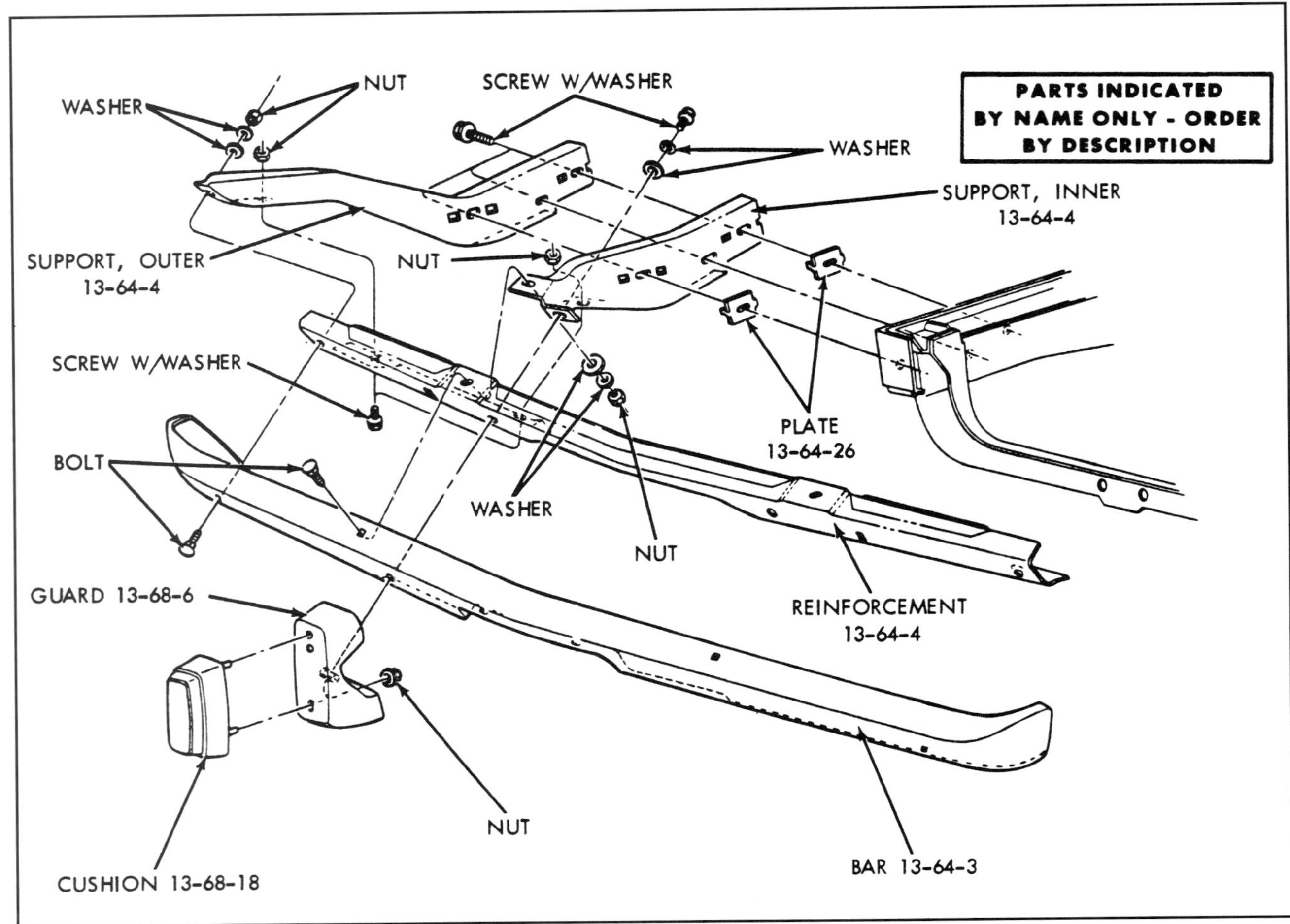

The 1973-1974 Barracuda front bumper.

tag to determine whether your Challenger came with the colored bumper. The option codes are the same as with the Challenger.

Bumper guards were still optional for both models, but they were not available for either model with the colored bumpers. The same bumper guards that were used on the 1970 Challengers were used again unchanged in 1971. However, those on the Barracudas were new and will not fit earlier models; even the black rubber cushion is different.

As explained above, the late-1971 chrome Barracuda bumper was held over and used on all 1972 Barracudas. Challengers used a brand new bumper listed as part number 3595039, and it, too, was the only bumper used. All colored bumper options were canceled. Although the bumpers were changed, the bumper guards remained the same parts used in 1971.

Due to more federal safety standards for 1973 models, both models got a new bumper, one which was used on 1974 models as well. They were heavier than previous years, as they had to pass a 5 miles per hour crash test without any body damage occurring to the car. Barracudas used part number 3686050 and the Challengers used part number 3686075. Bumper guards were also restyled and again each model used a unique set and they are not interchangeable. The guards protrude outward more than in previous years and the cushion was glued to a chrome backing plate. Both front and rear bumper guards were made standard equipment for both models, and the 1974 models used the same parts.

Rear Bumper

As with the front bumper, all 1967-1969 Barracudas used the same rear bumper each year for all body styles. As previously stated, bumper guards were available only in a group, so a car with rear bumper guards but without front bumper guards is considered incorrect. The rear bumper guards were the same throughout the three-year run, and unlike the front guards, these guards were designed to fit either side of the rear bumper.

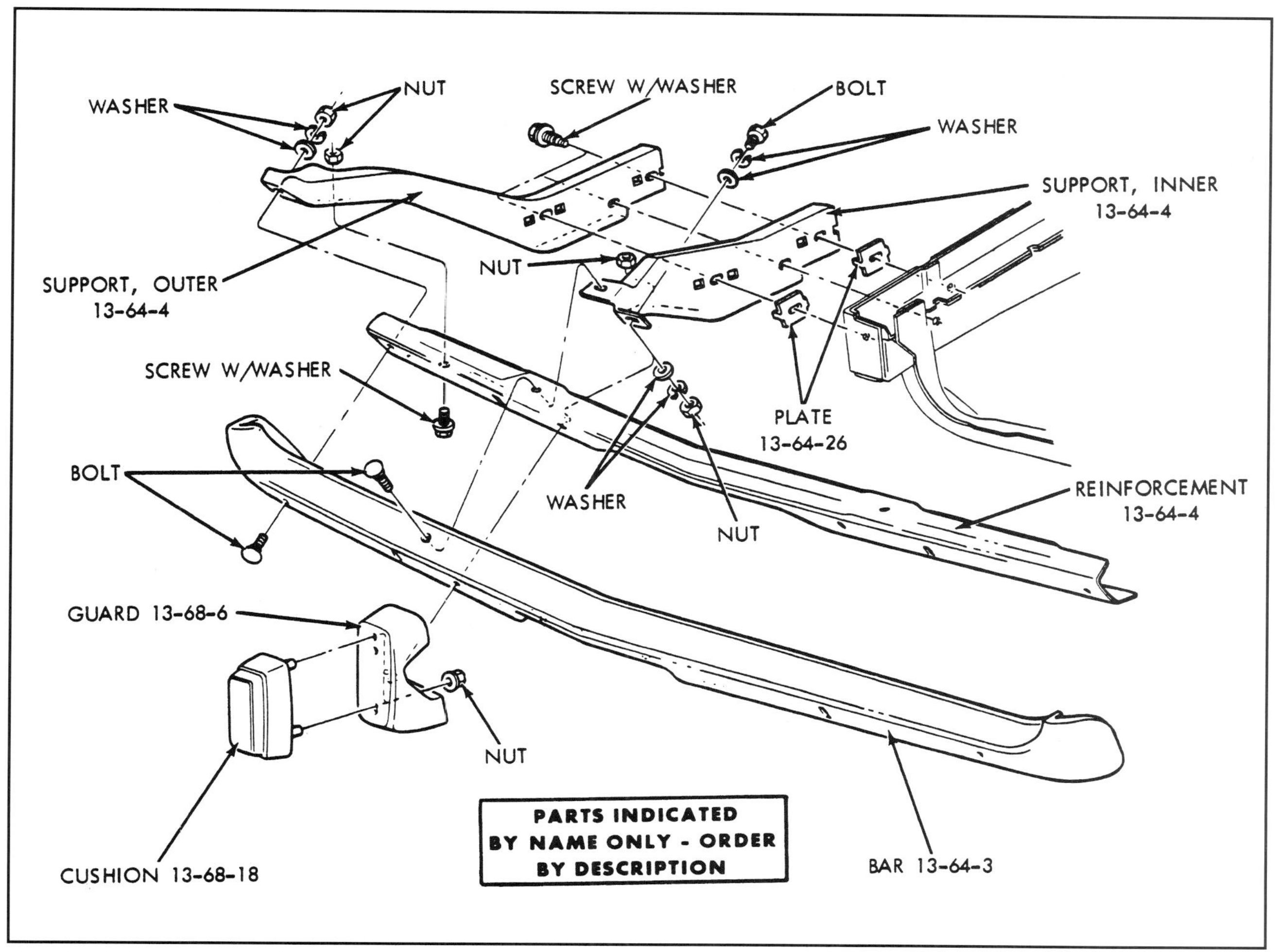

The 1973-1974 Challenger front bumper.

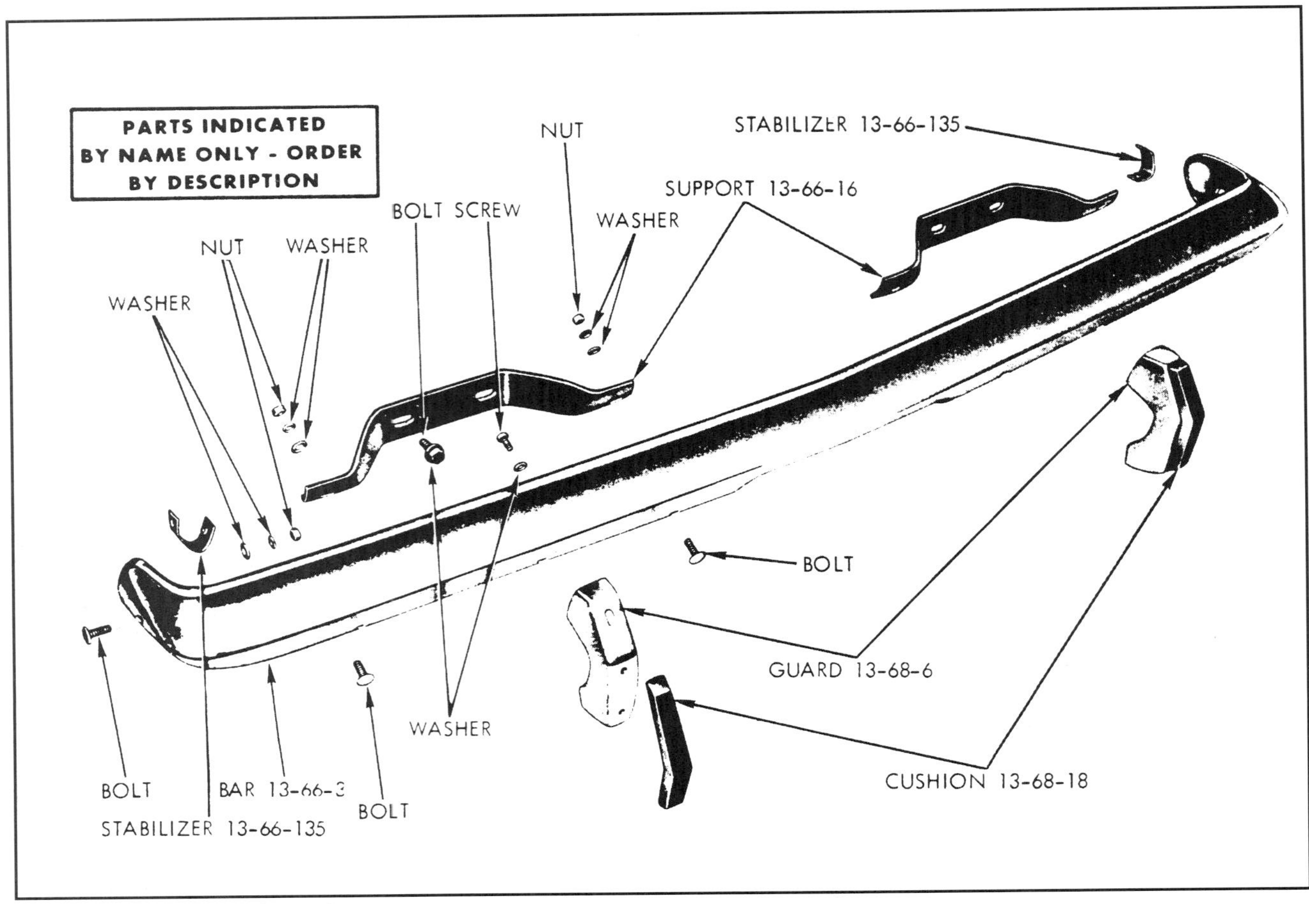

The 1967-1969 Barracuda rear bumper.

A chrome bumper, part number 2962300, was standard on all 1970 Barracuda models. However, with the A22 option, both a colored rear bumper and front bumper were available. The same colors that were available for the front bumper were also available for the rear bumpers. Moreover, there is an additional rear bumper listed as being available without a matching front bumper. The single rear bumper is for Limelight-colored cars.

Only one bumper, part number 2962350, was used on all 1970 Challenger models. No colored bumpers were available with this model this year. All Barracudas used part number 2962310. Rear bumper guards were made standard this year and were used with all bumpers, including the colored rear bumpers. Like earlier models, the guard is designed so it will fit either side of the bumper. The guards used no rubber cushion.

1971 Barracuda Rear Elastomeric Rear Bumpers

Exterior Color and Code	Bumper Color	Bumper Part Number
Rally Red, FE5	Red	2962391
Citron Yella, CY3	Citron Yella	3464883
In Violet, FC7	Plum	3464884
Tor Red, EV2	Tor Red	3464885

All but CY3 were canceled 4-15-1971; CY3 was canceled 7-1-1971.

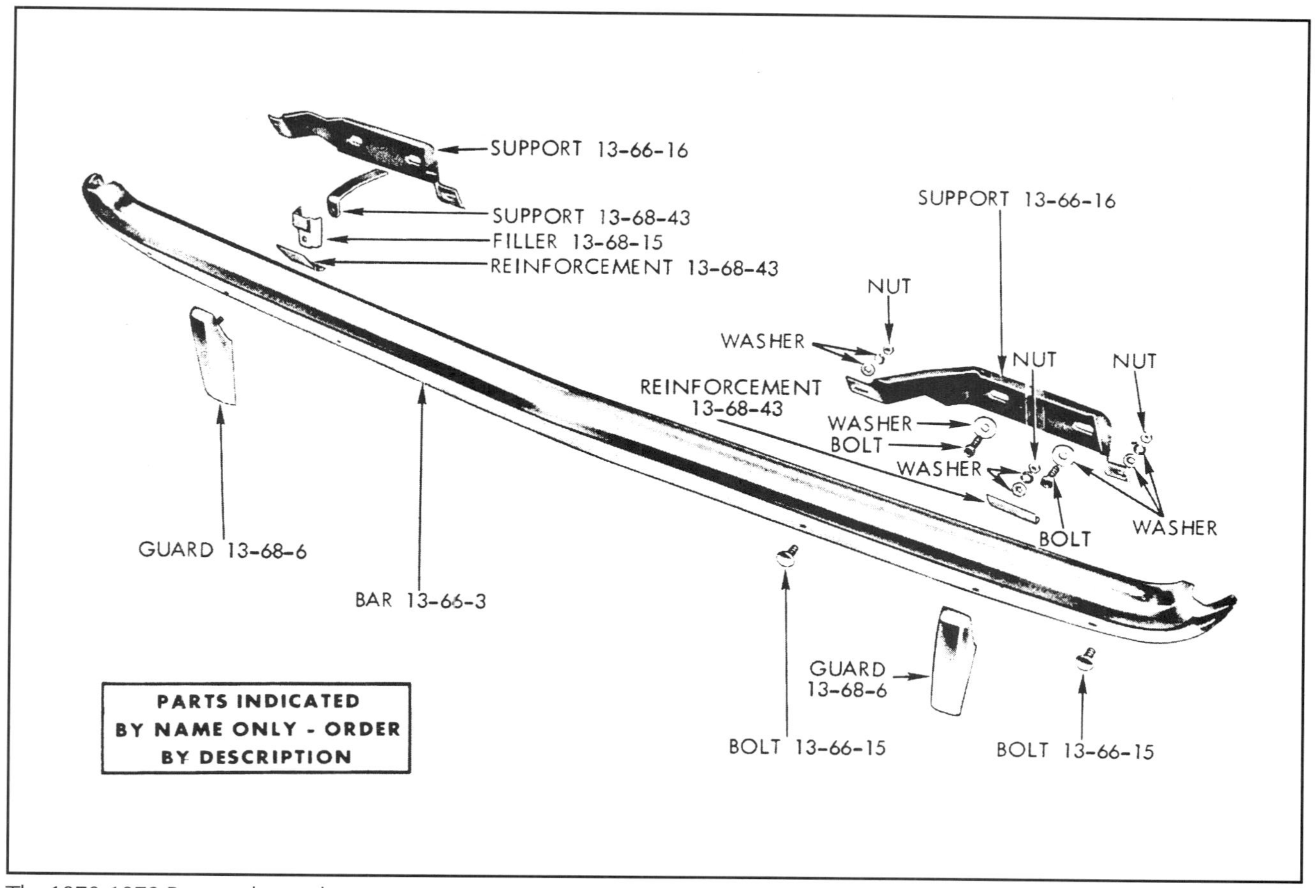

The 1970-1972 Barracuda rear bumper.

Challenger models used two different sets of bumper guards, with their use determined by body style. Base Challenger coupes (the rear quarter-windows will not roll down) used part numbers 2962366 (right) and 2962367 (left) and used no rubber cushion. All other models used part numbers 2962358 (right) and 2962359 (left), which did use a black rubber cushion. For correctness, the proper guards should be used. However, it is possible that the other type was installed on the car at the factory if there was a shortage at the factory. It is possible that your Challenger S.E. could have the solid chrome bumper guards like the Barracuda; rear bumper guards were standard items on all Challengers.

The standard chrome bumper for early-built Barracudas was the exact same chrome bumper used on 1970 models. Those built after June 1, 1971, used part number 359037, a change which, as with the front bumper, was made to satisfy safety standards. Also like the front bumper, the late-built cars' bumper was used on 1972 models all year.

Colored bumpers were again available for Barracuda models, but their color choice was cut to four exterior colors. This means that not all the colors offered with the colored front bumper were available with a matching rear bumper. Those cars painted True Blue Metallic (EB5) or Sassy Grass Green (FJ6) were not available with a colored rear bumper. See the accompanying chart for part numbers and colors that were available. Note that on April 15, 1971, orders for colored bumpers—except with the Citron Yella exterior (CY3)—were no longer being taken. After June 1, 1971, no cars with a colored bumper were built.

Two different chrome bumpers were used as standard equipment on the 1971 Challengers. Unlike its sister ship the Barracuda, the Challenger did not use a carryover bumper from the 1970 models. Early models used part number 3464073 until June 1, 1971, when part number 3595038 took its place. As with the Barracuda, this bumper was also used on the rear of all 1972 Challengers all year. A new option to Challengers this year was colored bumper groups.

Rear bumper guards were still standard in 1971 on all bumpers, including the colored bumper. However, the Barracuda used a new design. It still fit either side of the bumper, but it now used a black rubber cushion.

1971 Challenger Colored Rear Bumper

Exterior Color Code	Bumper Color	Bumper Part Number
Bright Blue, EB5	Bright Blue Met.	3464092
Citron Yella, CY3	Citron Yella	3464895
Plum Crazy, FC7	Plum Crazy	3464896
Hemi Orange, EV2	Ceramic Red	3464897

Note that the guards were not painted to match the colored bumpers. Instead, they were left bright. Challengers used the same two sets of bumper guards used on 1970 models.

To see if your car was built with both front and rear colored bumpers (rear colored bumpers were not available as a separate option), look for the option code A22 on your fender tag. Without this option code, it is incorrect for your car to have colored bumpers. If the code A21 appears, then only a colored front bumper should be used. If neither of these codes can be found, then your car used chrome front and rear bumpers—but watch for the build dates of 7-01-1971 to 08-31-1971, where the 1971 bumper was used.

Only a chrome rear bumper was used on both models in 1972. The colored bumper group was never offered for either model that year. The part numbers were the same as those used on the late-built 1971 models for both makes. Bumper guards were still used as standard equipment, and the Challenger still used the same two

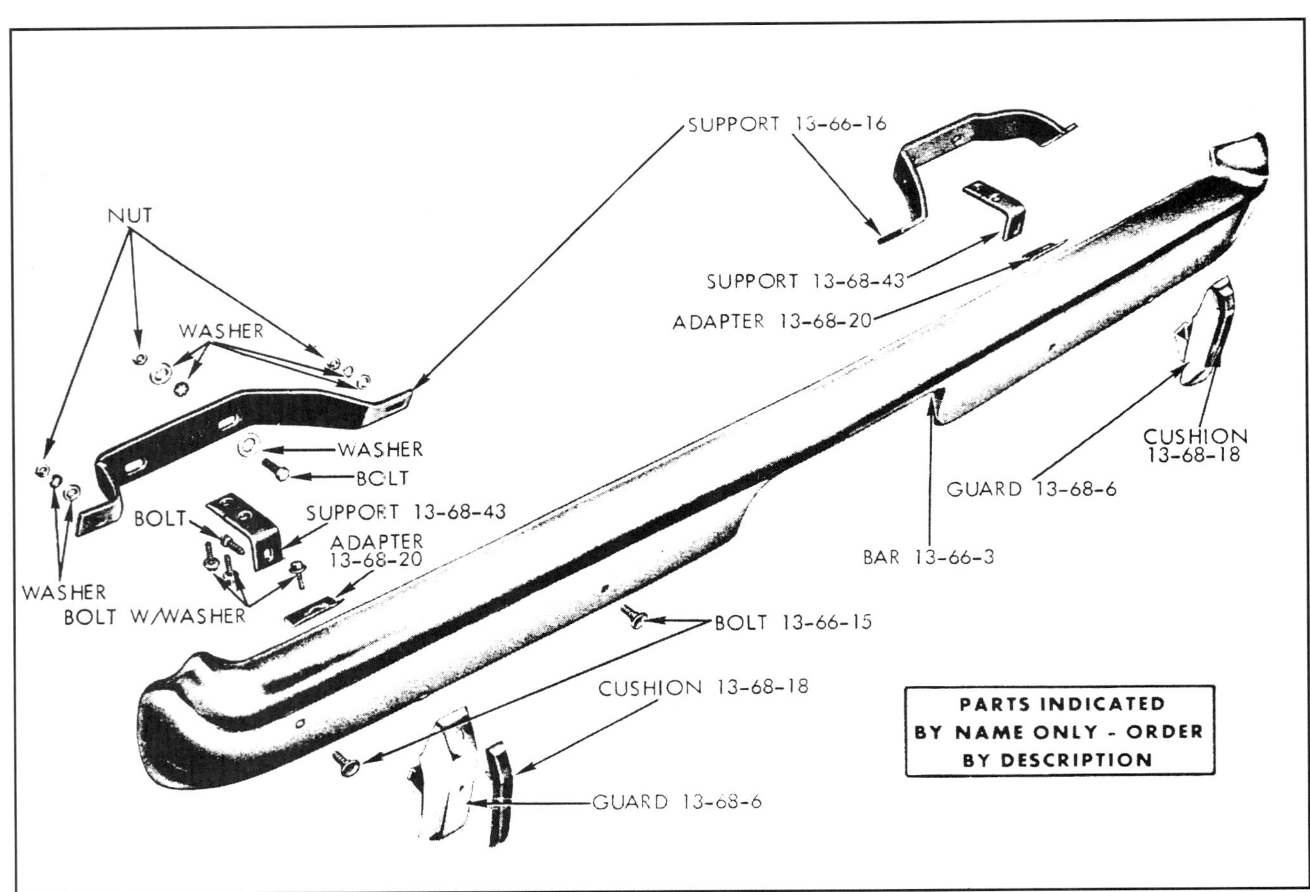

The 1970-1972 Challenger rear bumper.

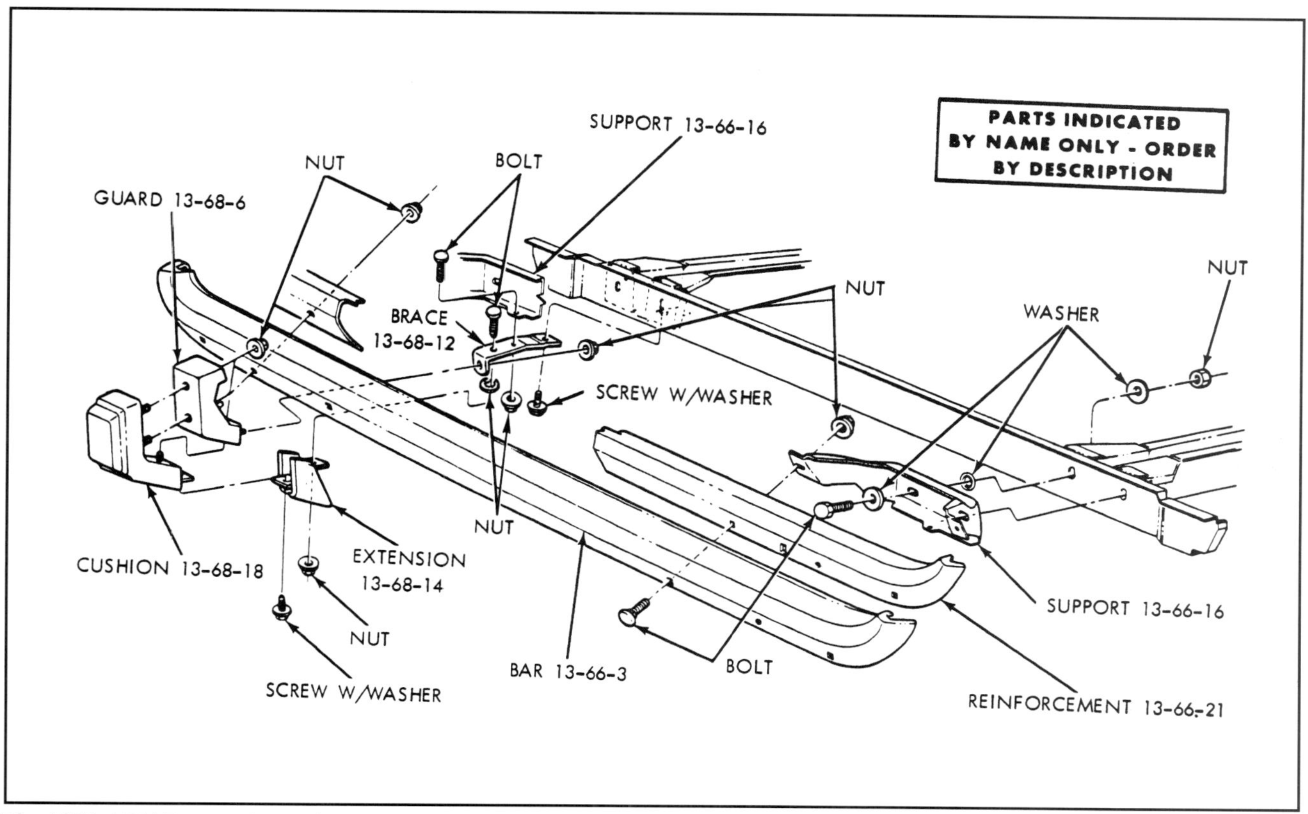

The 1973-1974 Barracuda rear bumper.

sets of guards it used in 1970 and 1971 models, one with a cushion and one without a cushion.

Likewise, the Barracudas also used two sets of guards, one with a black cushion and one without. Those with a cushion were the same guards used on 1971 models, and those without a cushion were the same parts used on 1970 models. Unlike the previous years, all models used both types, meaning either is correct on a given bumper. However, having one of each type on the same bumper is not correct.

New "big brother" government regulations in 1973 required that both models be equipped with new bumpers that can pass the mandated 5 miles per hour crash test. These new bumpers protrude farther from the car and were much heavier than previous versions. They were also not as sleek-looking. Challengers used part number 3686575 and the Barracuda used part number 3686550. These same two bumpers were used again on the 1974 models, and no colored bumpers were offered either year.

Rear bumper guards were restyled for the new bumper; they, too, were wider. Each model used a different set of guards and they will not interchange. All models in both makes used a rubber cushion. The cushions were designed like the guards and were unique to each side and each model. These same guards were used again for 1974 models.

Chapter 8

Interiors

Original Trim Color

The original type of seating, and the material and color of the interior trim can be determined by looking at the code on the fender tag. On 1967 and 1968 models, the code for the interior trim can be found on the bottom line under the letters "TRM." On 1969-1974 models, the interior trim code is located on the second line from the bottom, the second group of characters to the right. For 1969-1974 models only, the code for the interior paint is the group of characters next to the trim code.

1967 Barracuda seat trim. *Year One*

The trim code will begin with a letter that stands for the grade of trim. One of the following will be used to indicate the grade: H, High; X, Extra Low; D, Deluxe; P, Premium; or A, All Class. Next to the grade is a single digit or letter that indicates the type of material and the seating arrangement. The following codes were used:

1. Cloth and vinyl bench seat
5. All-vinyl split-back bench set (1967-1968)
4 All-vinyl split-back bench seat (1969-1971)
5. Cloth and vinyl bucket seats (1969-1974)
6. All-vinyl bucket seat
R. All-leather bucket seat

The last letter (or letters) and number in the code are for the color. Most codes changed year to year. To decode, see the interior combination chart for your model year.

1967 Seats

A split-back bench seat was standard in all models except the convertible. Standard in the convertible and optional in all other body styles were bucket seats. Whatever the seating arrangement, all seats were done in Coachman grain vinyl with multiple vertical pleated inserts in either white, dark blue, red, copper, black, or gold.

The rear seatback on the fastback features a dip in the middle where a special molding with a fish medallion was used. On the other side of the molding was a bright handle that allowed the seatback to be folded down onto the rear seat cushion. The hardtop and the convertible used a rear seatback that was fixed in place and straight across with no fish medallion.

1968 Seats

Standard again in the convertible was Coachman grain vinyl bucket seats. Bench seats were still standard in the two-door hardtop and fastback models, and they, too, are done in Coachman grain vinyl. Inserts in both seat types were of three wide vertical pleats, with the widest pleats in the center bordered on each side by narrower double pleats. The rear seat arrangement was the same as in 1967 models and its pattern matched that of the front seat. Seat colors were available in black, white, light blue, dark green, or maroon.

A new interior trim option (Deluxe trim) became available for all 1968 models with bucket seats. This upholstery used inserts that were similar in design to the standard trim, but the Deluxe trim used four vertical pleats with two narrow pleats in the middle bordered on each side by double stitching and the wider outer pleats on each side. Deluxe trim was available in the same colors as the standard trim, plus the addition of light gold. This option is easily recognizable by the letter D in the first position of the interior code on the fender tag.

1969 Seats

Split-back bench seats with a center armrest were standard on all models except the convertible. As in previous years, bucket seats were standard in convertibles and optional in all other body styles. Again both the bench and bucket seats were done in Coachman grain vinyl with multiple horizontal pleats. The seats were available in bright blue, white, black, dark green, or red. The Deluxe interior trim option returned for 1969 for all models with bucket seats. This year, however, this interior group, which was available only if the interior decor group package was ordered, used a completely different grain and pattern.

Deluxe trim seats used El Paso grain for the inserts, which featured vertical, center double pleats that were double-stitched on each side. Criss-crossing the vertical pleats were three double-stitched pleats. They were available in the same colors as the standard trim, with the addition of silver or saddle colors.

Also available this year, in two-door hardtop models only, was the floral pattern, commonly known as the Mod interior. Most books list only one pattern of yellow flowers with a green background being available, but the 1969 master catalog also shows that a pattern of yellow flowers with black background was also available. Note that most reproduction companies do not stock either of the floral patterns. You will most likely have to have these patterns custom made at an upholstery shop. Also listed as being available for the

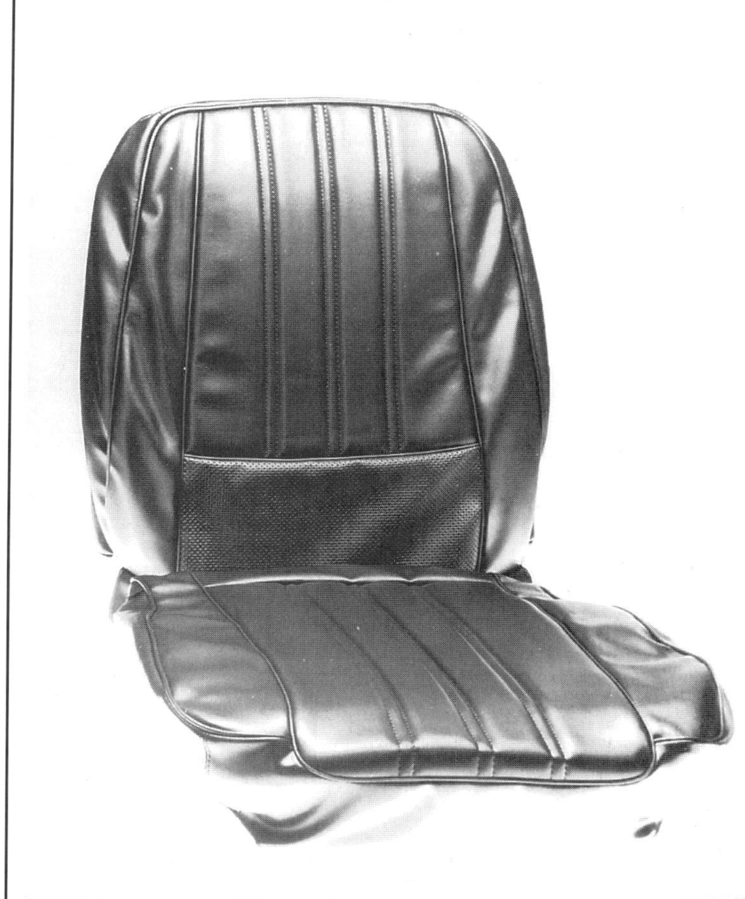

1968 Barracuda deluxe seat trim. *Year One*

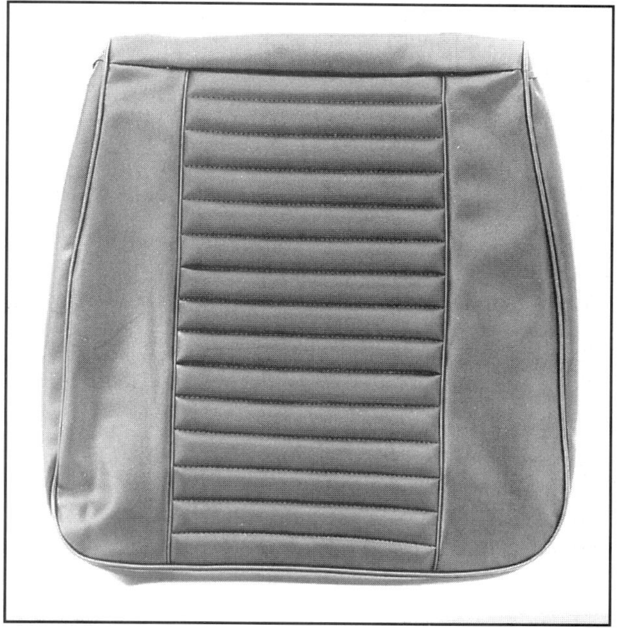

1969 Barracuda standard seat trim. *Year One*

1969 Barracuda deluxe seat trim. *Year One*

1970 Barracuda standard seat trim. *Year One*

fastback only was a saddle tan solid-back front bench seat. The inserts were done in fabric, and the skirts were done in matching Coachman grain vinyl. There is no matching rear seat listed as being available, so these seats were most likely placed in cars stripped down for racing applications only.

The folding rear seatback became an option for the fastback model. If the interior decor group was ordered, then the folding seatback was mandatory. Thus, it is impossible that your Barracuda came with the Deluxe seat trim and did not have a rear folding seatback, unless there was a mix-up at the factory. However, it is possible that your 1969 fastback could have come without a rear folding seat, or it could have come with a rear folding seat and without the interior decor group option.

1970 Seats

Split, high-back bench seats with a center armrest were standard in all Barracuda models except convertibles and the Gran Coupe, both of which had bucket seats as standard equipment. Bench seats and bucket seats used an insert pattern of thin multiple horizontal pleats near the front edge of the seating area and backrest. The inserts were done in Ranger grain vinyl and the skirts were done in Coachman grain vinyl. Colors were Brite Blue, dark green, or white. The bucket seats used in the convertible, which were optional in all models except the Gran Coupe, used the same grain, pattern, and colors used on the bench seats. Russet (dark red) or dark tan were two colors offered only with bucket seats.

Front bucket seats were standard in Gran Coupes, but they were done in leather trim, not vinyl. The pattern insert featured five vertical double-stitched pleats in the center of the seat cushion and the backrest, with four vinyl-covered buttons at the front edge of the inserts. Colors included black, white, or tan. The rear seat matched the pattern of the front seats but was done in Coachman grain vinyl with six vinyl-covered buttons in each seating area in the backrest. Effective August 9, 1969, leather trim became optional in all other Barracuda models.

Available as a credit option on the Gran Coupe were deluxe all-vinyl bucket seats, which looked nothing like the leather seats or the base Barracuda's trim. These seats used an insert pattern that featured two wide, vertical pleats in the center that were bordered by two narrower vertical pleats on each side. The inserts were done in Shallow Elk grain vinyl and the skirts were done in Coachman grain vinyl. Colors included; Black Frost (charcoal), red, Burnt Orange, tan, white, dark green, or gold. Another credit option for the Gran Coupe models was the combination cloth-and-vinyl seats in either black or Burnt Orange. The inserts were cloth and the skirts were Coachman grain vinyl.

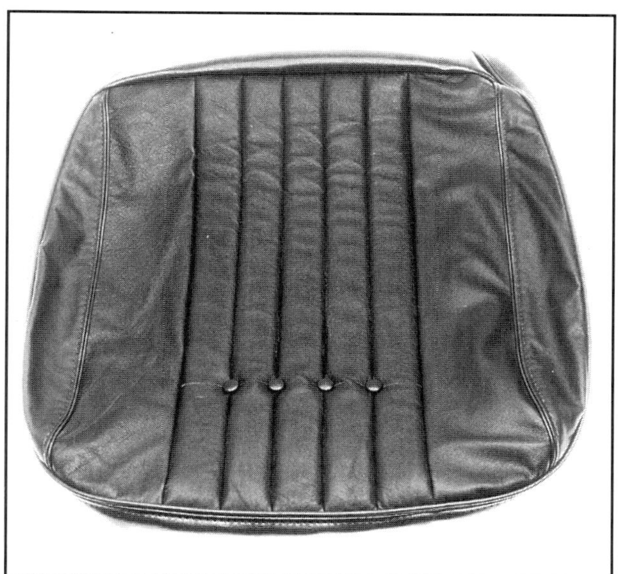

1970 Gran Coupe leather seat trim. *Year One*

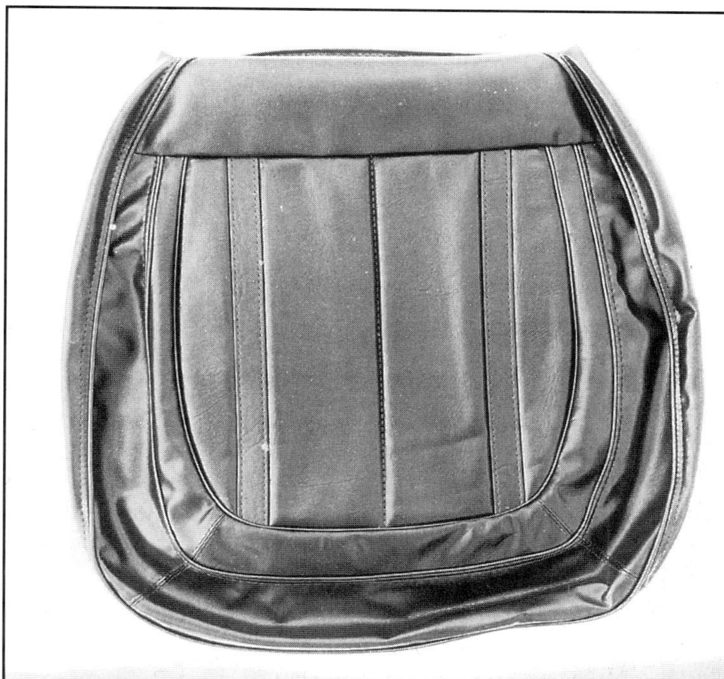

1970 Gran Coupe vinyl seat trim. *Year One*

Only base Challenger models came standard with a bench seat. The design, pattern, and grain were the same as those used on base Barracudas, and only black or Brite Blue were offered. Standard on all convertible and R/T models were front bucket seats, which were optional on the base hardtop. They used a pattern done in Regal grain vinyl that featured multiple horizontal pleats that were criss-crossed by two vertical pleats. Unlike the Barracuda, the pleats in the Dodge extended clear across the cushion. Colors included black, Brite Blue, dark green, white, Burnt Orange, red, or dark tan.

The Challenger S.E. came standard with leather-trimmed front bucket seats. They used a pattern insert of multiple vertical pleats surrounded by a seam in a semi-circle. Colors included dark tan, Burnt Orange, or black. Around August 9, 1969, leather trim was made optional on all other Challenger models. Cloth-and-vinyl bucket seats were a credit option in the S.E. and an extra-cost option in all other models. They were available in dark tan, Burnt Orange, black, or dark green. They featured a cloth insert with Coachman grain vinyl skirts.

1971 Seats

Standard again in all Barracuda models, except the convertible and Gran Coupes, were split-back, high-back bench seats with a center folding armrest. The pattern was very simple and plain, consisting of double vertical pleats in the center of each cushion and backrest, done in El Paso grain with Coachman grain vinyl skirts. Colors included black, Brite Blue, dark green, tan, or white. Bucket seats in the same pattern and grains were standard on all

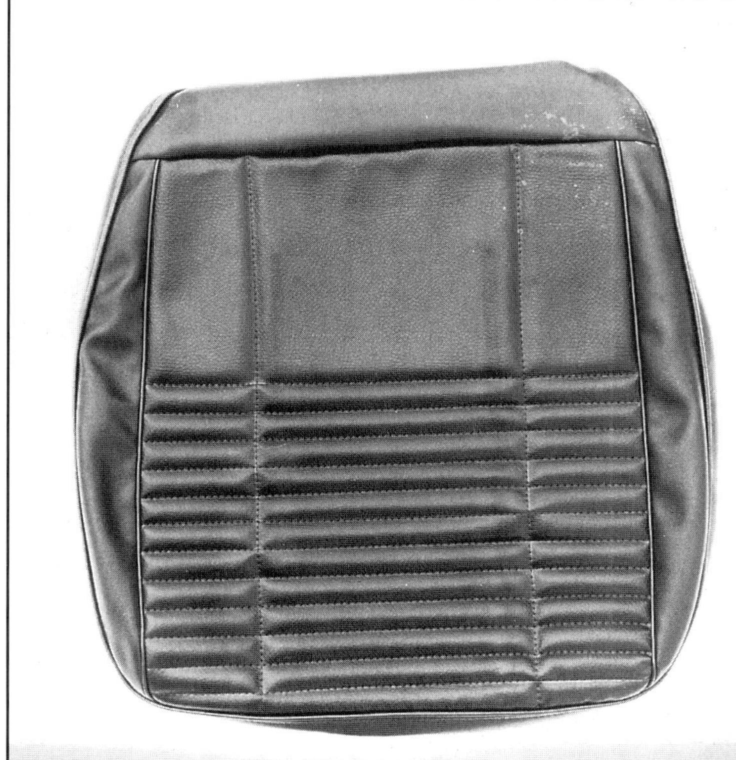

1970 Challenger deluxe seat trim. *Year One*

1971 Barracuda seat trim. *Year One*

convertibles and optional on all other models except the Gran Coupe. Colors were the same as with the bench seat except with the combination of black and Burnt Orange.

Leather trim remained standard in the Gran Coupe models, using the same pattern used in 1970 and available in black, tan, or gold. Leather trim was optional on the Cuda but was no longer available for the base Barracuda models and was limited to either black or tan. No gold leather trim was offered in the Cuda line. A combination black vinyl and black cloth seats were a credit option in the Gran Coupe line and an extra-cost option on all other models. Also available for all models was a seat with a combination of orange vinyl and black cloth inserts. Premium-grade all-vinyl bucket seats were also a credit option on the Gran Coupe models. Colors included black, Brite Blue, dark green, tan, or gold.

Base Challengers were standard with a split-back all-vinyl bench seat in the same pattern as those used on the 1971 Barracuda and were available in black or dark green trim only. All convertibles and R/T models were standard with all-vinyl front bucket seats. They used a pattern done in Belmont grain with skirts in Coachman grain vinyl. Low-ball base Challenger coupes used the same pattern and grain as those used on the Plymouths when bucket seats were ordered.

When the Formal roofline was ordered, black leather seats were included in the package, and no other trim

1972 E-body seat trim. *Year One*

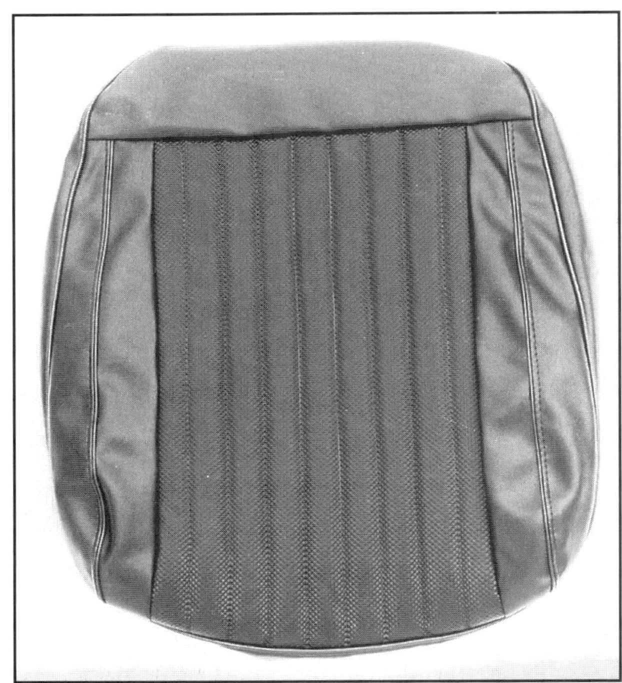

1973 E-Body seat trim. *Year One*

color was available. Cloth-and-vinyl bucket seats were again optional, but for two-door hardtop models only, and were offered in dark green, black, black-and-white, or dark green-and-white. The latter two seats used skirts of white Coachman grain vinyl with the alternate-colored (black or dark green) insert. The dark green-and-white trim was not available on the Challenger R/T models.

1972 Seats

All Barracuda and Challenger models now came standard with front bucket seats. Only all-vinyl seats were offered, and no combination cloth-and-vinyl or leather-trimmed seats were available as an option. Both makes used the same pattern, which featured Ranger grain inserts of multiple vertical pleats. Colors included BriteBlue, dark green, white, black, or gold.

1973-1974 Seats

Bucket seats were standard both years and both years they used the same pattern as in 1972 models, except the inserts were done in Empire grain vinyl and the skirts were of Coachman grain. Colors in 1973 were black, white, dark green, or bright blue. In 1974 only black, white, or dark bright blue were offered.

1967-1969 Instrument Panels

Each model year used a different instrument panel, but the same panel was used with or without air

The 1967-1969-style instrument panel. *Chrysler Historical Photo*

Here is the 1970-1974 Rallye dash. The Challenger style is shown here. *Chrysler Historical Photo*

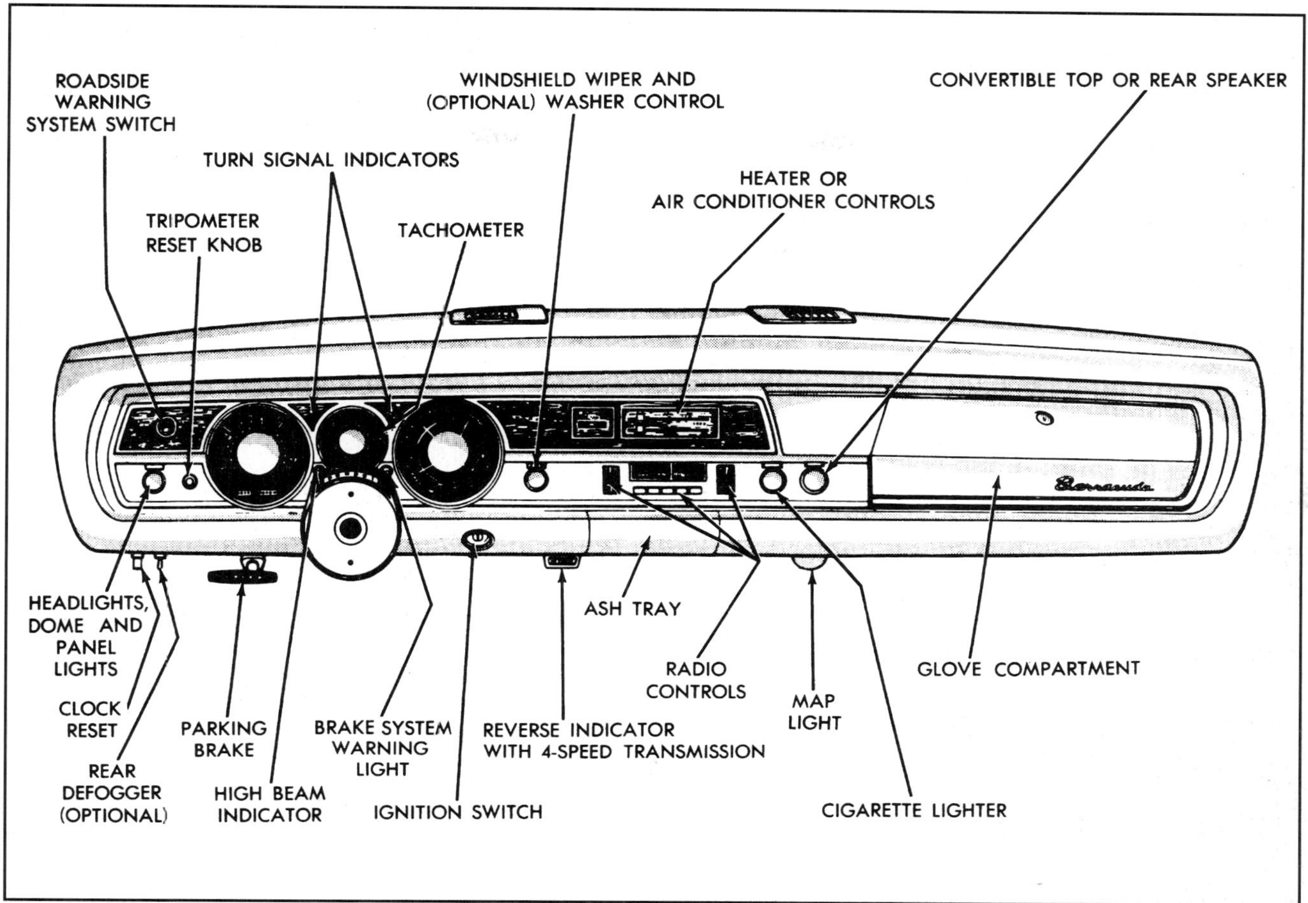

Typical 1967-1969 Barracuda instrument panel.

conditioning. The instrument panel was painted in a flat finish to match the seat trim. When white seats were used, however, the interior's corresponding color was used. For example, with the white-and-black interior, the instrument panel was painted flat black.

In those 1969 models with the flora print interior trims, the instrument panel was painted flat black with the yellow-and-black trim (F6P), or green with the yellow-and-green (F6J) seat trim. (See the accompanying chart for correct interior paint numbers and color names.) A dash pad was standard in all models and it was covered in vinyl that matched the color of the instrument panel.

All models used a folded black fiberboard glovebox insert. The 1968 and 1969 models used the same insert and glovebox door, but the 1967 models used different part numbers. Whichever the model year, the door should be painted the same color as the rest of the instrument panel in a flat finish.

A dull-aluminum-finish plate with the Barracuda script and a small fish symbol was used on the lower portion of the glovebox each year. The same plate, part number 2822370, was used in 1967 and 1968 with all instrument groups. In 1969 models, part number 2822370 was used only on those cars without the Rally instrument cluster. Those models with the Rally cluster used part number 2984620, and this molding still featured the Barracuda script and fish emblem, but it was painted flat black.

1970-1974 Instrument Panels

All Barracudas and Challengers used the same instrument panel with or without the Rally cluster, and with or without air conditioning all five years. As in the previous years, the instrument panel was painted to match either the seats or the corresponding color (see accompanying charts for correct colors) in a flat finish. A dash pad was standard in all models, and 1970 models used a pad with the model name, "Barracuda" or "Challenger," molded into the pad on the upper right-hand side.

For 1971 to 1974 models, the model nameplate was a separate part that was glued to the instrument panel in a space provided on the dash pad. Four different emblems

continued on page 218

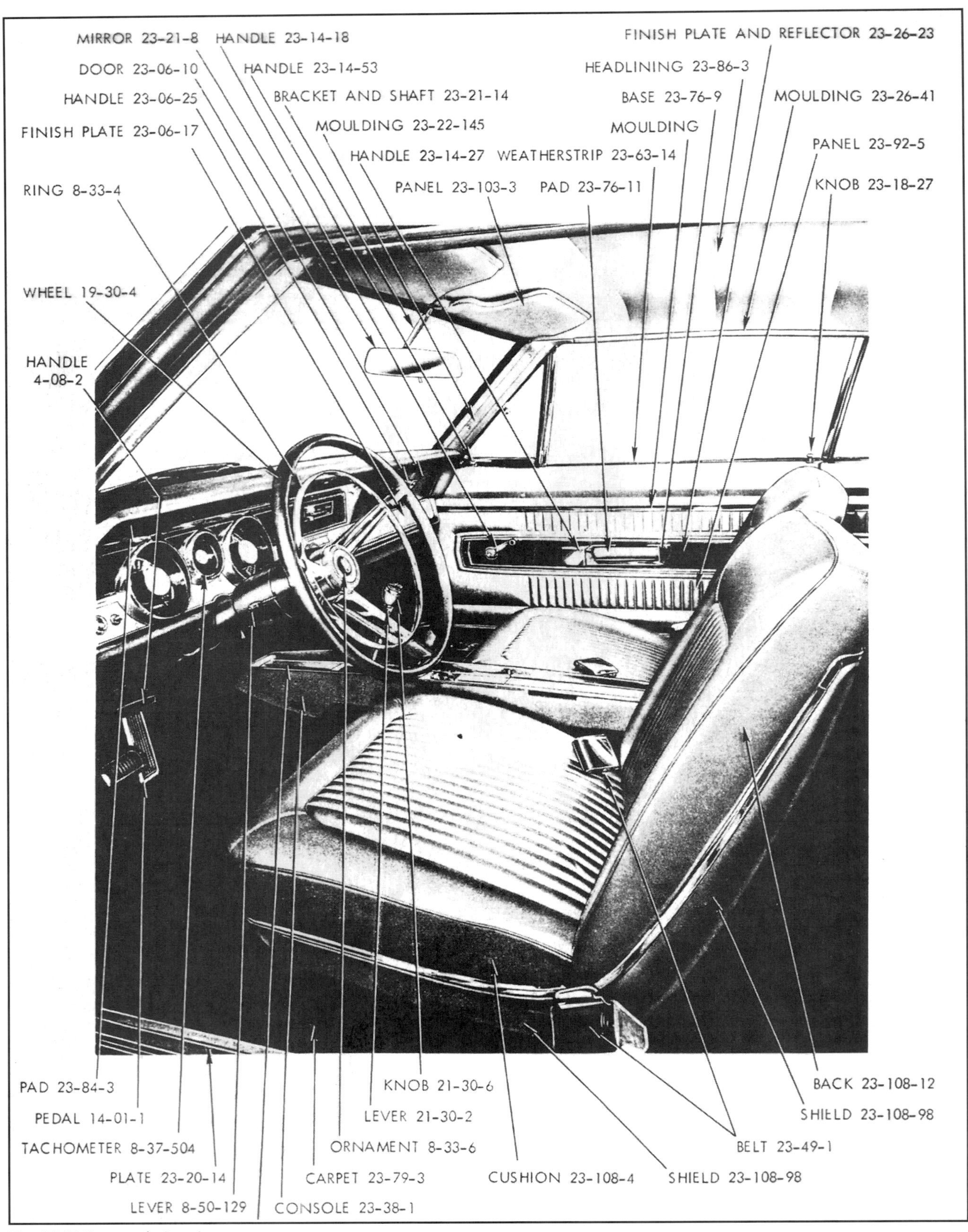

The 1967 Barracuda interior.

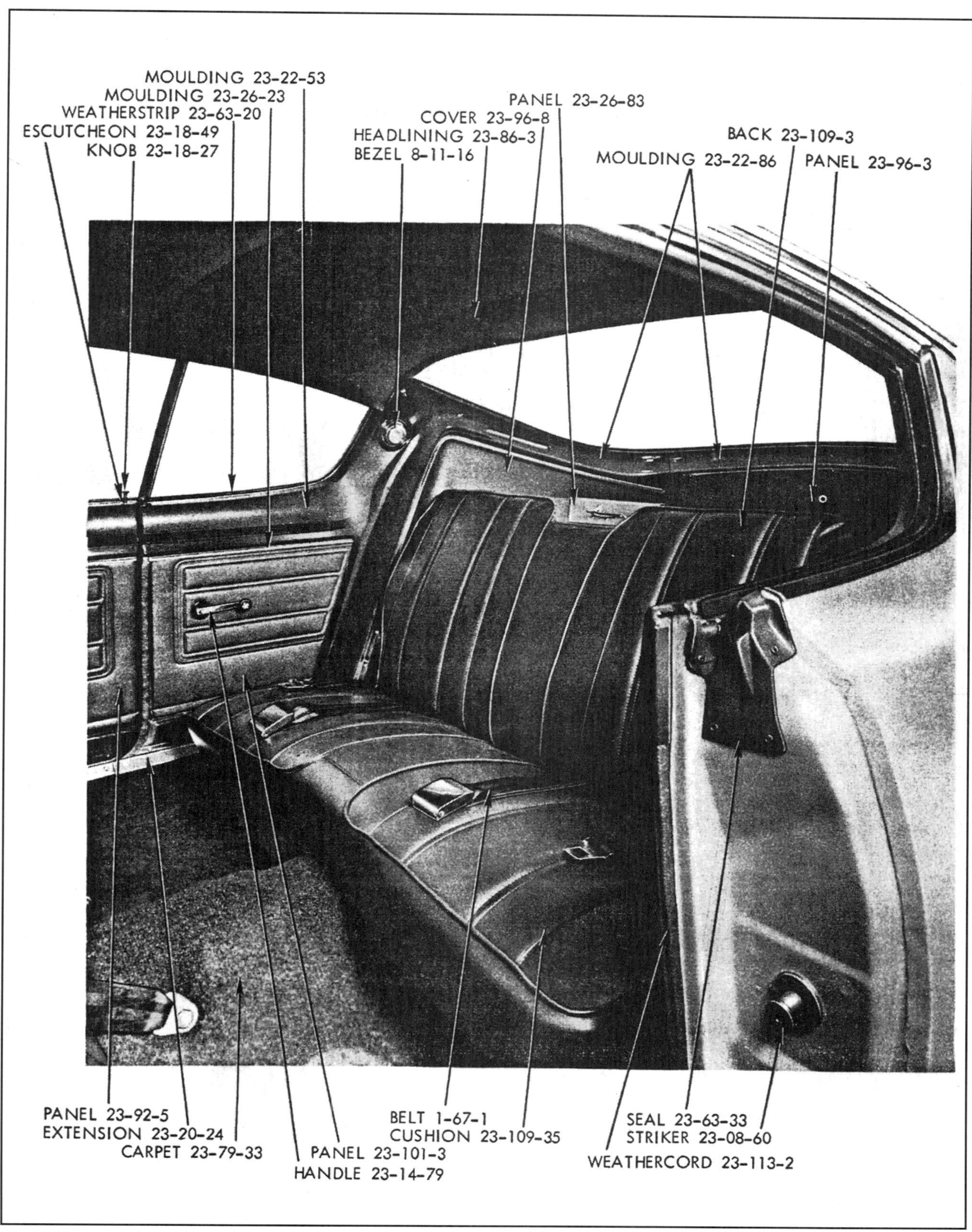

The 1968 Barracuda fastback rear seat.

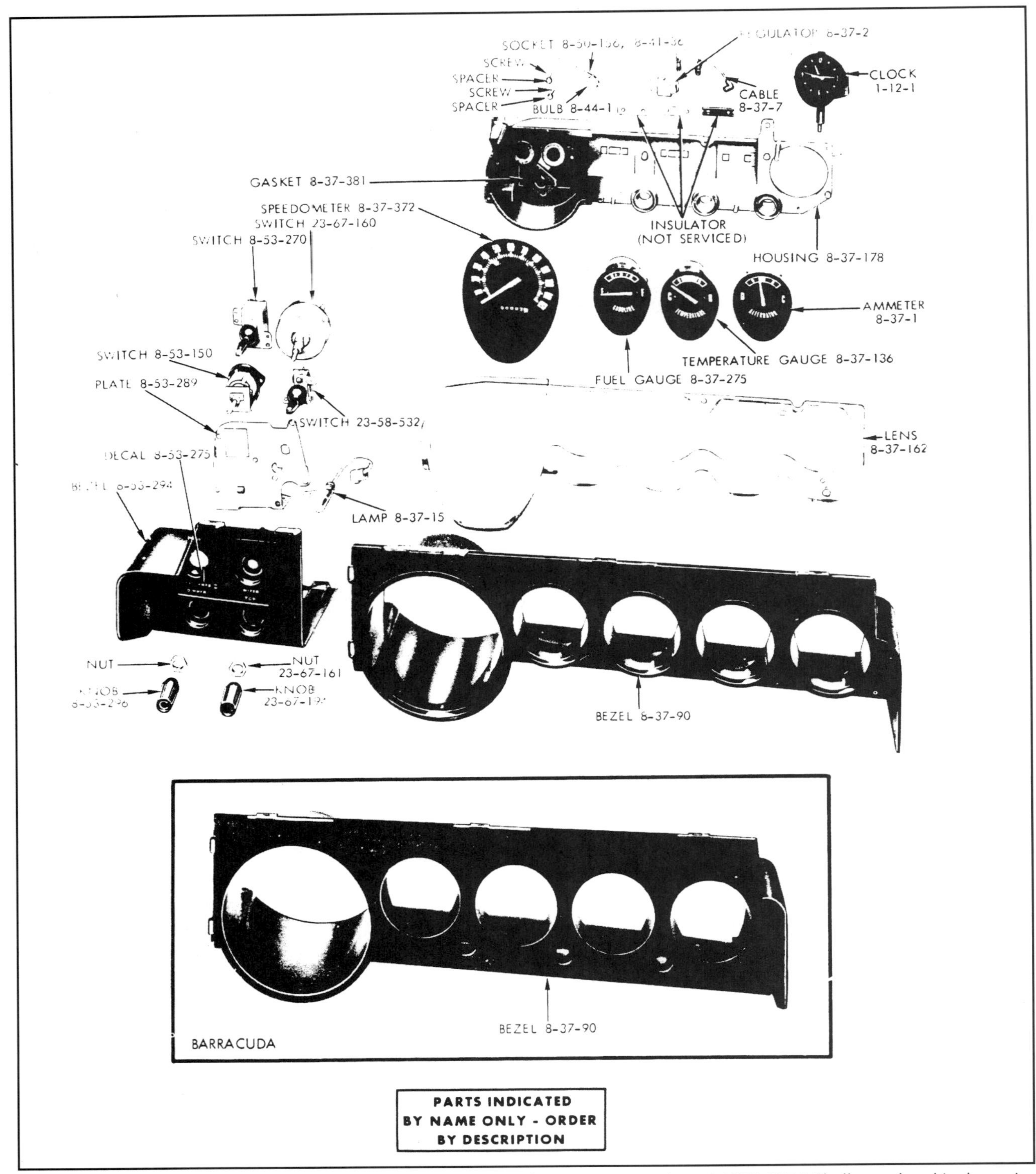

The 1970 Challenger instrument panel without the Rally cluster. The 1970 Barracuda and 1971-1974 Challenger bezel is shown in the insert. Note the difference in the bezels.

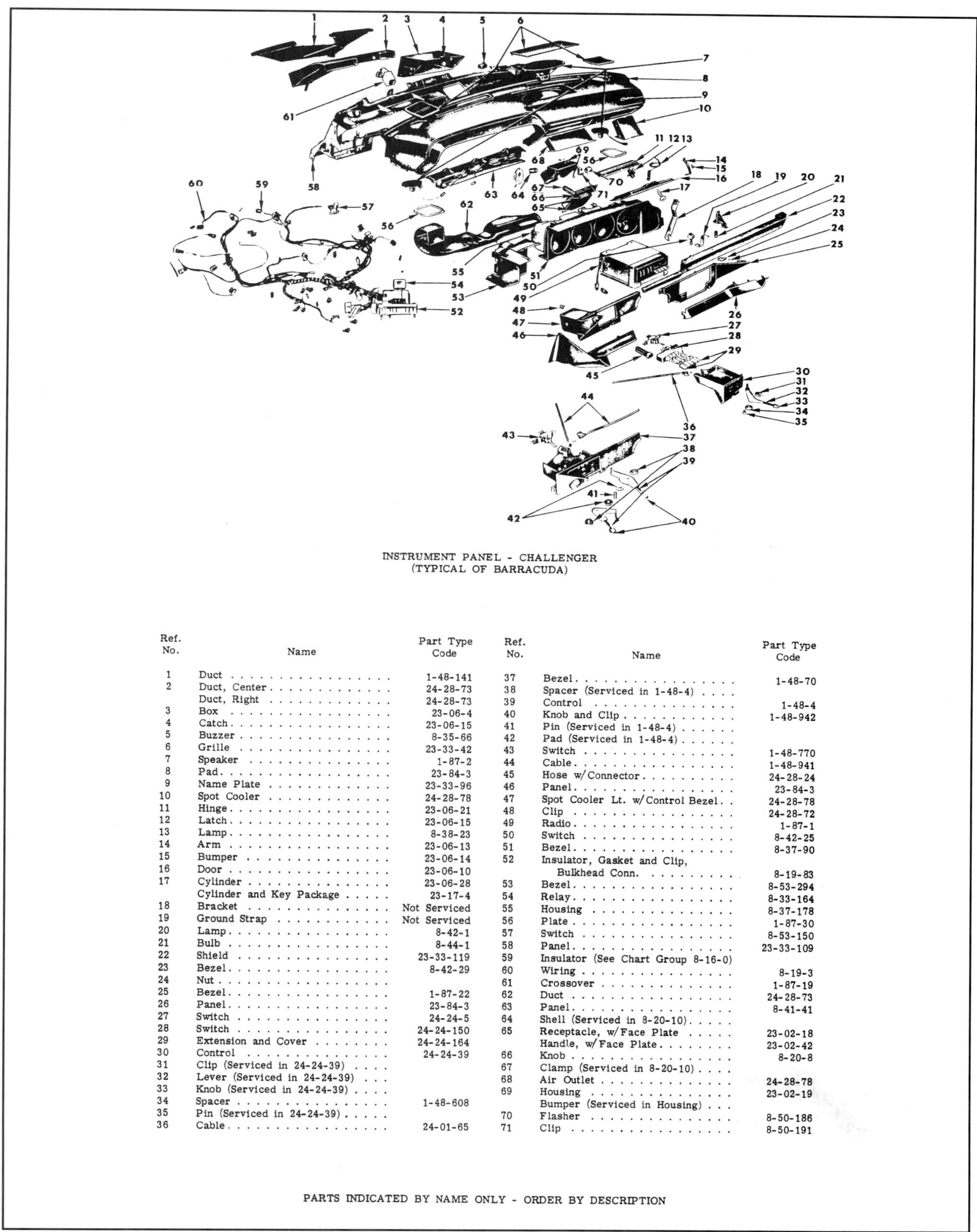

INSTRUMENT PANEL - CHALLENGER
(TYPICAL OF BARRACUDA)

Ref. No.	Name	Part Type Code	Ref. No.	Name	Part Type Code
1	Duct	1-48-141	37	Bezel	1-48-70
2	Duct, Center	24-28-73	38	Spacer (Serviced in 1-48-4)	
	Duct, Right	24-28-73	39	Control	1-48-4
3	Box	23-06-4	40	Knob and Clip	1-48-942
4	Catch	23-06-15	41	Pin (Serviced in 1-48-4)	
5	Buzzer	8-35-66	42	Pad (Serviced in 1-48-4)	
6	Grille	23-33-42	43	Switch	1-48-770
7	Speaker	1-87-2	44	Cable	1-48-941
8	Pad	23-84-3	45	Hose w/Connector	24-28-24
9	Name Plate	23-33-96	46	Panel	23-84-3
10	Spot Cooler	24-28-78	47	Spot Cooler Lt. w/Control Bezel	24-28-78
11	Hinge	23-06-21	48	Clip	24-28-72
12	Latch	23-06-15	49	Radio	1-87-1
13	Lamp	8-38-23	50	Switch	8-42-25
14	Arm	23-06-13	51	Bezel	8-37-90
15	Bumper	23-06-14	52	Insulator, Gasket and Clip, Bulkhead Conn.	8-19-83
16	Door	23-06-10	53	Bezel	8-53-294
17	Cylinder	23-06-28	54	Relay	8-33-164
	Cylinder and Key Package	23-17-4	55	Housing	8-37-178
18	Bracket	Not Serviced	56	Plate	1-87-30
19	Ground Strap	Not Serviced	57	Switch	8-53-150
20	Lamp	8-42-1	58	Panel	23-33-109
21	Bulb	8-44-1	59	Insulator (See Chart Group 8-16-0)	
22	Shield	23-33-119	60	Wiring	8-19-3
23	Bezel	8-42-29	61	Crossover	1-87-19
24	Nut		62	Duct	24-28-73
25	Bezel	1-87-22	63	Panel	8-41-41
26	Panel	23-84-3	64	Shell (Serviced in 8-20-10)	
27	Switch	24-24-5	65	Receptacle, w/Face Plate	23-02-18
28	Switch	24-24-150		Handle, w/Face Plate	23-02-42
29	Extension and Cover	24-24-164	66	Knob	8-20-8
30	Control	24-24-39	67	Clamp (Serviced in 8-20-10)	
31	Clip (Serviced in 24-24-39)		68	Air Outlet	24-28-78
32	Lever (Serviced in 24-24-39)		69	Housing	23-02-19
33	Knob (Serviced in 24-24-39)			Bumper (Serviced in Housing)	
34	Spacer	1-48-608	70	Flasher	8-50-186
35	Pin (Serviced in 24-24-39)		71	Clip	8-50-191
36	Cable	24-01-65			

PARTS INDICATED BY NAME ONLY - ORDER BY DESCRIPTION

Typical 1970-1974 E-Body instrument panel with Rally cluster

Continued from page 213
were used, and their usage depends on the build date. Early models, those built up until December 1970, used part number 2985884 for a Barracuda and 2985885 for a Challenger. Beginning on January 1, 1971, the emblems were restyled and used these part numbers: 3590126 for the Barracuda and 3590127 for the Challenger. Since the latter of these two were also used on all 1972-1974 models, this is what most reproduction companies offer, but they should not be installed on 1971 cars made before January 1, 1970. The latter two emblems used a separate backing plate that was black.

The dash pad itself was affected by the type of radio ordered and whether or not air conditioning was ordered. Those models with the stereo radio have provisions for three speakers, while all other radios have an opening for only one speaker. If air conditioning was ordered, then provisions for the outlets were cut into the pad.

A two-part-design (upper part number 2984457 and lower part number 2984456) glovebox insert was used all five years, and the two halves were stapled together. However, the glovebox doors differed according to the model year. The 1970 and 1971 models used part number 2984029, while the 1972-1974 models used part number 3590222. The door was painted in a flat finish to match the instrument panel all five years.

Door Panels and Other Interior Trim

The 1967 door panel was covered in vertical, pleated, Coachman grain vinyl separated horizontally across the middle by simulated walnut trim. In the center of the panel were the door handle and armrest. Front armrests were standard in all models, while the rear armrests were optional as separate equipment or as part of the interior decor group. Armrest bases were bright and the pads were color-keyed to match the door panels. Color-keyed carpeting was also standard in all body styles (see the accompanying combination chart to find the correct colors for a model). The area of the door that the panel did cover was painted in a high-gloss finish to match the door panel, except with white door panels, on which the paint color is the corresponding interior color.

For 1968 models, because of the addition of the Deluxe interior trim group, two different door panels were used. Those with the standard interior trim featured three horizontal pleats across the middle with no

A 1970-1974 Challenger inner-door panel.

map pockets. With the Deluxe interior trim, the door panels featured press-pleated map pockets and a strip of simulated wood-grain across the center, highlighted with chrome trim. Standard on all models were front armrests with bright-plated bases. Optional in all body styles except the convertible were rear armrests with bright bases. Rear armrests were also included in the Deluxe interior group. As in the previous years, the door frame was painted in a full-gloss finish that matched the door panel, except with white color door panels, where the corresponding interior color was used.

For 1969 models, two different panels were used again. With the standard interior trim, the door panels used a pattern of horizontal pleats in the center, while those panels used with the Deluxe interior trim featured a map pocket and an L-shaped, simulated wood-grain insert with chrome trim in the center. Both floral print designs were considered Deluxe trim, so they used the deluxe door panels, but they used a matching flora pattern instead of the wood grain. Front armrests were still standard with bright bases, and rear armrests were still optional in all body styles except the convertible and were part of the Deluxe interior group package. Once again, the door frame was painted to match the door panel in a high-gloss finish—except with the white interior trims or the floral print designs, where the corresponding interior trim color was used.

For 1970-1974 models, both the Barracuda and Challenger used a one-piece formed-plastic shell as a door panel. The panels were originally molded in a color that matched the interior seat trim color, including white. However, a used panel, or a reproduction panel can be

1967 Barracuda Interior Trim Color Combinations

Code	COLORS				COLORS		
	Seat	Door Panel	Door Frame	Door Armrest	Carpet	Headliner	Instrument Panel
H5B, H6B	Dark Blue	Dark Blue	Dark Blue 13040	Dark Blue	Dark Blue	Med. Dark Blue	Ensign Blue 9324
H5R, H6R	Dark Red	Dark Red	Med. Red 71545	Dark Red	Dark Red	Med. Dark Red	Derby Red 71390
H5X, H6X	Black	Black	Black 9000	Black	Black	Black	Jewel Black 9324
H5T, H6T	Tan	Tan 22712	Pale Tan	Tan	Buckskin Tan	Light Tan	Chestnut 22754
H5K, H6K	Copper	Copper	Copper 22710	Copper	Tan	Light Copper	Copper 22755
H5C, H6C	White	Dark Blue	Dark Blue 13040	Dark Blue	Dark Blue	Med. Dark Blue	Ensign Blue 9324
H5V, H6V	White	Red	Med. Red 71545	Red	Dark Red	Med. Dark Red	Derby Red 71390
H5W, H6W	White	Black	Black 9000	Black	Black	Black	Jewel Black 9324

Number below instrument panel color is the original Ditzler paint code number in a flat finish.
Number below door frame is the original Ditzler paint code in a full-gloss finish.

1968 Barracuda Interior Trim Color Combinations

Code	COLORS				COLORS		
	Seat	Door Panel	Door Frame	Door Armrest	Carpet	Headliner	Instrument Panel
HB5, H6B, D6B	Brite Blue	Brite Blue	Med. Dark Blue 2020	Bright Blue	Dark Blue	Med. Dark Blue	Baltic Blue 9324
H6F, D6F	Dark Green	Dark Green	Dark Green 43786	Dark Green	Dark Green	Med. Dark Green	Bayou Green 43925
H5X, H6X, D6X	Black	Black	Black 2033	Black	Black	Black	Jewel Black 9324
D6Y	Gold	Gold	Gold 2034	Gold	Med. Dark Gold	Med. Dark Gold	Laser Gold 23062
H5C, H6C, D6C	White	White	Med. Dark Blue 2020	White	Dark Blue	Med. Dark	Baltic Blue Blue 9324
H5W, H6W, D6W	White	White	Black 2033	White	Black	White	Jewel Black 9324
H5D, H6D, D6D	White	White	Dark Green 43786	White	Dark Green	Med. Dark Green	Bayou Green 43925
D6E	White	White	Gold 2034	White	Dark Gold	Med. Dark Gold	Laser Gold 23062
H5V, H6V, D6V	White	White	Brite Red 2029	White	Med. Red	Med. Red	Regatta Red 71688
H6R, D6R	Red	Red	Brite Red 2029	Red	Med. Red	Med. Red	Regatta Red 71688

Number under instrument panel color is the original Ditzler paint code number in a flat finish.
Number below door frame color is the original Ditzler paint code in a full gloss finish.

1969 Barracuda Interior Trim Color Combinations

Code	COLORS				COLORS		
	Seat	Door Frame	Door Panel	Door Armrest	Carpet	Headliner	Instrument Panel
H4B, LB2, G6B	Brite Blue	Brite Blue	Brite Blue 2019	Brite Blue	Dark Blue	Med. Blue	Baltic Blue 13705
H4X, L2X, H6X, D6X	Black	Black	Black 9000	Black	Black	Black	Jewel Black 9324
H4W, H6W	White	White	Black 9000	White	Black	Black	Jewel Black 9324
H4V, H6V	White	White	Brite Red 2029	White	Red	Red	Regatta Red 71688
H4C, H6C	White	White	Brite Blue 2019	White	Dark Blue	Med. Blue	Baltic Blue 13705
H4F, H6F	White	White	Dark Green 43786	White	Dark Green	Dark Green	Bayou Green 43925
L2R, H6R, D6R	Red	Red	Brite Red 2029	Red	Red	Red	Regatta Red 71688
D6U	Tan/Black	Tan	Black 9000	Tan	Black	Black	Jewel Black 9324
D6T, X1T	Tan	Tan	Lt. Bronze 2030	Tan	Dark Tan	Light Tan	Sienna Tan 23076
F6P	(1)	(1)	Black 9324	Yellow	Black	Black	Jewel Black 9000
D6P	Pale Yellow and Black	Yellow	Black 9000	Yellow	Black	Black	Jewel Black 9324
F6J	(2)	(2)	Dark Green 43786	Green	Dark Green	Dark Green	Bayou Green 43926
H6G, D6G	Green	Green	Dark Green 43786	Green	Dark Green	Dark Green	Bayou Green 43926

(1) = A pattern of yellow flowers replaced the simulated wood strip. Rest of panel was yellow.
(2) = A pattern of yellow flowers replaced the simulated wood strip. Rest of panel was green.
Note: F6J and F6P were available on two-door hardtop only.
Number below instrument panel paint name is the original Ditzler paint code in a flat finish.
Number below the door panel frame is the original Ditzler paint code in a high-gloss finish.

The Dodge tri-star emblem in an inner-door panel.

painted to match the trim in your car. The finish should be a flat gloss, and paint names and numbers are provided here to help you in restoring the proper shade and color. The Challenger's panel is more highly detailed and is longer than that used on the Barracuda, so they will not interchange. Armrest bases were part of the panels and both front and rear armrests were standard on all models.

No nameplate was used on the base Barracudas, but on the Cuda models the word "Cuda" was positioned on the front upper portion of the panel. Two Cuda nameplates were used: the 1970 and 1971 models used part number 3415645, while the 1972-1974 models used part number 3510863. The Gran Coupe models used a model script nameplate, part number 3415646, both years in the same position as the Cuda name.

A trim plate with the Dodge tri-star medallion was used in the middle of the door panel on Challenger models. Several different trim panels were used. All Challengers, except the S.E. used part number 3415312 in 1970 and part number 3509253 from 1971 to 1974. The Challenger S.E. model used special trim panels with Special Edition badges in the center, and this panel was listed as part number 3415843. Note that there was a slight change in the door panel design for Challengers in the 1972 models. The new panels were used until the end of the 1974 model year run. The Barracuda used the same door panel design all five years.

Headliners

A perforated headliner was used in all 1967-1969 Barracudas with a steel roof, but the fastback used a different liner than the hardtop. (See the accompanying combination charts for colors.) The 1970-1972 cars used three different styles of headliners. The 1970 and 1971 Gran Coupe, the 1970 Challenger S.E., and those 1971 Challengers with the formal roof used a one-piece felt-covered headliner. The other 1970 to 1972 models also used two

continued on page 229

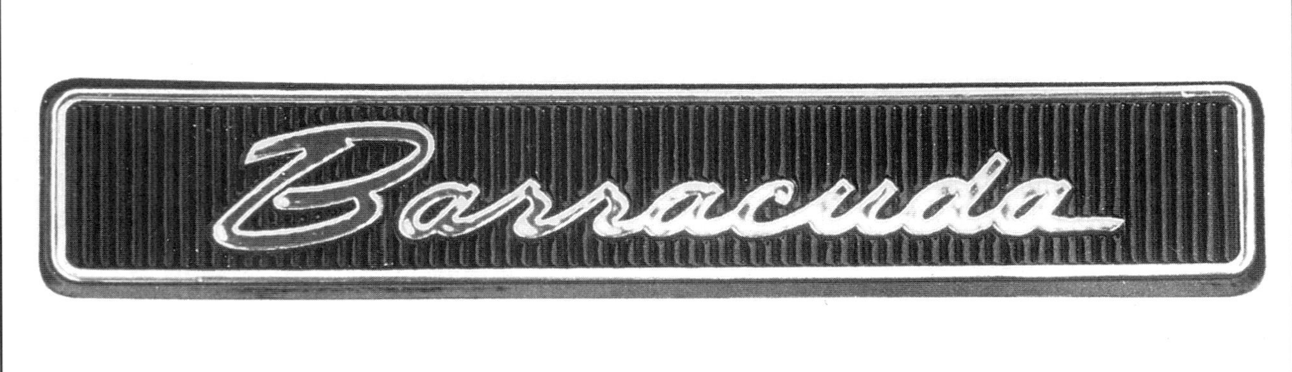

The 1971-1974 Barracuda dash pad nameplate. *Year One*

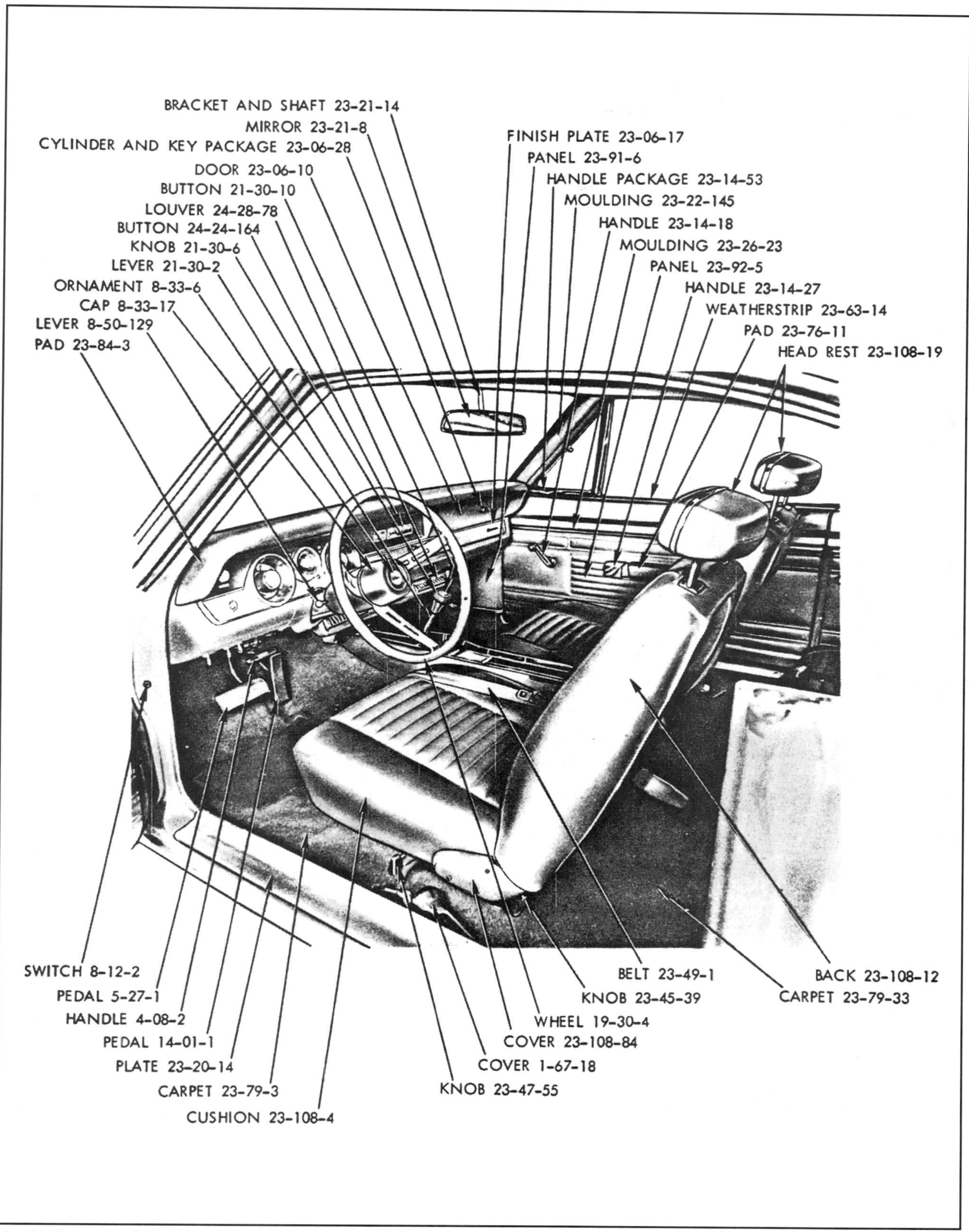

The 1969 Barracuda interior.

1970 Barracuda/Challenger Interior Trim Color Combinations

Code	COLORS				COLORS		
	Seat	Orig. Door Panel Col.	Panel Repaint Col.	Armrest	Carpet	Headliner	Instrument Panel
H4B, H6B, P6B, H5B	Brite Blue	Med. Blue	Thunder Blue Poly 13848	Brite Blue	Med. Blue	Med. Blue	Thunder Blue (flat) 13848
P5X, PRX, H6X	Black	Black	Jewel Black 9324	Black	Black	Black	Jewel Black (flat) 9324
P6E, H6E	Red	Red	Poppy Red 71764	Red	Dark Red	Red	Poppy Red (flat) 71764
P6F, H6F, H4F, H58	Green	Dark Green	Bayou Green 43925	Dark Green	Dark Green	Dark Green	Bayou Green (flat) 43925
P6K, P5K, HRK, H4K	Burnt Orange	Burnt Orange	Sunfire Orange 60557	Burnt Orange	Dark Burnt Orange	Dark Burnt Orange	Sunfire Orange (flat) 60557
P6T, PRT, H6T	Tan	Tan	Puma Tan 23219	Tan	Dark Tan	Light Tan	Puma Tan 23219
P6XW, PRXW, H4XW, H6XW	White	White	Dove White 8745	White	Black	White	Jewel Black (flat) 9324
P6EW, H6EW	White	White	Dove White 8745	White	Red	Red	Poppy Red (flat) 71764
P6FW, H6FW, H4FW	White	White	Dove White 8745	White	Dark Green	Dark Green	Bayou Green (flat) 43925
P6BW, H6BW, H4BW	White	White	Dove White 8745	White	Med. Blue	Med. Blue	Thunder Blue (flat) 13848
P6XY	Gold	Black	Jewel Black 9324	Black	Black	Black	Jewel Black (flat) 9324

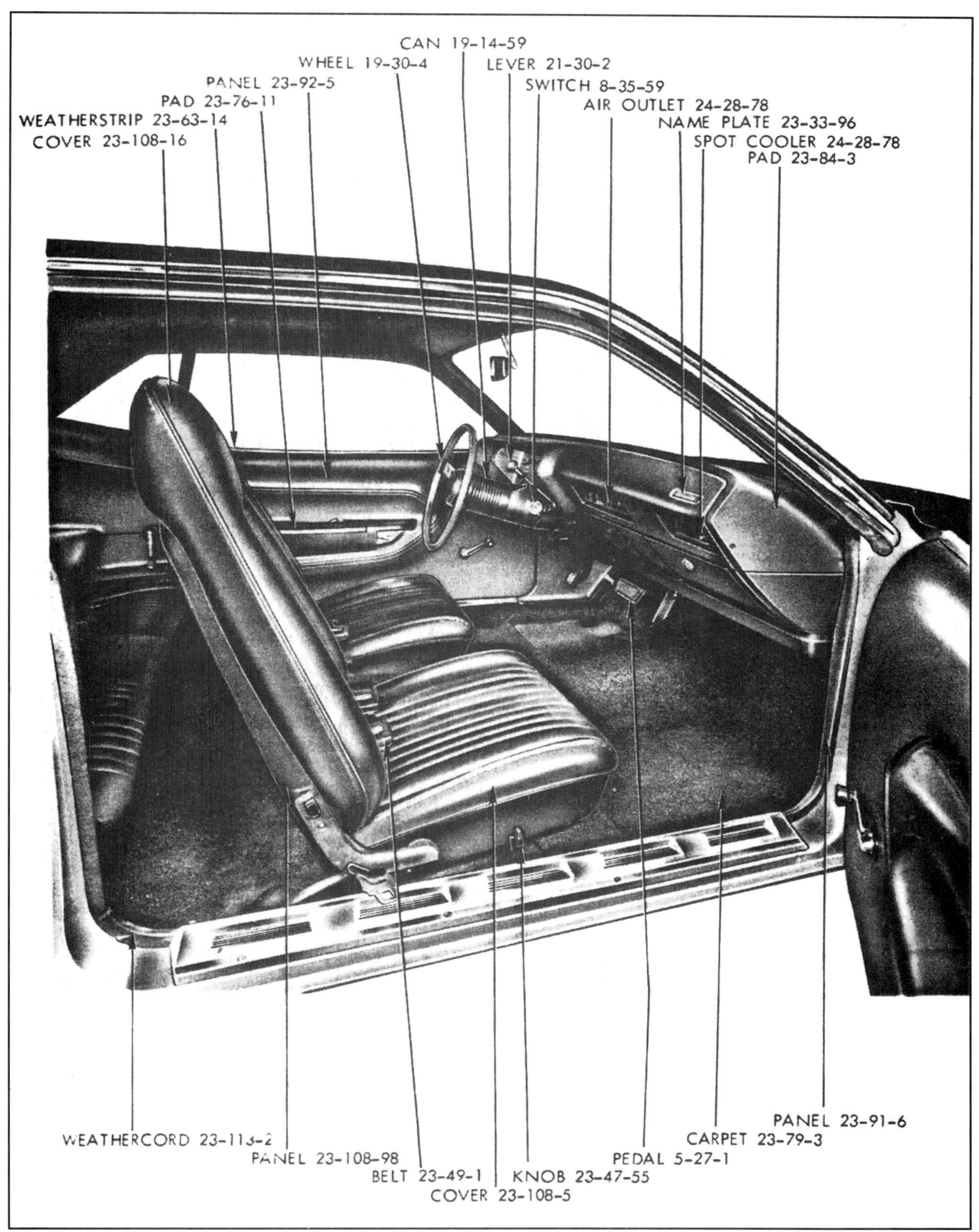

The 1970-1974 Barracuda interior, with, specifically, a 1972 interior shown here.

1971 Barracuda/Challenger Interior Trim Color Combinations

Code	COLORS				Carpet	Headliner	Instrument Panel
	Seat	Orig. Door Panel Col.	Panel Repaint Col.	Armrest			
H4B, H6B, P6B, L6B	Brite Blue	Brite Blue	Med. Blue Poly 14090	Brite Blue	Med. Blue	Med. Blue	Med. Blue Poly 14090
L6X, H4X, H5X, HRX, P5X, PRX, SRX	Black	Black	Black 9388	Black	Black	Black	Black 9388
L6F, H4F, H5F, H6F, P6F	Green	Dark Green	Dark Green 44290	Dark Green	Dark Green	Dark Green	Dark Green 44290
L6T, H6T, PRT, H4T, SRT	Dark Saddle	Med. Dark Saddle	Med. Dark Saddle 23428	Med. Dark	Dark Saddle Saddle	Med. Dark Saddle	Med. Dark Saddle 23428
L6XW, H6XW	White	White	White 8849	White	Black	White	Black 9388
H5XV, H6XV	Black &Orange	Black	Black 9388	Black	Black	Black	Black 9388
PRY, H6Y, P6Y	Gold	Gold	Med. Gold 23426	Gold	Med. Dark Gold	Light Gold	Med. Gold 23426
H5XX	Black & Charcoal	Black	Black 9388	Black	Black	Black	Black 9388
L5FW	White & Green	Green	Dark Green 44290	Dark Green	Dark Green	Dark Green	Dark Green 44290

Here is the 1971-1974 Challenger dash pad nameplate. *Year One*

1972 Barracuda/Challenger Interior Trim Color Combinations

Code	COLORS				COLORS		
	Seat	Orig. Door Panel Col.	Panel Repaint Col.	Armrest	Carpet	Headliner	Instrument Panel
A6B, B6B	Brite Blue	Brite Blue 14243	Brite Blue Poly	Brite Blue	Med. Blue	Med. Blue	Med. Blue Poly 14243
A6X, B6X	Black	Black	Black 9392	Black	Black	Black	Black 9392
A6F, B6F	Green	Dark Green	Dark Green 44482	Dark Green	Dark Green	Dark Green	Dark Green 44482
A6XW, B6XW	White	White	White 8849	White	Black	White	Black 9392
A6Y, B6Y	Gold	Gold	Light Gold 23589	Gold	Med. Dark	Light Gold	Med. Gold Gold 23589

1973-1974 Barracuda/Challenger Interior Trim Color Combinations

Code	COLORS				COLORS		
	Seat	Orig. Door Panel Col.	Panel Repaint Col.	Armrest	Carpet	Headliner	Instrument Panel
A6B, B6B	Bright Blue	Brite Blue Poly	Bright Blue 14096	Bright Blue	Med. Blue	Med. Blue	Dark Blue Poly 14090
A6X, B6X	Black	Black	Black 9388	Black	Black	Black	Black 9388
A6F, B6F	Green	Dark Green	Dark Green 44696	Dark Green	Dark Green	Dark Green	Dark Green 44696
A6XW, B6XW	White	White	White 8849	White	Black	White	Black 9388

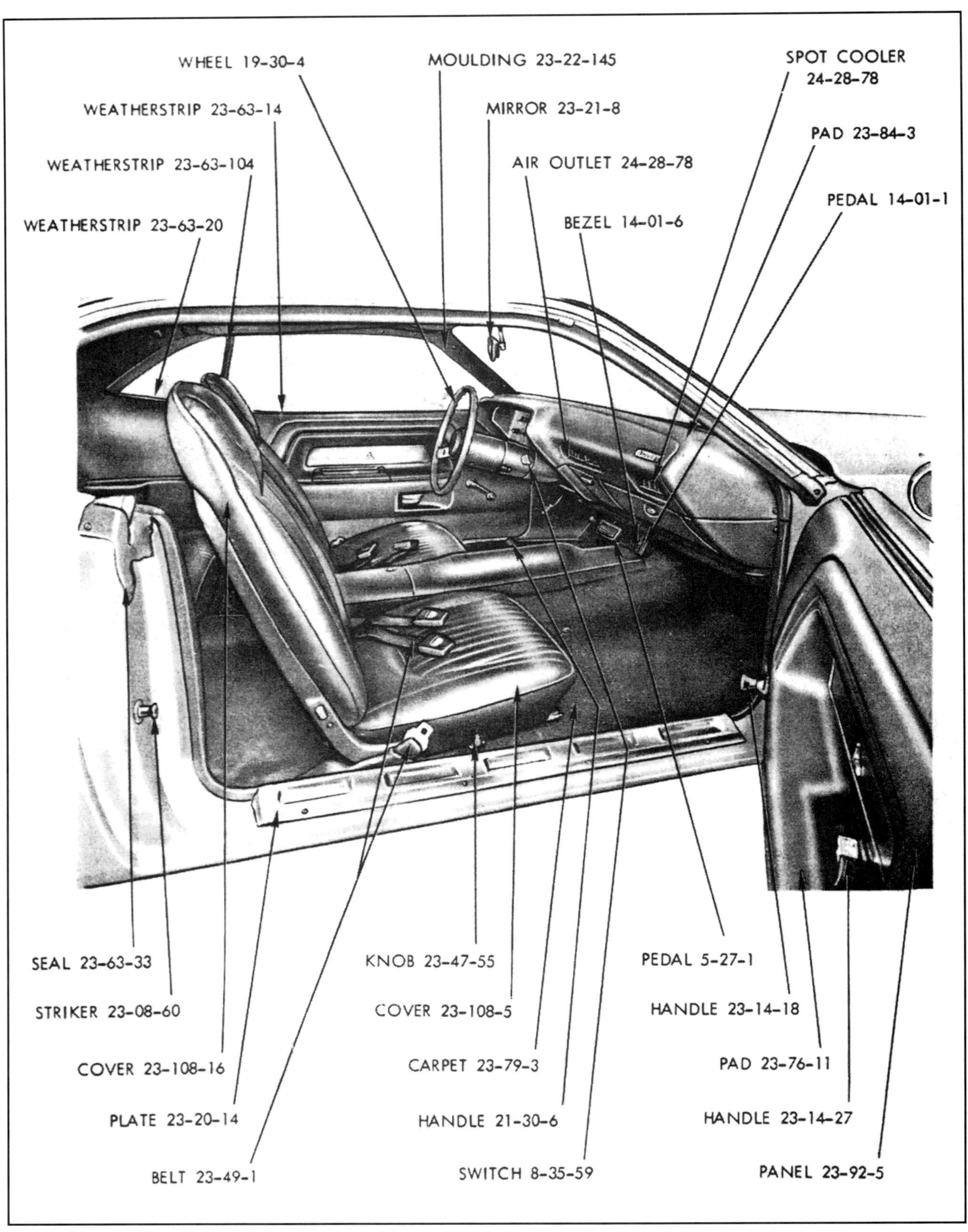

A 1972 Challenger interior, which was indicative of the 1970-1974 interiors.

Continued from page 222
different styles of headliners, the difference being the number of bows used. Those with five headliner bows used a perforated headliner, while those with six bows used a corduroy material pattern. When removing your old headliner, be sure to number the original bows, as each unit has adapted to the position it is in. If the bows are swapped around when reinserted, the new headliner may not fit correctly. If all-new bows are used, then there is no need to number them. The convertible used no headliner.

1967-1969 Instrumentation

Instrumentation all three years consisted of three round pods directly in front of the driver. To the far left-hand side was the speedometer. The standard speedometer was a 120 miles per hour unit with a black face with white numbers and marks. Each model year used a different speedometer. The 1967 models used part number 27771162, in 1968 it was part number 2889423, and in 1969 it was part number 2927718. Optional each year was the Rally cluster that replaced the 120 miles per hour speedometer with a 150 miles per hour unit that also included a trip odometer. Like the 120 miles per hour speedometer, each model year's speedometer used a different part number: 1967, 2771628; 1968, 2889424; and 1969, 2927719.

Export cars did not use a 120 miles per hour speedometer; instead, they had a 240 kilometers per hour unit. In 1967, the part number was listed as 2771630, and in 1968 and 1969, part number 2889426 was used. The Rally package was not available on export cars.

In the center of the speedometer is a smaller pod, and in standard form it was a blank panel. Options included either a clock, a tachometer, or a vacuum gauge called a performance gauge. In the United States, a tachometer was available only with a V-8 engine, but when a Barracuda was sent out of the country, a tachometer was also available with the six-cylinder powerplant. However, the tachometer used with a six-cylinder is not the same unit used with a V-8 engine. The tachometers below were used.

The performance gauge or vacuum gauge had a band that read from economy to a power range. Two different gauges were used: the 1967 and 1968 models used part number 2771653, and the 1969 models used part number 2927723. A performance gauge could not be ordered with a tachometer or a clock.

A clock with a bright reset knob was optional only in 1968 and 1969 models, and only if the vacuum gauge or tachometer was not ordered. Part number 2857678 was used for the clock both years.

At the far right was another round pod the same size as the speedometer. This pod held four smaller gauges: engine temperature, oil pressure, fuel level, and ammeter. In the upper left-hand corner of the pod was the ammeter, and only one gauge, part number 2771641, was used all three years. Just below the ammeter was the oil pressure gauge, and as with the ammeter, only one gauge (part number 2771640) was used all three years. In the upper right-hand corner was the fuel gauge, part number 2771638 all three years. The temperature gauge, part number 2771639, was used just below the fuel gauge all three years.

Bright trim was used on the standard bezel, and it has no provisions for the air conditioning outlet ducts. When air conditioning was ordered, provisions for the air ducts were cut out in the bezel. When the Rally cluster was used, a panel with simulated wood-grain trim was placed over the bezel, except in 1969, when a flat-black lower trim panel was used. The chart on the following page shows which bezels were used.

1970-1974 Instrumentation

The standard setup all five years included a large, round 120 miles per hour speedometer flanked by three smaller gauges for the fuel, temperature, ammeter, and a blank panel; oil pressure was handled by a warning lamp. Export cars again used a 240 kilometers per hour speedometer instead of the 120 miles per hour unit. A clock was optional with the standard instrumentation, and if in place, was placed where the blank panel was.

Speedometer usage was affected by the interior decor group option in 1970 and 1971 models, which added a wood-grain appliqué over the instrument panel bezel. Those without the wood-grain treatment used a different speedometer than those models with the

1967-1969 Barracuda Tachometers

Year	Engine	Part Number	Market
1967	Six-cyl.	2822556	Export Only
1967	V-8	2771656	U.S. or Export
1968-1969	Six-cyl.	2926019	Export Only
1968-1969	V-8	2857729	U.S. or Export

1967-1969 Barracuda Dash Panel Trim Plates

Years	Standard (120 miles per hour)		Rally (150 miles per hour)	
	Without A/C	With A/C	Without A/C	With A/C
1967	2822436	2822437	2771609	2771610
1968	2857665	2927706	2857662	2857663
1969	2927705	2927706	2927703	2927704

wood-grain appliqué. Those models without the appliqué in the United States used part number 2984966, while the exports used part number 2984967. With the wood-grain insert, part numbers were 2984964 in U.S. cars and 2984965 for export cars, both of which were used in 1972–1974 models.

A fuel gauge was just to the right of the speedometer in both models, but the 1970 Challenger used a different gauge than did the Barracuda. The Challenger used part number 2984159 while the Barracuda used part number 2984119. Yet in the 1971-1974 models, both the Challenger and the Barracuda models used the 1970 Barracuda gauge.

An engine temperature gauge was next to the fuel gauge. As with the fuel gauge, the 1970 Challenger used a different engine temperature gauge than those used in the Barracuda. As with the fuel gauge, both the Challenger and Barracuda from 1971 through 1974 used the 1970 Barracuda engine temperature gauge. In 1970 only, the Challenger used part number 2984160, while part number 2984120 was used in the 1970 Barracuda and all 1971-1974 models with the standard instrumentation group.

An ammeter in the 1970 Challenger was also unique and used part number 298416. The Barracuda ammeter used part number 2984121, as did all 1971-1974 Barracudas and the Challengers with the standard instrument group. To the far right of the ammeter was a blank panel unless the clock was ordered.

Two different clocks were used in 1970 models. Those without the wood-grain instrument panel used part number 2984952. Those with the wood-grain appliqué used part number 2984951; the latter of these was used in 1971-1974 models when the clock was ordered with the standard instrumentation group.

Several different bezels were used. In 1970, the Barracuda models used part number 2985801 while the Challenger models used part number 2984192. This bezel is the reason that different gauges were used in the 1970 Challenger models. All 1971 models used the Barracuda unit.

A point that is not widely known is that the 1970 Barracuda bezel was used on 1972 Challengers built until approximately January 1, 1972. After this date, Challengers used part number 3592242, which was used on both the Challenger and the Barracuda until the end of the 1974 model year.

Instrument panel wiring used a different part number each model year, but both the Challenger and Barracuda used the same harness. However, those models with the 426 Hemi in 1971 used a special wiring harness. If electronic ignition was ordered on the 426-ci engine, it required a special harness, as was the case when the speed control was ordered with the Hemi.

The optional Rally instrument cluster featured four large, round pods that housed all the gauges. To the far left-hand side was a 150 miles per hour speedometer in U.S. models and a 300 kilometers per hour speedometer in exports. A tachometer was just to the right of the speedometer, and to the right of the tachometer was a single pod that held four separate gauges for the fuel level, oil pressure, ammeter, and engine temperature. To the far right-hand side was a Rally clock.

The speedometer for 1970 models used part number 2984968 in U.S. models and 2984969 in export models. The part number was changed in 1971 models to 2985954 in U.S. cars and 2985955 in exports. The 1972 models used both the 1970 and the 1971 part numbers. Early models, those built up until October 17,1971, used the 1970 speedometers, and after this date, the 1971 units were used. This change applies to both the U.S. and exports cars. The 1973 and 1974 models used the 1971 part numbers.

A tachometer (part number 2984185) was used all five years with no change; it was used in both U.S. and export models. In the combination pod, the fuel gauge (part number 2984178) was mounted at the top. Below and to the left of the fuel gauge was the oil pressure gauge, listed as part number 2984181. The ammeter, part number 2984179, was mounted to the right of the oil pressure gauge. Above and to the right was the engine temperature gauge, listed as part number 2984180. All these gauges were used all five years and in both models.

The Rally instrument panel bezel was a two-part design, one area for the gauges and one for the headlamp and wiper controls. Both of the 1970 models used part number 2984192, but the 1971 models used two different bezels, and the difference is the grain of the wood. Early models, those built up to approximately February 1, 1971, used American Walnut, listed as part number 2985807; after that date, Kashmer Walnut was used, it was listed as part number 2985944. Early 1972 models used the 1970 bezel; cars built after October 17, 1971, and before November 15, 1971, used the late-1971 bezel. After November 15, 1971, part number 3592266 took its place and was used until the end of the 1974 model year.

The wiring harness was different each year, and to swap from the standard gauges to the Rally cluster, the wiring harness will also have to be changed. This is a feat you will not want to undertake, especially with a used wiring harness. Also note that there was a change in the wiring harness of 1972 models, with the change occurring around December 1, 1971. The early wiring harness will not fit cars with the late wiring harness. Also, those with a Hemi in 1970 or 1971 used a special wiring harness.

Inside Mirror

A prismatic inside mirror, part number 2299846, was standard in all 1967 Barracuda models. However, the mounting bracket differs between the convertible and other body styles. Convertibles used a chrome-plated bracket, while the bracket on the hardtop and the fastback was painted Alumna-Hide Silver (use Ditzler code DX-8555 to refinish). The mirror was changed to part number 2935490 in 1968, and the convertible continued to use a chrome-plated mounting bracket, while the hardtop and fastback used the silver-painted bracket. This mirror and the brackets were used again in 1969, but the brackets were restyled and will not fit 1967 models.

The inside mirror was again restyled for the 1970 models and was listed as part number 3454875. As in the previous years, the hardtops used a bracket painted silver, while the bracket used on the convertible was chrome-plated. The same mirror and brackets were used again in 1971 models.

Note that the mirror above was standard on all higher-trimmed cars, but the base coupes (those whose rear quarter-windows did not roll down) had a nonprismatic mirror, listed as part number 3548447, as standard equipment. The prismatic mirror was available as an option for the base coupe. All 1972 models had the prismatic mirror as standard equipment, but two different mirrors and brackets were used. Early models—those built before December 15, 1971—used part number 3586576, while those built after this date used part number 3695130. Brackets were painted Argent Silver (Ditzler DNA-8575) on models up to June 1, 1972, and used part number 3508523; after this date, part number 3695429 was used. The latter of these was used in 1973 and 1974 models.

Seat Belts

Two front and two rear lap belts were standard for all models and body styles. Shoulder belts were optional in

1967 Seat Belt Color Usage

Interior Color Code	Interior Color	Seat Belt Color
H5K, H6K	Copper	Dark Copper
H5R, H6R, H5V, H6V	Red, or White/Red	Med. Red
H5X, H6X, H5W, H6W	Black or White/Black	Black
H5T, H6T	Tan	Dark Tan
H5B, H6B, H5C, H6C	Blue or White/Blue	Dark Blue

1968 Seat Belt Color Usage

Interior Color Code	Interior Color	Seat Belt Color
H5B, H6B, D6B, H5C, H6C, D6C	Blue or White/Blue	Blue
H6F, D6F, H5D, H6D, D6D	Green or White/Green	Yellow Green
H6R, D6R, H5V, H6V, D6V	Red or White/Red	Dark Red
H5X, H6X, D6X, H5W, H6W, D6W	Black or White/Black	Black
D6Y, D6E	Gold or White/Gold	Gold

Note: Convertible with shoulder straps, or a hardtop or fastback with rear shoulder straps, used black belts with all interior trims.

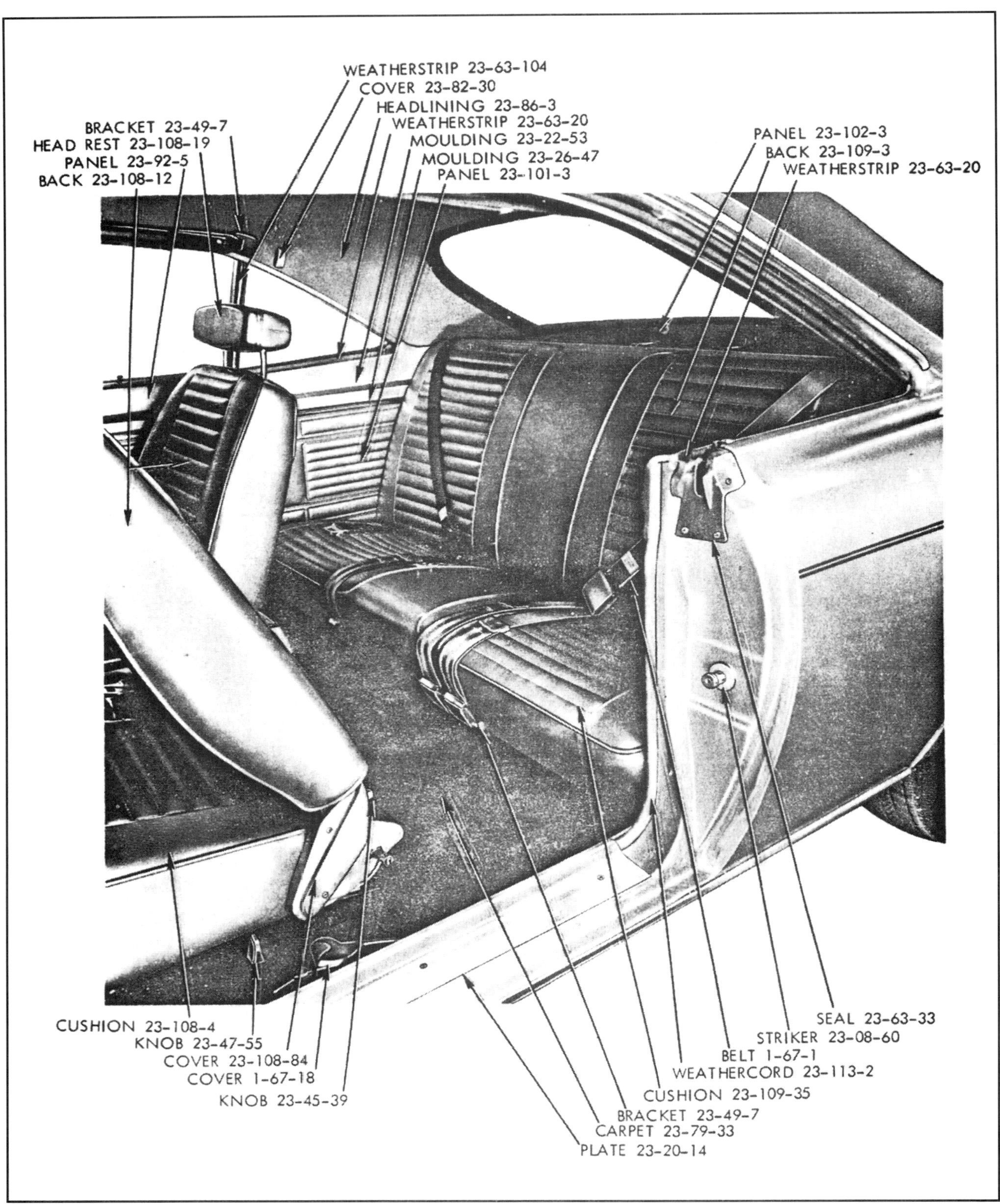

Rear seat shoulder belts, as seen in a 1969 model.

1967 and the early portion of 1968. Shoulder belts became standard on January 1, 1968, on all cars with a steel roof. Rear-seat shoulder belts were optional and saw limited usage. They were available for the fastback or two-door hardtop in 1968 and 1969, and the two-door hardtop in 1970 and 1971 only. Rear-seat shoulder belts are extremely rare, and on a musclecar they are rarer than Hemis.

Belts were usually but not always color-keyed to the interior carpet, and some cars used black seat belts. If rear shoulder belts were ordered, then only black belts were used, regardless of the interior trim color. It was not until near the end of the 1972 model year that solid black belts were used with all interior trims. Many feel this change to black seat belts took place in late-1971 models, but the belts are not solid black; they were tinted with either blue, green, or gold. Use the accompanying charts to find the proper color of seat belts used with your car interior trim.

1969 Seat Belt Color Usage

Interior Color Code	Interior Color	Seat Belt Color
H4B, L2B, H6B, D6B, H4C, H6C	Blue or White/Blue	Blue
HF4, H6F, F6J	White/Green or Flora Green	Green
D6T, D6U	Tan or Tan/Black	Champagne
H4X, L2X, H6X, D6X, D6P, F6P, H4W, H6W	Black or Yellow/Black, or Flora Black	Black
L2R, H6R, D6R, H4V, H6V	Red or White/Red	Red

Note: Convertible with shoulder straps, or a hardtop or fastback with rear shoulder straps, used black belts with all interior trims.

1970 Seat Belt Color Usage

Interior Color Code	Interior Color	Seat Belt Color
P6B5, H4B5, H6B5, P6BW, H4BW, H6BW	Blue or White/Blue	Blue
F6F8, H4F8, H6F8, P6FW, H4FW, H6FW	Green or White/Green	Green
P5X9, PRX9, H6X9, P6A8, P6XW, PRXW, H4XW, H6XW, P6XY, H6WX	Black, or Charcoal, or White/Black, or Gold/Black, or Black and White	Black
P6T5, PRT5, H6T5	Tan	Tan
P6E4, H6E4, P6EW, H6EW	Red or White/Red	Red
P6K4, P5K4, H6K4, HRK4	Burnt Orange	Orange

When equipped with rear-seat shoulder belts, all belts are black regardless of trim color.
Both standard and custom belts were available. Standard belt in black, green, or blue only.

1971 Seat Belt Color Usage

Interior Color Code	Interior Color	Seat Belt Color
H6B5, H4B5, P6B5, L6B5	Blue	Blue
H6F8 H4F8, P6F8, L6F8, H5F8, L5FW	Green	Green
H6T5, H4T5, P6T5, L6T5	Tan	Tan
L6X9, H6X9, H5X9, HRX9, H4X9, L6XW, H6XW, H5XW, H6Y3, H6XV, P6Y4, P6X9, SRX9, PRX9	Black, or White/Black, or Gold, or Black/Orange	Black

With rear shoulder belts, black belts were used regardless of interior color trim.

1972 Seat Belt Color Usage

Interior Color Code	Interior Color	Seat Belt Color
A6B5, B6B5	Blue	Blue/Black
A6F8, B6F8	Green	Green/Black
A6Y3, B6Y3	Gold	Gold/Black
A6X9, B6X9, A6XW, B6XW	Black or White/Black	Black

With rear shoulder belts, all belts were black regardless of trim color.

1973-1974 Seat Belt Color Usage

Interior Color Code	Interior Color	Seat Belt Color
All Codes	All Colors	Black

Trunk Compartment

The spare tire was concealed in a built-in well under the trunk floor of all 1967-1969 cars. A gray, houndstooth-pattern mat was used in the 1967 Barracuda trunk, except the fastback, which used color-keyed carpeting on the trunk floor and the back of the rear seatback. In 1968-1969 models, both the gray houndstooth and gray plaid mats were used in the hardtop and convertibles, and again the fastbacks used colored-keyed carpeting.

CAUTION
FOLLOW JACKING
INSTRUCTIONS

1967-1969 jack decal, which was placed on the base so it can be read from the front.

The 1970-1974 trunk compartment used no hidden spare, and the mat used a herringbone pattern. Although the patterns are the same, a mat from a Barracuda will not fit a Challenger, as the Challenger is wider. Some 1973 and 1974 models used a gray-and-black latex foam-backed mat instead of the herringbone rubber mat.

Because the jack fit under the spare in the trunk in 1967-1969 models, a special jack (part number 2808544) was used. The base of the jack was painted gloss black and positioned in the center of the spare wheel, where it was held with a large silver wing nut. A yellow caution decal was used on the base.

In 1970-1971 models, the Challenger used a different jack stand than the Barracuda, but the base was painted dark gray on both units. The "Caution follow jacking instructions" decal was restyled and positioned on the base. For 1972 to 1974 models, both the Challenger and the Barracuda used the same jack, but it was a different unit than the one used in either model in 1970 or 1971. Although the base was painted dark gray and the jack stand was painted dull silver, the jack itself was painted gloss black, as was the jack wrench.

2962995 **JACK INSTRUCTIONS** BARRACUDA-CHALLENGER

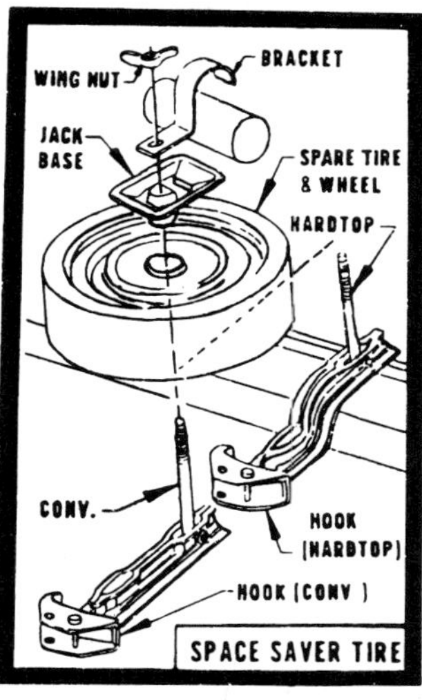

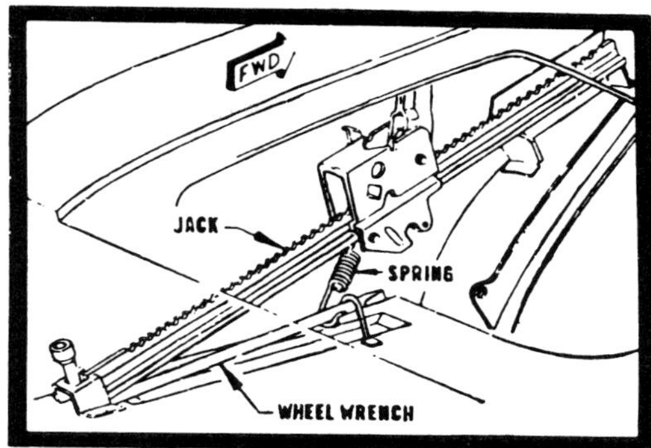

STORE JACK AND JACK BASE AS SHOWN

CAUTION: FOR CONVERTABLE MODELS, TO PREVENT REAR WINDOW BREAKAGE, CONVENTIONAL SPARE TIRE MUST NOT BE STORED IN FORWARD POSITION.

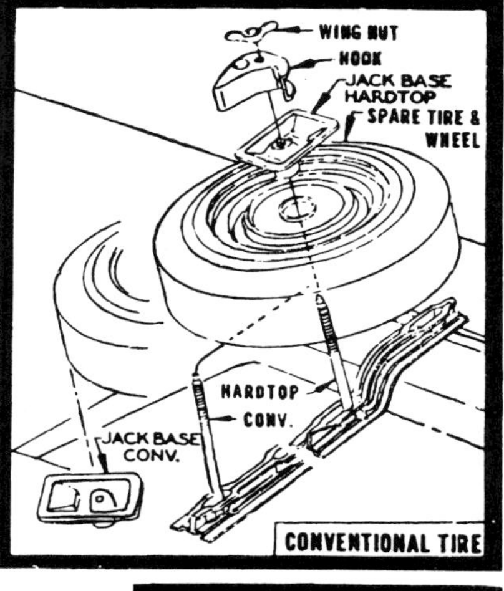

1. If possible, park car on level surface. Set parking brake.
2. Place in Neutral gear.
3. Block diagonally opposite wheel in direction of roll.
4. Remove spare wheel and jack from car.
5. Remove wheel cover. Loosen wheel nuts one turn.
6. Engage jack to bumper in vertical position as shown.
7. Jack up car.
8. Remove wheel; Replace with spare & tighten nuts.
9. Remove jack, tighten wheel nuts to 65 ft. lbs.

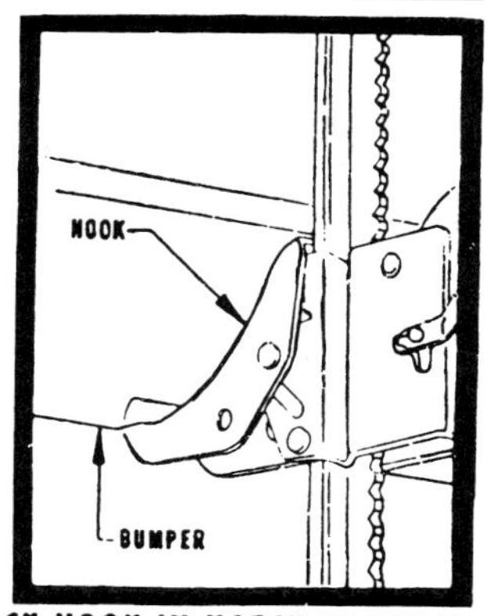

PLACE JACK HOOK IN NOTCH PROVIDED

CAUTION

THE BUMPER JACK IS A TIRE CHANGING TOOL ONLY.
DO NOT USE IT FOR WORKING UNDER CAR.

This 1971 jacking decal used blue-and-red lettering. It was portioned on the underside of the deck lid, usually in the center.

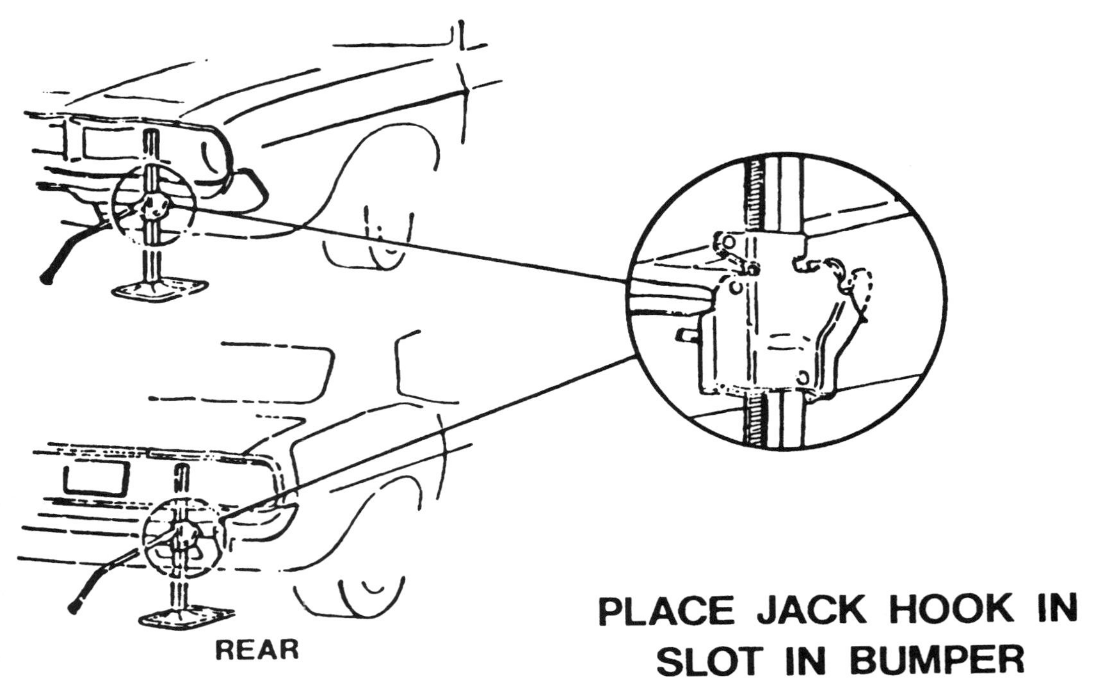

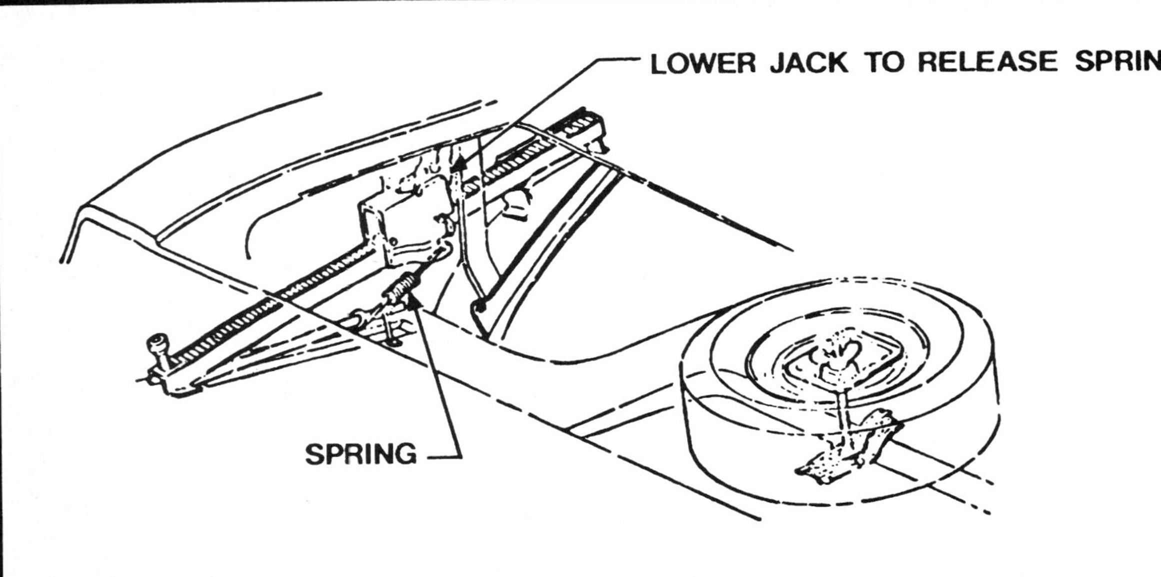

A 1972-1974 jacking decal. It was positioned the same as that of the 1971 model.

Chapter 9

Electrical Systems

Battery

The standard battery in the 1967-1969 Barracuda with a six-cylinder engine or a small-block V-8 was an A-24-A series 48-amp unit (part number 2444559). It used green-colored caps and had the words "Mopar Parts Division-Chrysler Corporation" printed on it.

The 1970-1972 models equipped with a six-cylinder came standard with a 46-amp battery listed as part number 2875951. This series A-21 battery also featured green caps. This battery was standard on cars with a 318-ci engine or a 340-ci engine from 1970 to 1973.

Standard with the 383-ci engine in 1967 to 1971 models was a 59-amp battery, listed as part number 2444562. This series A-24-B battery used yellow-colored

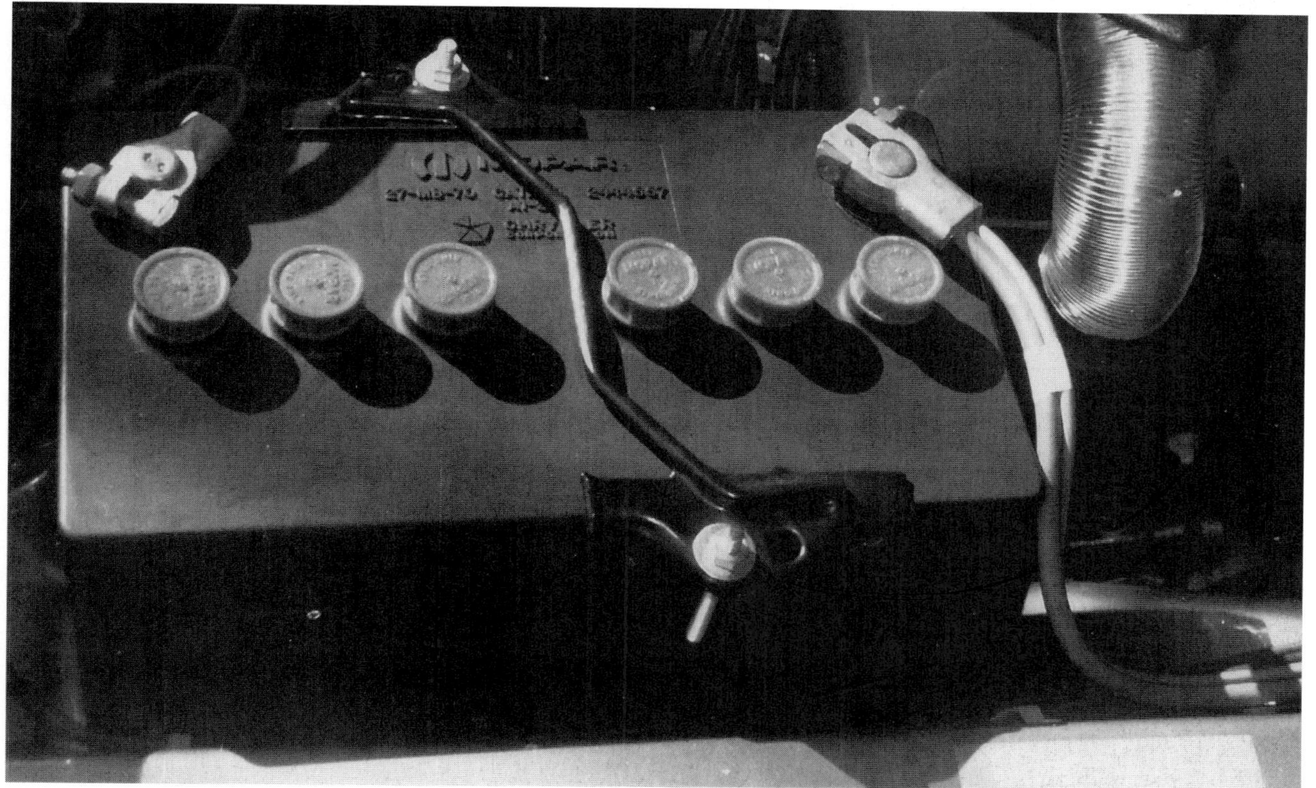

A reproduction of the powerful 70-amp battery.

caps and has no wording on the case. Those models with a 440-ci or Hemi engine in 1969 to 1971 came standard with a 70-amp battery listed as part number 2642969. This battery is a series A-27 unit and featured red caps and the word "Mopar" on top of the case.

Higher-rated batteries were optional each year in 1968 and 1969 models, and with a 318-ci or a 340-ci engine, the 59-amp battery was optional both years. The 70-amp battery was optional in 1969 models with the trailer-towing package. Since the trailer-towing package was not available with the 383-ci engine, a 70-amp battery was not available in these models. The 70-amp battery remained optional in 1970 to 1974 for all powerplants except the 440-ci or Hemi models, where it was standard. The part number for the 70-amp battery used in 1970 and 1972 models was the same as the 1969-1971 unit described above. In 1973 and 1974, it was listed as part number 3755069, but it still used red caps and the Mopar logo.

Original batteries are date-coded, and usually it is a two-digit code stamped on top of the negative post or into the case. The code will have the month represented by a single letter (A for January through M for December, with the letter I not used). The month code is followed by the last digit of the year: 6 for 1966, 7 for 1967, 8 for 1968, 9 for 1969, 0 for 1970, 1 for 1971, 2 for 1972, 3 for 1973, and 4 for 1974. Remember, this is the battery manufacturing year not the car's model year. Thus, it is possible that a battery stamped M6 (December 1966) could be used in your 1967 Barracuda. Batteries were shipped from the manufacturer to the assembly plant, so it is possible the code of M6 could have been installed in cars built in January or February 1967.

Battery Cables

Positive cables were six-gauge copper wires with a red-colored insulation cover all eight years. The head was natural aluminum with a spring-ring-type mount. This cable was routed from the battery to the starter motor. A red-colored 10-gauge piggyback wire was also used, and it was routed from the battery post to the starter relay.

Hemi-equipped models used unique-looking cables that contained a subharness that ran connecting wires to the oil pressure sending unit, starter relay, and the neutral switch when used with a four-speed manual transmission. The cable is covered in red vinyl, but black tape is used to hold the subharness to the battery cable. The lower portion of the cable was covered with an asbestos coating to protect the cable from the high underhood temperatures that a Hemi produces. Year One makes an excellent reproduction of this cable with the correct texture and white coloring of the original asbestos along with the correct black tape wrapping.

Special retaining straps were also used on the left-hand cylinder head to hold the battery cable away from the hot headers on the 426 Hemi. Two different lengths of straps were used. Either is correct as the usage depended on what was available as the car went down the assembly line.

Negative cables all eight years used a six-gauge copper wire with black-colored insulation, except 1969 models, where a four-gauge copper wire was used. Note that most reproductions are for the thinner six-gauge variety and in a concours event this will be considered incorrect for a 1969 model.

A single wire was used on 1967 to 1969 models, but beginning with 1970 and including later models, Chryslers used negative cable with two wires. The larger six-gauge wire was grounded to the engine block, while the smaller ten-gauge black wire was grounded to the body. This eliminated the ground strap used in the previous years.

The ground strap used in 1967-1969 Barracudas was a black covered wire with hoop ends, and it was attached to the right rear of the engine and to the firewall. Two different lengths were used: Those on cars without air conditioning measured 10 1/4 inches in length, while those without air conditioning used a longer cable that measured 12 3/4 inches. The ground strap was installed when the engine was painted and may have overspray on it.

Originally, the negative cable was in place when the engine was painted. Thus, paint will appear on the cable and wire looms where they run across the engine and the valve cover, leaving the area under the cable bare and free of paint. This may be correct and win you points in a concours showing, but it will look sloppy at all other showings. A much better method is to have two negative cables: one painted, the other left unpainted. To duplicate the assembly plant look, you can temporarily install the cable on the engine, then paint the engine. Then, when it's dry, remove the cable and paint the engine again to cover up the spots the cable shielded. If your engine has already been restored and you want to duplicate this look, mark the locations where the cable crosses the engine with masking tape. Then hang the cable up and lightly paint only the top portion of the cable using the same color as the engine, allowing a slightly heavier coat on the area that crosses the valve cover. Use this cable at concours showings. Leave the second cable unpainted and use it at all other showings and for everyday use.

Starter Motor

All models, except the 1967-1969 exports with the six-cylinder engines and four-speed manual transmissions, used a starter with 3.5 to 1 reduction built in. The export's six-cylinder with a four-speed transmission used

1967-1974 Starter Identification Numbers

Year	Engines	Type	ID Number
1967-1969	All*	Reduction	2095150
1967-1969	225-ci **	Direct	1889100
1968	Hemi	Direct	2642930
1970-1973	All	Reduction	2875560
1974	All	Reduction	3656575

* = Except exports; ** = Exports only.

a direct-drive starter. Starter motors can be identified by a number stamped on the outer case. The starter motor should be painted semi-gloss black, except the nose, which should have an unpainted, cast-aluminum appearance. The solenoid cover also had a two-tone finish: the front portion is flat black while the rear portion has a cast-aluminum appearance. The bolts that hold the two halves of the solenoid together should be painted flat black.

Alternator and Regulator

Standard in 1967 models was a 35-amp alternator, except those cars with the 383-ci engine, which came standard with a 46-amp alternator. All alternators without air conditioning used a 2 1/2-inch-diameter single-groove pulley. When air conditioning was ordered with a small-block, a 46-amp alternator with a dual-groove 3-inch pulley was used. Note that since the original alternator and pulley were mounted together, it is possible that a few cars with a 383-ci engine could have come with the double-groove pulley. This could be the case if supplies for the single-groove pulley ran out at the assembly plant. A 60-amp alternator was optional without air conditioning, and it, too, used the single-groove 2 1/2-inch-diameter pulley.

For 1968 and 1969 models, a 37-amp alternator was standard for all models, including the 383-ci-equipped cars. A 46-amp alternator was standard with air conditioning and used a double-groove 3-inch pulley. The 46-amp alternator was also optional on cars without air conditioning. The 60-amp alternator remained optional with or without air conditioning this year. With air conditioning, it used a double-groove, 3-inch pulley, and without air conditioning a single-groove 2 1/2-inch pulley was used.

Beginning in 1970, the alternator was stamped with an identification number. Standard for models equipped with a six-cylinder engine in 1970 and 1971 was a single-groove, 30-amp alternator stamped 3438171. All eight-cylinder-equipped models came with a standard 37-amp, single-groove pulley alternator that was stamped 3483172 (with a 2 1/2-inch pulley) or 3483780 (with 3-inch pulley). A 50-amp alternator was optional for all engines (for cars without air conditioning). The 50-amp alternator can be identified by the number 3438173 (with a 2 1/2-inch pulley) or 3438782 (with a 3-inch pulley). A 60-amp alternator was also optional with all V-8s and had the identification number of 3438174.

Standard on all 1970-1971 cars with air conditioning was a 37-amp unit. Although the output was not

1972 Alternator Identification Numbers Without AIR Emission Controls

Engine	Output (amps)	Pulley Diameter	No. of Grooves	ID Number
225-ci	34	2 1/2 in	1	3438803
All V-8	41	2 1/2 in	1	3438804
All	50	2 1/2 in	1	3438806
All	60	2 1/2 in	1	3656456
V-8 with A/C	50	3 in	2	3438811
All opt. with A/C	60	3 in	2	3438813, 3656459
All	60	2 3/4 in	2	3438812, 3656455

1972 Alternator Identification Numbers—California Cars Only (with AIR Emissions)

Engine	Output (amps)	Pulley Diameter	No. of Grooves	ID Number
V-8	41	n/a	1	3656217, 3656617
All	50	n/a	1	3656218, 3656618
All	60	n/a	1	3656219, 3656619,
3656471				

1973 Alternator Identification Numbers

Engine	Output (amps)	Pulley Diameter	No. of Grooves	ID Number
225-ci	34	2 1/2 in	1	3438803, 3755403
All V-8	41	2 1/2 in	1	3438804, 3755404,
3656645				
All	50	2 1/2 in	1	3438806, 3755406,
3755414, 3656614				
All	60	2 1/2 in	1	3438807, 3755407
All	65	2 1/2 in	1	3755192, 3755193
All	60	2 1/2 in	2	3438812, 3755412,
3656455, 3656570,				
				37555413, 3656713
All	65	n/a	2	3755190, 3755191

In 1974 models the alternators used a colored tag to identify the output. The following colored tags were used: yellow tag, 34-amp; red tag, 41-amp; green tag, 50-amp; blue tag, 60-amp; and black tag, 65-amp. Some 60-amp alternators used a parchment-colored tag.

changed, the identification number was changed. Remember that originally the alternator and pulley were assembled as a whole part, thus changing the part number. The following identification numbers were used: 37-amp, 3438176; 50-amp, 3438177 or 3438178; 60-amp, 3438179 with a 2 3/4-inch pulley; or 3438180 with a 3-inch pulley.

In 1972 and 1973, the alternator was still identified by an assembly part number cast into the case. As before, the output and type and size of the pulley will affect the identification number. However, those cars sold in California in 1972 used special alternators with different part numbers than cars delivered to other states.

Regulator

The 1967-1969 voltage regulator is box-shaped and has an identification number stamped on the housing. Two different units were used; most cars used the Chrysler-built unit with ID number 2098300, but some 1967 and 1968 models used the Essex Wire-built part that has the identification number of 2444980. The cover on both units should be painted gloss black. The base on the Essex unit should be painted flat black and left unpainted on the Chrysler-built unit.

One major drawback of the design above was that when the regulator developed a short, it had the tendency to drain the power out of the battery. So if you're wondering why your car's fully charged battery goes dead overnight, the regulator is probably the culprit. In 1970, Chrysler reduced the chance of this happening when it introduced the electronic voltage regulator. This unit required no mechanical adjustment nor did it use a coil wire as in previous years. It also used no points, thus reducing the chance of a short occurring and draining the battery. The new regulator was rectangular and was painted gloss black and mounted on the firewall. The words "Electronic Voltage Regulator" were printed on the case, and just below these words was the Mopar name and logo followed by an identification number of 3438150. This regulator was used with standard ignition or electronic ignition systems from 1970 to 1974.

Distributor

Three different designs of distributors were used: with single points, with dual points, and with no points or electronic ignition. The distributor can be identified by a number stamped on a tag attached to the body of the distributor. A date code can be found on the tag or on the body of the distributor itself. This code will consist of two or three digits. The first, or the first two digits, represents the week (1 to 52) of the year the distributor was made. The second or last digit is the last digit of the year (7 for 1967, 8 for 1968, 9 for 1969, and so on). Remember that the code may not agree with your car's model year. For example, the code 489, would be the 48th week in 1969 and thus be built for a 1970 model, while the code 118 would be the 11th week of 1968 and would be for a 1968 model. Usually, anything made after the 30th week in the year is for a car of the next model year.

All six-cylinder engines and cars with two-barrel V-8 engines with conventional ignitions used a black-colored distributor cap, while all four-barrel, multiple-carburetor cars, or those models with an electronic ignition

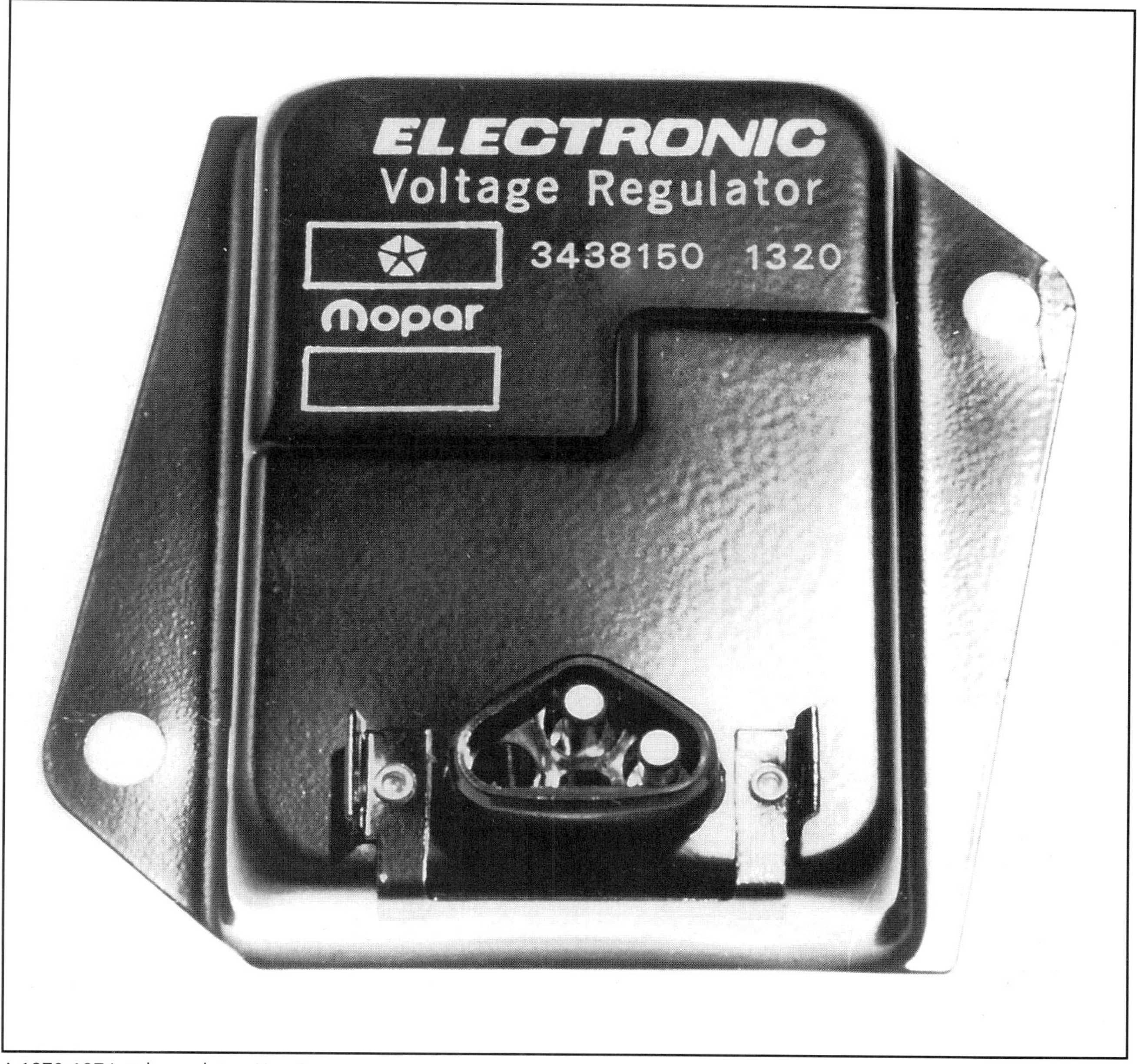

A 1970-1974-style regulator. *Year One*

system, used a tan cap. Listed below are distributor identification numbers. Note that more than one distributor manufacturer may have been used, or there may have been a change during the model year, so more than one distributor may be listed as available for an engine. Factors such as transmission and emission controls may also affect their usage, so read the charts carefully.

Distributors can be identified by this tag on the body. This one is for an early 1970 Six Pack model with manual transmission, and it was built on the 38th week of 1969.

Ignition Coil

Three different coils were used throughout the eight-model-year run. Most cars used the Chrysler-Prestolite-built unit, which was listed as part number 2444242 all eight years, although some models were

Coils have the part number on the case. This one is a reproduction of the 1967-1971 Chrysler-Essex unit. *Year One*

1967 Distributor Identification Numbers

Engine Displacement	Transmission	Without CAP	With CAP
225-ci six-cyl.	Manual	2444907	2642792
225-ci six-cyl.	Automatic	2444648	2642795
273-ci 2-bbl V-8	Manual	2642234	2642805
273-ci 2-bbl V-8	Automatic	2642238	2642805
273-ci 4-bbl V-8	All	2642242	2642358
		IBS-4013A**	IBS-4013B**
383-ci 4-bbl V-8	All	2642248	
383-ci 4-bbl V-8	Manual	————————	2642949
383-ci 4-bbl V-8	Automatic	————————	2642745

All units Chrysler-built except ** built by Prestolite

1968 Distributor Identification Numbers

Engine Displacement	Transmission	Point Type	ID Number
225-ci six-cyl.	Manual	Single	2875364
225-ci six-cyl.	Automatic	Single	2875366
318-ci 2-bbl V-8	All	Single	2875342
340-ci 4-bbl V-8	Automatic	Dual	2875105 IBS-4015A**
340-ci 4-bbl V-8	Manual	Dual	2875086 IBS-4015**
383-ci 4-bbl V-8	Manual	Single	2857356
383-ci 4-bbl V-8	Automatic	Single	2857358

All made by Chrysler except ** made by Prestolite; both types were used.

1969 Distributor Identification Numbers

Engine Displacement	Transmission	Point Type	ID Number
225-ci six-cyl.	Manual	Single	2875822
225-ci six-cyl.	Automatic	Single	2875826
318-ci 2-bbl V-8	All	Single	2875796
340-ci 4-bbl V-8	Manual	Dual	2875782 IBS-4015B
340-ci 4-bbl V-8	Automatic	Single	2875779
383-ci 4-bbl V-8	Manual	Dual	2875715 IBS-4016A**
383-ci 4-bbl V-8	Automatic	Dual	2875846 IBS-4016**
440-ci 4-bbl V-8	Manual	Dual	2875772
440-ci 4-bbl V-8	Automatic	Dual	2875758

All distributors are Chrysler-built except: ** = Prestolite-built.

1970 Distributor Identification Numbers

Engine Displacement	Transmission	Point Type	ID Number
225-ci six-cyl.	Manual	Single	2875822
225-ci six-cyl.	Automatic	Single	2875826
225-ci 2-bbl Export	Manual	Single	2875830
225-ci 2-bbl Export	Automatic	Single	2875833
318-ci 2-bbl V-8	All	Single	3438255
340-ci 4-bbl V-8	Manual	Dual	3438317
340-ci 4-bbl V-8	Automatic	Single	3438325
383-ci 2-bbl V-8	All	Single	3438231
383-ci 4-bbl V-8	All	Single	3438233
440-ci 4-bbl V-8	All	Single	3438222
440-ci 3x2-bbl V-8	Manual	Dual	3438314#
440-ci 3x2-bbl V-8	Automatic	Dual	2875982#
440-ci 3x2-bbl V-8	Manual	Dual	3438348+
440-ci 3x2-bbl V-8	Automatic	Dual	3438349+
Hemi	Manual	Dual	2875987 IBS-4014E**
Hemi	Automatic	Dual	2875989 IBS-4014F**

All units Chrysler-built except: ** = Prestolite-built; # = Before January 1, 1970; + = After January 1, 1970.

1971 Distributor Identification Numbers

Engine Displacement	Transmission Type	Point Type	Without NOX	With NOX
225-ci six-cyl.	Manual	Single	2875822	3438440
225-ci six-cyl.	Automatic	Single	2875826	3438442
225-ci 2-bbl Export	Manual	Single	2875830	Not used
225-ci 2-bbl Export	Automatic	Single	2875833	Not used
318-ci 2-bbl V-8	All	Single	3438255	3438453
340-ci 4-bbl V-8	Manual	Dual	3438522	Not used
340-ci 4-bbl V-8	Automatic	Single	3438517	Not used
340-ci 3x2-bbl	Manual	Dual	3438615 IBS-4018D**	Not used
340-ci 3x2-bbl	Automatic	Single	3438617 IBS-4018E**	Not used
340-ci 4-bbl V-8	Manual	Electronic ignition	3656151	Not used
340-ci 4-bbl V-8	Automatic	Electronic ignition	3438896	Not used
383-ci 2-bbl V-8	All	Single	3438534	3438544
383-ci 4-bbl V-8	All	Single	3438690	Not used
440-ci 3x2-bbl	All	Dual	3438577	Not used
Hemi	Manual	Dual	2875987	Not used
Hemi	Automatic	Dual	3438579	Not used
Hemi	Manual	Electronic ignition	3438891	Not used
Hemi	Automatic	Electronic ignition	3438893	Not used

** = Prestolite-built.

1972 Distributor Identification Numbers

Engine Displacement	Transmission Type	Point Type	Without Air Pump	With Air Pump
225-ci six-cyl.	Manual	Single	3656252	3656260
225-ci six-cyl.	Automatic	Single	3656257	3656266
318-ci 2-bbl V-8	Manual	Single	3656272	3656275
318-ci 2-bbl V-8	Automatic	Single	3656390	3656275
318-ci 2-bbl V-8	Manual	Electronic ignition	3656429	3656436
318-ci 2-bbl V-8	Automatic	Electronic ignition	3656587	3656436
340-ci 4-bbl V-8	All	Electronic ignition	3656278	Not used

1973 Distributor Identification Numbers

Engine Displacement	Transmission Type	Identification Number
318-ci 2-bbl V-8	All	3656763
340-ci 4-bbl V-8	All	3656771

All distributors are with electronic ignition.

1974 Distributor Identification Numbers

Engine Displacement	Transmission Type	Identification Number
318-ci 2-bbl V-8	All	3656763
360-ci 4-bbl V-8	All	3755486

All distributors are with electronic ignition.

equipped with the Chrysler-Essex-built coil. Where two coils were used, the 1967-1971 models used part number 2444241, while the 1973 and 1974 models used part number 2444211. Either a Prestolite or the Essex-type coil is correct, but part number 2444211 should not appear on a 1971-or-earlier model, and part number 2444241 should not be used on a 1973 or 1974 model. All three coils were black and have the part number, and the manufacturer's name is printed on each one.

Wipers

A two-speed wiper motor was standard all eight years in both models, but variable-speed wipers were optional. When the Shaker Hood scoop or the 426 Hemi was ordered, then variable-speed wipers were mandatory options. An identification number was stamped into the wiper motor's housing to identify the unit. The number may sometimes be hidden under a decal or sticker. Listed below are the original part numbers. Note, however, that the number of the original unit may not always match that of the part number; it may

Most wiper motors have an ID number on the case with which to identify them.

1967-1974 Wiper Motor Identification Part Numbers

Model Year(s)	Speeds/Type	Part Number
1967	2-speed	2808767
1967	Variable	2808801
1968	2-speed	2926168
1968	Variable	3004114
1969	2-speed	2770090
1969	Variable	2983116
1970-1971	2-speed	2926929
1970-1971	Variable	3431077
1972	2-speed	3431533*
		3431606**
1972	Variable	3431534#
		3431624##
1973	2-speed	3431606+
		3431718++
1973	Variable	3431665
1974	2-speed	3431790
1974	Variable	3431906

* = Up until May 2,1972;
** = Used after May 2, 1972; # = Up until September 1, 1971;
** = Used after September 1, 1971;
+ = Up until February 1, 1973;
++ = After February 1, 1973.

be off by a number or two. For example, a unit that is part number 2989921 may have a stamping number of 2989920 or 2989922.

Usually the housings on the two-speed wipers were painted gloss black and those with variable-speed wipers were left unpainted. The unpainted look can be duplicate and preserved by painting the housing stainless steel in a flat finish. Note that early-1967 models with the two-speed or variable-speed wipers used a gloss black housing with a white switch plate. Late-1967 models used a housing that was two-toned; part of it was aluminum in color and the other half was painted gloss black. The two-tone finish was also used on the 1968 model with variable-speed wipers.

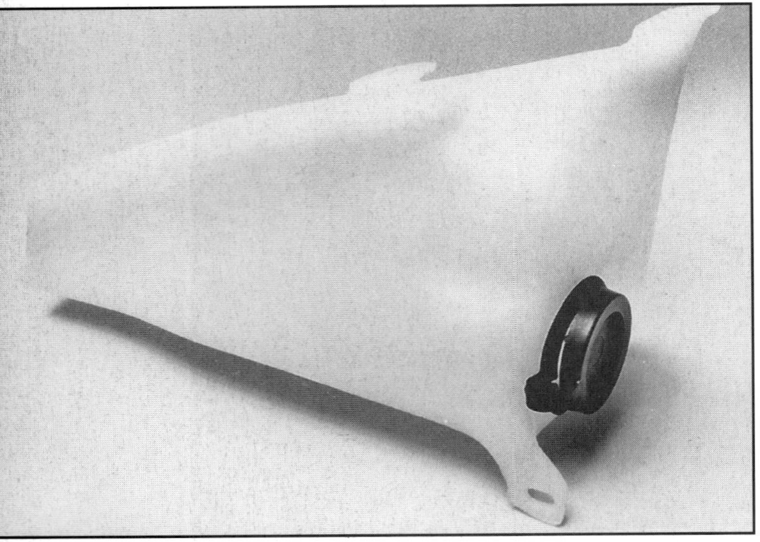

A 1970-1971 washer jar. *Year One*

Wiper Washer System

Electrical washers were standard on 1967 Barracudas. Foot-operated washers were standard from 1968 to 1974, except on cars with a Hemi or Shaker Hood. All 1970-1974 Challenger models, except those with a Hemi or the Shaker Hood, also came standard with a manual foot-operated washer pump. If the variable-speed wipers were ordered, then an electrical pump was used.

Those models with the foot pump have a small push-button pump mounted in the floor of the car just above the brake pedal. Check valves are built into the pump to control the direction of the fluid flow from the reservoir to the pump and from the pump to the nozzles. Washer fluid was held in a white plastic reservoir which has provisions for the hoses at the bottom of the tank. Those models with electrical washers have a pump mounted in the bottom of the washer jar.

Both the manual and the electrical washer jars have the same shape, but they will not interchange. The 1967-1969 reservoirs were square and used a black plastic cap. The 1970 and 1971 models use a design that is flat on top with a long, tube-like tank, while the 1972-1974 style was just the opposite. The filler neck on this latter model is long and flows into the tank. A black plastic cap imprinted with the words "Washer Fluid Only" was used on all models.

A 7/16-inch outside diameter ribbed hose was used from the washer jar to the foot pump on 1968 and 1971 models. Those cars with an electrical pump used ribbed hose with a 9/32-inch outside diameter from the reservoir to the connector. The 1972-1974 models—both those with the foot-operated and the electrical pump—used the 9/32-inch outside diameter ribbed hose.

Both models used a 3/16-inch outside diameter hose that ran from the connector, or foot pump, to the outlet nozzles. The 1967-1969 models used a nozzle design that was unique to each side of the car. The 1967 and 1968 models used the same set both years, but the 1969 model used different part numbers than did those earlier models. The 1970 to 1974 models used a nozzle design that would fit either side of the car, and the same nozzle was used all five years.

As for the foot pump, the 1968 models used part number 2889810. The 1969 models used two different pumps: early models (those built up to approximately February 3, 1969) used part number 2926927, while the later models used part number 3431058. Foot pumps used in the E-bodies were the same all five years and used part number 2983076. If the gloss black mounting bracket is removed, then the same pump can also be found in Dart or Valiant, including Duster models. With the mounting bracket, the pump is not interchangeable.

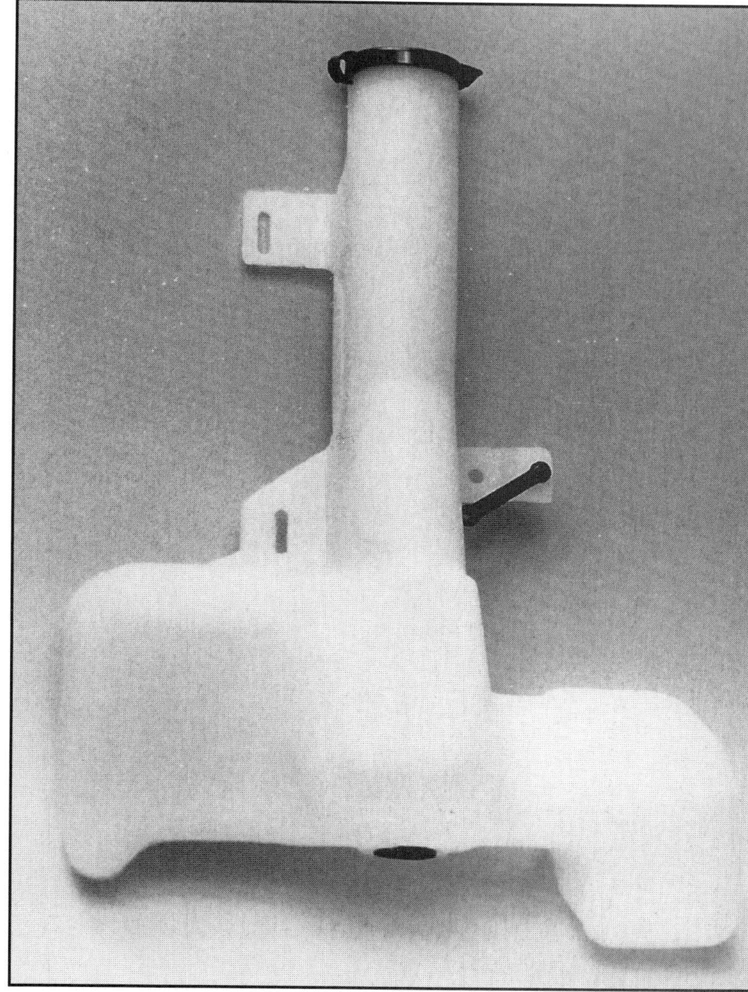

A 1972-1974 washer jar. *Year One*

Heater Motor

Two types of motors were used: those with the factory-installed air conditioning and those without the factory-installed air conditioning. Dealer-installed or hang-on-type air conditioning did not affect the heater motor, and the same motor was used without air conditioning.

All 1967 to 1969 Barracudas without the factory-installed air conditioning used the same motor, which was listed as part number 2837550. With the factory-installed air conditioning, part number 2808761 was used these three years. In 1970-1974, part number 2936602 was used in cars without factory-installed air conditioning, and part number 3514305 was used in 1970 to 1973 models. Most of the parts in 1974 models are the same as those used in the 1973 models, but the heater motor used with the factory-installed air conditioning

A typical example of the 1970-1974 heater controls.

1967-1969 A-Body and 1970-1974 E-Body Heater Cores		
Model Year(s)	**Without Factory A/C**	**With Factory A/C**
1967-1969	2277535	2277535
1970-1974	3503408	3441180

is an exception; part number 3837343 was used. All models with multiple carburetors were not available with factory-installed air conditioning, so only part number 2936602 was used with these models. The heater motor, whether with or without factory air conditioning, should be painted semi-gloss black.

Heater Core

Just as with heater motors, those models with the factory-installed air conditioning used different cores. Those models with the dealer-installed or hang-on air conditioning used the standard core. The above cores were used:

A 5/8-inch inside diameter hose was routed from the engine to the heater core and from the core to the engine in 1967 and 1968. In 1969 models, a preformed hose (part number 1595160) was used from the water pump to the core assembly. Both the inlet and outlet hoses used unpainted snap ring hose clamps at each end of the hose. At the firewall, the rings were installed pointing straight up. At the engine, the rings point forward toward the radiator.

Two different diameters of hoses were used on the 1970 to 1974 models. A 5/8-inch-diameter hose was used from the heater to the water pump, while a 1/2-inch inside diameter hose was used from the engine to the core. When air conditioning was ordered, the route was from the engine to the water valve. On 1970 models, a 5/8-inch diameter hose was used from the valve to the core, and from 1971, this hose was preformed and was 1/2-inch inside diameter. Snap rings were used at the end of each hose, including the hose from the water valve to the core.

The factory installed whatever hose was available when the car came down the line. Some hose may be stenciled with part numbers and the Mopar pentastar, while other vendors' hoses may be completely black with no part numbers and no logo. Note that hoses were installed when the engine was painted, so overspray may appear on the hoses, especially between the ribs on ribbed hoses. Hose brackets were painted gloss black.

Again, this can look sloppy on a show car, but because hoses can lose their sealing effectiveness when removed and installed several times, you should not use two different hoses. Choose one method and stick to it. If most of your showing is at national events, go for the overspray-on-the-hose look. If they are local events, go for the clean, unpainted hose.

Heater Vents and Controls

The 1967-1969 models used defroster vents on the top of the instrument panel. They were originally precolored to match the instrument panel. Each side is unique and right and left vents cannot swap sides. The vents can be repainted in the same finish as the instrument panel. Paint the vents separately before installing them in the instrument panel. Be sure to paint both sides and between the vents. An air brush or touch-up gun works better here than a full-sized paint gun.

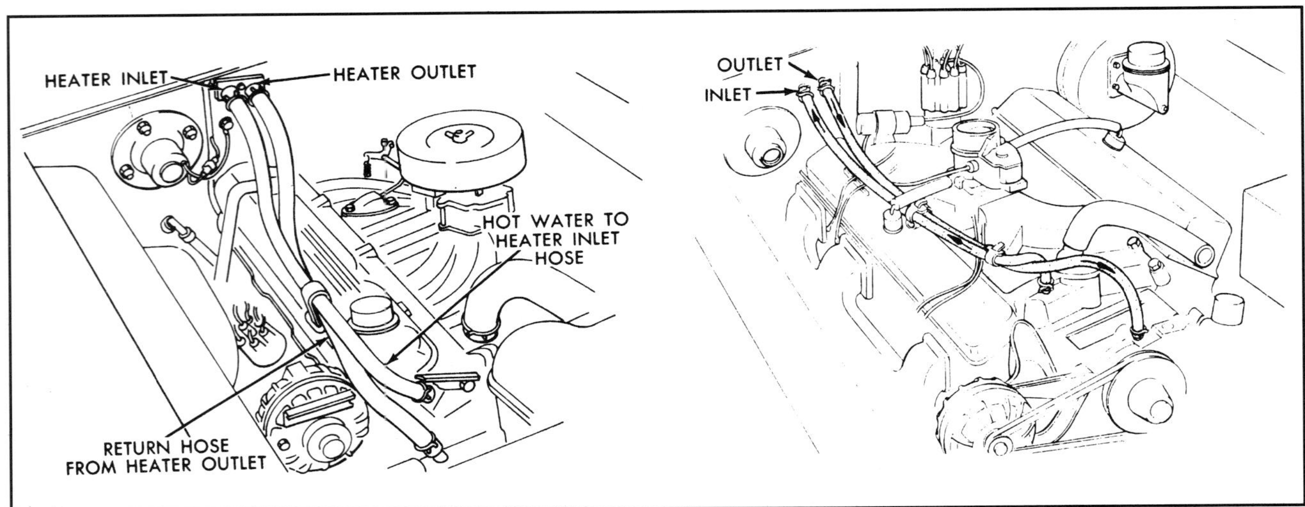

Heater hose routes for 1967-1969 six-cylinder engines (left), and V-8s (right).

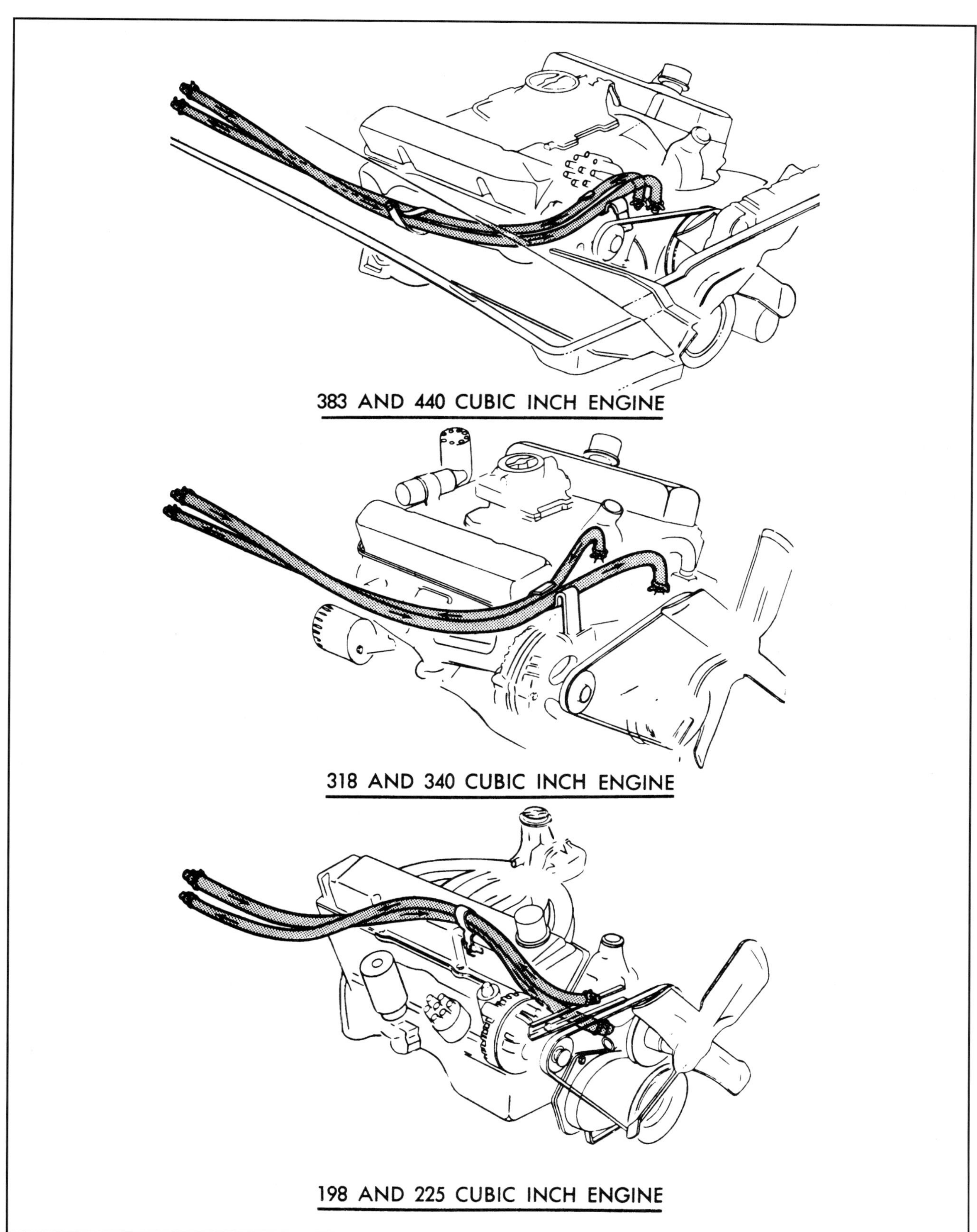

Typical E-body heater hose routes.

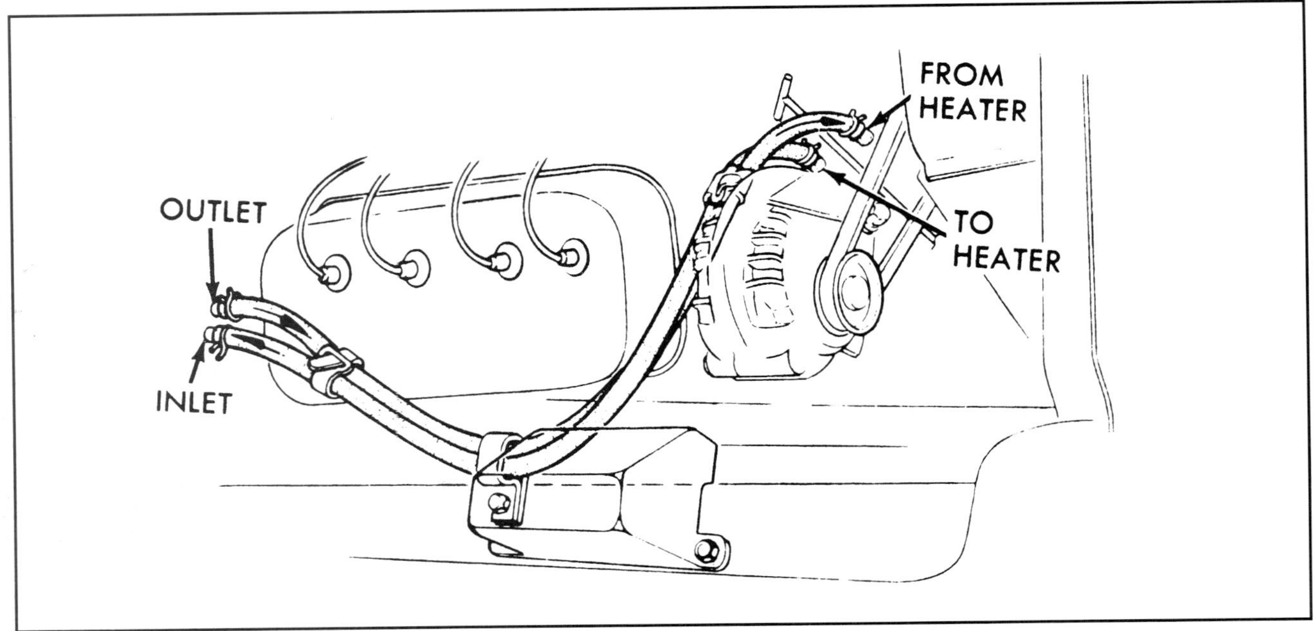

The Hemi heater hose routing.

Heater controls in the 1967-1969 models are located in the center of the instrument panel and the heater instruction panel was part of the instrument bezel. Thus, a car with air conditioning used a different bezel than those without it, and those with the decor interior group used different bezels than those models without this package.

On 1970-1974 models, the defroster vents are part of the instrument panel itself. Several different heater controls were used. The 1970-1971 Barracuda used a different heater switch than did the Challenger with the standard instrumentation. Barracudas without the Rally instrumentation group used part number 2884722 all five years, and it was also used on the 1972-1974 Challengers. However, the 1970-1971 Challengers used part number 2884717 with the standard instrumentation. Both models with the Rally cluster used part number 2884704 all five years.

A close-up of the 1970-1974 Barracuda instrument controls without the Rally Cluster.

Bezels used with the Rally cluster in both models were listed as part number 3431043 all five years for both models. Those without the Rally cluster group used part number 3431044, except the 1970 Challenger, which used part number 3431043. The 1971 to 1974 Challenger used part number 3421044. Due to the different design in the instrument bezel, a later-style bezel will not fit your 1970 Challenger.

If air conditioning was ordered, then a different set of controls was used. And like the heater controls, those cars with the Rally instrument group used a different part number than those without the package. Without the Rally instruments, part number 2884700 was used, and with the cluster, part number 2884701 was used. These parts were used until December 1971; after this date, part numbers 3502445 (without the Rally cluster) and 3502444 (with the Rally cluster) were used; these same part numbers were also used in 1973 and 1974 models.

Horns

Dual horns—a low note (part number 2808869) and a high note (part number 2808868)—were standard all eight years in both models. Both horns should be painted gloss black, including their mounting brackets. Original finish is a higher gloss than most underhood components. Eastwood's Fast Dry Gloss Black Engine Paint is an excellent match. Two different horn relays were used. The 1967-1969 models used part number 2822461 and the 1970 to 1974 models used part number 3467368.

Exterior Lighting

Headlamps

All Barracudas except the 1971 model used dual headlamps, while all Challengers and the 1971 Barracuda models used a quad-headlamp arrangement. There is some disagreement about which manufacturer supplied the headlamps. Most original cars used either G.E. (General Electric) or Westinghouse lamps. According to a former factory worker, the headlamps were placed in the parts bins, one on each side of the line, and whatever parts were available were what was used. So it is possible that General Electric parts could be on one side and Westinghouse parts on the other.

Dual headlamps were a combination of high and low beams, while on the quad-lamp arrangement, the outer headlamps were a combination of low and high beams, but the inner headlamps were for the high beam only. These inner headlamps will have the number 1 imprinted in the glass to identify them.

Barracudas with the single headlamp on each side with left-hand drive used part number 152291 all four years. When the car was sent overseas and converted to right-hand drive, a different headlamp (part number 152293) was used. The two cannot interchange due to the way the light shifts between high and low beams.

All Challengers and the 1971 Barracuda used part number 152285 as the inner high beam headlamp on both U.S. and export models. However, the outboard lamps were listed as part number 152286 with left-hand drive and 152287 on right-hand-drive models.

The headlamp switch on the 1967-1969 models was located on the lower portion of the instrument panel on the left-hand side. The switch (part number 2809087) and Brite knob (part number 2820135) were used all three years. The headlamp switch for the 1970-1974 models was located on the far left-hand side to the left of the wiper controls. One switch (part number 2947305) was used all five years and with both instrument panels. Just below the headlamp switch on 1970-1974 models is the instrument panel dimmer switch, and the same switch was used all five years. The outer bezels were a continuation of that used on the instruments.

Several different bezels were used depending on the options that were ordered and the body style. This is due to whether a switch was used below the windshield wipers. The power top button was located here on convertibles, and the rear defroster button was located here on hardtops when ordered with this option. If a convertible was not ordered with a power top, or a hardtop was not ordered with a rear window defroster, then no provision for a switch was offered. To further complicate matters, those models with Rally instruments used a different bezel than those without the optional gauge cluster. In addition, there was a change from American Walnut to Kashmer Walnut in February 1971 on the Rally cluster. In 1972, with the deletion of the convertible, the bezel choice was narrower.

The 1970 Rally Cluster instrument controls. Note the lack of provisions for convertible roof operation or the rear defroster. This is typical of 1971-1974 models, with black labels with white lettering.

Front Parking Lamps

Front parking lamps were standard each year. On 1967-1969 Barracudas they were mounted in the grille to duplicate the look of Rally lamps. Each year a different part number was used, and this number will appear on the lens.

In 1967, the lens (part number 2808995) was designed to fit either side. In 1968 models, the lenses were restyled and each side is unique and listed as part numbers 2809120 (right) and 2809121 (left). For 1969, the lenses (part numbers 2932838, right, and 2932839, left) were again restyled and included a small Barracuda medallion in the center of each lens.

In 1970, the Barracuda's front parking lamps were mounted above the grille insert in the grille frame. These

1970-1974 E-Body Instrument Panel Controls Bezel

Model Year(s)	Instrument Type	Options Used With	Part Number
1970	Rally	Power Top	2947823
1970	Rally	None	2947822
1970	Rally	Rear defroster	2947824
1971-1974	Without Rally	None	3488392
1971-1974	Rally	None	3488379
1971	Rally	Power Top	3488380
1971-1974	Rally	Rear defroster	3488381
1970 Barracuda	Without Rally	None	2947783*
			3488392**
1970 Challenger	Without Rally	None	2947791

* = Before February 1971; ** = After February 1971.

lenses were listed as part numbers 3420618 (right) and 3420619 (left). These lenses required a collimator to gather the light and spread it more evenly to the lens. For 1971, the Barracuda's front parking lamp was relocated to the outer ends of the front pan, and the lenses were listed as part numbers 3579174 (right) and 3579175 (left).

The Challenger used the same set of lenses from 1970 to 1972, but two different-colored lenses were used. The U.S. models used clear lenses listed as part numbers 3420554 (right) and 3420555 (left). Export cars used amber-colored lenses listed as part numbers 3420552 (right) and 3420553 (left). In 1972, the Barracuda's front turn lamps were still mounted in the front pan but were restyled and moved inward toward the center. The lenses were listed as part numbers 3621680 (right) and 3621681 (left); these same lenses were used in 1973 and 1974 Barracudas.

Sidelamps

No sidelamps were used on any of the 1967 models. In 1968, sidelamps became mandatory safety equipment, and these models used small, round-shaped lamps (not lenses). The entire assembly was listed as part number 2853647. The good news about this part is that it was used on the front fenders of all models except Darts, Chargers, or Furys. Look for four-door Coronets—there were thousands of these models made. Round-shaped lamps were also used on the rear quarter-panels; these lamps (part number 2853640), like the front lamps, fit either side, but their interchangeable nature was limited to Barracudas or Valiant models only.

In 1969, reflectors were used on the sides instead of lamps. The amber-colored front reflectors were listed as part number 2932922. This assembly was also used on full-sized 1969 Dodge models. Those models for sale in the United States got red-colored rear-quarter reflectors listed as part number 2932928, while those exported out used amber-colored lenses listed as part number 3420601. These part numbers included the reflector and natural bezel.

Much more interchanging of the front reflector is possible if only the reflector is swapped, as Valiants, Darts, Satellites, Coronets, Chargers, and full-sized Dodge models all used the same amber-colored reflector. Note, however, there was a change in part numbers after January 1969. Until then, part number 2930744 was used; after this date, part number 2930960 was used. Quarter-panel reflectors are also more interchangeable if only the reflector lens is changed, as it was used on Valiants and full-sized Chrysler models. Be careful when interchanging a reflector from a Newport model. Reflectors on this model were changed around January 1969 and the later style will not fit the Barracuda. The proper part number is 2930746.

As mentioned above, export models used an amber-colored reflector. Early exports used part number 2930774, while those produced after January 1969 used part number 2930960.

The 1970 and 1971 Barracudas used lamps again on the front. They used a design that included a lamp that held a small amber-colored lens, and this assembly was listed as part number 3403622. These lenses are the inner part and not the reflector that is visible from the outside. The reflector was included with the bezel. Two different bezels and reflectors were used: early-1970 models used part numbers 3403630 (right) and 3403631 (left). Those models built after June 1, 1970, used part numbers 3479380 (right) and 3479381 (left), and these were used on all 1971 Barracuda models.

Rear sidelamps were designed like the front marker lamps, but they used a red inner lens, listed as part number 3403638, which can be found on 1970-1971 Fury models. The bezel and rear reflector lenses were also change after June 1, 1970. Early-1970 models used part number 3403640 (right) and 3403641 (left). Those built after this date, including all 1971 models, used part numbers 3479386 (right) and 3479387 (left). When a Barracuda was exported, an amber-colored lens was used, and the part number is the same as that used on the front fender.

Challengers also used the same design and part numbers for 1970 and 1971. The assembly consisted of a lamp housing with an amber-colored lens and a gasket between the lens and the housing. A clear lens (part numbers 3420794, right, and 3420795, left) was placed over it. The rear lamps used a similar design; on U.S. models a red-colored lens, listed as part numbers 3420820 (right) and 3420821 (left), was used, while exports used an amber-colored lens, listed as part numbers 3420928 (right) and 3420929 (left).

Sidelamps were restyled for 1972 models and remained untouched until the end of the 1974 model year. Both the Challenger and Barracuda now used the same lens and lamp assembly. The amber-colored lenses were listed as part number 3587436 and were used at the front in U.S. models and at the front and rear on exports. U.S. models use a red-colored lens on the rear quarter-panels. There is great opportunity for interchange for the U.S. cars. The front and rear lenses can be found on all 1973 and 1974 Darts, Dusters, Valiants, Chargers, Satellites, and Coronets on all body styles except the station wagon.

Taillamps

Only one set of taillamps was used on all 1967 Barracudas no matter what body style. They used a housing that was painted Argent Silver and a red-colored lens (part numbers 2809020, right, and 2809021, left) that featured trim that corresponded with the trim on the rear panel. Back-up lamps were in the rear bumper. These lamps were listed as part numbers 2606818 (right) and 260619 (left).

For 1968, the taillamps were restyled and the back-up lamp was incorporated into the taillamp. The lenses were listed as part numbers 2809118 (right) and 2809119 (left). These lenses also used trim that fit in with that used on the rear panel. The taillamps were again restyled for 1969 models, and the lenses were listed as part numbers 2932728 (right) and 2932729 (left).

The 1970 Barracuda used taillamps that were square-shaped with two horizontal ribs across the red-colored lens; they were listed as part numbers 3420836 (right) and 3420837 (left). Two bezels were used with each taillamp assembly. They consisted of an inner bezel (part numbers 3403058, right, and 3403059, left) and the outer bezel (part numbers 3403236, right, and 3403237, left). When the bezels were installed, each taillamp looked like they were three separate units. As in the two previous years, the back-up light was part of the taillamp assemblies.

Challengers in 1970 used two taillight assemblies that were long and thin; the lens was listed as part numbers 3420556 (right) and 3420557 (left). A chrome bezel (part numbers 3403038, right, and 3403039, left) was used over each assembly. Unlike the Barracuda, the back-up lamp was not part of the taillamps but instead was placed between the taillight housing in the center of the rear of the car. The Dodge name was spelled out across the clear back-up light lens.

Taillamps used on the 1971 Barracuda were similar to those in 1970 but were smaller. The inner lens part numbers were now listed as 3478638 (right) and 3478639 (left), and outer bezels were part numbers 3478838 (right) and 3478839 (left); each taillamp looked like four separate lenses stacked on top of one another. Back-up lamps were placed to the side of the taillamps, and the red-colored lenses were listed as part numbers 3514364 (right) and 3514365 (left). Challenger taillamps were also restyled, and each assembly looked as if it were three individual units with the back-up lamps mounted in the center of each assembly. The lenses were listed as part numbers 3514392 (right) and 3420785 (left). No bezel was used on the taillamps.

From 1972 to 1974, the Barracuda used a design of twin round-shaped taillamps on each side with the inner lens supporting the back-up lens. The lenses were listed as part numbers 3587272 for the outboard lenses and 3587278 for the inner lens. This same set of lenses was used all three years. The Challenger taillamps were also restyled and used the same set of lenses for 1972 to 1974.

However, the Rally models used a different set of housings than those on base Challenger models. Rally models used part numbers 3587352 (right) and 3587353 (left), while the other Challenger models used part numbers 3587316 (right) and 3587317 (left). The difference is color. On those used on the Rally models, the outer edges of the housings were painted flat black. On base Challenger models, the taillamp housings were painted Argent Silver. A base Challenger housing could be used on a Rally model if it is accented in flat black. The lenses themselves are two separate units; the solid red lenses have part numbers 3621606 (right) and 3621607 (left), while the inner units use part numbers 3621604 (right) and 3621605 (left), and this includes the back-up lens.

Interior Lighting

Dome Lamp

An inside dome lamp was mounted in the center of the roof of all two-door hardtop models. Convertibles and fastbacks came standard with courtesy lamps. Those on fastbacks were mounted on the rear-quarter roof panels, and on a convertible they were mounted in the console.

The housing for two-door hardtops was listed as part number 2292994 and uses a white lens (part number 2292995 all eight years). This part can be for 1967-1974 A-bodies and 1967-1974 B-bodies, except the convertible or 1966-1967 Charger.

The fastback models in 1967 to 1969 used a lamp assembly with a white-colored lens and Brite bezel mounted in each on the roof quarter-panels. The same lamp, lens, and bezel assembly was used all three years. This assembly was unique to the Barracuda fastback and cannot be found on any other model. The convertible used a pocket-panel courtesy lamp listed as part number 2822471 in 1967 to 1969 models. This lamp can also be found in Dart convertibles. Again restyled in 1970, it was listed as part number 2926848 and was also used on 1971 models.

Challenger S.E. and Gran Coupe models used a special dome lamp that was part of the overhead console. The 1970 models used a different lamp (part number 2947912) than the 1971 models (part number 3488441). This lamp can be found in Fury sport models and Monaco 500 models with a map light. The overhead console was color-keyed to the interior. The same console was used in both models and matched the headliner. At the front of this console were indicator lamps for door ajar, low fuel, and unfastened seat belts. Brite trim was used to highlight the console base, which has a flat finish. Although the console was originally cast in color, it can be painted to match your trim. Use a flat gloss color.

Chapter 10

Options

This section covers the individual options that Chrysler offered each year. It covers factory options and some dealer-installed options. To be a correct dealer-installed option, the part or accessories must have been installed on the car before the original owner took delivery of the car or the car went out on the dealer's lot. Some options replaced the standard items that were covered earlier in this guide (such as disc brakes and power steering), while others are unique and are covered here.

Options are listed in alphabetic order according to their option code, which was used from 1969 to 1974. If an option was also available in 1967 or 1968, the number code is also given. However, the 1967-1968 codes are in no particular order. To find them for an option, you must know the option code used in later years for that option, or you'll find it in the section for those options offered only in 1967 or 1968.

Light Package: Code AO1, 1969-1974; Code 355, 1968

The light package was made available for the first time in 1968 models and remained an option until the end of the 1974 model run. This option was a package of separate options, of which some were not available as separate components. It was available on both the Barracuda and Challenger in 1970-1974, and except for a small number of revisions, it remained the same all seven years.

In all seven years the package consisted of an ashtray light, glovebox lamp, hood- or fender-mounted turn indicators, an ignition lamp with delay, and a trunk lamp. On fastbacks, however, no trunk lamp was used. Beginning in 1969 models, a headlamp-on warning buzzer was added to the package; this could also be ordered as a separate option but only if the headlamp delay switch was also ordered. In 1970, a map light and time-delayed instrument panel floodlight was added to the package.

Four different ashtray lamps were used. The 1968 models used part number 2864240; the 1969 models used part number 2947245; 1970-1972 models used part number 2947389; and the 1973 and 1974 models used part number 3488923. They are not interchangeable with each other from year-to-year.

Hood-mounted turn indicators in 1968 models consisted of a lamp with a single lead that required a hole to be drilled into the hood. An unpainted retainer was used to hold the Brite housing to the hood. The housing was designed so that it fit either side. In 1969, the lamps were restyled and the lamp and the housing were a single part.

For 1970, the signal lamps were placed on the front fenders instead of the hood. Two different lamps were used; all but those on a base Challenger with a 340-ci engine used part number 3420727, and those used on the base Challenger with a 340-ci engine used part number 2930781. The latter of these can also be found on 1970 Valiant models. The 1971 Challengers used the same part numbers they used in 1970, but the 1971 Barracuda used part number 3479261, which also was used on 1971 Valiant models.

Lamps were again restyled in 1972 and both models used part number 3587502. This assembly can also be found on a four-door Satellite (including station wagon models), and all Coronets and Chargers, but those from a *two*-door Satellite will not fit. Again restyled in 1973, the lamp was listed as part number 3679255 for both models and continued unchanged for 1974. These lamps can also be found on all full-sized 1973-1974 Dodge and Plymouth models.

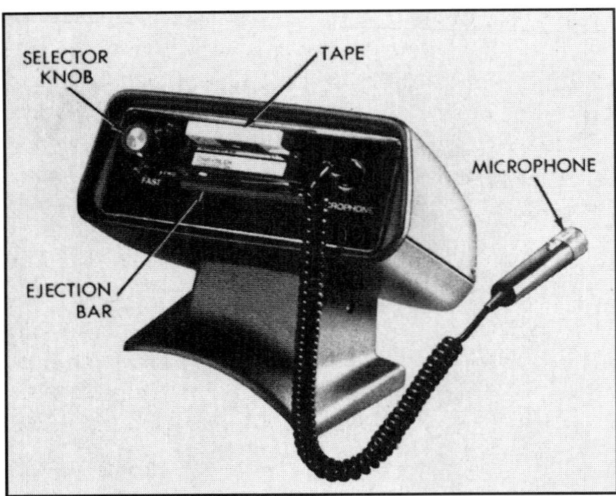

The 1971-1972 console-mounted tape recorder.

Four different ignition lamps were used; the 1968 models used part number 2864224, which can also be found in mid-sized 1968 models. The 1969 models used part number 2987108; this lamp can be found in all 1969 A-bodies. In 1970, part number 2947751 was used, which was also used in A- and B-body cars of the same year. From 1971 to 1974, part number 3488479 was used; this lamp can be found in all 1971-1974 car lines, *except* full-sized Dodge Plymouths with tilt steering. All ignition lamps featured a delay switch that would turn off a short time after the door was closed. On 1967-1968 models, the lamp was mounted above the key switch on the instrument panel, and for 1969-1974 models, the lamp was mounted on the steering column above the ignition switch.

Basic Group: Code AO4

This package included an AM radio, power steering, remote control mirror, and variable-speed washers. Note that this package was not available on cars with a 383-ci from 1967 through 1969 or the 440-ci in 1969. Since most of these components were covered in earlier sections, only the radios will be covered in detail here. The 1967 Barracuda, with the Basic Group package, used a model 236 AM radio. This radio, which was used in the Valiant line only, has the words "Solid State by Plymouth" printed on the dial. Thus a unit from a Dodge will not fit because it will not have the proper lettering.

An AM/FM radio, model 385, was available as a separate option or as an upgrade with the Basic Group package. This radio was used in all A-bodies, including the Dodge Dart and full-sized Chrysler models. The AM/FM radio is a rare option as most FM stations at the time played classical music and country and western, and not rock and roll—the music most young buyers listened to.

In 1968, a model 244 AM radio was used with the Basic Group package or as a separation option. The AM/FM radio, now model 398, was also available as a separate option or an upgrade with the Basic Group package. These radios are rare today, as they were used only in the 1968 and 1969 Barracuda models. Those from other lines will not correctly interchange.

In 1970 and 1971, the AM radio was listed as part number 2884853, and it used a unique styling as both the volume and tuning knobs were on the same side of the radio. Though the 1971 Charger and Satellite used this same knob arrangement, the radios are not the same. An AM radio with a stereo tape player was also available, and this radio had the same knob arrangement as the AM radio, but below the push buttons was an eight-track tape player. Also available was an AM/FM Multiplex radio. This radio used four thumb wheels instead of colored knobs; as with the other radios, the Brite thumb wheels were positioned on the left-hand side of the radio.

Two new options that appeared in 1971 models were radios that used a separate cassette tape player. The tape player sat on the console or the center (transmission) hump of the floor and was connected to the radio with a vinyl-coated cable. Two different lengths of cable were used: When the unit was mounted on the floor, a 44-inch cable was used, and a 9-inch cable was used when the tape player was mounted on the console. Either an AM radio or AM/FM Multiplex radio had to be ordered with the tape player. As with the other radios, these two units were designed for the E-bodies only, and while they're similar to those of a B-body, they will not interchange. However, the tape player itself was the same one used in all car lines.

The same AM radio that was used in 1971 was used again for 1972 to 1974. The floor-mounted tape player was also the same, but was available only with the AM/FM Multiplex radio with an input socket for 1972 and 1973. In 1974, the tape player was no longer available. A new AM/FM Multiplex radio appeared in 1974; it had the same design as the radio used in 1972 but has knobs, not thumb wheels. However, the AM/FM Multiplex radio with the thumb wheels did remain as an over-the-counter part for the 1974 Barracuda and Challenger models only.

A 60-inch manual-control antenna was used all eight years. However, some cars in 1969 to 1971 did use a 76 1/2-inch-long manual antenna. On all models except those with the fiberglass hood, the antenna was mounted on the right front fender. Those models with the fiberglass hood had the antenna mounted on the rear quarter-panel. The 1967-1969 models used the same antenna that was used on all A-bodies and 1968-1969 B-bodies.

With the 1970-1974 models, except those with the fiberglass hood, the antenna was designed specifically for the Challenger or Barracuda line only and will not interchange with other car lines. As previously mentioned, those models with a fiberglass hood had the antenna mounted on the rear quarter-panel. This antenna can be found on Dusters, Darts, and 1972-1973 full-sized Dodges, Plymouths, and Chryslers with a manual antenna. A power antenna was never offered for the Barracuda or Challenger as original equipment.

Axle Packages

Several different axle packages were available for the 1970 to 1974 models. However, after the 1971 model year, only one package remained available. In addition to different (lower) gear ratios, other components such as the maximum cool radiator and Hemi suspension were part of these packages.

High-Performance Axle Package: Code A31, 1970-1971

This was available only on 1970 and 1971 cars with the 340-ci or 383-ci 4-bbl engine. This package included 3.91 rear axle gears with a Sure Grip differential, a seven-blade fan, the maximum cool radiator, and the Hemi suspension.

The 1970 Challenger performance hood graphic option.

Super Performance Axle Package: Code A32, 1970-1971

This was available on Challenger R/T and Cudas with a 340-ci, 440-ci, or 426 Hemi powerplants with an automatic transmission. The package included: 4.10 gears with Sure Grip differential, a seven-blade fan, and maximum cool radiator. Hemi suspension is listed as part of the package, but it was standard with these models. Air conditioning was not available if this package was ordered.

Track Pack: Code A33, 1970-1971

This is the best-known axle package that Chrysler offered. It was available only on the Challenger R/T or

An optional rear wing spoiler.

Cuda models with the 440-ci or the Hemi engine with a four-speed manual transmission. It included the 3.54 gears in a Super Grip Dana axle, a dual-point distributor, a seven-blade fan, and maximum cool radiator. The reason this package is so well-known is that it was mandatory equipment with these models.

Super Track Pack: Code A34, 1970-1971

This is the pure performance axle package. It was available only on Cudas or Challenger R/Ts with 440-ci, Hemi, or 340-ci engines. It includes the same components as the A33 package but substituted 4.10 gears for the 3.54 gears and added power front disc brakes to the package. Of all axle packages, this is the most desirable to have on your car. As with all axle packages, it can be determined by decoding the fender tag. The axle option code will appear on the tag.

Performance Axle Package: Code A36, 1970-1974

Of all the packages offered, this was the only package that survived after 1971. It was available only for cars with a 4-bbl carburetor. It included: 3.55 rear axle gears with Sure Grip 8 3/4-inch differential, heavy-duty cooling, and the heavy-duty suspension.

Aerodynamic Spoiler Package: Code A45, 1970-1971

Available for late-1970 and 1971 models only as a factory option was a rear wing spoiler and a front chin spoiler. Due to an effort to reduce complexity in the assembly line, the spoiler package was dropped at the end of the 1971 model year. The spoilers remained optional as an over-the-counter part through Mopar Performance and could be installed by an owner or dealer. The only way a spoiler would be con-

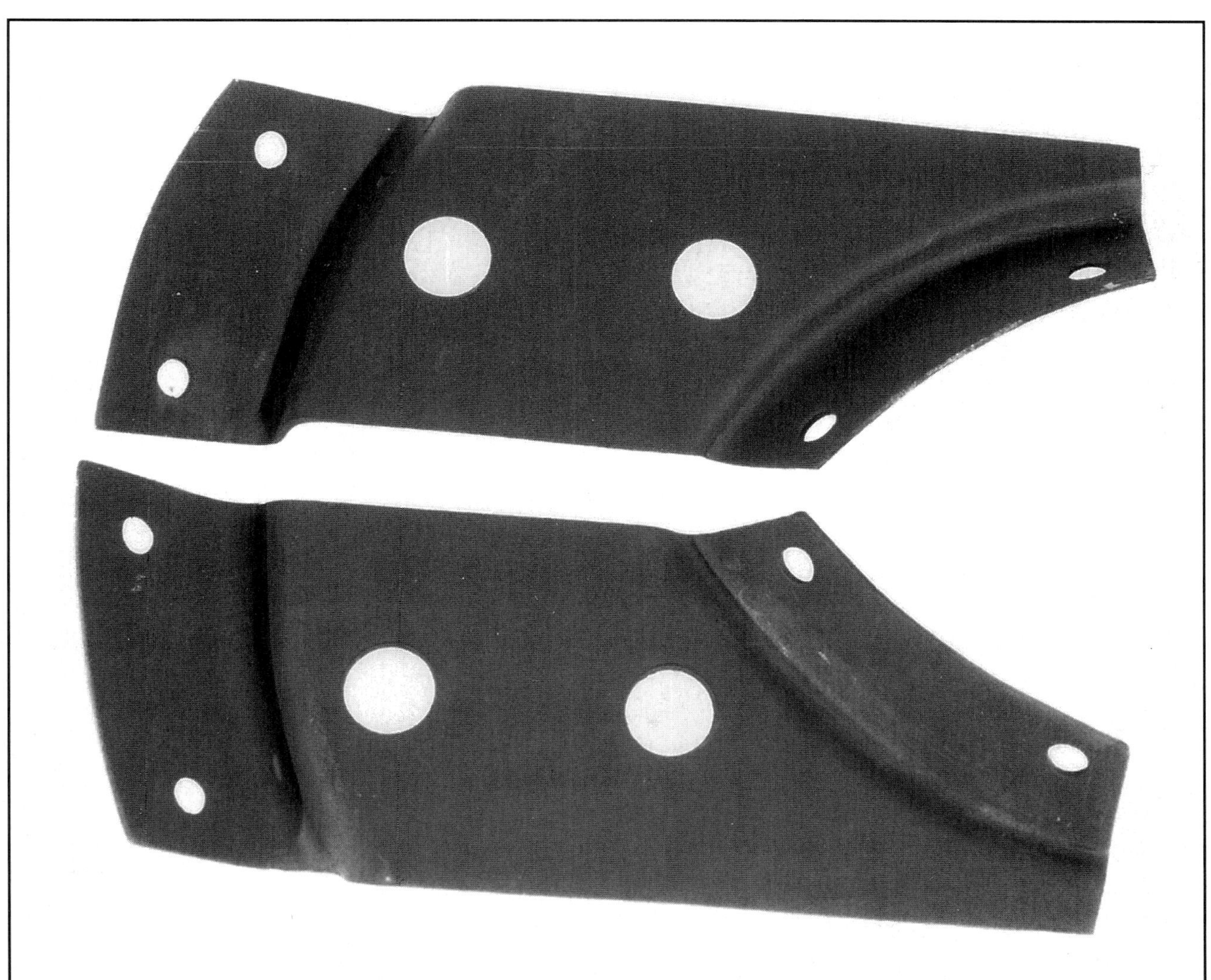

The under-deck lid spoiler brackets used on 1970 Barracudas with the early style deck lid. *Year One*

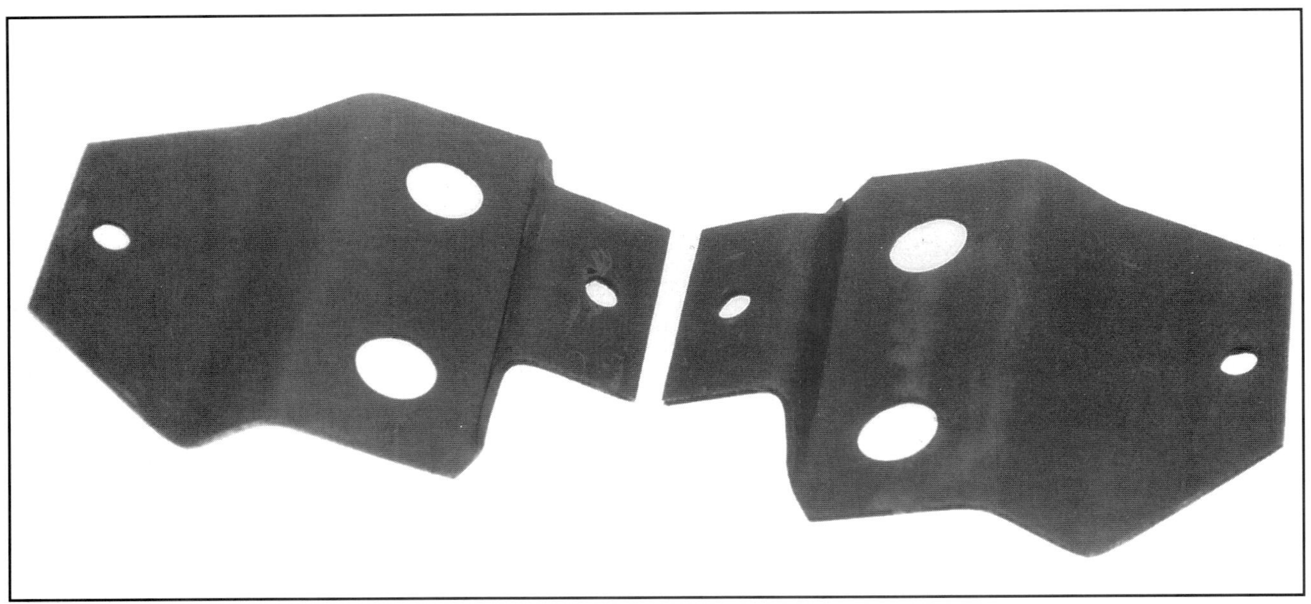

The under-deck lid spoiler brackets used with late-style deck lid. *Year One*

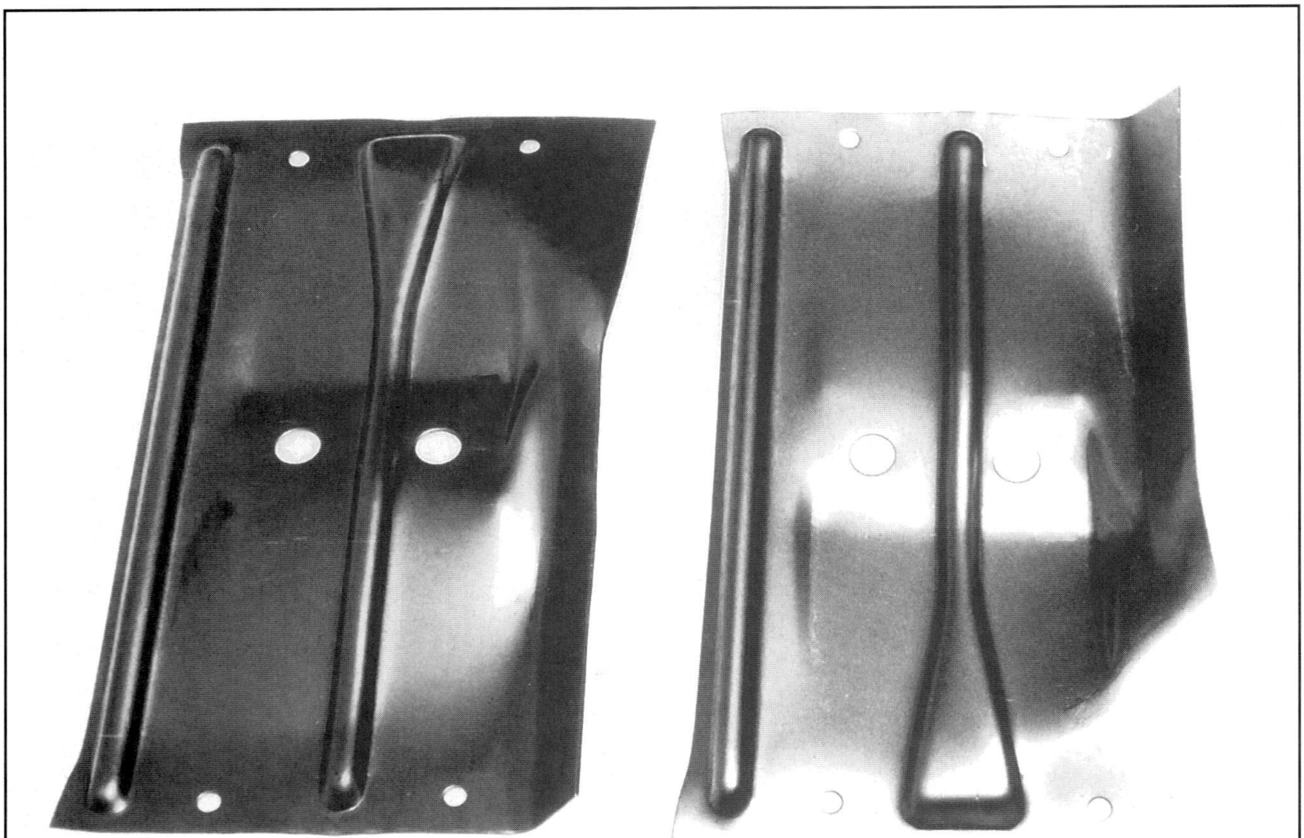

The under-deck lid spoiler brackets used on 1970-1974 Challengers. *Year One*

sidered correct on 1972 or later models is if a dealer installed it. This installation would have to be verified in writing and done before the original owner took delivery of the car.

The rear wing was available for all models in both years, except the AAR and T/A, and regardless of the exterior color, the rear wing was painted flat black. The Challenger T/A and the AAR Cuda included a rear lip-style spoiler as part of the Trans-Am package. These spoilers are covered in chapter 7 of this book.

The Barracuda and the Challenger used the same rear wing, but each model used different mounting hardware. Also, the 1970 Barracuda used different hardware than those on the 1971 models. The rear wing was available as a separate option, coded as option J81; this code will appear on the fender tag if the car came from the factory with this option. To get the front spoilers, the spoiler package had to be ordered, meaning no cars were built with a front spoiler but without the rear wing. The same sets were used for 1970 and 1971 models, but unlike the rear wing, each model used a different set. The A45 code will appear on the fender tag if both the rear and front spoilers were ordered.

Backlight Louver Package: Code A67, 1970-1971

This is a rare option that was available only on 1970 and 1971 models. The louvers themselves are different for each make and they will not correctly interchange, and those from a 1971 Charger or Satellite will not fit. A black vinyl roof and body-colored rac-

A view of some twin front spoilers.

ing mirrors were required options with the louvers. Special rear window moldings painted flat black were part of the package. This option, like spoilers, was deleted from the line-up in 1972 to reduce complexity in the assembly line. It was also illegal in some states and may be illegal in even more states today. State officials claim louvers restrict visibility, so it would be wise to check with your local Department of Motor Vehicles (DMV) before installing these louvers. You might have a legal leg to stand on if you can prove these were original items on your car. Look for the option code A67 on your fender tag, denoting that this option was originally ordered and installed on your car when it was new.

Floor Console: Code C16, 1969-1974 Code 486, 1967-1968

A center floor console was optional all eight years on both models. However, on 1969 Barracudas with a 383-ci or 440-ci with automatic transmission, a console was a mandatory option. The 1967 to 1969 models used the same console all three years, but there were two different consoles, one for the four-speed transmissions and the other for cars with automatic transmissions. The base should be painted to match the instrument panel, but the finish should be a semi-gloss instead of flat. See the adjacent chart for proper color code numbers.

Front finish plates were also fitted according to the type of transmission; the four-speed used part number

A look at the rear-window louver setup.

1967-1969 Console Paint Code Numbers

Model Year	Interior Code	Color Name	Ditzler Paint Code Number
1967	H6B, H6C	Academy Blue	13060
1967	H6K	Copper Brown	22735
1967	H6T	Jewel Black	9028
1967	H6R, H6V	Medium Red	71495
1967-1969	H6W, D6X, D6W D6P, D6U, F6P	Jewel Black	9028
1968	H6B, D6B, H6C, D6C	Bahama Blue	13370
1968	H6F, D6F, H6D, D6D	Velvet Green	43137
1968	H6V, D6V, H6R, D6R	Aztec Maroon	50755
1968	D6E, D6Y	Saber Gold	81583
1969	H6B, D6B, H6C	Majesty Blue	13686
1969	H6V, H6R, D6R	Rally Red	71687
1969	H6F, F6J	Bayou Green	43929
1969	D6T	Buckskin Tan	23061

2589600, while those with automatics used part number 2589599. In 1969, the plates were given new part numbers. Those with automatic transmissions used part number 2877233, while those with a four-speed manual used part number 2877234. The console lid was also changed, and the 1967 and 1968 models used part number 2589596 while the 1969 models used part number 2877232. The difference is that the 1969 units have simulated-wood trim while the earlier panels have a flat-black finish.

Consoles were completely restyled for 1970 models and consisted of a two-part design. The lower portion of the base was determined by the type of transmission in use. Manual transmissions used part number 3526FX9, and those with automatics used part number 3505FX9. These two bases were used for both models in 1970 and 1971. The upper portion of the base was used with all types of transmissions; however, the 1970 and 1971 models used different part numbers. The 1970 models used part number 3504FX9, while the 1971 used part number 3504GX9, but they are visually the same.

In 1972, the lower and upper portions of the console were restyled. Again, two different lower portions were used, and cars with a manual transmission used part number 3542GX9 while those with automatics used part number 3541GX9. The upper portion was restyled and given part number 3500HX9, and as in 1970 and 1971, it was used with all types of transmissions. Both the upper and lower portions were used again on 1973 and 1974 models.

The part numbers listed above show that the upper and lower portions were molded in black plastic. Originally, the console was painted to match the instrument panel but in a low-gloss finish. A finish plate was used on top of the upper portion of the base. The part number was based on the type of transmission used. The 1970 models used a part number 3415508 with an automatic transmission, and with a manual transmission they used part number 3415507. The 1971 to 1972 models used part number 3509152 with a four-speed and part number 3509153 with automatic transmissions. Both sets of these trim panels used simulated-wood vinyl tape, but the 1970 models used a lighter shade than the other model years. The trim plate was again restyled in 1973, with a manual transmission using part number 3550074 and automatics using part number 3550076. Both of these trim panels continued unchanged into 1974. For correct restorations, the proper base and trim panels for the proper model year should be used. Listed below are the paint color code numbers use to correctly refinish your car's console.

Rear Window Defroster: Code 418, 1967-1968; Code H31, 1969-1974

A rear window defroster was available all eight years for the two-door hardtop models only. The setup was the same all eight years and consisted of an inlet grille mounted in the rear shelf panel. The air was funneled down to a motor that heated it up, then pushed it through a plastic duct hose to an outlet duct. This outlet duct was also mounted in the rear shelf panel. The motor was painted gloss black, as was the blower housing. The intake wheel and the outlet

1970-1974 Console Paint Color Code Numbers

Model Year(s)	Interior Trim Codes	Paint Color Name	Paint Code Number
1970	P5X9, PRX9, H6X9, P6XW, PRXW, P6XY, H6XW, L6XW, HRX9	Jewel Black	9324
1970	P6B5, H6B5, P6BW, H6BW, H5BW	Thunder Blue	13848
1970	P6T5, PRT5, H6T5	Puma Tan	23219
1970	P6F8, H6F8, P6FW, H6FW,	Bayou Green	43925
1970	P6K4, H6K4	Sunfire Orange	60557
1970	P6E4, H6E4, P6EW, H6EW	Poppy Red	71764
1971-1974	H6X9, P6X9, P5X9, H6XW, H6XW, A6X9, B6X9, H6XV, H5X9, H5XV, PRX9, SRX9	Black	9388
1971-1974	H6B5, P6B5, A6B5, B6B5	Brite Blue	14096
1971-1974	H6F8, P6F8, L6F8, L5FW	Dark Green	44696
1971	H6T5, P6T5, L6T5	Medium Dark Saddle	23428
1971-1974	P6Y4, A6Y3, H6Y3, B6Y4	Light Gold	23467
1971	L6B7, H6B7	Medium Blue	14090

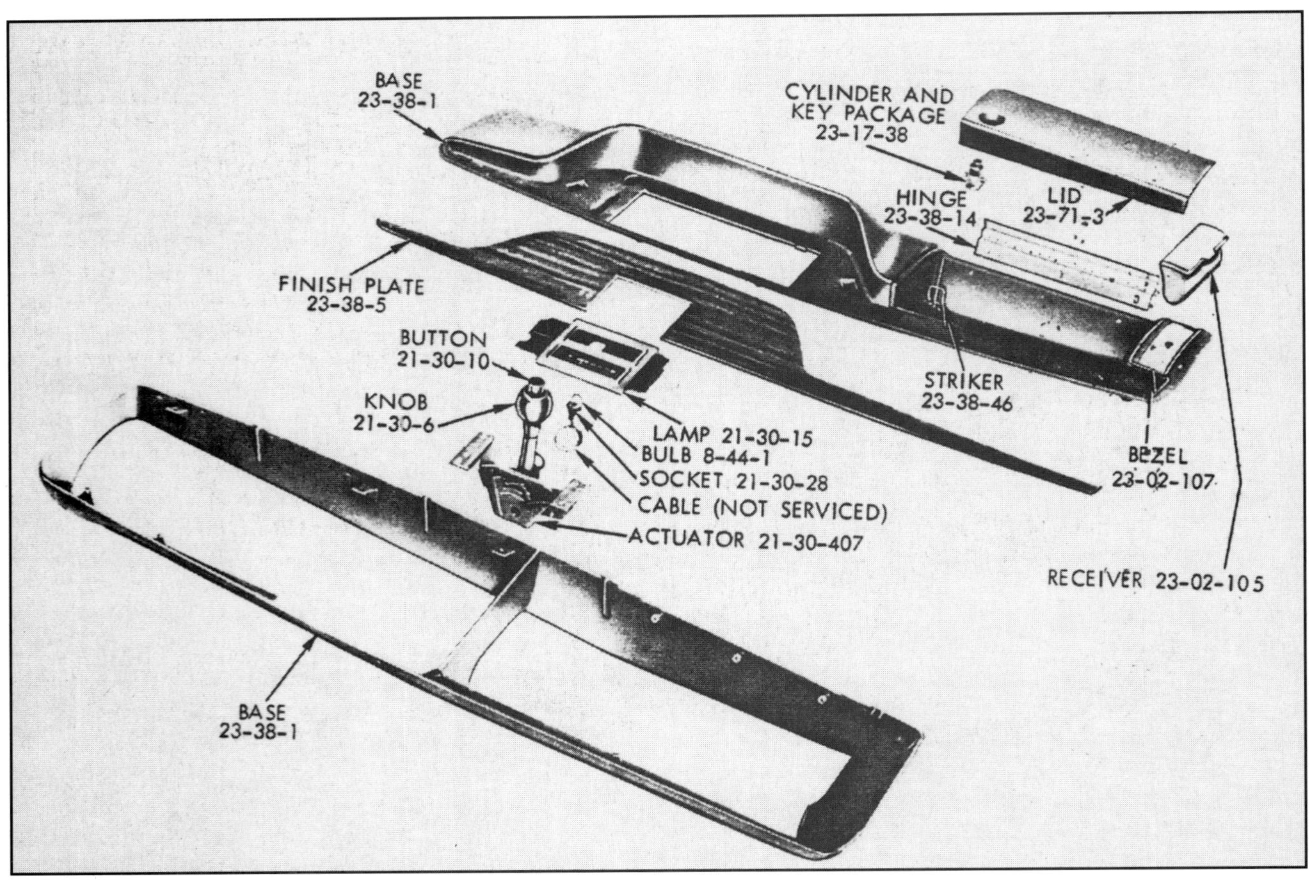

The 1970-1974 console.

duct should be painted flat black. The intake and outlet bezels should be painted to match the rear shelf panel in a flat finish. This is same finish used on the instrument panel.

Air Conditioning: Code 411, 1967-1968; Code H51, 1969-1974

Air conditioning was an immensely popular option consisting of several different components. Due to the complexity of the option, only the major parts will be covered here. Air conditioning was available all eight years for all models with these exceptions: 1967-1969 Barracuda with 383-ci; 1969 Barracuda with 440-ci; 1967-1971 Hemi cars; 1970-1971 440-ci 3x2-bbl; 1970-1971 340-ci 3x2-bbl; 1967-1968 Barracuda with a V-8 and a three-speed manual transmission; and 1969 225-ci with the trailer package.

Several different air compressors were used, and the part number of the compressor will appear on the identification tag that is on the compressor. The compressor, drier, mounting brackets, and the pulley should all be painted gloss black; underhood black from Eastwood works well. Compressor pulleys are identified by their diameter, number of grooves, and an identification number. Air-conditioning hose routes vary with the model year and engine usage.

Road Lamps: Code L34, 1970-1971

Available only for Barracudas in 1970 and 1971 were two round lamps mounted just below the front bumper, one on each side of the license plate holder. The lamp assembly was listed as part number 3403840 both years and will fit either side of the car. However, the mounting brackets are different for each side of the car and for each year. The 1970 models used part numbers 3403838 (right side) and 3403839 (left side), while the 1971 models used part numbers 3479316 (right) and 3479317 (left). The switch for the road lamps was mounted under the instrument panel to the left of the driver. A bezel that read "Road Lamp" was used both years.

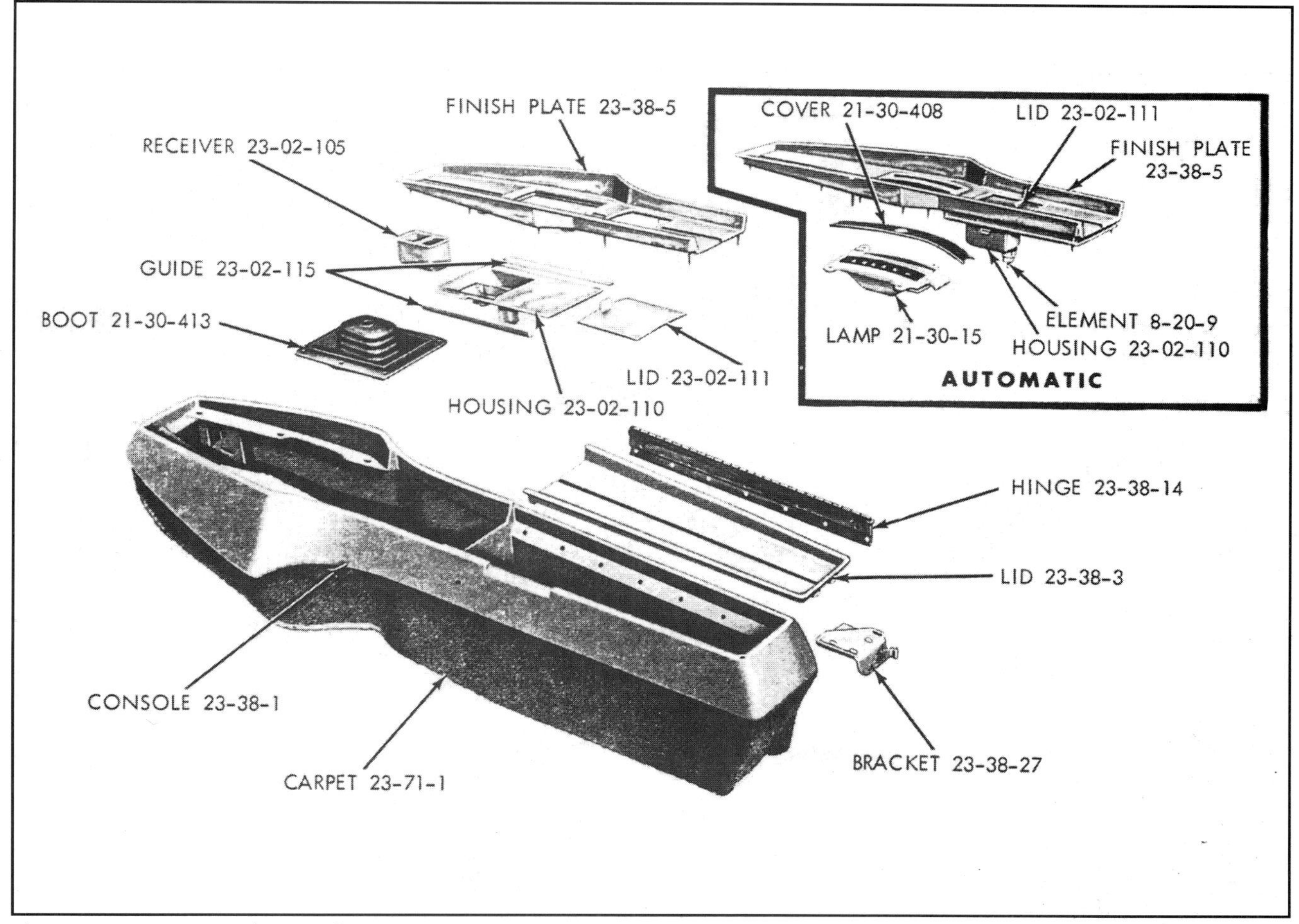

The 1967-1969 Barracuda console.

Compressor and Pulley Hub Identification

Model Year	Compressor ID Number	Pulley Diameter	Pulley Grooves	Pulley Part Number
1967	2815760	6-5/8 six-cyl.	Single six-cyl	2521824
		7-1/4 V-8	Single V-8	2521963
		7-1/4 V-8	Dual V-8	2521923
		6-3/4#	Single #	2006396
1968	2843800	6-5/8 six-cyl.	All are single groove	2521824
	2843801	7-1/4 V-8		2521963
	2843802	6-5/8# six-cyl.		2003058
	2843803	6-3/4# V-8		2870253
	2843805			
	2865391			
1969	2951193	6-5/8 six-cyl.	Single	2521824
	2951194	7-1/4 V-8	Single	2521963
	2951195	5-3/8 all	Dual	2837163
	2951220			
	2951268			
	2951271			
	2953349			
	2953368			
	2953388			
	3462019			
	2960782			
	2941998			
	3462350			
	3462419			
	3462420			
	2961920			
	3461919			
	3462920			
	2962998			
	3512062			
	3491270			
	3491271			
	3484252			
1970-1971	2951193	6-5/8	Single	2521824
	2951194	5-3/8	Dual	2837163
	2951195			
	2951220			
	2951268			
	2951271			
	2953349			
	2961947			
	2953368			
	2953388			
	3462019			
	2960782			
	2941998			

Compressor and Pulley Hub Identification (cont.)

Model Year	Compressor ID Number	Pulley Diameter	Pulley Grooves	Pulley Part Number
(1970–1971)	3462350	6-5/8	Single	2521824
	3462419	5-3/8	Dual	2837163
	3462420			
	2961920			
	3461919			
	3462920			
	2962998			
	3512062			
	3491270			
	3491271			
	3484252			
	3512706			
	3512707			
1972	3462998	6-5/8	Single	2521824
	3512706	5-3/8	Dual	2837163
	3502610			
	3502608			
1973-1974	3502608	6-5/8	Single	2521824
	3502610	5-3/8	Dual	2837163
	3502716			

= Dealer-installed air conditioning.

Body Sill Moldings: Code M25, 1969-1974; Codes 544 and 529, 1967-1968

Sill moldings were extra-cost items for the 1967 Barracuda. These moldings had a Brite finish and were listed as part numbers 2809694 (right) and 2809695 (left) for all body styles. They were positioned under the bottom of the door along the side of the car. In 1968, the moldings extra-cost items for all body styles, but four different sets of moldings were used. The standard-width moldings used part numbers 3004232 (right) and 3004233 (left), but note that part numbers 3004228 (right) and 3004229 (left) were also used.

The custom-width moldings (part numbers 3004234, right, and 3004235, left) were approximately 5 feet and 1/4-inch in length (60.25 inches). Extra-wide moldings used part numbers 2932588 (right) and 2932589 (left) and were nearly 5-1/2 feet in length (66 inches). No moldings were recommended if sport stripes were ordered.

If the molding is missing, count the number of retainers to determine which molding, if any, was used. The standard-width molding was held on with 20 retainers and 2 nuts. The custom-width moldings used 10 screws and 10 nuts. The extra-wide moldings were held on with 12 retainers. By counting the retainers or drilled holes where the retainers mount, you can learn which sill moldings were installed on your 1968 Barracuda. If there are no retainers or drilled holes in the doorsills, then no molding was ordered and you should not install one.

Custom sill moldings were available on the 1969 Barracuda except with the Cuda package. Part numbers were listed as 2933236 (right) and 2933237 (left). These moldings were narrow and blacked-out with flat black paint. Because these moldings ran along the same plane as the Cuda stripes, they could not be ordered with the Cuda package.

Sill moldings were optional on the 1970 Barracuda models. These moldings, part numbers 3549646 (right) and 3549647 (left), had the simulated look of side exhaust pipes or fish gills. They were held on with 11 screws and 7 retainers. Sill moldings were standard on the Gran Coupe models and were listed as part numbers 3419786 (right) and 3419787 (left). These moldings are narrower and do not have the fish-like gills as those on a Barracuda; they were also held on with 14 retainers and 4 screws.

A Barracuda road lamp.

Sill moldings were optional for all Challenger models except the T/A, and they were listed as part numbers 3419792 (right) and 3419793 (left). They were held on by nine retainers, two nuts, and two screws. These same moldings were also optional on 1971 Challenger models. The one 1971 Challenger T/A that was built did not use these moldings.

Until 1971, all moldings were designed so they were unique to each side of the car. In 1971, the Barracuda molding was restyled and part number 3579148 fit either the left- or the right-hand side of the car. This molding was held on with seven retainers and nine screws. The Gran Coupe continued to use a special molding, and unlike the other Barracudas, these moldings were unique to each side. The part numbers were listed as 3579146 (right) and 3579147 (left). Each molding was held on with seven retainers and two screws.

For 1972, all Barracuda and Challenger models used the same molding, listed as part number 3579148, which is the same molding used on base 1971 Barracuda models.

In 1973, the molding was again restyled and given part number 3744364 and was used on both the Challenger and the Barracuda. This molding continued unchanged into 1974.

Power Sunroof: Code M51

This is one of the rarest of options installed on the 1970-1972 models, and it was available on hardtop models only, except the Challenger S.E. and those Challengers with the formal roof option (A78) in 1971. The standard roof was cut to accept the sunroof, and a vinyl roof was required to hide the patchwork, so no models with a sunroof were built without a vinyl roof.

A small motor (part number 3412549 in 1970 and 1971 and 3571510 in 1972) was connected to a drive pulley and a gearbox that control the sliding door in the roof. The door itself rode on plastic sliders and was activated by a switch, or a crank, when the motor failed or the ignition was not on. Due to the modified roofline on the Challenger and the inside overhead console, the sunroof could not operate properly with the formal roof option. Thus, this op-

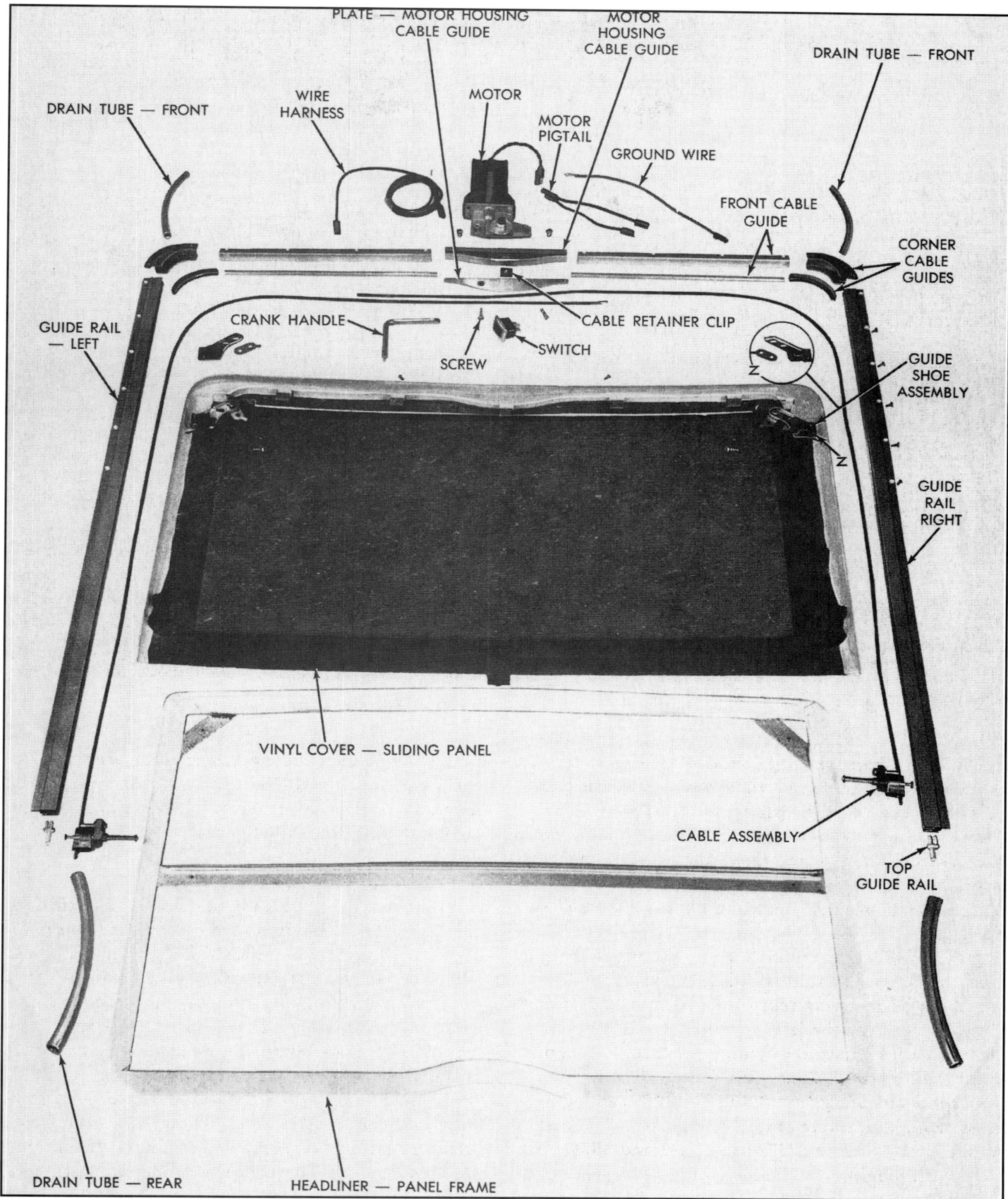

Sun roof components.

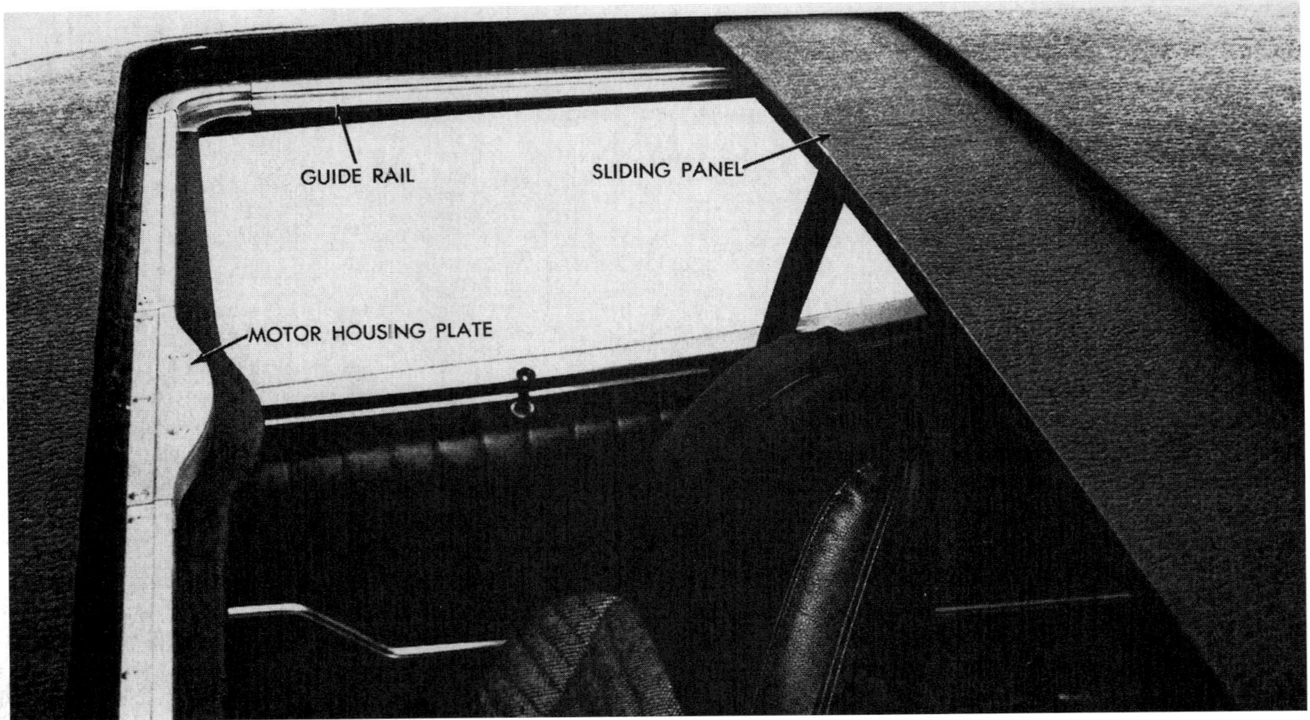

The sun roof in the open position. The Duster shown was typical of the E-bodies.

tion was never available on this model. It was available on the Gran Coupe, but the overhead console was deleted.

Wheel Liners: Code J35, 1967, Code 558, 1967-1968

Red fender inner liners were available for the 1967-1969 models as a dealer-installed option. They were available only for the two-door hardtops or fastback, and no convertibles were built with these inner liners. The same liners, part numbers 2856306 (right) and 2856307 (left), were used all three years.

Index